MACROECONOMICS
1979
READINGS ON CONTEMPORARY ISSUES

EDITED BY
PETER D. McCLELLAND

CORNELL UNIVERSITY PRESS ITHACA AND LONDON

Copyright © 1979 by Cornell University

All rights reserved. Except for brief quotations in a review, this book, or parts thereof, must not be reproduced in any form without permission in writing from the publisher. For informations address Cornell University Press, 124 Roberts Place, Ithaca, New York 14850.

First published 1979 by Cornell University Press.
Published in the United Kingdom by Cornell University Press Ltd., 2-4 Brook Street, London W1Y 1AA.

International Standard Book Number 0-8014-9870-8
Library of Congress Catalog Card Number 77-6193
Printed in the United States of America

FOREWORD

To the student

When you signed up for a course entitled Macroeconomics you probably had two expectations. The first was that you were about to study many of those problems featured in the national news media. Inflation, unemployment, prospective energy shortages, the inadequacies of our present welfare system—these are but a few of the macroeconomic issues encountered almost daily as you read the newspaper or watch the evening news on television. Probably your second expectation, fostered by the same sources, was that your studies would help you to understand why economists have sharply differing opinions on how these problems should be attacked. If your course reading were confined to a textbook—any textbook—you would be in for a disappointment. These books invariably include little about contemporary problems, and even less about the national debate on how to solve them. The reasons are rather simple. Each author has his own opinion on the ideal solutions, and his text, not surprisingly, tends to emphasize that point of view. As for contemporary issues, no textbook that appears today (never mind last year) can possibly deal with them, because the lag between finished manuscript and appearance in the bookstore is usually twelve to eighteen months, sometimes longer.

This reader's main objective is to remedy these two defects. Assembled in late May of 1979, it attempts to give empirical flesh to those theoretical skeletons that you will be learning about in lectures and from the textbook. It also emphasizes, wherever possible, different points of view on how to solve some of our most pressing macroeconomic problems. It cannot promise you a definitive resolution of those problems. But it should give you a sense of why they matter, and why macroeconomic theory is relevant in attempting to solve them. The ultimate hope is that you will emerge from this reader and your course with a sense of how crucial these issues are to the future well-being of our nation and its citizens.

Ithaca, New York

To the instructor

Teaching macroeconomics to undergraduates is a demanding assignment. The lecturer who strives to integrate textbook theory with national problems is constantly bedeviled by the speed with which the leading contemporary issues change—from inflation to unemployment to energy and back to inflation again, to mention but one of several recent sequences. Also in a constant state of flux are the mechanisms that dominate current analysis of these problems. The unabashed Keynesian approach tempered by a belief in the Philips Curve has given way to such disparate topics as Okun's Law, rational expectations, and the merits of monetary targets. In the popular press, there is no shortage of commentary on both problems and associated causal mechanisms. The difficulty is that several dozen articles from different sources cannot be incorporated easily (or at all) into the reading list of a course in which enrollment may run to hundreds. At least not without creating pandemonium in the library. This book attempts to solve this impasse. Readings were culled from a range of material in May, assembled in early June, and with the aid of photo offset made available in bound form by mid-August. The result is viewed by both the editor and Cornell University Press as merely a first step. Our intention is to modify this volume annually, in terms of both topics covered and articles included. We hope that you will help us with that modification. If you have any suggestions, I would appreciate hearing from you (Economics Department, Cornell University, Ithaca, N.Y. 14853). Such ongoing interaction with those who study and teach the subject will be a crucial ingredient if the annual readers are to satisfy the instructor while achieving that most important of objectives: fostering the student's interest in, and understanding of, contemporary American macroeconomic issues.

Peter D. McClelland

CONTENTS

Foreword

I INFLATION AND UNEMPLOYMENT

1. The Trouble Is Serious. (Time, April 30, 1979.) A recent poll indicates a growing national concern with economic problems, particularly inflation, but no clear consensus on how to solve them. — 9

2. Runaway Inflation: Can Carter Corral It? (U.S. News & World Report, March 12, 1979.) A review of the problem, possible causes, and possible solutions. — 12

3. Edward Meadows, Our Flawed Inflation Indexes. (Fortune, April 24, 1978.) How is the rate of inflation measured, and what are the major defects of these measures as indicators of changes in the aggregate price level? Edward Meadows reviews the three main inflation indexes: the Consumer Price Index, the Wholesale Price Index, and the GNP deflator. — 16

4. Sharon P. Smith, An Examination of Employment and Unemployment Rates. (Federal Reserve Bank of New York Quarterly Review, Autumn, 1977.) How are employment and unemployment rates calculated, and why is one measure more reliable than the other? An economist with the Federal Reserve Bank of New York examines these two key measures of economic activity and suggests some of the reasons why measured unemployment has been so high in recent years. — 21

5. The U.S. Structures Itself to Live with Inflation. (Business Week, January 29, 1979.) The persistence of inflation over the past decade and a half has led to some marked changes in the behavior of businesses, labor unions, financial institutions, and consumers. Business Week outlines the major transformations and suggests how they may undermine the government's ability to fight inflation. — 26

6. Marcelle V. Arak, Indexation of Wages and Retirement Income in the United States. (Federal Reserve Bank of New York Quarterly Review, Autumn, 1978.) The previous article raised the possibility of "the indexation of the whole U.S. economy." What is indexation, who is now affected by it, and what are the dangers as this process spreads? An economist with the Federal Reserve Bank of New York suggests the answers. — 33

7. Henry C. Wallich, Honest Money. (Federal Reserve Bank of Dallas Voice, August, 1978.) The case for fighting inflation is explained by a member of the Board of Governors of the Federal Reserve System. — 41

8. Living with Inflation: Consider the Alternative. (Dollars & Sense, May–June, 1978.) The case against fighting inflation is explained by a leading left-of-center journal concerned with contemporary economic problems. — 45

9. Juan Cameron, "I Don't Trust Any Economists Today." (Fortune, September 11, 1978.) The persistence of problems such as inflation and a slowdown of productivity growth has been accompanied by a lack of consensus among economists concerning causes and desirable remedies. The unsurprising result is confusion in Washington concerning which economic policies to pursue. — 48

10. Albert E. Burger, Is Inflation All Due to Money? (Federal Reserve Bank of St. Louis Review, December, 1978.) What causes inflation? This article attempts to give an explanation and justification of the monetarist's answer to that question: a too rapid increase in the money supply. — 51

11. Is There Really Too Much Money? (Dollars & Sense, February, 1979.) A left-of-center analysis of the causes of the present inflation emphasizes what monetarists emphasize—a rapid growth in the money supply—but draws different conclusions. — 56

12. Walter W. Heller, The Realities of Inflation. (Wall Street Journal, January 19, 1979.) A former chairman of the Council of Economic Advisors attacks the monetarist's explanation of inflation and emphasizes instead "structural and institutional factors." Singled out for special scrutiny are transient factors generating higher prices and "the underlying wage-price spiral . . . that changes only gradually." — 59

13. Paul W. McCracken, Our Unmysterious Inflation. (Wall Street Journal, April 23, 1979.) Another former chairman of the Council of Economic Advisors argues that the present price rise is a "classic inflation." Excessive aggregate demand is straining productive capacity, in part because the lag in productivity growth has slowed the expansion of supply in recent years. — 61

14. John Kenneth Galbraith, On Post Keynesian Economics. (Journal of Post Keynesian Economics, Vol. 1, 1978.) The previous article argued that inflation would "not be brought to heel until markets impose strong disciplines on wage and price increases." The present article emphasizes the limited ability of the market to provide that disciplining force. — 62

II MONETARY AND FISCAL POLICY

15. Peter D. McClelland, A Layman's Guide to the Keynesian-Monetarist Dispute. Articles in the first section illustrate one of the dilemmas of current macroeconomics. Economists have widely different views on how inflation and unemployment should be attacked, and those differences show no signs of being resolved. There are two main reasons for this disagreement. One stems from a difference in values. Some economists emphasize equity considerations; others, the preservation of certain freedoms. The second major reason for disagreement is differing views on how the economy works. This article attempts to summarize the main arguments in the theoretical dispute between the two dominant schools of thought in contemporary macroeconomics. — 65

16. Joseph A. Pechman, Introduction and Summary. (Excerpted from Chapter 1 of The Brookings Institution, *Setting National Priorities: The 1980 Budget.*) A detailed review of monetary and fiscal policy in general and President Carter's 1980 budget in particular is presented from a Keynesian perspective. — 68

17. Robert Lekachman, Playing to the Haves: Carter's Dangerous Budget Act. (The New Leader, February 12, 1979.) The President's economic policies are analyzed from a left-of-center perspective. — 80

18. Irving Kristol, Can Carter Reap a Windfall? (Wall Street Journal, April 13, 1979.) The President's economic policies are analyzed from a right-of-center perspective. — 83

19. Richard J. Levine, Fed Plan to Slow Money Growth Further Is Signaled in Policy Report to Congress. (Wall Street Journal, February 21, 1979.) The central bank spells out its priorities and policies for 1979 and beyond. — 84

20. Karen W. Arenson, Can the Fed Stem the Tide? (New York Times, November 12, 1978.) Recent changes in the practices of financial institutions may pose a threat to the effectiveness of monetary policy. Arenson outlines why. — 85

21. Interest Rates: A Bargain at 10%? (Dollars & Sense, January, 1979.) Are the present high interest rates indicative of a restrictive monetary policy or of adjustments in financial markets to a rapid rate of inflation? Dollars & Sense discounts the first and emphasizes the second. — 87

22. Paul A. Samuelson, The Last Days of the Boom. (Newsweek, April 30, 1979.) Economic prospects and appropriate government policies are assessed from a Keynesian perspective. — 90

23. Milton Friedman, The Fed: At It Again. (Newsweek, February 19, 1979.) Economic prospects and appropriate government policies are assessed from a monetarist perspective. — 91

24. Sidney Weintraub, Proposal for An Anti-Inflation Package. (Challenge, September-October, 1978.) One of the authors of a tax-based incomes policy (TIP) presents an updated version of his plan. — 92

25. Joseph A. Pechman, Can Tax-Based Incomes Policies Work? (Challenge, November-December, 1978.) One major objection to TIP proposals is that they would be extremely difficult to administer. A leading expert on taxation explains why. — 94

26. Nancy Ammon Jianakoplos, A Tax-Based Incomes Policy (TIP): What's It All About? (Federal Reserve Bank of St. Louis Review, February, 1978.) Another objection to TIP proposals is that they are predicated on the wrong view concerning the causes of inflation. An economist with the Federal Bank of St. Louis presents the monetarist's critique. — 96

27. R. Alton Gilbert and Jean M. Lovati, Disintermediation: An Old Disorder with a New Remedy. (Federal Reserve Bank of St. Louis Review, January, 1979.) What is "disintermediation," how has it changed in recent years, and how have those changes affected the housing market? Two economists with the Federal Reserve Bank of St. Louis review the recent history and document some of the effects. — 101

28. Randall C. Merris, Automatic Transfers: Evolution of the Service and Impact on Money. (Federal Reserve Bank of Chicago Economic Perspectives, November-December, 1978.) A new development in banking practices has implications for monetary policy. An economist with the Federal Reserve Bank of Chicago suggests why. — 107

29. Automatic Transfer and NOW Accounts Compared. (From Randall C. Merris, Automatic Transfers, Federal Reserve Bank of Chicago Economic Perspectives, November-December, 1978.) Two recent changes in banking practices are compared. — 110

30. Recent Developments Enabling Depositors to Use Interest-Earning Balances for Purposes Previously Requiring Non-Interest-Earning Demand Balances. (From Alfred Broaddus, Automatic Transfers from Savings to Checking, Federal Reserve Bank of Richmond Economic Review, November-December, 1978.) The Review lists the major revisions since September, 1970. — 110

31. Anne Marie Laporte, Behavior of the Income Velocity of Money. (Federal Reserve Bank of Chicago Economic Perspectives, September/October, 1977.) Laporte charts the recent upward trend in velocity and explains how this movement is caused by changes in the practices of financial institutions. — 111

III WAGE AND PRICE REGULATION

32. Jimmy Carter, Anti-Inflation Program. (Vital Speeches of the Day, November 15, 1978.) The President explains why inflation is a threat, how he plans to attack it, and the role to be played by "voluntary wage and price standards" and a "real wage insurance policy." 114

33. Those Mystifying Guidelines. (Time, March 5, 1979.) The President's wage and price guidelines have raised complex problems for business and labor leaders who would understand them and for bureaucrats who would enforce them. Time outlines some of the difficulties. 118

34. Ralph E. Winter, Braking the Spiral? Wage-Price Guidelines Just May Help a Bit, Many Executives Say. (Wall Street Journal, February 15, 1979.) Businessmen note some of the positive results, and some of the unsolved problems, in the early stages of the President's efforts to enforce wage-price guidelines. 120

35. Robert Lekachman, The Case for Controls. (The New Republic, October 14, 1978.) Lekachman outlines the case against controls, and then indicates why he still favors them. Much of his argument rests upon perceived defects in the market system. 122

36. Michael E. Trebing, The Economic Consequences of Wage-Price Guidelines. (Federal Reserve Bank of St. Louis Review, December, 1978.) Trebing explains the monetarist argument against any form of controls, including the President's wage-price guidelines. Much of his argument rests upon a belief in the effectiveness of the market system. 126

37. Wage Insurance Embarrassment. (Wall Street Journal, January 16, 1979.) Jimmy Carter's proposal for a "real wage insurance policy" seemed to be doomed from the start. A Wall Street Journal editorial suggests why. 132

38. Robert T. Falconer, The Minimum Wage: A Perspective. (Federal Reserve Bank of New York Quarterly Review, Autumn, 1978.) Another form of wage regulation is the minimum wage. This article outlines the history of the policy and the arguments for and against its continuation. 133

IV TAX REVOLTS AND CONSTITUTIONAL AMENDMENTS

39. Anita A. Summers, Proposition 13 and Its Aftermath. (Federal Reserve Bank of Philadelphia Business Review, March/April, 1979.) What has sparked the recent "tax revolts," and will they culminate in a state-initiated constitutional amendment to limit the federal budget? An economist with the Federal Reserve Bank of Philadelphia attempts to assess some of the causes of discontent and some of the options for fiscal reform. 137

40. Shades of the Founding Fathers. (Time, February 19, 1979.) A large number of states have voted to call a Constitutional Convention to approve an amendment requiring a balanced federal budget. This article examines how that prospect is viewed by various constitutional lawyers, politicians, and economists. 144

41. Pro and Con: A Constitutional Ban on Red Ink? Interviews with Edmund G. Brown, Jr., and Gardner Ackley. (U.S. News & World Report, January 29, 1979.) A leading advocate of a balanced budget amendment explains why he favors it, and a leading economist explains why he views the balanced budget amendment as a "disastrous and irresponsible proposal." 146

42. The Balanced Budget Mania. (Dollars & Sense, April, 1979.) The Time article outlined the objections of monetarists to a balanced budget amendment. The Ackley article presented a Keynesian perspective. The present article assesses the same proposal from a more radical perspective. 148

V ENERGY, GROWTH, AND PRODUCTIVITY

43. What Decontrol of Oil Will Mean. (Newsweek, April 16, 1979.) Newsweek outlines what the present control system is, how the President proposes to modify it, and what the likely effects will be from those modifications. 151

44. Jai-Hoon Yang, The Nature and Origins of the U.S. Energy Crisis. (Federal Reserve Bank of St. Louis Review, July, 1977.) As a complement to the previous article, Yang gives a detailed history of U.S. energy policy and offers an explanation of present difficulties which emphasizes how previous government intervention has distorted the forces of supply and demand. 154

45. George J. Church, Looking Anew at the Nuclear Future. (Time, April 16, 1979.) What role should nuclear power play in meeting U.S. energy needs of the future? Time outlines some of the relevant questions and some of the possible answers. 165

46. G. William Miller, The Role Of Productivity Gains in Solving National Economic Problems. (Federal Reserve Bank of Dallas Voice, December, 1978.) The chairman of the Federal Reserve outlines the history of the slowdown in productivity growth, suggests the major causes, and offers possible solutions. 167

VI POVERTY, WELFARE, AND INCOME DISTRIBUTION

47. Richard Freeman, Black Economic Progress since 1964. (The Public Interest, Summer, 1978.) What have been the major changes, why have they occurred, and what are the implications for present policy? In a carefully documented study, Freeman explores these and other issues, and suggests some of the answers. — 174

48. Elliott Currie, The New Face of Poverty. (The Progressive, January, 1979.) The focus of the previous article was largely upon advances made. The focus of the present one is upon advances not made, combined with some bleak speculation about the probable trend in government policies designed to alleviate poverty. — 188

49. America's War on Poverty—Is It a No-Win Struggle? (U.S. News & World Report, January 22, 1979.) Have the antipoverty programs of the past decade succeeded, and if not, why not? U.S. News & World Report explores the conflicting evidence and ongoing disagreement among the experts concerning the answers. — 191

50. Nick Kotz, Feeding the Hungry. (The New Republic, November 25, 1978.) Kotz argues that federal programs aimed at alleviating hunger among the poor, while far from perfect, have achieved a definite success. — 195

51. Young Blacks Out of Work: Time Bomb for U.S. (U.S. News & World Report, December 5, 1977.) One of the most pressing social problems of the nation has, to date, been little affected by government policies. This article outlines the major policies and indicates why they have had so little success. — 198

52. Martha S. Hill and Mary Corcoran, Short and Long Run Unemployment Burdens. (Economic Outlook U.S.A., Autumn, 1978.) A special study attempts to identify the pattern of long-term unemployment, who is persistently unemployed, and why. — 202

VII INTERNATIONAL

53. Federal Reserve and Treasury Support the Dollar. (Federal Reserve Bank of Dallas Voice, November, 1978.) A summary of why the dollar declined in recent years, and how the Treasury and the central bank intervened in November, 1978, in an effort to strengthen the dollar. — 205

54. Our Sick Dollar Starts to Regain Its Health. (U.S. News & World Report, April 30, 1979.) After a prolonged slide, the value of the American dollar has been rising. U.S. News & World Report summarizes some of the explanations for this reversal. — 210

55. Bruce K. MacLaury, OPEC's Billions. (The Brookings Bulletin, Fall, 1978.) The article reviews the international adjustments required by OPEC surpluses of the past, and forecasts adjustment problems of the immediate future. — 212

56. Trade Wars 3: The Politics of Oil. (Excerpted from Dollars & Sense, February, 1979.) From a perspective left of center, Dollars & Sense assesses the impact of OPEC actions upon the price of oil, its supply, and the value of the U.S. dollar. — 217

57. Henry C. Wallich, Evolution of the International Monetary System. (Challenge, January-February, 1979.) A member of the Board of Governors of the Federal Reserve reviews how recent "dissynchronized" business cycles among the world's major countries have contributed to international monetary instability and why current American government policy should make for greater stability. — 220

1

The Trouble Is Serious

That is the state of the nation, says a majority in a TIME *poll*

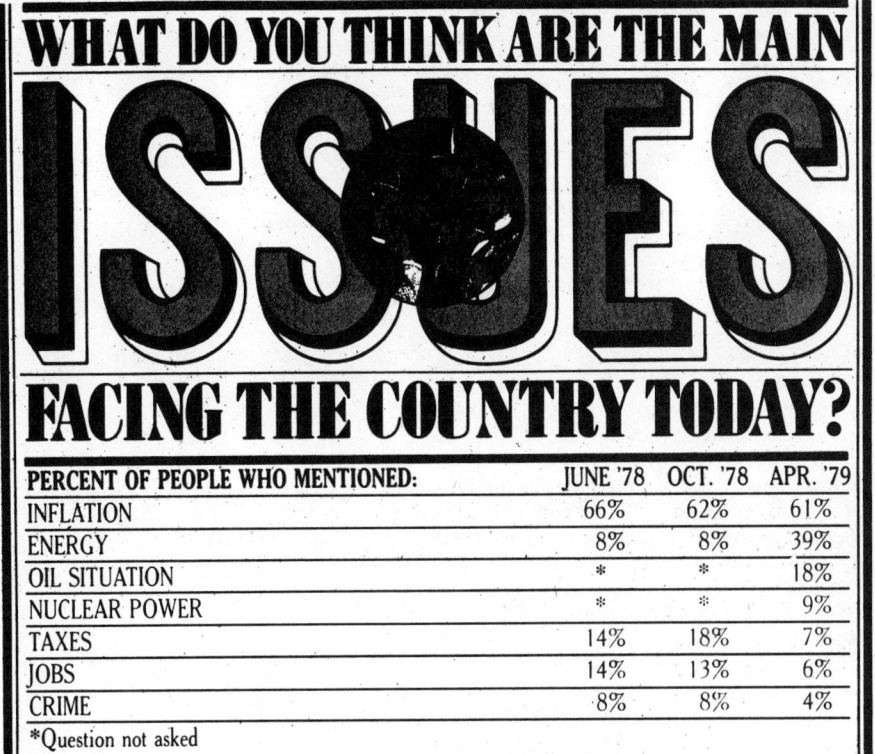

WHAT DO YOU THINK ARE THE MAIN ISSUES FACING THE COUNTRY TODAY?

PERCENT OF PEOPLE WHO MENTIONED:	JUNE '78	OCT. '78	APR. '79
INFLATION	66%	62%	61%
ENERGY	8%	8%	39%
OIL SITUATION	*	*	18%
NUCLEAR POWER	*	*	9%
TAXES	14%	18%	7%
JOBS	14%	13%	6%
CRIME	8%	8%	4%

*Question not asked

STATE of the NATION

	APR. '78	OCT. '78	APR. '79
U.S. PROBLEMS ARE NO WORSE THAN USUAL	51%	44%	31%
THE U.S. IS IN DEEP AND SERIOUS TROUBLE	41%	49%	64%

Optimism and self-confidence are as inherently American as the right to the pursuit of happiness. Just two years ago, most people responded to a TIME poll by saying they believed that the nation's problems were no worse than usual, that inflation would probably subside or a least get no worse, and that newly elected President Carter was a man in whom they could fully place their trust. That sunny view of the nation's affairs has been giving way to a gloomy and even slightly fearful mood. Haunted by anxiety about continually rising prices, which hit a painful annual rate of 9.5% during the first quarter of this year, plus a heightened concern about energy supplies and nuclear safety, Americans have turned increasingly sour on their own prospects. Specifically, they have become more pessimistic that Carter or any other politician will be able to cure the most pressing of their problems, inflation.

These are among the findings of a survey of 1,024 people completed this month for TIME by the opinion research firm of Yankelovich, Skelly and White, Inc. The poll found that a record low 23% of those questioned feel things are going well in this country, compared with 45% in June 1977. The poll also found that Carter, who rose substantially in popularity in the wake of his Camp David meetings last September with Anwar Sadat and Menachem Begin, has again fallen into low esteem in the country. The President has lost important ground to all his political opponents.

The main concern of Americans polled continues to be the rate of inflation and the apparent inability of the Government to cope with it. Nearly two-thirds of those questioned placed inflation at the very top of their list of worries, while more traditional fears like crime in the streets dropped sharply. The state of general gloom seemed to be deepened by the people's belated realization that the nation's energy problems are genuine. Sixty-three percent said they now worry a lot about an energy shortage, indicating that Carter has perhaps convinced the nation of the severity of this problem, if not of his competence to solve it.

Out of these apprehensions comes the belief by 64% of the sample that "the country is in deep and serious trouble," an opinion shared by only 41% one year ago.

On a more personal level, concern about paying bills has risen, as has anxiety about the inability to save for the future. Nearly half of those questioned reported having to dip into what savings they have to make ends meet. More than one-third have trimmed their gifts to charity because of higher living costs. Twenty-one percent say they have taken second jobs, and 32% of the men say their wives have gone out to work to bring in extra money.

All over the country, Americans have begun making small changes in life-styles to deal with rising prices. In Pittsburgh, for example, Newspaper Reporter Helen Kaiser abandoned her dream of having a band perform at her wedding next month. Says she: "I've decided to tape the music in advance and play it over the speaker system." While stores in citadels of wealth like Beverly Hills report booming business, others in similar areas in Texas say that even their wealthier clients are cutting back. One Neiman-Marcus saleswoman has just transferred from the high-fashion department to a moderately priced dress section where, she says, "I see all my old customers."

The basic problem for most people is the price of food. Says Judy Carey of Little Rock, Ark.: "For one thing, I quit buying ground beef. The junk food had

Reprinted by permission from TIME, The Weekly Newsmagazine; Copyright Time Inc. 1979.

to go. And we're using leftovers wherever we can. Yesterday we had a chef's salad for dinner. Sunday it was a casserole because we can get two meals out of it." Philadelphia Quality Control Technician Leo Valz has tired of supplying expensive snacks for his three children. Solution: do-it-yourself pizzas costing $16 for 24 shells, a big can of tomato sauce and a big bag of cheese. Says Valz: "A nighttime snack doesn't break our backs any more. I just wish they sold make-it-yourself steaks."

Some consumer groups advocate that a one-day-a-week beef boycott be organized to resist meat increases, which amounted to 110% at an annual rate for hamburger in the past three months. But beef producers retort that this will only aggravate the long-run shortage by discouraging the building of new beef herds. One Georgia grocery-store manager reports on his customers' switching to cheaper meats: "They're not boycotting beef, they just can't afford it."

Second on most people's list of price problems comes the cost of fuel. For new car buyers, this produced a high demand for gas-saving automobiles. In New England, the use of wood to replace high-priced oil has grown so much that last week New Hampshire was forced to establish a lottery for woodcutting privileges in state-owned forests.

What could be done? The Yankelovich survey showed that the public favors a variety of rather stringent measures to curb inflation. Half of those surveyed said mandatory price controls would help check inflation, even though popular opposition is usually considered one of the main reasons why controls haven't worked well in the past. Slightly more than half of the respondents said some sort of restriction on the use of credit cards would help, as would putting a ceiling on housing prices.

A pronounced protectionist sentiment also emerged from the survey. Fifty-seven percent said adding a tax to imported goods to bring them into line with American-made products would help control prices. On the other hand, more than 60% rejected limiting the availability of mortgages as a way to control housing prices, and nearly 90% turned down a tax increase as a way of reducing total demand for goods.

To the extent that Americans perceive government spending to be a cause of inflation, they want it cut back. Despite the opposition of most political and economic leaders, they favor by a ratio of 50 to 31 the controversial idea of a constitutional amendment to balance the federal budget. And if it turned out that peacemaking efforts abroad required increased taxes, half the respondents would rather have that part of the budget cut. As for their personal spending, 63% said they would accept a pay freeze if they could have stable prices rather than continued inflation.

As pervasive as is the concern about

prices, the prospect of high unemployment seems no less frightening. By 38% to 29%, respondents said they would rather deal with high inflation than high joblessness. At the same time, only 6% said they felt loss of jobs was a currently urgent issue and only 2% volunteered that a recession was of immediate concern.

When asked to choose between conflicting energy policies, 53% said they would prefer gasoline rationing to an increase of 50¢ per gal. in the price of gas. Some 75% said that increasing all oil prices, as President Carter plans, would not help discourage excessive use. Nearly two-thirds felt that closing gasoline stations would do nothing to limit the consumption of gasoline.

On the question of nuclear power, Americans were predictably undecided. With the Three Mile Island nuclear plant accident still fresh in their minds, 42% said the dangers of a nuclear accident concerned them a lot. Yet when confronted with the choice of building more nuclear power plants "even in neighborhoods such as your own" or facing a serious energy shortage, more than half said they would prefer building more plants.

Beyond the choices and concerns about the national economy lies a more difficult and perhaps more damaging problem: the corrosive effects that continued inflation have on the political and psychological atmosphere. Throughout the country, people are finding that despite rising incomes their economic situation is either stagnating or worsening, leading to feelings of having been cheated. Observes Dubuque University Sociologist Wayne Youngquist: "Inflation takes all the old rules and invalidates them. It creates an unstable, speculative, spendthrift mentality and causes the erosion of social values. As a result, the electorate is extremely volatile. Voters have become like unguided missiles as they try to figure out how to have an effect."

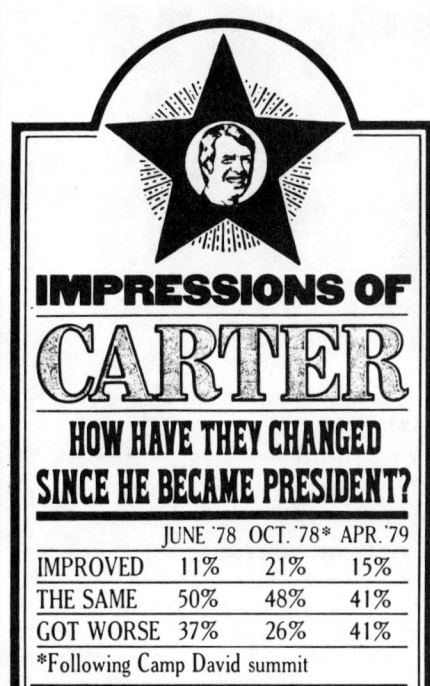

IMPRESSIONS OF CARTER
HOW HAVE THEY CHANGED SINCE HE BECAME PRESIDENT?

	JUNE '78	OCT. '78*	APR. '79
IMPROVED	11%	21%	15%
THE SAME	50%	48%	41%
GOT WORSE	37%	26%	41%

*Following Camp David summit

According to the Yankelovich survey 53% of the people questioned agreed fully with the statement: "People who work hard and live by the rules are not getting a fair deal these days." More than a third agreed that "people like yourself are powerless to change things in the country."

Plainly, this resentment is not unguided. It is targeted directly on Jimmy Carter. Most striking is the decline in the trust the President inspires in the country, a political quality that has been the hallmark both of his candidacy and his two years in office. Less than a majority of those polled said they think Carter is a leader they can trust. Even among Democrats, only 48% gave the President their undiminished loyalty, and 50% or more in each section of the country said they had doubts and reservations about his trustworthiness.

In the first few months of his presidency Carter impressed many people with his performance; 82% now say their impressions of Carter have either remained the same or worsened. More than one-third of those who voted for him in 1976 say their opinion of Carter has declined since his election.

The prime factor behind this decline is his handling of the economy. Forty-two percent gave his economic policies as the reason for lowering their opinions of the President. Thirty-one percent blamed his overall lack of leadership and 23% listed his management of the energy situation. Asked specifically if they had a lot of confidence in the President's handling of the economy, a mere 8% said yes, compared with 33% when he took office.

The results on the energy question were a disappointment for the President as well. Only 14% expressed a lot of confidence on that score, while 41% said they had no real confidence at all.

The post–Camp David surge in the President's popularity has not been repeated after his triumph in the Middle East. While half of the sample reported some confidence in Carter diplomacy, only 27% said they had a lot of confidence, and slightly less than a quarter said they had no confidence at all. Any hope the President has of bolstering his flagging popularity with new foreign policy triumphs, like the impending SALT II agreement, thus seems rather empty.

The SALT treaty itself still does not command support from a majority of the country, but the trend since last June seems to be toward greater acceptance. Forty-one percent now say the treaty should be signed, compared with only 32% nearly a year ago, while the percentage of those who feel the treaty is too risky has declined in the ten months from 56% to 48%. Some 37% still feel that the Soviet Union would be the chief beneficiary of the treaty.

As the President's popularity has declined, the mood of pessimism in the country has increased, creating ominous signals both for a second Carter term and for inflation itself. Fifty-one percent now believe that with Carter in the White House inflation will get worse, as compared with less than 10% who think that he will be able to stop inflation. That kind of lack of expectations is self-fulfilling; economists say that people alter their lifestyles in anticipation of ever higher prices. This pessimistic mood extends beyond the Carter presidency. Not more than 17% feel that any other President, Republican or Democrat, will be able to stop the inflationary spiral. ∎

2

RUNAWAY INFLATION

Can Carter Corral It?

The cost of living is going up faster than almost anyone expected. The government's anti-inflation plan hasn't done a thing yet to slow the wage-price race, and the experts—along with consumers—are groping for new answers.

The surge of inflation bedeviling the U.S. is turning into a stampede in spite of everything President Carter is trying to do to bring it under control.

Food, energy, utilities, housing, tuition, hotel and restaurant prices—almost every product or service is going through the roof.

One economist after another, as a result, is backing away from earlier predictions that inflation would slow substantially in 1979. Carter, himself, at his February 27 news conference, said that "inflationary pressures do exceed what we had anticipated."

The President's guidelines for wage and price increases are in danger of collapse. Fears are growing that, to get the boom and the wage-price spiral under control, the Federal Reserve System may have to step harder on the credit brakes and bring on a recession.

Not only did consumer prices rise more in 1978—9 percent—than in any year since 1974 and speed up in January, but costs have continued to soar in one industry after another in recent weeks, and these increases will soon be passed along to the public.

A steeper rise. Oil price increases that were expected to come gradually throughout the year have now been bunched, to a large extent, in the first two months. Some industry experts expect the base price set by the Organization of Petroleum Exporting Countries to rise 20 percent this year, instead of the 14.5 percent that OPEC was aiming at last December.

Costlier oil means higher rates for electricity and transportation. Gasoline, on average, is likely to cost motorists close to 80 cents a gallon this summer, at least 10 cents more than now. Predictions are widespread that unleaded fuel will pass the $1-a-gallon mark in 1980.

Bus and trucking companies, airlines and railroads are also paying more for fuel and boosting their charges accordingly. The Interstate Commerce Commission has just given railroads permission to raise freight rates on a long list of commodities, including cotton, wheat, soybeans and paper products, and the industry is expected to seek a much bigger, across-the-board boost later this year.

Farm experts say that food prices will rise substantially more than they figured when the year began.

In many areas, rental houses and apartments are increasingly scarce, reflecting a low level of apartment construction in recent years and the massive conversion of older units into condominiums. That translates into pressure for higher rents.

Before the nuts and bolts. Prices paid by industry for basic ingredients are rising.

Shoe factories are paying 94 cents a pound for top-grade hides, up from 70 cents at the beginning of January.

At 90 to 95 cents a pound, copper for wiring, plumbing and all sorts of household gadgets has rarely been so expensive—up nearly 20 cents a pound in just two months.

Other metals—lead, zinc and aluminum—have joined the parade. Tin, platinum and gold are selling at record or near-record prices.

Scrap steel, a major ingredient for making new metal, now costs $107 a ton delivered in Chicago, up $20 since the start of this year. The steel industry, also facing higher prices for other materials, already has announced one

What's Happening To Your Dollar

The dollar that bought 100 cents worth of goods and services in 1967

Today buys only 49¢ worth

And a year from now will buy just 44¢ if present inflation rates continue

Source: U.S. Dept. of Labor

round of price increases this year, and a second is expected next summer that will show up in 1980 auto models.

Silver for photography, jewelry and flatware is selling for $7.85 an ounce in New York. A year ago: less than $5.

Higher prices for imported raw materials and finished products—everything from ores to autos to wines and perfumes—continue to work their way through the economy as a result of the dollar's decline in value in foreign markets last year.

The price of money. Companies all across the nation are paying more, sometimes record rates, for credit, a major cost of doing business. South Central Bell Telephone Company, with a top credit rating, has just paid 9⅝ percent to borrow on a new issue of bonds, its highest cost in more than three years.

Higher borrowing costs will, in time, force state and federal regulators to allow telephone, gas and electric companies to boost the rates they charge to other businesses and homeowners.

Price cuts, meanwhile, are few and far between. Coffee has come down markedly during the past year. Airlines have reduced some fares since the government relaxed its regulations.

Why is inflation proving such an intractable foe? Largely because of an economic boom that shows few signs of slowing down and, more recently, a revolution in Iran that has shut off oil exports from that country and caused shortages around the globe.

The bad news on prices faced by industry and consumers spells trouble also for the President's efforts to impose guidelines to limit wage and price increases.

Already, federal officials are trying to find a way to make the lid on pay more palatable to the unions without appearing to give up the fight.

Alfred Kahn, the man in charge of the President's anti-inflation campaign, has wondered aloud how the federal government can expect workers to settle for a 7 percent increase in income at a time when the government officially forecasts a 7.4 percent jump in the cost of living and when most economists fear that inflation will be much worse than that.

A top federal economist calculates the basic rate of inflation—not counting unusual factors that sent food and oil prices soaring in recent weeks—at about 8 percent a year.

With prices rising even faster than that, people who get pay raises of 7 percent in keeping with the federal standard will lose purchasing power at least in the first half of this year, Kahn recently conceded.

A labor leader's view. That prospect complicates the government's task of preventing a major, perhaps fatal, breach in the guidelines when the Teamsters' master freight agreement expires on March 31. Roy Williams, union vice president, warned on February 27: "As long as the price index keeps going up and they don't put any

MACROECONOMICS, 1979

curb on inflation, our members are going to be harder to deal with."

Thus far, few unions have publicly accepted the guidelines.

Douglas Fraser, president of the United Auto Workers, has indicated that his union might do so—but only if prices do not continue to skyrocket.

Where business stands. Among the large corporations, acceptance has been widespread. At latest count, 207 companies out of 500 that were asked to promise compliance with the price and wage restraints have told the Council on Wage and Price Stability that they will do so. Officials predict the vast majority of the other firms also will go along.

Kahn, however, complained in a speech to business leaders in Detroit that some companies are moving too quickly to put into effect the maximum amount of price increase allowed by the guidelines for the first half of this year. The National Association of Purchasing Management also suggested that the guidelines may actually be encouraging some companies to hike prices now instead of waiting until later in the year.

Most economists figure that the guidelines will have only marginal impact on inflation even if they do hold. Most of their appraisals suggest that inflation will, at best, slow down very gradually and continue for years to be much worse than this country was accustomed to before the "soaring '70s."

The President's advisers still say it is possible that prices will be rising at an annual rate of less than 7 percent by the end of this year, compared with more than 11 percent in January. They count on more-normal weather and greater hog production to check the rise in grocery bills later in 1979.

Finally, the Carter administration expects very slow economic growth in the second half of this year, so that it will become more difficult for some companies to raise prices or wages. Officials suggest that, once the government is seen to be in earnest, "inflationary expectations" will be lowered, and people will no longer be buying ahead and demanding pay raises to protect themselves against the threat of runaway prices.

The guidelines are supposed to help bring about that change in attitude.

Inflation's Treadmill

Even if your income keeps up with inflation, chances are that you will wind up with less buying power. Reason: income-tax rates that rise as income climbs, and Social Security taxes that have been boosted steadily. For example, counting only the impact of federal taxes—

1974 Income		1979 Income After Taxes			Change in Buying Power of Income After Taxes
Total	After Taxes	Total	Current Dollars	1974 Dollars	
$ 7,500	$ 6,611	$ 10,650	$ 9,519	$ 6,704	+1.4%
$ 10,000	$ 8,605	$ 14,200	$12,232	$ 8,614	+0.1%
$ 15,000	$12,628	$ 21,300	$17,623	$12,411	−1.7%
$ 20,000	$16,718	$ 28,400	$23,185	$16,327	−2.3%
$ 30,000	$24,528	$ 42,600	$33,670	$23,711	−3.3%
$ 50,000	$38,438	$ 71,000	$51,780	$36,465	−5.1%
$100,000	$68,668	$142,000	$94,418	$66,492	−3.2%

Note: Assumes 42 percent total increase in inflation and income and that all income is earned by one spouse in family of four; deductions are the higher of 20 percent or the standard-deduction/zero-bracket amount.

A slowdown in business, short of an actual recession, is a major part of Carter's strategy. The President is counting on the Federal Reserve System to keep interest rates high but not tighten the screws on credit so severely as to bring on a recession. Carter is also banking on a more conservative Congress to help him hold down federal spending, reduce the deficit, and thus keep the government itself from piling fuel on the inflationary fires.

So far there are few signs that this strategy is working. The economy continues to expand at a fast clip. Latest reports tell of increases in orders received by industry for durable goods, including business equipment, machinery and machine tools. As some economists see it, this means that the Federal Reserve may, after all, have to press harder on the credit brakes even at the risk of bringing on a slump, if it is to be successful in checking inflation and keeping the dollar afloat in the international money market.

Another hurdle. The government is also finding it impossible to fight inflation single-mindedly. To placate growers and their allies in Congress, the White House recently agreed to boost the price floor under raw sugar from 15 cents a pound to 15.8 cents.

Also, steps are being taken to restrain imports of steel, textiles and some other items. The aim is to forestall a wave of "protectionism" in Congress that might wreck plans for a new world trade agreement. One result, however, will be less competition holding down domestic prices.

Meanwhile, efforts to protect industries from excessive costs of government regulations are running into

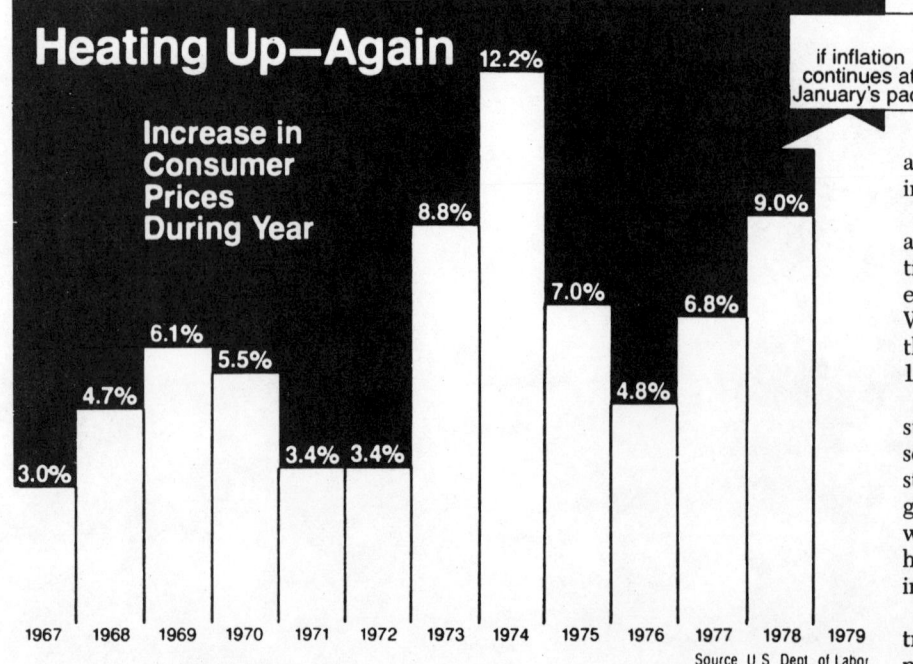

Heating Up—Again
Increase in Consumer Prices During Year

1967: 3.0% 1968: 4.7% 1969: 6.1% 1970: 5.5% 1971: 3.4% 1972: 3.4% 1973: 8.8% 1974: 12.2% 1975: 7.0% 1976: 4.8% 1977: 6.8% 1978: 9.0% 1979: if inflation continues at January's pace

Source: U.S. Dept. of Labor

U.S.NEWS & WORLD REPORT, March 12, 1979

trouble. Federal regulators—and some key lawmakers—say there is little leeway under the law to consider the economic impact of federal rules intended to reduce pollution and increase safety. So-called public-interest groups are threatening to go to court if standards are eased. So far, Carter is reluctant to tackle this problem head-on by suggesting a change in the laws.

A White House demand that agencies draw up a calendar of proposed regulatory actions with cost estimates for each evoked no response from many agencies, only vague generalizations from some others. The Occupational Safety and Health Administration, for example, said its plans for regulating carcinogenic substances, which industry claims may cost more than 40 billion dollars, will have "no direct economic impact."

How economists see it. What more could the government do to curb inflation? Economists, by and large, feel Carter is trying to do the right things. But many of them want to see evidence of more determined leadership. Some feel his budget is still too large.

Most private forecasters are raising their estimates of how much prices will climb in 1979. Raymond Jallow, senior vice president and chief economist at the United California Bank, Los Angeles, says he now expects prices to average 8 to 8½ percent higher than in 1978. He initially estimated the rise at less than 7 percent.

Says Norman Robertson, chief economist of the Mellon Bank in Pittsburgh: "Progress toward a lower inflation rate is likely to be slow, erratic and more than a little uncertain. In fact, for 1979 as a whole, I am concerned that the rise in retail prices may come uncomfortably close to 10 percent."

The forecast from Data Resources, Inc., in Lexington, Mass., is 9 percent from the fourth quarter of last year to the fourth quarter of this year.

Economists at Merrill Lynch Economics, Inc., in New York, are more hopeful about the chances of a marked slowing of inflation. They estimate the price rise during this year at only 6.7 percent. That figure implies an even slower pace by the end of 1979. However, this group is also counting on "a recession of moderate depth lasting six to nine months" to eliminate much of the inflationary pressure.

Whether events will bear out any of these forecasts is a big question. Prices have surprised the experts time and again in the 1970s as inflation proved to be more virulent than economists reckoned. There's no clear-cut evidence yet that Carter will be able to cure this disease. □

3

The gross national product, the various inflation indexes, and the employment statistics were once tucked away in the daily financial section, where they could be pondered by businessmen and economists and ignored by the general public. Now these same numbers are the stuff of which front-page headlines and televised congressional hearings are made. A blip in an important index may create strong public pressure for remedial action —and the pressure may persist after the blip has been erased by a revision in the data. Communities stand to gain or lose millions in federal aid from a change in the local unemployment rate, and an uptick in inflation triggers multimillion-dollar adjustments in wages and pensions.

In this three-part series, FORTUNE *takes a look at how the principal economic indicators are compiled, how accurate they are, why they are being endlessly revised, and how they might be made better. The subsequent articles will deal with the unemployment rate and the G.N.P.*

Verena Brunner, an attractive blonde field economist for the Labor Department, begins her day at a small, scruffy supermarket in New York City's Spanish Harlem. The *ambiente* is cordial there, and staccato Spanish punctuates the air as Miss Brunner quietly goes about her business, moving past bins of melons and mangos, searching for a predetermined list of groceries that make up part of the consumer price index. Miss Brunner isn't buying; rather, she's on a "quality assurance" mission for the Bureau of Labor Statistics. She has replaced the regular data collector for the day to make sure the "regular" hasn't been doing sloppy work or "curbstoning" (the BLS term for faking it, while sitting, presumably, upon a curbstone).

As Miss Brunner travels from the ghetto grocery store far uptown to a department store on the fashionable East Side and a half dozen more establishments throughout midtown Manhattan, store clerks recognize her by the dark blue notebook she carries under her arm. Emblazoned with the legend, "Consumer Price Index," it's

Research associate: Patricia Hough

the trademark of the 500 BLS data collectors across the country who visit stores selected by computers in Washington and note the prices of various items also picked by the computers in accord with sophisticated statistical techniques.

The grand result is our chief indicator of inflation, and possibly the single most important statistic produced by the government. The consumer price index, designed to measure the price change of a fixed market basket of goods and services over time, influences consumers' confidence and investors' plans. A change of 1 percent in the index can trigger a billion dollars' worth of income transfers, affecting about half the population. All 31 million Social Security recipients have their payments tied to the C.P.I. by a cost-of-living escalator, as do 2.5 million retired members of the civil-service and the military.

Changes in the index also directly affect

Our Flawed Inflation Indexes

by EDWARD MEADOWS

Illustration by James Flora

Reprinted from the April 24, 1978 issue of Fortune Magazine by special permission; © 1978 Time Inc.

MACROECONOMICS, 1979

The consumer price index and other official measures of prices aren't as accurate as they should be, and they have a persistent upward bias.

the food-stamp allotments for 20 million recipients, the subsidies for the 25 million children who are served food under the National School Lunch Act and the Child Nutrition Act, and benefits for millions more who partake of health and welfare programs with "poverty level" eligibility requirements tied to the C.P.I. Then, too, there is the growing number of private contracts governed by a C.P.I. escalator. The contracts cover such various matters as rent, child-support payments, and, most notably, the wages of nine million unionized workers whose cost-of-living escalators are tied to the C.P.I.

Those union workers loom large in the life of the C.P.I., for the index was born a child of labor's needs, being first used by the government to adjust the wages of shipbuilders during the World War I inflation. Every change in the C.P.I.'s methodology since then has been suspiciously watched by the unions, out of fear that the index may suppress wages by underreporting inflation. In fact, most economists agree that the problem is just the opposite: because of sundry inherent biases, the index has been exaggerating inflation for decades.

The quality problem

No one seriously denies that the biases exist; the debate is over their magnitude. Yale economist Richard Ruggles offers one of the larger estimates. He suggests that if the C.P.I. had taken improvements in the quality of products into account, prices would be seen to have fallen steadily from 1949 to 1966, whereas the C.P.I. had them rising 36 percent in that period. (Ruggles concedes that prices *have* been going up since 1966, though less than the index indicates.) The C.P.I. simply fails to adjust adequately when the higher price of, say, a color TV set reflects only the higher costs of building improved circuitry. The consumer may be paying more, but he's getting more too. And while the BLS continues to price that particular model, the consumer is free to switch to a cheaper one.

The BLS does attempt to allow for some of the changes in quality by subtracting the cost of a new feature from the increased price. But this works only when the improvement is apparent and easy to value. It ignores improvements that don't raise costs, or that actually lower them.

In many cases, of course, quality is subjective, and attempts to measure it can be contentious. A case in point, famous in BLS folklore, arose in 1971 when automobiles acquired antipollution equipment. The BLS decided that the anti-smog gear represented a price increase without a quality increase, since performance wasn't improved and maintenance became more expensive. But an interagency committee set up by the Office of Management and Budget overruled the bureau, arguing that society as a whole would benefit from cleaner air. The cost of the equipment was kept out of the C.P.I., and the decision still rankles at the BLS. Says John Layng, the assistant commissioner in charge of price statistics: "That was one of the big ones we lost."

A pervasive source of upward bias is found in the market basket itself, which remains fixed for far too long. The brand-new index, released for the first time in February, is in fact based on a consumer-expenditure survey conducted in 1972-73, when the Census Bureau interviewed 20,000 families to see how they disposed of their money. Obviously the survey shows how Americans spent their incomes *before* the quadrupling of oil prices and before the dramatic food price increases of the mid-1970's. But economists know that, if one effect of price increases is to lower people's real income, the other effect is to cause switching from higher-priced goods to lower-priced substitutes. This "substitution effect" grows stronger over time, as alternative products evolve.

Shiskin's improvements

The commissioner of the Bureau of Labor Statistics, Julius Shiskin, admits the obsolescence of the C.P.I.'s "new" market basket. He and other economists acknowledge that the problem lies in the practice of conducting consumer-expenditure surveys only once every ten or more years. That was okay in former, more stable periods of price behavior. But in the volatile 1970's, more frequent studies are needed.

And, indeed, the bureau now has money in its budget to begin an ongoing survey. According to Commissioner Layng, the data collection will start next year, and information from the continuous expenditure survey will be incorporated into the index by the mid-1980's. (The BLS has also embarked on a continuing point-of-pur-

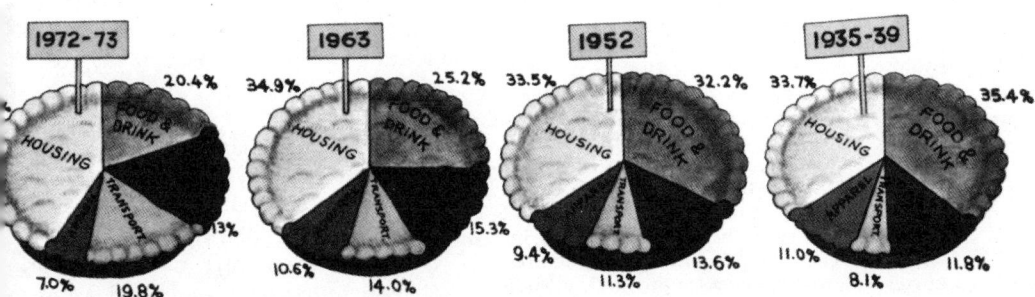

Once a month the Bureau of Labor Statistics computes the price of the "market basket" of consumer goods and services that make up the consumer price index. Family budgets have changed a lot over the years, with food accounting for a shrinking percentage of total purchases and housing and transportation for a growing share. But the market basket is revised only once every ten years or so, and the "new" C.P.I., based on a consumer-expenditure survey taken in 1972-73, is already out of date.

Wholesale Prices Run a Wayward Course

chase survey to ensure that its data collectors are checking retail outlets typical of the ones where most consumers shop.)

Oddly enough, the issue generating the most heat on the BLS these days is relatively unimportant. From its inception, the C.P.I. has measured the price experiences not of everyman but of two specific groups —urban wage earners and clerical workers, who between them make up only about 40 percent of the population. As part of the recent overhaul of the C.P.I., the BLS began publishing a second index, covering the entire urban and suburban civilian population. The broader index is obviously a good idea, but organized labor is up in arms, suspecting some long-range plot to phase out the older index and perhaps understate the effect of inflation on the working man. It is too soon to know how closely the two indexes will track each other, but in the first two months they moved in close tandem—that is to say, upward more than they would have had the biases been stripped out.

Part of the spiral?

There is no way to ascertain how strong that upward bias might be, though there is a fair amount of support for Professor Ruggles's estimate, which on the basis of quality changes alone works out to better than 2 percent a year. Even more problematic is what role the C.P.I. may have in *causing* inflation by triggering excessive increases as a result of those escalator clauses, which feed the wage-price spiral. Wages are hard-fought matters, and it is at least conceivable that the unions would be getting increases of the same size even if there were no C.P.I. at all. Still, given the importance now attached to these numbers, they should be as good as the taxpayers' money, in reasonable quantities, can buy. Continual revision of the market basket will help, and a number of economists, including Northwestern University's Robert J. Gordon, argue that there are mathematical techniques that the BLS could use to isolate the price effect of quality improvements from other price changes. "These days," he notes, "computer time

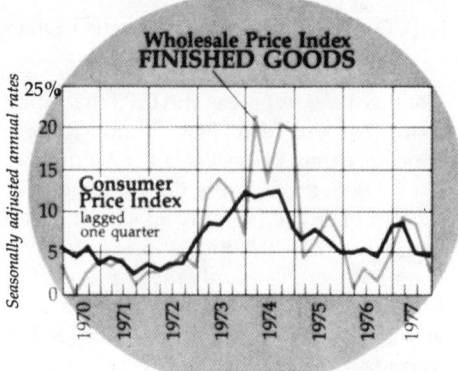

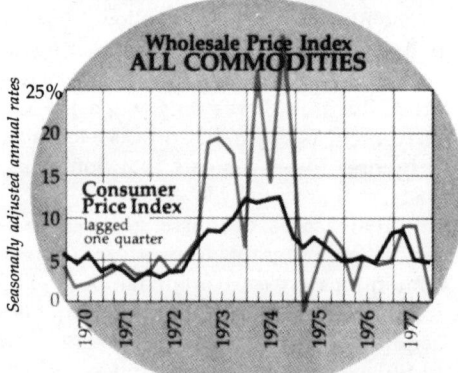

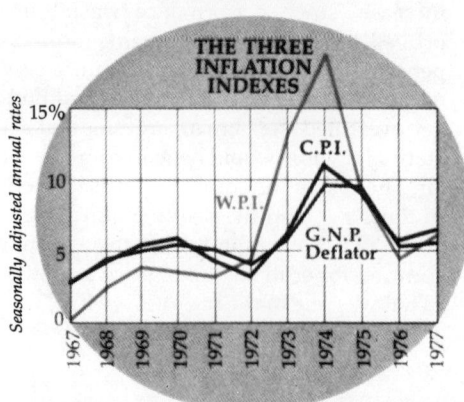

The wholesale price index is frequently used by journalists as an indicator of what will be happening to consumer prices later on. The top two charts measure the soothsaying ability of two different versions of the W.P.I.—the "finished goods" and "all commodities" indexes —by comparing them with the consumer price index, which is lagged here by one quarter. The "finished goods" index, which counts only goods ready for sale to distributors, does a better job than the "all commodities" W.P.I., which contains a grab-bag of raw materials, intermediate goods, and finished goods. Neither, however, is awfully close to the mark. At bottom is an unlagged comparison of the three major price indexes—the C.P.I., the all-commodities W.P.I., and the G.N.P. deflator. It's obvious that the W.P.I. runs a wayward course.

is cheap and the technique could be adopted for a few important product categories with little additional expense." It might be just as well, all the same, to keep George Meany in the dark until the bugs are worked out.

The broadest measure

Journalists and Wall Streeters may chart the flight path of the C.P.I., but economists have traditionally preferred the "implicit price deflator of the Gross National Product." That mouthful refers to the price index that results when statisticians in the Commerce Department's Bureau of Economic Analysis "deflate" current-dollar G.N.P. to a constant-dollar amount. They begin by dividing the various subcategories of current-dollar G.N.P. by the relevant price indexes. For instance, the C.P.I. indexes are used to deflate various classes of consumer outlays; the wholesale price indexes are used for some classifications of capital goods; special indexes, such as the telephone-equipment index provided by A.T.&T., are used to deflate special categories. Then the "deflated" sums are added, to arrive at a single figure for *real* G.N.P. When this figure is divided into current-dollar G.N.P., what falls out is the deflator.

The virtue of the G.N.P. deflator is its breadth of coverage, which also, however, encompasses some rather broad categories of error. The deflator picks up errors from the C.P.I. and the wholesale price index, and it adds a few of its own. Services loom large, since they account for almost half the G.N.P., and there is no good way to measure changes in the quality of services. So far, the BEA hasn't really tried; it simply attributes all increases in the cost of haircuts or government to inflation.

The G.N.P. deflator also suffers from a chronic tardiness that makes it less useful for short-term analysis. It is first released with the early G.N.P. estimates, about twenty days after the end of the quarter. These estimates involve much guesswork, and users must wait for the third or fourth revision before the figures begin to settle down. That's because many of the private and governmental sales data the BEA reies on to compute G.N.P. just aren't available in time for the initial quarterly estimates and some not for a considerable time afterward. In the meantime, BEA statisticians make estimates based on recent trends. Their early estimates aren't necessarily any better than those made by private forecasters, but because of the official auspices, they carry a lot more weight.

Adding to the deflator's short-term unreliability is the distorting effect of the frequent shifts in U.S. spending patterns. If housing, where prices have gone up much faster than the overall average during the past few years, falls on its face for a quarter, the deflator will be held down because that higher-priced item is less important in the total G.N.P. These problems are corrected for in two specialized BEA indexes —which do not, however, make the newspaper front pages.

The least reliable measure

If the C.P.I. and the deflator have their problems, they are paragons of statistical science compared with the other main inflation indicator, the wholesale price index. The W.P.I. is put to many important uses —as a "materials escalator," for example, in at least $100 billion worth of long-term contracts, and to revalue corporate assets at replacement cost, as required by the Securities and Exchange Commission. The Justice Department pores over breakdowns of the W.P.I., looking for evidence of monopolistic practices. And of course the news media see the W.P.I. as a forecaster of consumer prices. Yet Yale's Professor Ruggles, who recently completed a major study of the W.P.I. for the Council on Wage and Price Stability, concluded that the index "fulfills its functions so badly that a major effort should be made to replace it."

How does the wholesale price index err? Let us count the ways. Even its name is misleading, for the W.P.I. doesn't measure wholesalers' prices. Instead, it gauges prices from producers in mining, manufacturing, and agriculture. To measure those price changes, the BLS sends out forms each month to about 3,000 firms that have volunteered to report their prices on about 10,000 items. The quotations are used to construct separate price indexes for 2,800 commodities. These are then combined into averages, weighted by the quantity of goods shipped back in 1972.

However, the BLS adequately prices only 27 percent of the products made by the 550 major U.S. industries, and many of the price changes listed in the W.P.I. are based on reports from only one or two firms. Worse than that, the selection of the items to be priced is arbitrary and frequently out of date. Professor Gordon points this out as a major source of upward bias in the W.P.I. The index for office machinery, he notes, has shown increasing prices just during those years when electronic computing equipment offered dramatic reductions in price per computation. Whereas in 1952 it cost $1.26 to do 100,000 multiplications, now they can be done for less than a penny. Yet the W.P.I. has missed the price drop, because most types of modern office equipment, including computers, aren't even priced by the BLS.

A candid admission

"The W.P.I. is based on very thin data," admits Commissioner Layng. "We have pushed the data base too far, basing 2,800 price series on 10,000 quotes." And if the price quotes are too few in number, their quality is highly suspect, for many companies habitually report only their list prices. These may equal transactions prices when demand is strong. But in the doldrums of recession, producers shave prices through cash discounts, or by offering free shipment to the buyer's warehouse, or by any number of other devices. Thus, industrial prices rise and fall more sharply with fluctuating demand than the W.P.I. indicates.

"Businessmen are too secretive about their prices," complains Layng. "We think we're getting good price quotes, but it's hard to tell. Price is a sensitive topic to most businessmen." He concedes that the BLS doesn't always get to the bottom of the matter. "For instance, in the steel industry there are firms that have large sales forces with some pricing latitude. Now, we go into the accounting department for detailed prices, but it may not be aware of the discounts used by salesmen."

Double and triple counting

Layng has pointed out that the W.P.I. is biased because it gets its reports mostly from the bigger firms, leaving out smaller and perhaps more competitive ones. Upward bias creeps in because the W.P.I., like the C.P.I., isn't properly adjusted for quality improvements. Professor Gordon finds this bias especially strong when it comes to durable goods such as electric appliances, which, he notes, have grown increasingly energy efficient and reliable.

The W.P.I.'s biggest distortion of all comes from double, triple, and even more redundant counting of price changes. If the price of cotton rises, and the price hike is passed on to yarn producers, and by them to cotton-fabric producers, and by them to finished-cotton-fabric makers, and finally to shirtmakers, the price increase will have been counted five times in the W.P.I.

The problem led Layng's predecessor, Joel Popkin, to upgrade three supplementary series—for raw goods, intermediate goods (those sold from one producer to another for further processing), and finished goods ready for sale to distributors. Late last year the BLS officially recognized the deficiency of the original "all commodities" W.P.I. by announcing that it was switching emphasis from this measure to one of Popkin's improved indexes, the finished-goods series. And in belated recognition that W.P.I. was something of a misnomer, the BLS this month is changing the name of its three-way tabulation to the Producer Price Indexes.

Guided by Ruggles's report, Layng and his technicians at the BLS have outlined a program of major overhaul for the W.P.I. They want to cover many more industries, gather larger samples of prices, use scientific sampling techniques to replace the judgmental procedures now in force, attempt better reporting of transaction prices, and further eliminate multiple counting. Unfortunately, the reform plan is a piecemeal affair, dependent on future funding by Congress. The best the BLS can do with present funds is to enact the easiest revisions, and even those wouldn't come to fruition till the mid-1980's.

Time for repairs

So it's evident that our price indexes are imprecise guides at best, and highly flawed ones by any reckoning. Their manifold errors could seriously mislead the policymakers. Yet, because they are now so much used by prognosticators, contract negotiators, and Presidents, they can't just be left to the statisticians either.

If these figures are to bear the heavy informational burdens thrust upon them, they'd better be as good as they can be. It's clear that they can be improved by some relatively simple expedients, and this does seem to be one place where Congress can spend to good advantage by amply financing complete and competent upgrading of all the price indexes. Meanwhile, it's wise to take abrupt gyrations in the numbers with a skeptical and stoic calm.

4

An examination of employment and unemployment rates

The persistence of high rates of unemployment after more than two years of economic recovery has increased the controversy over what the best measure of labor market conditions is. The usefulness of the unemployment rate, the traditional measure, has been called into question; the employment ratio is the most frequently recommended alternative. Too frequently, the debate has implied that an absolute choice must be made between the two statistics. Such a view is mistaken, for no single measure can hope to provide a complete assessment of labor market conditions.

At the outset, it must be recognized that each measure suffers from some shortcomings. The unemployment rate has the most deficiencies, and because of them that rate has become an increasingly imperfect measure of labor market conditions. Analysts are therefore regarding the unemployment rate with increasing reservations, and some have suggested that the employment ratio be given more emphasis in the analysis of the labor market as it reflects demand pressures in the economy as a whole.

The two measures defined
The unemployment rate refers to the percentage of the civilian labor force that is seeking work but does not have a job.[1] This widely used statistic is not the only unemployment rate that the Bureau of Labor Statistics (BLS) regularly reports. A number of other unemployment rates, such as the percentage of household heads in the labor force who are unemployed, the percentage of teenagers in the labor force who are unemployed, and the percentage of the labor force out of work for fifteen weeks or longer are also available for evaluating labor market conditions. No matter whether the total or a segmental unemployment rate is examined, all these rates are intended to represent the proportion of labor force participants that offer labor for sale but are unable to find employment at the current level of wages. Thus, each measures the unutilized or excess supply of labor in the market at existing wages.

The employment ratio, in contrast, is defined as the proportion of the noninstitutionalized *population* in the working ages—16 years of age and older—that is employed, and it thus measures the extent of utilization of potential labor resources.[2] Employment ratios analogous to many of the published unemployment series may be constructed. These ratios measure the proportion of labor resources whose services have been purchased in the labor market.

A rate of unemployment supposedly indicates the extent of utilization of available rather than potential labor resources. The unemployment rate is also used to help assess the hardship experienced by workers who are willing to work and are available for work but are unable to find jobs. But whether the unemployment rate indicates hardship or need as precisely as one would like has come to be questioned. Its accuracy is impaired in several ways. The measured rate can be considered too low because it fails to include "discouraged workers", that is, the people who do not seek work if they do not believe they are likely to obtain jobs and thus leave the labor force temporarily or remain outside it. Similarly, the rate fails to include those who want to work full time but are forced to work part time because of economic conditions. In-

[1] The civilian labor force refers to all noninstitutionalized individuals 16 years of age and over who are employed or are without a job and seeking work.

[2] If the employment ratio were defined as the proportion of civilian labor force that is employed, it would simply be the mirror image of the unemployment rate. In that case, it could be obtained by subtracting the unemployment rate from 100. But then, any statistical or institutional factors that caused defects in the unemployment rate would cause the same defects in an employment ratio based on the civilian labor force. That is why the employment ratio uses the relevant population rather than the labor force in the denominator.

Reprinted from Federal Reserve Bank of New York *Quarterly Review*, Autumn, 1977.

stead, all part-time workers with jobs are treated as employed whether or not they would prefer full-time work.[3] The measured rate can be considered too high because of the expansion in the coverage of such programs as unemployment insurance as well as the rise in benefit levels. Applicants must remain in the labor force to receive these benefits even though they may not be seriously looking for jobs. Such behavior imparts an upward thrust to the unemployment rate. And the increases in these programs have also served to weaken the tie between the unemployment rate and "hardship".

Changing participation rates and their impact
The employment ratio avoids to a greater degree than the unemployment rate a statistical problem that is caused by changing labor force participation rates, *i.e.*, the proportion of the population 16 years of age and over who are at work or are looking for work. Changes in these participation rates have altered the composition of the labor force in recent years. The changes suggest that a basic structural alteration in the pattern of choice among work in the market, work at home, and the amount of leisure desired is under way, particularly in certain demographic groups. As a result of these changes, a larger proportion of the labor force now consists of women and teenagers. Indeed, the secular increase in labor force participation rates (see top panel, Chart 1) is attributable largely to this change in behavior by women and teenagers. And these groups in the labor force are among those that traditionally have experienced higher than average rates of unemployment. It is now recognized that for this reason alone a given rate of aggregate demand will be associated with a higher level of unemployment than in the past.[4]

Experience shows that rates of labor force participation respond to a host of influences. In the short term, the rate of business activity may have the most effect. On the one hand, the rate of participation in the labor force typically increases during upswings in economic activity because individuals perceive increased job opportunities. If, as sometimes happens, the growth of the labor force is faster than that of employment, the resultant increase in the unemployment rate should not be construed as a sign of weakening economic conditions. On the other hand, if during an economic decline workers become discouraged and leave the labor force, the resulting tendency toward a lower unemployment rate should not be construed as a sign of improving economic conditions.

Changes in the long-term trend of labor force participation rates also affect the interpretation of the two measures. Should the rate of participation in the labor force and the age-sex composition of the population

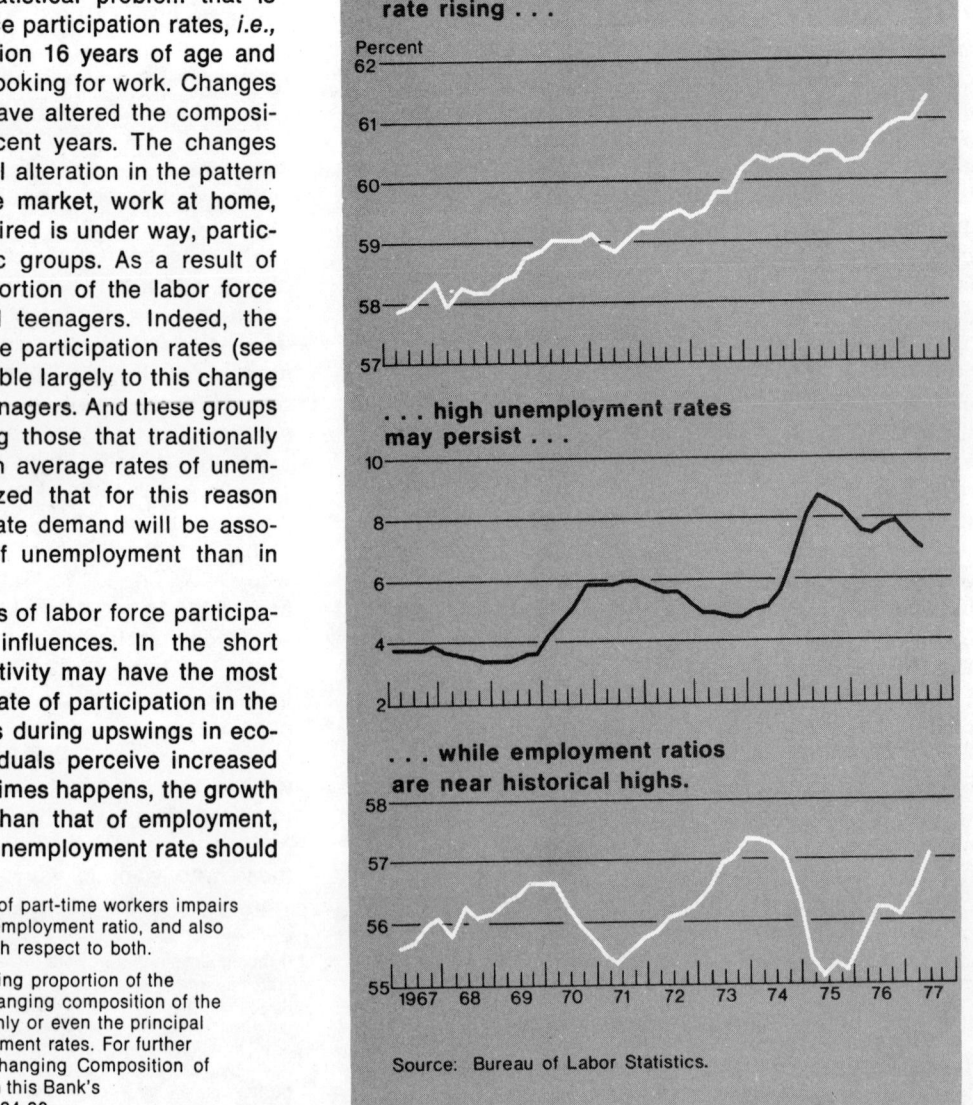

Chart 1
With the labor force participation rate rising . . .

. . . high unemployment rates may persist . . .

. . . while employment ratios are near historical highs.

Source: Bureau of Labor Statistics.

---

[3] It should be noted that this treatment of part-time workers impairs both the unemployment rate and the employment ratio, and also creates difficulties of interpretation with respect to both.

[4] While it can be shown that an increasing proportion of the unemployment rate stems from the changing composition of the labor force, this by no means is the only or even the principal explanation for today's high unemployment rates. For further discussion of this point, see "The Changing Composition of the Labor Force" by Sharon P. Smith in this Bank's *Quarterly Review* (Winter 1976), pages 24-30.

remain constant for a considerable period, the unemployment rate and the employment ratio would suggest similar assessments of labor market conditions. However, if the labor force participation rate changes, the unemployment rate and the employment ratio can yield different assessments. Among all the possible scenarios, here are two. If the labor force participation rate is rising, then the employment ratio may suggest stable labor market conditions although the unemployment rate would be increasing. If the labor force participation rate is falling, the unemployment rate may suggest a strengthening of labor market conditions although the employment ratio would be declining. It thus seems clear that when changes in labor force participation rates occur, whether for cyclical or secular reasons, *both* the unemployment rate and employment ratio ought to be looked at to obtain more accurate appraisals of labor market conditions.

The relationships being discussed are highlighted in Chart 1, which shows quarterly data for the labor force participation rate, the civilian unemployment rate, and the employment ratio. During periods when labor force participation rates are more or less constant, as they were during most of 1970-72, a rise in the unemployment rate and a decline in the employment ratio suggest worsening labor market conditions. In fact, whenever these statistics move in opposite directions and participation rates are roughly the same, both statistics yield similar labor market appraisals. In recent years, however, it has been more typical for the labor force participation rate to rise—it went up strongly from 59.8 percent at the end of 1973 to 62.3 percent in September of this year. Consequently, the present employment ratio of 57.3 percent is associated with an unemployment rate of 6.9 percent; in 1973, the same employment ratio was accompanied by an unemployment rate of only 4.8 percent.

Characteristics of the two measures
The employment ratio is in general less subject to error than the unemployment rate. Because the impact of measurement error on the unemployment rate appears to be increasing, the unemployment rate is becoming the less reliable measure with which to assess labor market conditions.

Unemployment data are collected in a survey of households, and one individual usually responds for all members of the household. As a result, the recorded employment rate is affected by the accuracy of replies by the individuals who report on the labor force status of all members of the household. It has been observed that reports given by most households show higher unemployment when they have recently been added to the survey sample than in later interviews. This is documented in a study by Robert E. Hall.[5]

Because of the difficulty of determining whether individuals actually are looking for and are available for work, a count of the employed is likely to be much more accurate than a count of the unemployed.[6] Moreover, because the employment figure is much larger than the unemployment figure, sampling errors that are to be expected in either statistic introduce a smaller possibility of error into the employment ratio than the unemployment rate. Seasonal fluctuations also are much smaller in employment than they are in unemployment.

In addition to these statistical problems, the unemployment rate is affected by institutional influences. Among the most publicized are those that occur as a consequence of unemployment compensation and of work registration requirements in certain welfare programs. To be eligible to receive benefits under the above programs, individuals are required to register as unemployed with the United States Employment Service or to register for manpower training.[7] These individuals are defined by the BLS to be unemployed, since registration with a public employment service is viewed as a means of actively seeking employment. However, these programs, like any income-maintenance plan, also create disincentives to seek employment in a more active fashion than by merely registering for employment to obtain benefits. As a result, it is likely that some recipients of benefits under these plans are voluntarily unemployed—that is, they basically choose not to work—and so would not be counted in a more precise measure of unemployment.

A number of analysts have attributed much of the present high rate of unemployment to Government benefits programs. Ehrenberg and Oaxaca, as well as Feldstein,[8] have suggested that a large portion of un-

---

[5] "Why is the Unemployment Rate So High at Full Employment?" *Brookings Papers on Economic Activity* (3, 1970), page 375.

[6] The BLS defines the employed as those who, during the survey week, worked either as paid employees or in their own profession or business, worked without pay for fifteen hours or more on a farm or a family-operated business, and those with jobs but not at work because of a labor-management dispute, illness, vacation, etc. The unemployed are defined as those who did not have a job during the survey week but were available for work and (according to the survey respondent) actively looked for a job at some time during the four-week period immediately prior to the survey.

[7] Some welfare recipients are exempt from these work registration requirements. These include certain categories such as the ill or incapacitated (with medical verification) and mothers or other members of the household charged with the care of children under age 18.

[8] See Ronald Ehrenberg and Ronald L. Oaxaca, "Do Benefits Cause Unemployed to Hold Out for Better Jobs?" and Martin Feldstein, "Unemployment Compensation: Its Effect on Unemployment", both in the *Monthly Labor Review* (March 1976).

employment is voluntary, because the high levels of unemployment compensation enable unemployed workers to engage in a longer period of search before taking another job or simply to enjoy leisure-time activities. Moreover, Feldstein believes that the present system of unemployment compensation costs some employers less in contributions to unemployment programs than the benefits that are paid to the employees they lay off. He concludes that this system thereby encourages employers to organize production so as to exaggerate seasonal and cyclical variations in unemployment and to create more temporary jobs than would otherwise exist.

Clarkson and Meiners maintain that the single most important factor contributing to the high level of unemployment is the change in certain welfare eligibility requirements.[9] They argue that the current overall unemployment rate has been inflated by as much as 2.1 percentage points because of the work registration eligibility requirements that were introduced in 1971 into the Aid to Families with Dependent Children (AFDC) program and into the food stamp program. In their view, these registrants represent a group of individuals who either are largely unemployable or have no need or desire to work but are counted as unemployed because they have to register to obtain benefits.

Clarkson and Meiners estimate a "corrected" unemployment rate by omitting from both the unemployment and the civilian labor force figures all those work registrants who have been required to register to be eligible for AFDC or food stamp benefits. This is undoubtedly an overadjustment since many welfare recipients actually do want a job. Indeed, nearly a fourth of all the AFDC recipients who register for work with the public employment service are exempt from registering. Moreover, a study of AFDC recipients indicates that nearly half of them have had recent labor market experience.[10] These facts cast doubt on the assumption that none of the welfare recipients are employable or seeking a job. In sum, while it appears that the work registration requirements of the welfare programs inflate the unemployment rate, the extent of overstatement is likely to be considerably less than the 2.1 percentage points suggested by Clarkson and Meiners.

An increasing awareness of the foregoing sorts of problems is reflected in the new unemployment insurance benefits bill signed into law on April 12, 1977.

---

[9] Kenneth W. Clarkson and Roger E. Meiners, "Government Statistics as a Guide to Economic Policy: Food Stamps and the Spurious Increase in the Unemployment Rates", *Policy Review* (Summer 1977).

[10] Robert George Williams, *Public Assistance and Work Effort* (Research Report Series No. 119, Industrial Relations Section, Princeton University, Princeton, N.J., 1975).

Under this legislation, individuals may be denied unemployment compensation if they do not actively seek work, do not apply for suitable work to which they are referred, or do not accept an offer of suitable work. Contrary to past practice, under the new law individuals may be required to accept positions that are significantly different in tasks and pay from their past jobs if the position is within the individual's "capabilities", if the individual is offered either the Federal minimum wage or more than the unemployment benefit, if the job does not entail unreasonable travel, and if it does not endanger the individual's "morals, health, or safety". It is too early to ascertain the extent to which the law may affect labor market statistics.

The need for further study

All in all, the unemployment rate tends to be inaccurate for both statistical and institutional—including legislative—reasons. In addition, the possible size of any error seems greater than for any associated with the employment ratio. In large part, this is because it is simply easier to identify clearly those who are working than to identify clearly those who want to work and are seeking work, since it is difficult to determine how many of the latter are in fact available for work. Further study of labor supply behavior under various income maintenance programs is necessary to formulate techniques that will eliminate from the unemployment numbers those who are really voluntarily unemployed.

Although at present the unemployment rate is a less accurate measurement than the employment ratio, this does not imply that the unemployment rate should be abandoned as a means of assessing labor market conditions. Instead, it calls for action to correct the shortcomings in all statistics relating to the labor market. For this reason, the Emergency Jobs Programs Extension Act of 1976 (Public Law 94-444) established a new National Commission on Employment and Unemployment Statistics. (The last major evaluation of employment and unemployment statistics was made fourteen years ago.) The new commission is charged with the responsibility of evaluating the present statistics as well as with making recommendations for their improvement.

In seeking the proper statistics to assess labor market conditions, the measure chosen should depend on the question being posed. For example, the Employment Act of 1946 calls for the Federal Government to take all feasible action to encourage the "conditions under which there will be afforded useful employment opportunities, including self-employment for those able, willing, and seeking to work, and to promote maximum employment, production, and purchasing power". To find out whether maximum—or full—

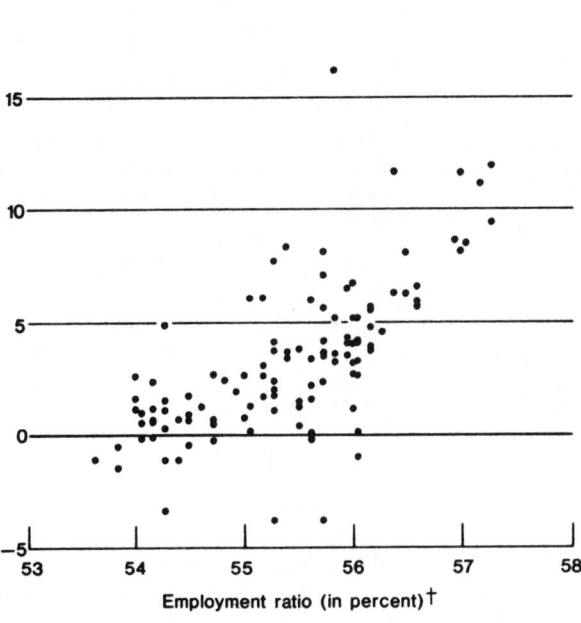

Chart 2
Relationship between the Consumer Price Index and the Employment Ratio

*Change from previous quarter (at annual rate), 1948-77.
†By quarters, 1948-77.
Source: Computations based on data from the Bureau of Labor Statistics.

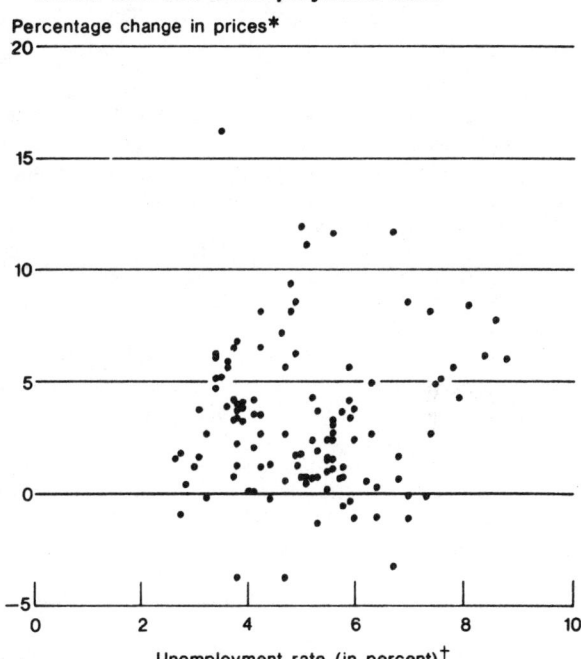

Chart 3
Relationship between the Consumer Price Index and the Unemployment Rate

*Change from previous quarter (at annual rate), 1948-77.
†By quarters, 1948-77.
Source: Computations based on data from the Bureau of Labor Statistics.

employment has been achieved, the unemployment rate is conceptually the more appropriate measure, although its inaccuracies seriously compromise its relevance at the present time.

If, however, the primary interest is the relation between wage changes or inflation and the condition of the labor market, the employment ratio may be the better statistic to use because increasing inaccuracy of the unemployment rate has weakened the relationship between that statistic and excess demand. This has been pointed out by Geoffrey Moore[11] and is illustrated in Charts 2 and 3, which show a much stronger association between the percentage change in the consumer price index and the employment ratio than between the percentage change in the consumer price index

[11] "Employment, Unemployment, and the Inflation-Recession Dilemma", *AEI Studies on Contemporary Economic Problems* (1976).

and the unemployment rate. Of course, the observation of correlation between these statistical series does not prove the existence of any causal relationship between them.

If the unemployment rate included only the involuntarily unemployed, the rate could be interpreted as an indirect measure of the inflationary pressures resulting from excess demand. This, in fact, is the interpretation that underlies the Phillips curve relation. In that relation, wages are expected to rise when there is excess demand—which is taken to be indicated by a low unemployment rate—and the rate of wage increase is expected to be the faster the greater the excess demand. However, if the unemployment rate is increasingly affected by the inclusion of the voluntarily unemployed, this relationship becomes blurred and the employment ratio may provide a better indication of demand pressures.

Sharon P. Smith

5 THE U.S. STRUCTURES ITSELF TO LIVE WITH INFLATION

President Carter's war against inflation is no better than a long shot to succeed. The 14 years of high and volatile inflation since the Vietnam war turned hot in the summer of 1965 have put an end to a century of relative price stability in the U.S. In the years since, inflation has become institutionalized—deeply imbedded in the soul of the U.S. economy.

The traditional view is that inflation is a self-limiting process: Once it starts, imbalances are created in the economy that force spending cuts by consumers and business, slow down economic growth, and force business and labor to reduce prices and wages. This is the old idea that an inflationary boom contains within it the "seeds" of a subsequent economic decline.

The notion that inflation is a self-limiting process may have been true in the years before 1965. But in the years since, the private sector of the U.S. economy has adapted to inflation, so it no longer disrupts spending patterns nearly as much as it once did. The incomes and spending levels of business, labor, and consumers have held up better in the current inflation that began in late 1975 than they did in the earlier post-World War II inflations—those associated with the Korean war, the Vietnam war, and the 1973 quadrupling of the price of oil by the Organization of Petroleum Exporting Countries.

Easing the burden

At the same time, a political process that still responds to the deep desires of the public has brought about changes in government policies that ease the burden of adjusting to inflation.

Washington talks against inflation, but rather than cut back spending or tighten credit to combat it, the government usually opts to make inflation more comfortable to those who otherwise would suffer most from it. Thus the two federal programs that together touch the lives of virtually every citizen have been changed in a way that allows real income to keep pace when inflation is accelerating. The Social Security system has been formally indexed to the change in the price level so that benefits automatically rise when prices rise. The federal income tax has been informally indexed in the view of many economists. Congress has, in effect, kept cutting tax rates as inflation has pulled people into higher tax brackets. As a consequence, the inflation-adjusted burden of taxation has stayed about constant over the past 15 years.

Equally important have been regulatory changes that have prevented the bouts of high interest rates that are part and parcel of an inflationary environment from curbing spending by business and consumers—such changes as allowing savings institutions to pay higher rates for funds, thereby protecting the flow of financing to the housing industry. Even the bite of the Federal Reserve Board's monetary policy has been eased by such things as the ability of business to hedge against higher interest rates in the newly minted market in financial instrument futures.

The institutionalization of inflation has resulted in four key changes that together are likely to vitiate the effectiveness of traditional monetary and fiscal restraint in curbing inflation:

The U.S. economy has become far more inflation-prone. In the past, outbreaks of inflation were caused by shocks external to the workings of the economy itself—such things as crop failures or war or, in the 1973-75 bout of inflation, by the quadrupling of the oil price. The current inflation stands in sharp contrast. Even though there has been no specific shock to the price system, the overall inflation rate since 1975 has been almost as high as that during the OPEC inflation—6.9% vs. 7.9% and higher than during the Vietnam or Korean wars.

The level of business activity has become better insulated from the dampening effects of restrictive monetary policy. Despite a four percentage point rise—almost a doubling—of short-term interest rates last year, economic activity continued to climb. This knocked out the standard forecast of a late 1978 slowdown and casts doubt on the widespread forecast of a slowdown or recession in the second half of 1979. Already, most economists have pushed their timetable for recession forward. Only months ago most forecasters saw a first-half recession; now they see the recession in the second half. But economists who have been once burned can be twice burned.

The costs of fighting inflation have soared. Economists measure those costs in terms of a curve thrown to them by a British economist, A. W. Phillips. The Phillips curve provides an answer to such questions as: How much would unemployment have to rise in order, for example, to cut the inflation rate by one percentage point? Statistical estimates of the size of the required rise in the unemployment rate vary, but economists who agree on little else have agreed that the rise in unemployment required to achieve even a modest drop in inflation is much higher now than in the past.

The political will to fight inflation has been sapped. Because the economy is now so much better adjusted to inflation than it used to be, it costs so much more to fight rising prices. This changes the outcome of political decisions—which are still made, as the British philosopher John Stuart Mill pointed out, on the basis of a "calculus of pleasure and pain." At the beginning of 1979 that calculus tells President Carter that the political payoff to fighting inflation is big among virtually all constituencies. But the implications of Mill's political calculus is that while the anti-inflation constituency is a mile wide, it may be no more than an inch deep.

The anti-inflation constituency

That the anti-inflation constituency may be no more durable than a toy balloon is not yet visible. Right now, the fight against inflation seems worth making to most voters.

On one hand, four years of rapid economic growth has led to an 11 million rise in employment and huge jumps in money wages and business profits. On the other is the concern of business and families that money does not go as far as it once did.

Says economist Lester C. Thurow of the Massachusetts Institute of Technology: "People get dissatisfied if someone deposits $75 on their doorstep, and then takes $60 away from them in the form of higher prices. They may convince themselves that their real standard of living has gone down. Everyone thinks how enjoyable life would be if there were no inflation and money income would go up at the same rate."

But a mountain of evidence suggests that money income will not continue to go up at the same rate if the fight against inflation begins to get serious. The pleasures of Carter's program will soon be balanced and perhaps overbalanced by pain. In the most recent spurt of serious inflation fighting, in 1974 and 1975, the inflation rate was cut by about half from a high of 12.4% in the first quarter of 1974, to a low of 6.5% in the fourth quarter of 1975. But what most people have conveniently forgotten is that the sharp fall in the inflation rate was bought at the expense of the worst recession since the Depression. The response to that recession was extremely stimulative monetary policy in 1976 and

Reprinted from the January 29, 1979, issue of BUSINESS WEEK by special permission. Copyright © 1979 by McGraw-Hill, Inc., New York, N.Y. All rights reserved.

1977, and that policy put the economy so firmly back on the inflation merry-go-round that the rise in wholesale prices is in double digits again.

The burden of proof is on those who believe that the war against inflation that has been launched by President Carter will yield better, more enduring results. The speed with which inflation has become institutionalized has intensified in the past few years. Businessmen, consumers, and labor have all learned to live more easily with inflation. And the loopholes that both Washington and the private sector have created so that the economy can escape the effects of overall budget and monetary restraint have multiplied.

The role of consumers

Ironically, the evidence that the economy is adjusting to inflation is emerging in the very sector where both policymakers and economists believe that inflation bites deepest: consumer spending. The idea that inflation so undermines the economic well-being of consumers and creates so much uncertainty that it inexorably leads to a sharp downturn in economic activity is based largely on what happened in the double-digit inflation days of 1973 and 1974. Before then, economists could show that, in the main, inflation was neutral in its impact on total consumer demand. But in that siege of inflation, consumers cut back spending, especially on such big-ticket items as automobiles. A drop in consumer spending became the major force pushing the economy into recession.

In this inflationary period, however, consumers have made no such cuts. Indeed, despite an acceleration of the inflation rate in 1978, the consumer has emerged as the engine of strong economic expansion. Says F. Thomas Juster, director of the University of Michigan's Survey Research Center: "It's crystal clear that there has been a far stronger element of advance buying and a correspondingly weaker element of uncertainty and retrenchment over the last 18 months than in 1973 and 1974."

Back then, as prices unexpectedly pushed ever higher, explains Juster, the advance-buying psychology was swamped by the uncertainty factor, and consumers retrenched sharply. "The consumer was uncertain as to whether his nominal income would keep up with inflation," says Juster. If income did keep pace, then the most the consumer lost was the opportunity to buy at a low price. But if it did not, to continue a high level of spending would have resulted in overcommitment, and that would have been a disaster.

It is in large part because the U.S. did survive the last inflation cum recession so well—topping it with the current

Thurow: People should realize that incomes are rising despite inflation.

expansion—that fighting inflation now is so hard. "They went through 1973-74, and the world didn't come apart," says Juster. "People are less concerned now about their ability to forecast inflation, because whatever happens, their money incomes keep pace more or less." Juster believes, therefore, that the same level of inflation this time around would generate less uncertainty and retrenchment than it did in 1974.

According to Carol Brock Kenny, vice-president of research at Loeb Rhoades, Hornblower & Co., today's inflation is hurting less not only because the current rate is somewhat below 1974's but also because the composition of inflation has changed. "Consumers, especially those in the low- and low-middle income categories, really could not adjust to the unexpected quantum leap in energy prices in 1974," she says. Although a good deal of the current inflation is in food prices, Kenny maintains that there has been a lot of substitution of lower-priced foods for those that have moved up in price, changes that the price indexes do not affect. "A lot of people have substituted eggs, cheese, and pasta for meat, but there was no substitution possible when it came to heating their homes," she notes.

Phillip D. Cagan, of Columbia University and the National Bureau of Economic Research, points to a very basic reason why today's inflation is creating less hardship than the 1973-74 inflation. Real income and purchasing power were then reduced, he says, because that inflation was generated from abroad when OPEC boosted the price of crude oil. This, in effect, imposed a sudden tax on consumers. But, says Cagan, "the current inflation is more or less internally generated. The economy now is at virtually full employment, and the monetary growth rate has been high. The money and income are there, so from a rational viewpoint there is no reason whatever for the consumer to cut back," says Cagan.

Like Cagan, Ronald A. Glanz, economist and automobile industry analyst for Paine Webber Mitchell Hutchins Inc., emphasizes monetary policy in contrasting 1974 with the present inflation. In 1974 tight money played a key role in bringing about the sharp decline in consumer spending. Many consumers were shut out of the automobile market, as lending standards were raised substantially, and mortgage money dried up almost completely, he notes. "This time there is lots of money around, and consumers are taking advantage of it." When money does threaten to run out—in the mortgage market, for instance—the government has changed the rules so that the endangered sector is again made liquid.

Taking on debt

Furthermore, because interest payments are tax-deductible, consumers have an incentive to continue spending by using credit. For example, says Glanz, a consumer in the 40% marginal tax bracket finds that an auto loan, which currently carries an 11.4% interest rate, really costs the borrower only 6.8%, well below the current inflation rate. "It costs nothing to buy today rather than next year. Interest rates are low, and the consumer therefore feels better off. As long as he can borrow to buy now and pay back in tomorrow's cheaper dollars, he has been able to transfer the bite of inflation to the lenders," says Glanz.

Consumers are buying in advance to beat price rises, and in the process they are taking on debt in unprecedented doses. Consumer debt as a percent of disposable income hit a record 17.8% in November. Nevertheless, as measured by the amount of debt consumers owe compared with the total value of their wealth, the consumer is in a stronger financial position now than at any time since the early 1960s and is vastly better off than in 1973. Part of this improvement in consumer wealth is because of the shift the consumer has made from putting money into financial assets, such as stocks and bonds—which have done poorly in the inflation—to buying such tangible assets as automobiles and houses.

Indeed, homeowners have seen their houses appreciate by 31% over the past two years, more than twice as fast as the rate of inflation. It is little wonder that the consumer surveys show that advance buying is strongest in housing and is at the highest level in two decades.

More and more people are buying houses, both new and existing ones, to beat inflation. Five years ago the amount of new mortgage money roughly equaled the value of new home construction. Last year new mortgages far outstripped that value, indicating that consumers are leveraging their buying to the hilt to reap large capital gains. And, indeed, as prices have risen, more people have taken those gains. The sales of existing houses have increased dramatically over the past few years. In 1976 sales of existing homes averaged about 3 million a month, at an annual rate. In October and November of last year, that figure was up 43%, to a 4.3 million-a-month rate. And according to Alan Greenspan, president of Townsend-Greenspan Inc., realized capital gains on homes are running at an annual rate of $60 billion.

The 51 million families that own homes are obviously far better off in this inflation than in 1973-74, when it became almost impossible to sell a house because of the lack of mortgage money. But even those families that do not own homes are faring better now. Real incomes have risen over this expansion, in sharp contrast to the experience of 1974. From 1976 to 1978, real disposable per capita income increased at an annual rate of 4.3%, compared with a 3.8% decline in 1974.

To cope with inflation and maintain their standard of living, more households are becoming two-wage-earner families. According to Kenny, 44% of all households had two salary checks coming in 1970. By 1977 this had risen to 53%. And the sharpest increase occurred in the under-35 age group, in which home-ownership is relatively low. Says Kenny: "By and large, this group has not been indexed to inflation through home ownership And it has compensated for it by sharply increasing the number of wage earners." It is precisely this group that has made the sharpest gains in employment in the current economic expansion.

Not only have most working consumers been able to maintain their standard of living in this current inflation, but even those who rely on government benefits have had their inflation-eroded dollars shored up by increased payments. The Social Security system, which paid out $94 billion to some 34.5 million people in 1978, has been indexed to inflation since 1975. And this formal indexation combined with legislated boosts have raised, for example, the average monthly benefit for a single retired worker from $162 in 1972 to $261 in 1978, an increase of 61%—about in line with the rate of inflation. Supplemental Security Income (SSI), which goes to some 4.3 million elderly poor and disabled, is also indexed to the consumer price index, and the government's food stamp program is indexed to food prices. Aid to Families with Dependent Children (AFDC), which is administered by the states, is not indexed to inflation and payments to families have risen only 25% over the last five years. Nevertheless, the shrinkage in the average family size from 3.6 per family to about 3 means that AFDC payments per family member have about kept pace with the rate of inflation.

Taxpayers have long complained that the tax system allowed inflation-bloated income to push them into higher brackets, raising their tax burden. But here the evidence suggests that legislated tax cuts and increased itemization of deductions have muted the inflationary impact. "From the early 1960s to 1975 the federal income tax system was more than indexed to inflation," says Joseph A. Pechman of the Brookings Institution. "And from 1975 it has been pretty close, although the middle class has not done all that well." According to calculations by Thurow of MIT, federal income taxes actually fell from 10.9% of personal income in 1972 to 10.6% during the first half of 1978.

Short-term contracts

Not all wage earners have suffered the same erosion of spending power because of inflation. Some workers, especially those who are members of unions with industrywide bargaining leverage—such as the Auto Workers, the Steelworkers, and the Teamsters—have so far been protected relatively well from inflationary effects by contracts providing for an automatic cost-of-living adjustment (COLA) as the consumer price index rises. These workers have by no means overcome the psychological impact of a world that seems to have gone awry with soaring inflation, but their income is indexed so that they fare far better when inflation rises than do workers without COLAs.

The number of workers covered by COLAs has risen and fallen with the rate of inflation ever since the United Auto Workers and General Motors Corp. negotiated the first COLA in 1948. Last year 5.8 million workers, or 60.4% of those in major collective bargaining units of 1,000 or more workers, had COLA protection. The number was down slightly from the 1977 peak of 6 million, largely because the United Mine Workers traded away its COLA clause for improved health and pension benefits. The general trend since the early 1970s, however, has been toward an increase in COLA coverage in big-industry bargaining. And more than 3 million other workers in small union units, nonunion companies, and government jobs get wage boosts triggered by rises in the CPI.

Yet COLA coverage may have reached the saturation point, and this could result in a significant turning point for collective bargaining in the U. S. Unable to win COLAs in some industries and dissatisfied by which COLAs in others keep up with actual price gains, organized labor may well embark on a trend back to the short-term contract of one or

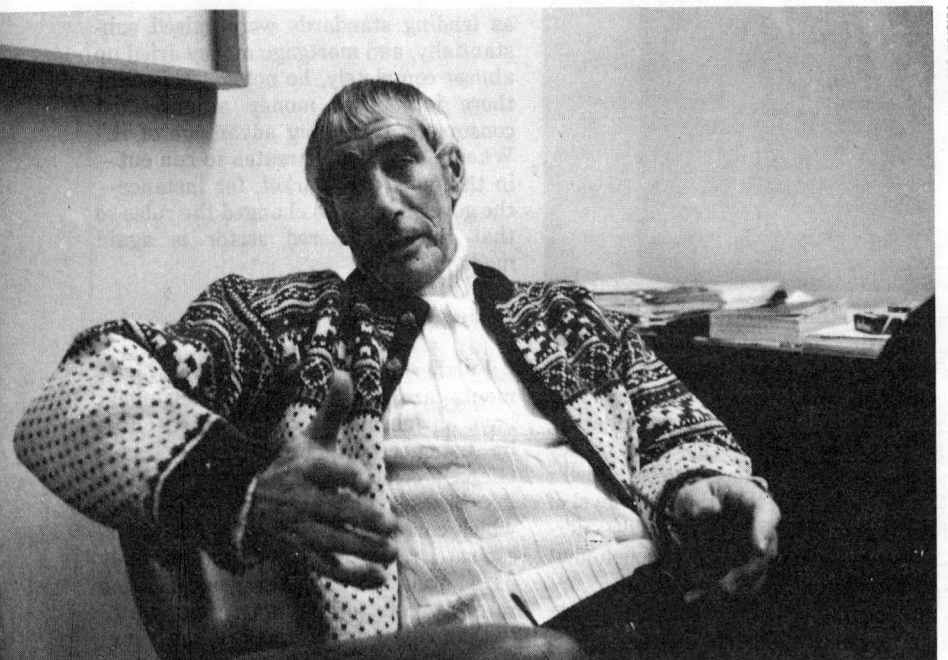

Juster: Consumers are less concerned about inflation now than in 1973-74.

two years that was common 30 years ago. If this trend develops—and management is certain to fight it—labor relations in the U.S. could return to the relatively primitive days of the late 1940s, when year-by-year bargaining in the major industries produced a never-ending round of strikes and threats of strikes.

A number of unions, including the UAW and the electrical unions, have already raised the possibility of reviving the short-term contract because of their frustrations in COLA bargaining. Where contracts do not contain COLA provisions, it is largely because organized labor is fragmented and weak and unable to win long strikes. In these industries, companies resist demands for COLAs because they want to avoid the unpredictability pacts have covered periods of about three years. A general trend back to the one-year agreements, or to two-year contracts with wage reopeners at the end of the first year could have a big impact on the economy because of the numbers of workers involved. As of Jan. 1, 1956, for example, nearly 2 million workers were covered by one-year pacts, compared with probably fewer than 200,000 in 1979.

Some economists would welcome a return to the short-term labor contracts, arguing that these more accurately reflect changes in the economy than the long-term pacts with COLAs and deferred wage increases. The latter have done much to institutionalize inflation in the economy, these economists say. Others contend, however, that a preponderance Schroder, Naess & Thomas agree: "I sense a positive change in the secular relationship between profits and the rest of the economy," says Conlan. "In the past two years we've been constantly surprised by the size of earnings gains. Companies are passing on rises in materials and unit labor costs with alacrity. And I suspect profits will prove less vulnerable in the economic slowdown when it materializes."

Corporate profit margins have held up, notes Cohen, because companies have become a "lot more careful" about inventory levels, capital investment, and debt acquisition. "Last time around they bought in advance of rising prices and thus contributed to the inflation they were trying to hedge against," he says. "When the bust came, they lost their

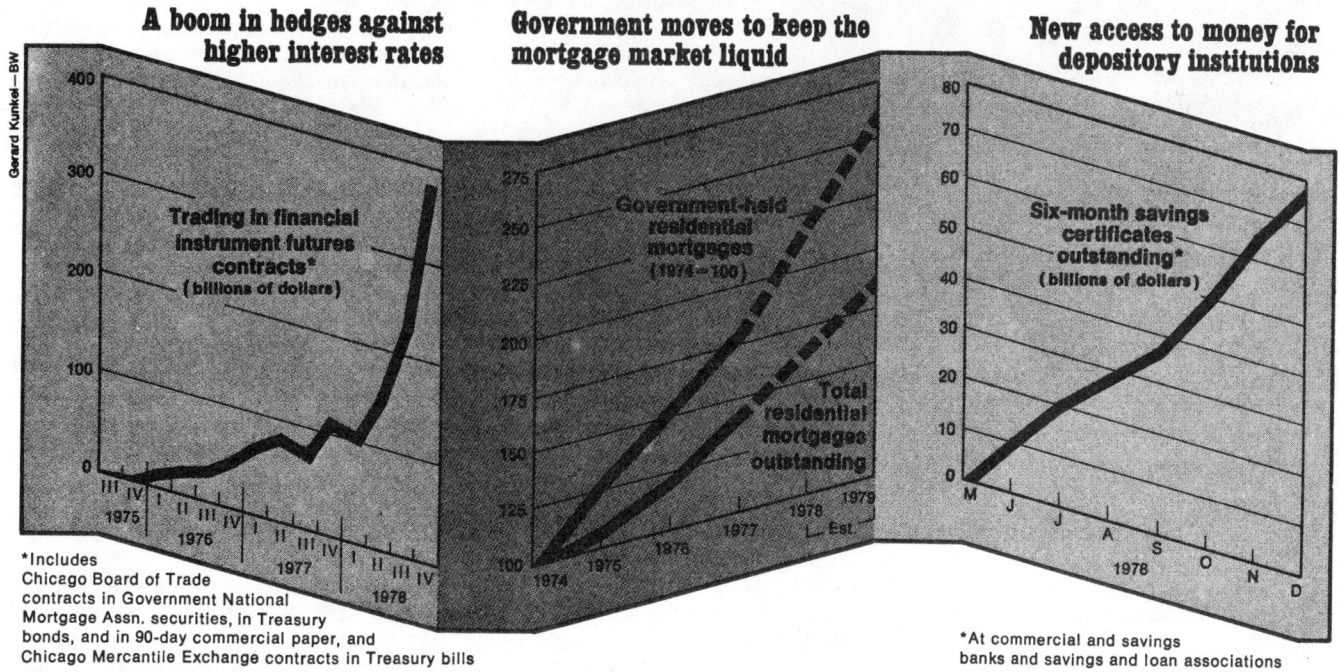

Three ways around inflation for the financial markets

A boom in hedges against higher interest rates — Trading in financial instrument futures contracts* (billions of dollars)
*Includes Chicago Board of Trade contracts in Government National Mortgage Assn. securities, in Treasury bonds, and in 90-day commercial paper, and Chicago Mercantile Exchange contracts in Treasury bills
Data: Chicago Board of Trade, Chicago Mercantile Exchange

Government moves to keep the mortgage market liquid — Government-held residential mortgages (1974=100); Total residential mortgages outstanding
Data: Commerce Dept., Salomon Bros.

New access to money for depository institutions — Six-month savings certificates outstanding* (billions of dollars)
*At commercial and savings banks and savings and loan associations
Data: Federal Home Loan Bank Board, BW estimate

of labor costs under COLAs and because they simply do not want to add the principle of automatic wage escalation to their labor contracts. With inflation moving toward a double-digit rate, the nation is likely to see sharply increased strike activity this year, as unions demand COLA protection for those not yet covered and improve the COLA payments of those already covered by removing caps and changing the formula. In the auto industry, for example, workers receive a 1¢-per-hour increase for each 0.3 point rise in the CPI, based on a quarterly review. They thus recover 80% to 85% of the real wages lost to inflation. The UAW has signaled that it intends to press for 100% recovery in bargaining later this year with the auto companies.

Since the mid-1950s, most major labor of one-year pacts, which anticipate future inflation rates with flat wage increases, can be highly inflationary if the negotiators "guess" wrongly on inflation. Finally, the rhythm of industrial life would be considerably changed if major industry contracts must be renegotiated on an annual basis.

Corporations may talk a good anti-inflation line, but after a decade of high prices, they clearly have learned to tolerate a heavy dose of it. "Businessmen don't like inflation, and for good reason," says Irwin L. Kellner, economist and senior vice-president of Manufacturers Hanover Trust Co. "But there's no question that they have learned to survive and even thrive in the current inflationary environment."

Economists Don R. Conlan of Capital Strategic Services and Morris Cohen of shirts. This time, it looks like it is the consumer who is being profligate while business is behaving responsibly."

A recent analysis of the financial data of some 700 companies by Data Resources Inc. dramatizes U.S. business' new-found financial stability. According to Fred Plemenos, director of DRI's industry financial services operation, the data reveal that aftertax profit margins of nonfinancial corporations deteriorated from a high of 8% or 9% in the mid-1960s to a low of 4.75% in 1975, but they have now moved back up slightly and have more or less stabilized in the 5½% range. "Now that margins are no longer eroding," says Plemenos, "sales growth is being translated into income growth." Indeed, DRI's computer projections suggest that while sales growth between now and 1985 will be lower than in the past, aftertax earnings growth will be higher.

DRI's analysis also charts the remarkable improvement in corporate balance sheets. Aside from a handful of exceptions—specifically the steel, oil, utilities, and telecommunications industries—most industries maintained a positive net cash flow from 1974 through 1977 (the last year analyzed), Plemenos reports. It is consumers and government that are the worrisome debtors today, not business. "Companies have been managing their net cash flow," Plemenos says, "making sure it stays positive and they stay liquid. By and large they've been funding their expansion with internally generated funds. As a result, debt-to-equity ratios are still in reasonably good shape."

Griggs: The Fed has failed to perceive the changes that have limited its ability to control inflation.

The escalator clause

Such behavior may seem to violate the rule that borrowing can be smart strategy in an inflationary environment, but DRI's Otto Eckstein argues that long-term interest rates have been adjusted upwards in recent years to discount almost fully anticipated high rates of inflation. "Considering the exposure that debt can entail in cyclical downturns," he says, "debt aversion now makes good economic sense." Similarly, Plemenos notes that "companies realize that current high interest-rate carrying charges probably far outweigh any gains that inventory-building could bring as an inflationary hedge, particularly with the risk of a near-term recession."

Financial management is not the only area that has changed in the new inflationary climate. Companies are paying a lot more attention to pricing and the need to pass through costs rapidly. In many cases this has simply resulted in more frequent price adjustments—as in the auto industry, which recently shifted from annual to quarterly price boosts. "In the past we would make money at the beginning of the model year and lose it at the end," says R. K. Brown, executive vice-president of Chrysler. More frequent price boosts, adds Thomas A. Murphy, chairman of General Motors Corp., "enable us to make more adaptations to the realities as they unfold."

In other cases, inflationary adjustments are either automatic or contractual. Many utility bills, for example, are automatically adjusted to reflect changing fuel costs. Office building leases commonly contain escalator clauses to cover rising utility bills, real estate taxes, and labor costs. Several copper producers have abandoned the old list price system and are tying their tabs to the price on New York's Commodity Exchange.

Escalator clauses are particularly common in long-term sales contracts covering commercial construction, military hardware, and capital goods. Says Joseph T. Bailey, chairman of Warner & Swasey Co., the big Cleveland machine tool maker: "Some of us in the industry have been quoting price escalators, and some of us have tried simply to anticipate cost increases in setting contract prices. About 90% of our backlog is protected by escalators or estimated cost increases."

At the same time, however, companies are taking a closer look at the escalator clauses in their contracts with their suppliers to ensure that future price rises really reflect cost increases. Curtis Rockwell, purchasing director at Carrier Corp.'s Carlyle Compressor Div., for example, negotiated a long-range purchase contract for electric motors that for the first time allows the supplier to raise his price only if he can prove specific cost increases. "We were concerned that we would get hit with so-called inflationary increases with little substantiation," explains Rockwell.

Corporations have also learned to fine-tune their salary adjustments to stress productivity in the age of inflation. In the wake of the 1973-74 inflationary surge, for example, many companies raised white-collar salaries across the board, but now experts report a "retreat" from wholesale cost-of-living adjustments. "Automatic indexing seems fair on the surface, but it really takes care of inefficient people," says Charles E. Fancher, president of Imperial Reading Corp. Imperial Reading, in fact, is one of a number of companies that is keying its incentive compensation plan so that sales gains do not trigger incentive payments unless they represent higher volume rather than simply inflated prices.

In short, U. S. business has grown no fonder of inflation in recent years, but it has developed ways of coping with many of the inefficiencies and excesses that an inflationary climate can inspire. In the industrial sector, for the most part, these developments appear to be salutary. The nation's financial sector, however, is clearly another matter.

The revolution in financing

Nowhere has the adaptation to inflation been more pronounced than in the nation's financial markets. And that is perhaps the most crucial development of all, because it is money that feeds inflation, and it is by controlling the growth of money that the Federal Reserve attempts to combat inflation. Between what Washington has done for the financial markets, including housing, plus what the private sector has done on its own, inflation does not hurt as it once did, and the Fed's efforts to slow inflation have proven increasingly ineffectual. There has been a revolution in finance, and to William N. Griggs, senior vice-president with J. Henry Schroder Bank & Trust Co., "the Fed has failed to perceive it."

The changes include:

■ The easing of ceilings on what financial institutions can pay for money. Most dramatic was the introduction last summer of six-month savings certificates, by which banks and thrift institutions can beat out even the U. S. Treasury for funds, a development that has done the most to weaken the Fed's grip on monetary policy.

■ The astonishing growth of trading in interest rate futures, which has gone from zero in late 1975 to $378 billion today.

■ The movement to floating rate loans by financial institutions. Because banks now merely pass on the higher costs of funds to borrowers, high interest rates have lost much of their bite.

■ The rapid growth of those sections of the financial markets that lie outside the Fed's jurisdiction. These include nonbank institutions that make loans in competition with banks, as well as banks that have left the Fed system.

■ New lending techniques such as five-year car loans and graduated mortgage payments.

■ The proliferation of foreign banks in the U. S. This has been matched by the growth of U. S. bank activities overseas, with access to funds that the Fed cannot control.

■ The housing sector's fast-growing

ability to tap the national money markets through the sale of mortgage-backed securities, the sale of mortgage pools to federal agencies, and the use of the six-month savings certificate.

By far the most important single development affecting the financial markets in recent years has been the astonishing success of these savings certificates, which carry rates pegged to the yield on six-month Treasury bills. Because of them, the housing sector now is very well protected. In all previous business cycles, mortgage lenders suffered from disintermediation—massive withdrawal of funds—whenever open market rates rose above passbook ceiling rates. With no money to lend to builders, housing collapsed, a recession followed, and demand cooled off. This time around, housing has flourished even as rates have soared.

Important as they are, however, the certificates are only a part of the story. Mortgage lenders are also insulated from high rates by long-term savings certificates, such as the eight-year 8% accounts that were introduced last June that have substantially lengthened the average maturity of deposits. Largely because of such accounts, passbook deposits at thrift institutions—which can be withdrawn at a moment's notice—today make up less than 30% of all deposits, from 44% in 1974 and 88% in 1966.

And on Jan. 4, the Federal Home Loan Bank Board authorized a pilot program under which a savings and loan association in New Jersey will be allowed to issue mortgage-backed commercial paper. Under the program, City Federal, of Elizabeth, in early February will start issuing up to $60 million of the notes in minimum denominations of $100,000 and maximum maturities of 270 days. By allowing thrifts to compete in the commercial paper market, which had formerly been the preserve of giant banks and corporations, housing will be further insulated from high rates.

Further, the growth of these new instruments seems inevitable. Several S&Ls have asked the Federal Home Loan Bank Board for permission to follow City Federal's lead. Beyond that is the possibility that the bank board may soon permit S&Ls to enter the Euromarket through large-denomination mortgage-backed certificates of deposit. The bank board is also propping up housing by encouraging thrifts to borrow from it. Last year advance borrowing by S&Ls increased by about $12 billion, compared with a rise of $4.2 billion in 1977.

Until the six-month certificates were introduced last year, the most important insulator of housing had been the packaging of mortgages into pools of negotiable bond-like instruments that were sold to institutional investors. Since they were introduced in the late 1960s, after the housing collapse of 1966-67, some $80 billion of such "pass-through" securities have been created and marketed both privately and through the government agencies such as Government National Mortgage Assn. and the Federal Home Loan Mortgage Corp. By continuing to supply funds to the mortgage market, these securities are "institutionalizing inflation and higher interest rates," contends Solon Patterson, president of Montag & Caldwell, an Atlanta investment advisory firm. "If that money had not gone into those securities, it could have been lent to somebody else, maybe to business."

To keep housing afloat, mortgage lenders have also been coming up with new payment schedules, such as variable rate mortgages, which have had a spec-

Fred W. McDarrah

Harrington: The clamor to cut government growth will end as unemployment rises.

tacular success in California. Currently, some 250,000 such mortgages, totaling $15 billion, or 26% of the portfolios of state-chartered S&Ls in that state, are variable rates. Twenty other states have also approved their use. Undoubtedly, VRMs are likely to become more popular, because the bank board has authorized federally chartered S&Ls in California to offer them, and the board is expected to do the same in other states.

In short, governmental policies have prevented housing from becoming the victim of a classic downturn by indexing it to inflation. But as a result, housing is now taking down a disproportionate share of credit, and this has helped push rates up to unprecedented levels.

Still, housing is only a part of the story. In recent years, controls that have been eased include usury laws in many states, coupon ceilings on Treasury bonds, various rate ceilings on savings accounts, and the 46-year-old ban on the paying of interest on checking accounts. "These controls happen to be our principal mechanisms for cooling off an overheated economy," says Albert M. Wojnilower, an economist for First Boston Corp. "Their removal goes far in explaining why, in every business cycle, inflation and interest rates surge to higher crests than in the preceding cycle."

The stop-go pattern

Rates are not only higher this time around, but they also have a far different meaning. In 1974 an institution offering a 10% mortgage was signaling that no money was available at any price. Today, rates approaching 11% indicate absolutely nothing about the availability of money.

Consequently, the government has mistakenly believed that rates were biting when they were not. But because such high interest rates make a recession look imminent, the Fed prematurely eases and then is forced to tighten monetary growth. This stop-go pattern builds inflation into the economy.

Finally, the impact of high interest rates on the big users of money is increasingly being muted by the booming market in interest-rate futures. With such instruments, financial institutions can inexpensively protect themselves from even today's sky-high rates.

There is concern about what the futures market will do to the underlying market in Treasury issues, at $500 billion the largest and most stable financial market in the world. One fear is that the cost and timing of the Treasury's financings will be adversely affected by futures contracts that increase the volatility of rates. The other is that the underlying market may be manipulated by speculators. "To the extent that people on the fringe speculate, that doesn't add to the efficiency of the financial markets," warns James G. Wilson, senior vice-president of Pittsburgh's Equibank.

Concern there may be, but it has not done a thing to slow growth in financial instrument futures. The first financial futures, Ginnie Maes, were sold on the Chicago Board of Trade in late 1975. Since then, the Chicago Mercantile Exchange has introduced futures in three-month Treasury bills, and the Board of Trade has added Treasury bonds and 90-day commercial paper. Late last year the American Stock Exchange opened an exchange to trade financial futures, and the New York Stock Exchange is mulling over a similar move. Overall, the value of contracts traded has grown from zero to more than $378 billion in three years.

Undoubtedly, the market would have grown even faster if the Fed and the

Treasury had not asked the Commodity Futures Trading Commission to delay the approval of other applications. The two agencies and the CFTC want the ban continued until they complete a study on the relationship between financial futures and their underlying markets, expected to be completed in March.

A likely scenario

While regulators worry, more and more corporations are discovering the market. "These companies are more practical than philosophical," says Lawrence M. Backes, an interest-rate futures specialist for Merrill Lynch, Pierce, Fenner & Smith Inc. "They don't care what causes the moves in rates. They just want protection. And they're now using the futures markets the way the big grain companies have been using them for years." Adds Wilson of Equibank: "Financial futures are not speculative. They are a hedge."

The use of financial instrument futures may be the most sophisticated wrinkle of all in a process that is going on in every nook and cranny of the U. S. economy—the institutionalization of inflation. And that is precisely why President Carter's goal of getting the inflation rate down to 7% by the end of 1979 with only a mild increase in unemployment, and only a slight decline in business activity is unlikely to be met.

Some economists, in fact, believe that the U. S. now faces a deep recession no matter what Washington does now, and that efforts to forestall it will only worsen its impact when it finally comes. "You can postpone a hangover by getting even drunker," says George A. Christy, professor of finance at North Texas State University. "Instead of having a fairly mild recession this year to recover from a 10% inflation rate, you may have a much deeper recession in 1980 and 1981 from an even higher inflation rate."

Yet there is still another scenario and, based on all that has occurred over the past 15 years, it may be the most likely scenario of all: no severe recession this year, or in 1980 or 1981, either, and no slowing in the rate of inflation. Because the cost of fighting inflation has risen, while the pain of living with inflation has eased for most people, not only the ability of the government to deal with inflation—but also its will—has been compromised. The minute unemployment begins to rise, says Michael Harrington, political scientist at the City University of New York, "the clamor for fighting inflation by cutting the growth of government spending will end." And that may well mean the inexorable acceleration of the process that has already begun: the indexation of the whole U. S. economy. ∎

6

Indexation of wages and retirement income in the United States

Should wages be automatically adjusted in line with the cost of living? Should pension benefits be tied to a price index? These questions have been debated at union meetings, labor contract bargaining sessions, and in the legislatures of local, state, and national governments. Economists, too, have examined indexation and raised some provocative questions about the desirability of indexation from the viewpoint of inflation and unemployment.

The idea of indexing income is more than two centuries old and has been used in many nations. During the American Revolution, Massachusetts linked soldiers' pay to an index composed of beef, corn, wool, and leather prices. In nineteenth century Britain, some firms offered wage scales which were tied to the prices of certain staple commodities. In Belgium, many wage indexation plans date back to the 1930's. Then, during the two decades following World War II, a large number of other European countries experimented with wage indexation of one form or another; Israel and Brazil also put extensive indexation programs into effect. In the United States, several major unions negotiated wage escalators during the 1950's. Over the past ten years, however, a new surge of interest in cost-of-living protection has developed in the United States, as the inflation rate accelerated sharply. Among unionized workers, escalator clauses have now become more common. As for the retired, social security benefits are now indexed, and many of those who worked for Federal, state, or local governments are entitled to price-linked retirement benefits.

Is indexation a desirable thing? Indexation may make the individual feel more secure about the purchasing power of income. But, under some circumstances, indexation of wages might make layoffs more common and actually reduce workers' well-being. As regards inflation, there is the question of whether indexation would make it easier to curb inflation or whether it would aggravate it.

What is the purpose of indexation?

Indexation ties the dollar size of a payment to an index of prices. For example, wage indexation typically provides for the hourly wage rate to rise automatically by 1 cent whenever the consumer price index increases by a certain amount. The basic purpose of this linkage is to provide an automatic mechanism for protecting the purchasing power of income if prices should rise. Its major use has been in long-term contracts, particularly long-term union contracts. Indexation is not so common in short-term wage contracts, since wages and salaries can adjust to changing prices without long delays.

In long-term union contracts, indexation is basically an insurance policy protecting the worker against unexpectedly high rates of inflation. Insight into the nature of wage indexation can be gained by considering the wage negotiations in two contracts which differ only in one respect—one has a cost-of-living adjustment clause or "COLA" and the other does not. In the wage contract without a cost-of-living escalator clause, the negotiating parties must *estimate* the likely inflation rate and provide for a wage pattern that reflects this inflation adjustment. For example, if prices are expected to rise at a 6 percent annual rate, and the parties decide on a real wage increase of 2 percent a year, annual wages would be slated to rise 8 percent in each year of the contract; 8 percent would allow a 6 percent "purchasing power adjustment" plus a 2 percent "real" increase. Consider next a contract with a cost-of-living clause which provides that the wage rate will increase by the same percentage as the cost of living. (The hypothetical escalator for this example gives 100 percent protection, whereas most

Reprinted from Federal Reserve Bank of New York *Quarterly Review*, Autumn, 1978.

escalator clauses fall short of complete protection. See page 18.) For this wage contract, only the real wage increase of 2 percent per year would need to be specified; the COLA would provide whatever adjustment in the nominal wage rate that was necessary for an annual real wage increase of 2 percent.

In the contract without the COLA, the actual real wage increase depends upon the inflation rate. If prices rose at 6 percent per year over the duration of the contract, workers would get a 2 percent real wage increase. In contrast, if prices rose at a 7 percent annual rate, they would gain a real wage increase of only 1 percent per year (the 8 percent increase in wages less the 7 percent increase in prices), a full percentage point less than expected.

The importance of a COLA clause depends upon the duration of the contract. In a short contract without a COLA, say of one-year duration, the loss (or gain) would typically be small. For example, a 1 percent per year error in the price forecast would cost the worker a dollar amount equal to only ½ percent of annual wages over the course of a one-year contract. (The real wage falls short by a full 1 percent only at the end of the year.) The same incorrect inflation estimate over a three-year contract, however, would cost the worker a total of 4½ percent of annual wages: ½ percent in the first year, 1½ percent in the second, and 2½ percent in the third.

For employees whose expenses depend upon current prices, a COLA clause reduces the employee's uncertainty about the likely purchasing power of wages from his job over the ensuing contract period. Does it also reduce the uncertainty of the employer? If the employer's expenses and sales revenues were closely related to the general price level upon which the COLA is based, real profits might be more certain under a contract with a COLA: both the price of the goods sold and the wage rate paid would move together. In an alternative contract without a COLA, the employer could do better than one with the COLA, if prices rose at 7 percent, but might also do worse if prices rose at only a 5 percent rate.

Thus, under generalized inflation—all prices increasing at the same rate—indexation might insure both parties against unexpected loss. However, higher inflation usually absorbs some resources, detracting from the economy's productivity, so that it is rarely possible for everyone to remain as well off. Of great concern to the firm is the possibility that inflation will not proceed at the same pace in all sectors. If the prices of other goods rise more rapidly than expected while the price of the goods the firm is producing does not, the COLA clause would erode real profits.

Who has cost-of-living protection in the United States?
Escalator clauses of one form or another appear in a wide variety of circumstances today. According to the Bureau of Labor Statistics, about half of the United States population is affected in some way. Food stamp allotments are based upon an index of food costs, eligibility for some governmental assistance programs is based upon a poverty line linked to the price level, and business contracts for the delivery of goods and services may specify that payments depend upon the level of certain prices. The focus here is on two major concerns of the typical American worker—whether his or her wage rate keeps pace with inflation and what the outlook is for the purchasing power of retirement benefits.

Wage COLAs
The union sector in the United States consists of 19.4 million workers. Of this group, more than 8½ million workers are covered by contracts that call for automatic adjustments of wage rates based upon changes in the cost of living.[1]

In "major" bargaining agreements—private nonfarm sector agreements which cover 1,000 or more workers —COLA clauses are fairly common. Of the roughly 10 million workers who are covered by such agreements, about 6 million currently have some form of escalator clause. The United Automobile Workers was the first major union to gain cost-of-living protection; its COLA with General Motors Corporation dates back to 1948. Since then, there have been ups and downs in the number of contracts containing COLAs. Periods of inflation typically have led to the adoption of escalator clauses, while periods of price stability have resulted in the dropping of such clauses (chart). After the run-up of prices associated with the Korean war several other major unions got COLAs, and by 1958 some 4 million workers covered by major agreements had cost-of-living provisions. Then, in the early 1960's several large unions, including the steel and communications workers, dropped the COLA from their contracts, and the number of workers covered by COLAs declined to below 2 million in 1963.

Beginning in the late sixties, however, accelerating inflation created renewed interest in cost-of-living provisions. The steel and communications workers had their COLA clauses reinstituted, and other large unions obtained cost-of-living provisions. Particularly noteworthy was the surge in COLA coverage between 1974 and 1976; 2 million workers covered by major

---

[1] A good review of wage escalator clauses may be found in an article by Nicholas S. Perna, "The Contractual Cost-of-Living Escalator", *Monthly Review* (Federal Reserve Bank of New York, July 1974), pages 177-82.

Inflation Rate and the Number of Workers Covered by Escalator Clauses (Private Nonfarm Agreements Involving 1,000 or More Workers)

*Preliminary for 1978
Source: United States Department of Labor, Bureau of Labor Statistics.

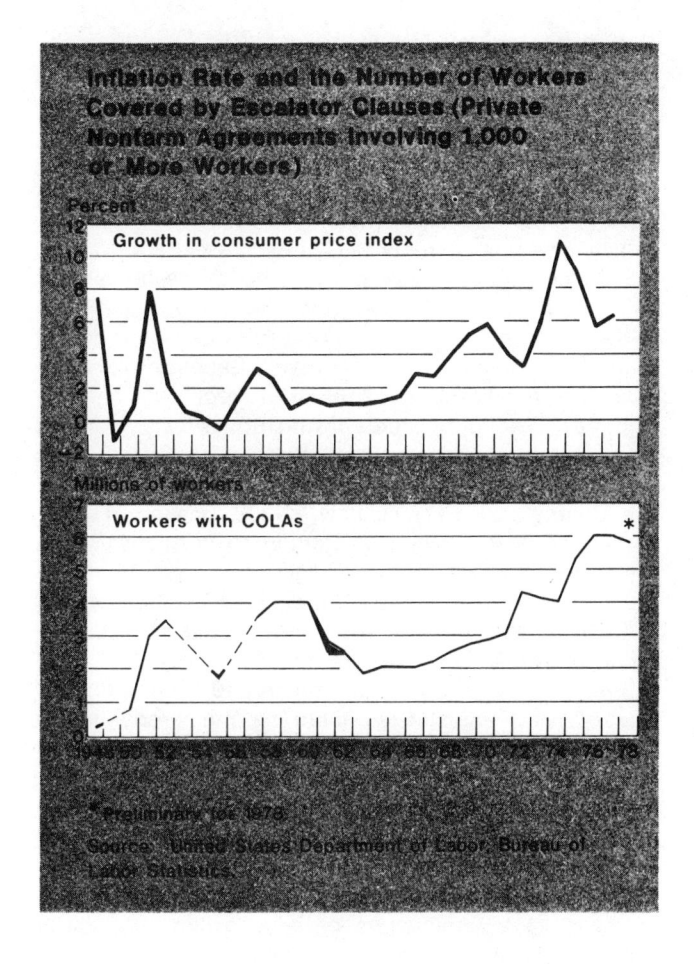

agreements obtained COLAs, bringing the total to 6 million workers for this sector of the union work force. There are now many private-sector industries in which virtually all major labor contracts contain COLAs (Table 1).

As might be expected, unions with longer contracts are more frequently covered by escalators. In bargaining units with three-year contracts, for example, about 71 percent of workers were covered by COLAs in 1978, whereas in bargaining units with annual contracts only 9 percent of workers have COLAs.

COLA clauses have also been obtained by unions representing workers employed by state, county, and city governments. The Bureau of Labor Statistics surveyed the collective bargaining agreements of many of these governmental units in 1975.[2] About 25 percent of the state, county, and local government workers covered by the survey had wage escalators.

[2] *Characteristics of Agreements of State and Local Governments* (Bulletin 1947). The survey covered all states and those counties and cities with population of 100,000 or more but excluded agreements covering workers in public education.

Federal Government workers do not have a COLA clause for salaries, although since 1967 they have normally received an annual structural increase which was judged to be comparable to wage increases in the private sector. (See article on Federal pay scales beginning on page 7 of this issue.) However, the Postal Service, now a quasi-independent agency, does have a COLA clause in the agreements with four postal unions which represent about 570,000 employees.

What are the escalator clauses that cover American workers like? Although, in principle, an escalator clause could be designed to compensate the employee fully for rises in the price level, most escalators provide substantially less than 100 percent protection. One feature which leads to less than full compensation is the adjustment formula. This is usually specified as 1 cent per hour for each 0.3 or 0.4 percentage point rise in the consumer price index—over half the workers with escalators under major contracts have this type of formula. Another popular type of formula gives cost-of-living increases in the *base wage*. These types of formula seldom compensate high wage workers fully and usually do not compensate even the average worker fully for cost-of-living changes. For example, consider a worker with hourly earnings of $7.75 per hour in July 1977. Between July 1977 and July 1978 the consumer price index rose 7.7 percent. By the 1 cent per 0.4 percentage point formula, the COLA would be 35 cents, equivalent to a 4.5 percent wage increase. With the 1 cent per 0.3 percentage point formula, the worker would get a 47 cent COLA, equivalent to a 6.1 percent wage increase.

Second, many COLAs require that the rate of inflation exceed a minimum level (called the "trigger" level) before workers get any adjustment at all; others specify a range within which the usual escalator formula does not hold; and some escalators have "caps" or maximums on the size of the allowable cost-of-living adjustment. Almost 1½ million workers covered by major contracts in 1978 had capped escalators.

Finally, there is generally some time lag between the occurrence of inflation and the compensation for it. Of workers covered by major agreements, about 2½ million receive annual adjustments and 0.9 million receive semiannual adjustments; only 2.3 million get quarterly adjustments. If inflation accelerates, the time lag in receiving the corresponding wage adjustment causes some loss in real income. One analyst estimated that these features have restricted wage increases from escalator clauses to about 50 percent of the consumer price index rise.[3]

[3] H.M. Douty, *Cost-of-Living Escalator Clauses and Inflation* (Council on Wage and Price Stability, August 1975), page 28.

Another way that unionized workers with long-term contracts have tried to reduce price uncertainties is through "reopener" clauses which allow renegotiation during the contract period under certain circumstances. In fact, some contracts specify that cost-of-living increases greater than some amount permit reopening. Although in some circumstances the reopening will produce a wage adjustment similar to a COLA clause, other factors such as market conditions and firm profits may come into play when the wage discussion reopens. Because of this, reopener clauses may avoid some of the problems associated with COLAs. (See page 21.)

Table 1

Industries with Escalators Covering Over 50 Percent of the Workers

Collective bargaining agreements in the private nonfarm sector covering 1,000 or more workers

Industry	Workers covered by escalator clauses (in thousands)	(in percent)
Metal mining	51	97.5
Anthracite mining	2	100.0
Bituminous coal and lignite mining	120	100.0
Ordnance and accessories	25	74.3
Tobacco manufactures	28	94.9
Printing and publishing	37	58.1
Rubber and plastic products	86	89.8
Primary metal industries	555	96.1
Fabricated metal products	70	79.1
Machinery, except electrical	267	89.5
Electrical equipment	432	91.6
Transportation equipment	1018	94.8
Railroad transportation	472	100.0
Local and urban transit	115	97.6
Motor freight transportation	551	98.1
Transportation by air	101	62.3
Transportation services	2	100.0
Communications	679	93.7
Wholesale trade	44	61.8
Food stores	400	72.6
Finance, insurance, and real estate	51	65.1

Source: United States Department of Labor, Bureau of Labor Statistics, *Monthly Labor Review* (January 1978).

Retirement income COLAs

Many retired workers receive social security benefits plus a pension from their previous employer. Old-age and survivors benefits provided by the social security system have been adjusted upward many times since 1965, and public-sector employees frequently do receive cost-of-living pension adjustments. However, private pension plans with COLAs are extremely rare.

Adjustments that have been made to the benefits of retired persons collecting social security are shown in Table 2. Until 1972, each of these increases required special legislation. Now, however, benefits are automatically increased annually to reflect cost-of-living changes. Belgium, Canada, France, Germany, Norway, and Sweden also provide automatic cost-of-living adjustments to social security payments. According to the United States Public Law 92-336, passed in 1972, automatic cost-of-living adjustments are paid in years when there is no legislation giving a general social security benefit increase.[4] Special legislation raised OASDI benefits in the years 1972-74; the first cost-of-living increase was effective June 1975. Cost-of-living adjustments were also paid in 1976, 1977, and 1978. A cost-of-living adjustment would be made only if the consumer price index were at least 3 percent higher than it was when the most recent adjustment was made.

In February 1978, about 18 million people were receiving retirement benefits from the social security system. Also, those qualifying for survivors benefits and disability benefits under OASDI—about 16 million persons—got similar cost-of-living adjustments. The social security system as a whole, therefore, is providing 34 million people with price-linked benefits in 1978. By 1985, about 40 million persons will be receiving such benefits, according to projections.

Because social security benefits were frequently changed prior to their indexing in 1972, there never was a long lag between inflation and an increase in benefits. What then was accomplished by indexing benefits? The price linking of social security benefits may prevent the temporary losses in real income of the retired that could occur when special legislation was required and may thereby make people feel more secure. In addition, it may save the United States Congress some time.

The situation regarding private pensions is very different: their purchasing power has been greatly eroded. Very few companies provide indexed pension benefits. Indeed, a 1972-73 Conference Board survey indicated that only 4 percent of the firms questioned provided

---

[4] The 1977 amendments to the Social Security Act corrected a feature that "double-indexed" newly retired people's benefits, giving payments which rose with wages *and* with prices.

Table 2

The Consumer Price Index and OASDI* Benefits for a Person Who Retired in 1959

Date	OASDI benefits* Percentage change	Cumulative‡	Consumer price index Percentage change	Cumulative‡
January 1965	7.0†	7.0	7.8†	7.8
February 1968	13.0	20.9	9.3	17.8
January 1970	15.0	39.0	10.8	30.6
January 1971	10.0	53.0	5.1	37.2
September 1972	20.0	83.5	5.8	45.2
March-June 1974	11.0	103.7	16.4	69.0
June 1975	8.0	120.0	9.4	84.9
June 1976	6.4	134.1	5.9	95.8
June 1977	5.9	147.9	6.8	109.1
June 1978	6.5	164.0	7.5	124.8

* OASDI = old-age, survivors, disability, and hospital insurance system under the Social Security Administration.

† Since 1959. There were no adjustments between 1959 and 1965.

‡ Because of compounding, exceeds the sum of the items in previous column. For example, (1.07) (1.13) = 1.209 which yields the 20.9 percent for the second item in column (2).

Sources: OASDI benefits: *Social Security Bulletin*, selected issues. Consumer price index for all urban consumers, seasonally adjusted: Bureau of Labor Statistics.

pension benefits that were price linked.[5] (However, 17 percent of the plans did allow some portion of the pension to be taken in the form of an annuity, whose annual payment would vary with an investment portfolio of stocks and bonds.) The tremendous erosion of pension purchasing power in recent years has led some firms to raise voluntarily the pensions of the already retired. However, such adjustments have been insufficient to maintain purchasing power. Few unions have expressed interest in obtaining indexed pensions. And those indexed pensions that have been negotiated typically provide only for new retirees.

There are two major exceptions to the general lack of price linking for pensions. One is the College Retirement Equities Fund (CREF), a nationwide plan for college teachers that was established in 1952 by the Teachers Insurance and Annuity Association of America (TIAA). Many United States colleges make pension contributions to this plan on behalf of their faculty, rather than provide their own pension plans. CREF invests pension money in common stocks and pays retirement benefits based upon the earnings of its portfolio. When it was established, economists believed that the stock market would keep pace with the cost of living so that CREF would in effect provide a price-linked pension. As it turned out, however, stock prices have not kept pace and CREF beneficiaries have not received dollar benefits sufficient to compensate for the cost of living. The pension plan for retired railroad workers is the second major exception to the general lack of price linking for pensions in the private sector; this plan did in fact provide a pension with price protection. Railway workers have been covered by special Federal legislation since 1937 and so in many respects are more similar to public employees than to private ones. According to the 1974 amendments to the Railroad Retirement Act, retired railway workers receive a substitute for social security, which provides identical price-linked retirement benefits, plus an added payment which is partially price linked.[6] About 1 million workers are receiving retirement benefits under this program.

In sharp contrast to the private sector, the public sector does provide extensive cost-of-living protection to retired workers. The first COLA for Federal pensions was legislated in 1962. However, no adjustment was called for in the years 1962, 1963, and 1964 under the original wording. The procedures were changed in 1965,

---

[5] Mitchell Meyer and Harland Fox, *Profile of Employee Benefits* (Conference Board, 1974).

[6] Prior to the 1974 amendments, many railway workers received both social security and a full pension from the railway retirement system.

1969, and again in 1976.[7] According to the 1976 legislation, increases based upon the June-December consumer price index change are given each March 1 and increases based upon the December-June change are given to retired civil service workers each September 1. Retired military personnel are also entitled to indexed pensions. About 2.8 million retired Federal civil service workers and military personnel and their survivors were receiving such pensions at the beginning of 1978.

At the state and local level, there is some indexation of pension plans, although considerably less than at the Federal level. A recent Bureau of Labor Statistics study of the municipal pension plans of twenty-seven large cities found that about one third of the plans provided benefits connected to movement in the consumer price index. However, most of these cost-of-living adjustments were limited to a maximum of 5 percent a year.

Why have private companies not indexed their pension plans, while the Federal Government and many state and local governments have indexed theirs? Perhaps this difference reflects the fact that retired persons are voters and so retain influence on Government decisions whereas their influence on the company and/or union ceases when they retire. The company management and union leadership may feel that it is not in their interest to distribute money to the retired that might instead be used to boost the pay of current workers.

The outlook for indexation
Because the union sector is relatively small in the United States, compared with many other industrialized countries, escalator clauses *per se* are unlikely to apply to the bulk of the work force. For example, there is a total of 19.4 million unionized workers, compared with a work force of 100 million. This comparison, however, understates the possible impact of wage indexation in the United States. For one thing, there is a tendency to maintain wage differentials by giving similar increases to nonunion employees in the firm and for some nonunion firms to give cost-of-living adjustments to keep in line with other firms' wages. Second, governmental units frequently award civil service workers increases comparable to those in the private sector. As for the future, there are some unions without COLAs who have expressed some interest and there are some groups who would like to tie the minimum wage to the general wage level. Further wage indexation may, therefore, occur unless inflation abates.

There is very little indexation of private pensions currently, and it is not apparent whether there will be much movement in this direction. The public sector, which had been fairly generous with providing price-linked retirement benefits, appears to be under pressure to cut costs. In addition, many localities have discovered that their pension plans are underfunded even under current provisions. Finally, there is new awareness of possible pitfalls in designing pension escalators; benefits were inadvertently indexed for both prices and wages, *i.e.*, "double-indexed", in the 1972 Social Security Act and there was a "kicker" in the 1969 civil service retirement amendments which overindexed pension benefits. These factors suggest that public pension plans will probably not move further toward indexation very fast in the near future. As far as private pensions go, there is relatively little movement toward indexation, although this may change if inflation continues at current high levels. There has already been an increased awareness of the possibility that pension benefits may become severely eroded. Combined with the rising average age of the work force, this may cause wider interest in pension indexation. On the other hand, if people work longer years because of the rise in the mandatory retirement age, erosion of pension values will be a less serious problem.

Consequences of indexation
Economists and policymakers, union leaders, and corporate representatives have all argued about the desirability of indexation. The differences in opinion arise not only from differences in their respective interests but also from certain implicit assumptions about how the economy works and what causes prices to change.

One important characteristic of indexation is that it speeds up the response of prices and wages to changes in the economy. In some circumstances this faster response may be desirable, but in other circumstances it is not.

Several economists, including Milton Friedman and JoAnna Gray, have argued that the fast response is desirable in the case where the money supply grows faster or slower than expected.[8] Without indexation, nominal wages are set to provide some compensation for expected inflation. If nominal wages have been set to provide for a large inflation adjustment, then a deceleration in money growth and in price inflation would

---

[7] The 1969 amendment (Public Law 91-93) gave an extra 1 percent each time there was an adjustment to compensate for the time lag. However, because this 1 percent became part of the base, there was overcompensation for the cost of living.

[8] See Milton Friedman's article "Using Escalators to Help Fight Inflation", *Fortune Magazine* (July 1974), pages 94-96, 174-76, and JoAnna Gray's article "Wage Indexation: A Macroeconomic Approach", *Journal of Monetary Economics* (April 1976), pages 221-35.

cause the real wage rate to rise. Under these circumstances, firms could no longer afford to maintain the same employment and output. In contrast, with indexed wages, a slowing of money growth and inflation would not have this effect on the real wage and employment. Therefore, the indexed wage scenario is less likely to produce changes in employment and output when the money supply shifts.

Friedman goes one step further, arguing that a tight monetary policy to curb inflation would be more palatable in an indexed economy, because a reduction in money supply growth would cause less unemployment. If money growth were reduced, the inflation rate might actually be lower under indexation. The Friedman argument is indeed intriguing, and there are some economists who agree with his argument and are in favor of wage indexing for just this reason. However, others point out that numerous political forces impinge on our policies toward inflation. If large well-defined groups who have strong lobbying power are protected against accelerations in inflation, the pressures to restrain it could be much moderated. Already, a large fraction of the union sector and a substantial portion of workers in the government sector have wage and salary protection. Moreover, through social security, many of the elderly receive price protection, and those who had government jobs commonly have indexed pensions. These groups who could contribute to an effective campaign against inflation no longer have a big incentive to do so.

A more fundamental difficulty with indexation is its affect on the economy's ability to adjust to changes in output, productivity, or international competitiveness —situations which usually require a change in the real wage rate. Consider, for example, the situation in 1973-74. Food prices skyrocketed in 1973, because world grain harvests were much smaller than normal. The price of petroleum, an important United States import, was doubled by the Organization of Petroleum Exporting Countries in the fall of 1973 and again in early 1974. As a result, the overall cost of living, which includes food and energy, increased much more than the price of domestic nonagricultural goods. United States producers of nonagricultural goods could not afford to maintain the same employment if workers insisted on wage increases commensurate with the overall cost of living. Yet, with wage indexation, wages increase automatically with the overall cost of living. This forces nonagricultural business to lay off workers, leading to more unemployment. Furthermore, if monetary and fiscal policy are more stimulative—to ease the unemployment problem—then there is much more inflation in this scenario of wage indexation.

The damage on the price front might be offset during periods when farm prices fall or when imported goods become cheaper. However, in the short run, indexation does make changes in the supply of certain goods and services much more painful for the economy, both in terms of unemployment and in terms of inflation. Indeed, Finland abandoned wage indexation in 1968, shortly after it devalued, to prevent some of these consequences.

The faster response of wages produced by indexation has led to criticism on other grounds. Some people argue that an economy without indexation has a second line of defense against rampant inflation. They postulate the following example: the demand for goods and services expands beyond the economy's ability to produce, and prices begin to rise. Clearly, one defense against this excessive demand situation is restrictive fiscal and monetary policies. But sometimes there are difficulties in sizing up the near-term situation, or there are delays in obtaining necessary legislation. (And, in some cases, political forces prevent the implementation of restrictive policies.) In these cases the redistribution of real income caused by inflation might help to curb it: If wages were not indexed, the price rise would lower the real income of workers who have wage contracts and raise the real profits of firms and the real tax revenue of the government. (The government gains both from inflation *per se* and from the fact that corporate profits are taxed at a higher marginal rate than the typical wage or salary income.) As a result of their real income loss, workers will cut their purchases of goods and services. But the gainers of real income—business firms and government—do not usually step up their purchases much when real income is higher than expected. The cut in spending by workers therefore exceeds the rise in spending by business and government and, on balance, total spending declines, helping to curb inflation.

Turning to a different perspective, some people argue that indexation permits the lengthening of union contracts, thereby saving on negotiation time and the danger of strikes. However, longer term contracts build in a real wage structure for the length of the contract that may turn out to be unsuitable. For example, suppose the demand for good A increases and that for good B declines. Typically, wages in industry A will increase, as the industry tries to attract workers, while wages in industry B fall relative to the average. A long-term contract tends to postpone the relative wage decline in industry B and may therefore lead to more layoffs and higher unemployment. Generalizing this phenomenon, changes in relative demand and supply for various goods could lead to more unemployment under a system of long-term contracts.

To the extent that escalator clauses provide only

partial cost-of-living compensation, all these problems may not be very serious at the present time. However, if indexation becomes more widespread and fuller price protection for those with escalators develops, the economy may have a higher unemployment rate and periods of more rapid inflation.

Problems with the consumer price index as the basis for COLAs

While the potential increases in inflation and unemployment have concerned the majority of analysts, some economists are concerned about the use of the consumer price index in escalator clauses. They point out that at least some of the other problems mentioned above could be either aggravated or mitigated by the particular price index that is used.

From the perspective of the consumer, the consumer price index fails to measure the true cost of living on a number of scores. One problem is that sales taxes and property taxes are treated as consumer prices; income taxes, on the other hand, do not affect the index. Therefore, if a state or local government replaced an income tax with an excise or property tax or vice versa, the index would change when in fact there was no change in the cost of living. Or, if a state or local government were to impose a new excise or property tax and undertake provision of some service that was formerly provided by the private sector, the index would rise, even though the consumers' true purchasing power at the current level of income is in fact unchanged. Thus, decisions that should be based upon efficiency considerations may be hampered; with indexing based upon the consumer price index, these decisions will have wage and price ramifications.

Perhaps more important are factors that cause changes in the consumer price index to overstate changes in the true cost of living. For one thing, the index uses the same market basket of goods and services to determine the price level at different times. But, other things being equal, people will try to substitute cheaper goods for the ones whose prices have risen more rapidly. Thus, the fixed market basket probably gives too much weight to items with rapid price increases.

Another source of upward bias is the way the cost of home ownership is calculated. When inflation accelerates and higher inflation is expected to continue, the mortgage interest rate, like other interest rates, tends to rise. As currently calculated, home-ownership cost reflects the rise in home prices and the entire rise in mortgage interest rates even though most of the interest rate increase is offset by the greater expected appreciation in home prices. Thus, the rise in the cost of home ownership is overstated. (The Bureau of Labor Statistics is currently working on a revised "user cost" of homes to correct for this problem.)

Turning to even tougher criticism, it is argued that price linking should not be based upon a cost-of-living index at all. A cost-of-living index will reflect import prices, but domestic producers are in a poor position to give wage increases based upon import prices. (More detailed arguments on this issue can be found on page 22.) Instead of a cost-of-living index, some economists propose that a price index of domestic goods and services be used. While this would have advantages from some viewpoints, there has been little enthusiasm on the part of workers when it was proposed in other countries.

Conclusion

The worsening of inflation in the United States over the past decade has sparked interest in the price linking of wages and retirement incomes. Many Americans are now favorably disposed toward indexation, regarding escalator clauses as a good protection mechanism against inflation. From an economy-wide perspective, however, the merits of indexation are questionable. In many circumstances, indexation could have undesirable effects on inflation and unemployment. There are some circumstances where it could protect the incomes of those who have escalator clauses with relatively few harmful ramifications for unemployment and inflation—in economywide inflation where all prices are rising in proportion. In such general inflation, however, there would be other groups who suffer inequities and certain economic costs that could not be avoided. Consequently, indexation will not make inflation either equitable or costless. Moreover, if indexation reduces the political pressures to curb inflation, price inflation could be worse in an economy with indexed wages. Faster inflation would, of course, be more costly for the nation as a whole.

Marcelle V. Arak

7

Honest Money

Remarks by

Henry C. Wallich, Member
Board of Governors of the Federal Reserve System
Washington, D.C.

at the

M.B.A. Graduation Exercises
of the
Fordham Graduate School of Business
New York, New York

June 28, 1978

As you prepare to arise from this seat of learning, the years of intake end, and the moment of output is at hand. You may well suspect that you will never know so much as you do now. For a while, you may feel like those great minds who forget more in a year than some learn in a lifetime. Education, after all, is what remains when all the detail has been forgotten. And if you find yourselves close to some leader of business or government, you may be contributing to great achievement. Nothing is impossible to the man with a competent assistant.

At this time, you are presumably looking at your future role in the world in the broadest possible sense, including a moral sense. Today I would like to talk to you about one aspect of your future that has a moral dimension, although it is technically an economic problem. I mean the breakdown in our standards of measuring economic values, as a consequence of inflation. Nothing that is stated about dollars and cents any longer means what it says. Inflation is like a country where nobody speaks the truth. Our failure to deal effectively with inflation results largely from our failure to regard it as a moral issue.

Inflation as deceit

Inflation introduces an element of deceit into most of our economic dealings. Everybody makes contracts knowing perfectly well that they will not be kept in terms of constant values. Everybody expects the value of the dollar to change over the period of a contract. But any specific allowance made for inflation in such a contract is bound to be a speculation. We do not know whether the most valuable part of the contract may not turn out to be the paper it is written on. This condition is hard to reconcile with simple honesty.

If our contracts were made in terms of unpredictably shifting measures of weight, time, or space as we buy food, sell our labor, or acquire real estate, we would probably regard that as cheating, and as intolerable. Yet the case is much the same when we are dealing with monetary values.

Nor are we dealing with small differences between promise and performance. At the going rate of inflation of about 8 percent, a year at a leading college that today costs $7,000 will cost $32,630 by the time your children approach college age. If you buy an average home, by the time your present life expectancy ends, your heirs could sell it for almost $2.5 million. Of course, the only sure thing about these calculations is that they will not ma-

Reprinted from Federal Reserve Bank of Dallas *Voice*, August, 1978.

terialize. Inflation is not stable, nor is it predictable. But I hope the illustrations make their point.

The moral issues posed by inflation go beyond what I consider deceit. Inflation is a means by which the strong can more effectively exploit the weak. The strategically positioned and well organized will gain at the expense of the unorganized and the aged. Because inflation is unpredictable, its effects also cannot be predicted and safeguarded against.

Inflation is a means by which debtors exploit creditors. The interest rate may contain an inflation premium, but when you consider that it is taxable to the creditor and tax deductible to the debtor, the scales obviously are ill-balanced. The small saver, moreover, by law is not even allowed to obtain an adequate inflation premium. Interest rate ceilings on savings deposits see to it that he will be a sufferer from inflation. The unpredictability of inflation, again, makes any inflation premium a speculation.

In the eyes of economists and of government, inflation becomes a means of exploiting labor's "money illusion," i.e., its supposed failure to anticipate inflation correctly. The device through which this mechanism operates is the well-known "Phillips Curve," i.e., the alleged trade-off between unemployment and inflation. It is believed that labor will respond to a seemingly large wage offer that subsequently is eroded by inflation. If labor fails to notice the trick, it will keep working for less than it really had demanded, and employment will be higher. A government pretending to serve a nation's interest by, say, misinforming the people about its military plans would be harshly taken to task. Why should trading on the people's money illusion be regarded any differently?

As it happens, the attempt to trade on money illusion has backfired because labor turned out not to be money blind. Mounting inflation was increasingly perceived and, as it came to be perceived, to accelerate. In consequence, we got both high inflation and high unemployment. Deceit revealed and rejected nevertheless remains deceit.

Business accounting is made deceptive by inflation. Inventory profits and profits due to a depreciation schedule that does not take adequate account of replacement costs grossly exaggerate true earnings. The government permits a remedy for the former—through LIFO—but not for the latter. The effects on profits of a firm's net debtor or creditor position are ignored. Taxes and dividends are paid from profits that may not exist or, if they can be shown to exist by appropriate accounting adjustments, are not backed up by cash flows. In addition to misleading the stockholder and the public, these conditions push firms into higher leveraging. Business thus becomes more speculative.

Meanwhile, planning ahead becomes more difficult for business. Investment lags, because long-term commitments involve risks that inflation makes incalculable. The need to guard against these unknowable risks compels both parties to any transaction, buyer and seller, employer and employee, lender and borrower, to introduce a risk premium into their pricing. Each must demand a little more or offer a little less than he would under noninflationary conditions. That reduces the range of possible bargains and the level of economic activity. Fewer jobs, less output, in the private sector are the results.

Inflation also undermines the honesty of our public policies. It allows the politician to make promises that cannot be met in real terms, because as the government overspends trying to keep those promises, the value of the benefits it delivers shrinks. A permissive attitude toward inflation, allowing the government to validate its promises by money creation, encourages deceitful promises in politics.

Inflation threatens the market system, property, and democracy

Finally, inflation becomes a means of promoting changes in our economic, social, and poltical institutions that circumvents the democratic process. Such changes could be forced upon a reluctant nation because inflation may end up making the existing system unviable. One instance is the diminishing ability of households to provide privately for their future. Personal savings, insurance, pension funds—all become inadequate. Money set aside in any of these forms for old age, for sickness, for education could be wiped out by accelerating inflation. One may indeed ask whether it is not an essential attribute of a civilized society to be able to make that kind of provision for the future. But that is not the point I want to stress. Rather, I want to emphasize that the increasing uncertainty in providing privately for the future pushes people seeking security toward the government.

Today, the best hedge against inflation is to be retired from the Federal Government. That guarantees a reliably indexed pension which may outgrow the pay of the job itself. Social security is the next best thing, although at a much lower level. Every other form of pension, even if indexed, is exposed to the risk that the employer, or the private sector as a whole, may not be able to perform. A government pension is riskless, short of a strike at the Bureau of Engraving and Printing.

A similar trend toward bigger government threatens at the level of productive enterprise. Inflation, as I have noted, distorts corporate accounting and cash flows. It creates liquidity and profitability problems. Strong firms become less strong; less strong firms become marginal. Dependence upon and eventually absorption by government may be the ultimate outcome. Countries like Italy and Great Britain are already on their way to this solution.

In the United States we have not yet reached that condition, though the increasing passage of the railroads into government hands is a danger signal. But the role of government nevertheless has expanded as the private sector has retreated before the impact of inflation. Mounting regulation, tax burdens, and other impediments, of course, have also contributed their part.

Not long ago it was taken for granted that at full employment the private sector should be strong enough to produce a surplus in the Federal budget. It was expected, in other words, that the inherent impulses of private consumption and especially investment would generate a level of aggregate demand sufficient to absorb capacity output. Today this has become very doubtful. Capital formation is too weak, consumption too low, to generate enough demand to sustain the economy at full employment without the crutches of a Federal deficit.

We might be able to change this by appropriate tax reform that would stimulate investment. We could adopt policies that would cut down our enormous trade deficit that is sucking purchasing power out of the country. But inflation is an obstacle on either of these courses. Tax reform is unlikely to call forth large-scale business investment so long as inflation beclouds the outlook. Policies to improve the trade balance will avail little if inflation reduces our competitiveness.

Thus, by one route or another, inflation creates a vacuum in the private sector into which the government moves. By making the performance of the economy inadequate, inflation is likely to induce expanded government activity. The same result may follow if inflation leads to the imposition of wage and price controls. Indeed, if enduring controls were imposed, which I do not expect, our market economy would be on the way out. Of the three great dimensions of our society—private rather than public ownership, decision making by the market rather than by central planning, and democracy rather than authoritarianism—private ownership and market decision making will then be in retreat. No one can say how long, under such conditions, a shift also in the third dimension, away from democracy and toward authoritarianism, can be avoided.

The sources of inflation

What can be done? Before we look for remedies, we must examine the causes. Inflation is like cancer: many substances are carcinogenic, and many activities generate inflation. The sources of inflation can be diagnosed at several levels. The familiar debate about the sources of violence provides an analogy. Do guns kill people? Do people kill people? Does society kill people? Some assert that money, and nothing but money, causes inflation—the "guns kill people" proposition. Some assert that the entire gamut of government policies, from deficit spending to protectionism to minimum wage to farm price supports to environmental and safety regulations, causes inflation—the "people kill people" proposition. Some argue, finally, that it is social pressures, competition for the national product, a revolution of aspirations, which are at the root—the "society kills people" proposition. The first view holds primarily responsible for inflation the central bank, the second the government in general, the third the people that elect and instruct the government.

In addition, time preference—the social discount rate—enters into the equation. Inflation usually is the final link in a chain of well-meant actions. The benefits of a tax cut, of increased public spending, are felt within a few weeks or quarters. The penalty, in terms of inflation, may not come until after a couple of years or even later. Inflation is the long-run consequence of short-run expediencies. Life, to be sure, is a succession of short runs, but every moment is also the long run of some short-run expediency of long ago. We are now experiencing the long-run consequences of the short-run policies of the past. These consequences are as unacceptable as rain on weekends, and just as easy to change. If we continue to meet current problems with new short-run devices, the bill will keep mounting.

We will not defeat inflation if we always take the short view. We will then always find that the cost of fighting inflation is always too high, the short-run loss of output and employment too great. We shall find ourselves ignoring inflation, in the hope that it will somehow not grow worse. That is pure self-deception. Cancer ignored does not become stationary, and neither does inflation. Inflation ignored accelerates.

A plan for action

A long view is needed on inflation. It is a view very different from that of the politician, who is under enormous pressure to do quickly something that looks good. Harold Wilson said that in politics one week was a long time. More charitably, the pressure is until the next election. If the people will not instruct their elected representatives to do the things that are needed to end inflation, if they turn them out of office because the remedies take time and are temporarily painful, we will keep getting a little more employment and output now at the expense of much more unemployment and loss of output later. And we will get more inflation all along the way, down to its ultimate consequences.

We need to make the ending of inflation our first priority. That must be our overall policy. In the current circumstances, to implement it, we need to take a number of steps, some of which I shall list here.

(1) We need to recognize that we are currently very close to full employment and accordingly must slow down the growth of the economy, gradually but firmly, to its long-term rate of $3^{1}/_{4}$ to $3^{1}/_{2}$ percent.

(2) We must limit the pending tax cut to what is needed to offset the effect of inflation on income brackets, perhaps of the order of $10 billion.

(3) We must work to bring the budget deficit for 1980 below $40 billion.

(4) Monetary policy must prevent increases in money growth that would fuel inflation and must gradually bring the growth of the monetary aggregates down to levels commensurate with the real growth rate of the economy.

(5) We must stop adding to inflation by government actions such as protectionism, regulation, farm price supports, minimum wage increases, and high government construction costs.

(6) We must promote competition, through antitrust action, and productivity, through tax changes that stimulate investment.

(7) We must maintain as strong a dollar internationally as our balance of payments will permit.

(8) We would be wise to adopt an incomes policy that employs the tax system and the market mechanism, free from the taint of wage and price controls, commonly referred to as TIP.

The President's program of voluntary de-escalation of price and wage increases deserves everybody's support. But in our highly competitive environment, voluntary sacrifices on the part of labor and business have their limitations. We should view the program as a supplement to, not a substitute for, a comprehensive anti-inflation program.

If inflation is a moral problem, we require a moral solution; that is, a recognition that public policies have led to serious inequities affecting people in different and unequal ways and a commitment to new policies that will correct the cumulative distortions and contribute to desired economic progress. The policies I have proposed require taking a long-run view of inflation. Nothing will stop inflation overnight, and in the short run the gains will always seem dearly won. But without such a long-run approach, the damage will mount and the ultimate costs will escalate.

You, as you assume your roles in the productive sector of our nation, are in a better position than anyone to take such a long-run view. You have nothing to gain from the expedients of the past. You have a lifetime interest in the honest, non-inflationary, productive performance of the American economy.

8

LIVING WITH INFLATION: CONSIDER THE ALTERNATIVE

It's springtime, and Jimmy Carter is falling in love with one of Jerry Ford's old sweethearts: the dream of controlling inflation. He's quite shy about the whole affair, and has rejected the suggestion from some of his advisors that he launch a dramatic, all-out public campaign against rising prices. Still, he did take to the airwaves in mid-April to announce the following anti-inflation schemes:

• Federal white-collar employees will be limited to a 5.5% pay increase, less than had been budgeted for them this year. Top Carter appointees will have salaries frozen for a year.

• Carter's ceiling on total federal spending will be strictly enforced, with vetoes if necessary.

• Logging on federal lands will be increased, to ease lumber shortages.

• Businesses and unions will be urged to hold price and wage hikes below the average rate of increase for the last two years.

• Finally, Congress will be urged to pass a hospital cost-control bill and other Administration proposals.

This is great news if you're buying lumber, unless you also happen to be a federal white-collar employee. But for most of us, the impact of Carter's new romance with "fiscal responsibility" is less clear. Will the new policies be enacted? If so, will they really cure inflation? And will the cure be better or worse than the disease?

Asleep at the Wheel?

It's easy, at this point, to be skeptical about any new Carter plans. Our president has made it perfectly clear that his policy pronouncements should be taken with a grain of indecision. From the on-again, off-again tax cut, to the no-surprises 1979 Budget, to the indifference about the falling dollar and the ho-hum urban policy Carter's approach has been to promise them anything but give them about what they got last year.

This is no mere character defect, but rather a result of the fundamental indecision in U.S. ruling circles today: there is no clear consensus among business and government policymakers about how to solve the economy's problems. In the absence of such a consensus, economic policy is dominated by the conflicting pressures of myriad interest groups, some of which are likely to block almost any significant change.

In this environment, a presidential promise is an attempt at verbal pacification, a measure of what seems popular to say, as often as it is an indication of what will be done. So perhaps the news from the White House should be rephrased. Jimmy Carter has announced that it now seems popular to emphasize fighting inflation — a change from last year, when fighting unemployment was still more fashionable.

There are some real changes in the economy that lie behind this change in attitude. The official unemployment rate has inched downward from 9% three years ago to "only" about 6% today. That's still a recession by 1960's standards, but apparently it's what now passes for prosperity. Meanwhile, inflation, which had slowed down to less than a 3% annual rate of increase in early 1976, has recently speeded up to around 7%.

But the simple fact of more inflation and less unemployment doesn't mean that everyone *should* be worrying about inflation. The widely-held belief that poor and working people suffer the most from inflation is at best a half-truth. On the one hand, it is true that the rich have more savings to fall back on, and probably more ability to increase their incomes to compensate for inflation.

On the other hand, the things that poor and middle-income people buy have not, on average, been going up in price any faster than the things rich people buy. Moreover, inflation has often been associated with times of rising employment, while anti-inflationary policies usually throw more people out of work.

Something for Everyone

It is often taken for granted on the left and among liberals that prices have been going up faster on necessities than on luxuries, and that inflation is therefore a particularly severe problem for the poor. To test this idea, *Dollars & Sense* examined the impact of inflation on the budgets of households at three different income levels (see box, next page). From 1967 to January 1978, there was an 84.7% increase in the average price of the items in a low-income

Dollars & Sense magazine, 324 Somerville Ave., Somerville, MA 02143 (monthly, $7.50/yr.).

household's budget, 85.5% for median-income households, and 86.0% for the rich.

In short, there is no significant difference in the rate of price increase experienced by people at different income levels. Inflation, in recent years, has included something for everyone. Therefore, inflation should have little impact on the distribution of income — which is consistent with the fact that there has been almost no change in the distribution of income during the recent years of rapid inflation (see *D&S* #29).

While inflation itself may hit rich and poor budgets equally hard, the causes of inflation are often particularly good for the poor: the same forces which cause inflation often cause an expansion in employment opportunities. Inflation occurs when demand exceeds supply; that is, when the total amount that businesses, government and workers are trying to buy is greater than the amount of goods and services being produced.

Increased spending by business often (though not always) means that employers are creating more jobs; increased deficit spending by government will also generally lead to growth in employment. And increases in the number of people working — as well as the higher wage levels that workers are able to win when unemployment rates are low — lead to more consumption spending by working people.

Thus inflation is frequently (certainly not always) associated with low unemployment. Conversely, the government's favorite remedy for inflation, reducing total spending, reduces employment as well. When the government spends less (or raises taxes, which reduces private spending), fewer goods and services are bought, leading business to cut back on production and employment. With lower employment, workers as a whole spend less, further reducing the demand for goods and services. Eventually this lowers demand enough to slow the increase in prices.

Some observers claim that this mechanism, the "tradeoff" between inflation and unemployment, no longer works since both inflation *and* unemployment have been high in recent years. But in the last major attempt to use it, the "tradeoff" did work: President Ford traded millions of workers' jobs, in the 1974-76 recession, for a reduction in the rate of price increase from over 13% annually in the first quarter of 1974 to under 3% annually in the first quarter of 1976. While failing to permanently "Whip Inflation Now," Ford did demonstrate that by causing the greatest economic slump since the 1930's it was possible to temporarily whip inflation two years later.

CALCULATING INFLATION'S IMPACT

To examine the impact of inflation, we used the budgets for different income groups from the U.S. Bureau of Labor Statistics 1972-74 survey of consumer expenditures, the latest such data available. We looked at three income levels: $5,000 to $6,000; $10,000 to $12,000; and $25,000 and over. (Median household income in 1973 was $10,530.)

The technique we used can best be explained by an example. Suppose that the poor spend 2/3 of their income on food and 1/3 on clothing. Then the average price rise for the poor would be 2/3 of the food price increase plus 1/3 of the clothing increase. Suppose that the rich spend 1/2 their income on food and 1/2 on clothing; then their average price rise would be 1/2 the food increase plus 1/2 the clothing increase. If food goes up faster in price than clothing, then prices are rising faster for the poor, since they spend more of their incomes on food.

Actually, we used three income levels and 13 expenditure categories: food at home, food away from home, alcohol, tobacco, rent, homeownership, utilities, housekeeping and house furnishings, transportation, health care, clothing, personal care, and recreation. The result was that from 1967 to January 1978 prices rose 84.7% for the lower-income group, 85.5% for the middle group, and 86.0% for the rich. Looking only at January 1975 to January 1978, there is even less difference in the three rates.

The reason for these near-identical results is that some of the things going up fastest in price make up a larger share of rich people's budgets (such as homeownership and food away from home), while others make up a larger share for the poor (such as utilities and health care). A similar pattern holds for the items with the slowest price increases.

We also looked more closely at food eaten at home. Dividing it into 15 smaller categories, and carrying out the same kind of calculation, we found that from 1967 to 1977 food prices increased 92.9% for the lower-income group, 92.8% for the middle group, and 90.4% for the rich. (The rich are more heavily into beef, which has had slower-than-average price increases, accounting for the small difference here.)

These calculations should be interpreted with caution. It is particularly unfortunate, but unavoidable, that they are based on surveys done before the big food and fuel price increase of the mid-1970's, and that they do not include information on how budget patterns have actually changed in response to inflation: they reflect only how inflation has affected average 1973 budgets.

Sources: *Bureau of Labor Statistics*, Bulletin 1959, Report 455-4, press releases.

The terms of the inflation-unemployment tradeoff seem to be growing worse — it takes more unemployment than it used to in order to achieve the same amount of reduction in inflation. This is caused by the growing dependence of the economy on international trade, which introduces some inflation that is beyond U.S. control, and by the steady increase in monopoly power of large corporations, which makes them able to resist price decreases in recessions.

Why Not the Best?

Given the choice between inflation and unemployment, why not always choose inflation? People are better off with jobs and rising prices, after all, than with no jobs and constant prices; if those are the choices, it should always be politically popular to favor full employment and accept inflation as an unfortunate side effect. One drawback to this approach is that many people are on fixed incomes. Before the introduction of cost-of-living increases for Social Security benefits in 1972, this was probably a politically decisive number of people.

Concern for retired people, or for workers whose wages haven't been keeping up with inflation, however, is hardly the most important obstacle to a permanent full-employment-with-inflation economy. There are two major reasons why capitalism won't work that way for long. First, a prolonged period of low unemployment increases the bargaining power of labor, and allows workers to make gains in wages and working conditions at the expense of profits; this occurred most recently in the late 1960's, when total profits, corrected for inflation, began dropping after 1966, while total wages continued to climb.

At today's levels of unemployment, a "wage squeeze" on profits is not likely to occur. A second problem with a permanent-inflation economy is more serious. As international trade has become more important to U.S. business, rapid inflation here puts U.S. goods at a competitive disadvantage. Capitalists need to control inflation in order to win the foreign trade wars just as they need periodic bouts of unemployment to discipline labor and prevent a wage squeeze on profits; for both these reasons, a permanent inflation/full employment economy is unacceptable to them.

But as any used-car salesman knows, you can't always sell the naked truth. Imagine Jimmy Carter going on TV to tell us that three million people are going to be laid off in order to keep up profits and productivity and to out-compete the Germans. Capitalism not only needs to throw people out of work periodically; it also needs a way to mobilize mass popular support for doing so. And so far, a great national campaign against inflation has been the most successful technique anyone in Washington has found.

The View from Below

Anti-inflation politics do strike a responsive chord in many people. For those on fixed incomes, and for those whose wages don't, or just barely do, keep up with inflation, the hope that the government will control price increases is always appealing. Yet it is almost always a false hope. There is some evidence that workers, by fighting hard, can make wages keep up with inflation. On average, wages have been going up as fast as prices over the last decade or so. And the important case of Social Security shows that fixed-income programs can be changed to include cost-of-living adjustments.

There is no evidence, on the other hand, that the government can control peacetime inflation by any means except a recession — which leaves almost all workers, employed and unemployed, worse off. Other anti-inflation measures frequently mentioned include "jawboning," a form of public prayer for self-restraint by businesses which has no measurable effect on the world; and wage-price controls, which have worked only when the U.S. was fighting World War II and the Korean War, but which fell apart within a year or two when attempted in the early 1970's.

So despite the obvious hardships caused by inflation, most workers are better off living with it, fighting for wage increases to keep up with it, and fighting *against* the usual anti-labor form of anti-inflation policies.

Meanwhile, back in the White House, what of Jimmy Carter's newfound love for controlling inflation? Shy and indecisive as he is, he doesn't seem ready to do anything about it yet; he just wanted us all to know that it's on his mind. If inflation, or the balance of trade, continue to get worse, he may decide to make a more serious proposal. But if we're lucky, his springtime romance may turn into nothing more than a midsummer night's dream.

While inflation itself may hit rich and poor budgets equally hard, the causes of inflation are often particularly good for the poor: the same forces which cause inflation often cause an increase in employment.

9

There's high-level perplexity in Washington about the signals the economy is giving off. Says one Senator who's heard too many conflicting views:

"I Don't Trust Any Economists Today"

by JUAN CAMERON

It's certainly nothing new when outside commentators say that those people in Washington who are trying to manage the economy don't understand what's going on. What *is* new is that a lot of those people in Washington now admit they don't understand what's going on. Perplexity about the economy is rampant these days, even at very high levels—or perhaps especially at very high levels. "Our old rules of thumb no longer work," says Lyle Gramley, a member of Jimmy Carter's Council of Economic Advisers. "And we haven't been able to develop new ones."

A great deal of the current confusion in Washington, to be sure, is traceable to President Carter's apparent inability to adopt a coherent set of economic policies and stick to it. (See "A Record of White House Wobbles," page 33.) But even apart from the Administration's flip-flops, there is puzzlement about the behavior of the economy. Gone are the days, not so long ago, when economists could pride themselves on being, as Nobel laureate Kenneth Arrow once put it, prescribers of rationality to the social world. Seldom is heard the old tone of crisp confidence with which economists often counseled Presidents and Congresses.

A remarkable comment on the new perplexity comes from Secretary of the Treasury W. Michael Blumenthal, who is both a Ph.D. in economics and a former chief executive of a major corporation, Bendix. Says Blumenthal: "I really think the economics profession is close to bankruptcy in understanding the present situation —before or after the fact." That's quite a statement for the chairman of the Administration's Economic Policy Group. Blumenthal thinks there are serious deficiencies in our understanding of how today's inflation affects the economy. And there is no clear grasp, he adds, of how monetary policy works in the face of the huge international investment flows and fluctuating exchange rates.

A game of hunches and guesses

His feeling that economic realities have outrun economic understanding, Blumenthal finds, is shared by finance ministers in Germany, Japan, and other industrial nations. "The Germans don't know why they have such a slow rate of growth. And the Japanese are at their wits' end about what to do about their large trade surplus."

The uncertainties, Blumenthal says emphatically, have made the econometric models that policymakers depend on increasingly unreliable. "I tell the President, when we come to him with predictions about how a certain tax cut will affect unemployment, to listen—then forget it. We can't predict with any certainty what will occur, for the models are as confused as we are about the tradeoffs."

Indeed, Carter and his political assistants, groping their way through today's economic perplexities, have moved from their early overconfidence to a view of economics as a high-risk game of hunches and guesses. Some months ago, the President quipped that he knew a fortune-teller in Georgia who was a better forecaster than his own economic wise men. Congressmen and Senators, struggling to set spending and tax policies, voice concern about the conflicting and equivocal advice they have been receiving from Administration economists, and those on the outside, too. After hearings on the fiscal 1979 budget, a member of the Senate Budget Committee, Republican Pete Domenici of New Mexico, went so far as to say: "I don't trust any economists today. Their theories are out of date."

Certainly the events of the past two years have left economists scratching their heads. They have seen a lengthy recovery take place without a business investment boom. The old relationship between the money supply (measured by M_1), G.N.P. growth, and interest rates has changed. Consumers, apparently taking on more

Reprinted from the September 11, 1978 issue of Fortune Magazine by special permission; © 1978 Time Inc.

mortgage debt to finance other kinds of purchases, have confounded forecasters with the strength of their demand. And inflation has roared on in an economy that, by historical measures, has had enough slack to prevent such price pressures.

The law wasn't working at all

A real shocker came in the first quarter of this year, when the number of jobs rose by one million although there was no real growth in G.N.P. Taken by itself, the improvement in the employment picture was good news, and was hailed as such, but it was also puzzling.

Over a considerable span of years, the unemployment rate had roughly conformed to a rule of thumb known as Okun's Law (after Arthur M. Okun, chairman of the Council of Economic Advisers toward the end of the Johnson Administration). According to Okun's Law, the unemployment rate declines only when growth in real G.N.P. is running above the normal trend rate (around 3.5 or 4 percent)—and then it declines by only one-third of a percentage point for each full point of G.N.P. growth in excess of the trend rate. Well, in the first quarter of this year, Okun's Law obviously wasn't working at all. With output flat, the unemployment rate should have gone up; instead, it went down—to 6.2 percent, a decline of 0.4 from the last quarter of 1977. "I am baffled," says Okun. "For the moment, it's clear Okun's Law has been repealed—or at least suspended."

Some of Washington's leading economists find a bit of comfort in the notion that the failure of the economy to follow its predicted course may be due to statistical aberrations that later revisions in the data will clear up. Maybe so; but others argue that the explanation of the confusion in economics probably lies outside economics. While established economic laws and relationships have not been repealed, the political and social context in which they function has changed momentously over the past decade or so.

Charles Schultze, chairman of the Council of Economic Advisers, disputes the view that Keynesian theories, which have dominated fiscal policy since World War II, no longer hold. Both the current recovery and the preceding recession, he says, were "testimonials to the power of fiscal and monetary tools" first to restrain and then to stimulate the economy. "Our forecasting models may be inaccurate," he says, "and our judgments sometimes wrong, but the tools at our disposal are clearly good enough to avoid a reemergence of excess demand." He concedes, however, that there are obstacles to using these tools in a setting like today's, marked by inflation and slow growth.

Alan Greenspan, Schultze's predecessor, agrees that nothing has happened to alter the general thrust of what John Maynard Keynes wrote in the 1930's. The problem, he feels, is that relationships formulated when inflation was running between 1.5 and 4 percent simply don't hold when prices are rising by 8 to 10 percent a year. "We have no guidelines from peacetime periods to describe this phenomenon," Greenspan says. "What we are finding today is that, as we depart from past experiences, the whole policymaking decision process, and the whole structure of the economy, is far more complex than we had proposed."

"Something strange going on"

Today's most worried-over economic puzzle is what has happened to productivity, which seems to have entered a period of markedly lower growth. From 1950 to 1968, private nonfarm productivity grew at an annual rate of about 2.7 percent. Then for the next nine years, through 1977, it slowed to about 1.4 percent. This year, says the CEA's Schultze, the rate of productivity growth has inexplicably plunged below 1 percent at a time when the economy was expanding. For months

In these days of economic perplexity, many members of Congress are uncertain whether to step on the gas or the brakes.

now, Schultze has had his staff working in vain to find an answer. As one of his economists says: "Something strange has been going on out there. We have taken the numbers apart, but we still can't tell what's the matter."

Treasury Secretary Blumenthal thinks the explanation lies in higher energy prices, and more particularly in the haphazard growth of federal regulations during the past decade. "If a company has to devote 20 percent of its available capital to anti-noise and anti-dust equipment," he says, "that money is clearly not available for new machinery and facilities that will promote efficiency and cut costs." The influx into the labor force of large numbers of women and young workers, short on skills and education, is widely thought to be another important factor.

Adding workers instead of machines

The slowdown in productivity is related, of course, to this year's surge in employment and the drop in the unemployment rate. One theory is that employers are meeting rising demand for output by adding a lot more workers instead of investing in new plant and equipment. A more questionable explanation is that businessmen may, in effect, be stockpiling labor in anticipation of still higher demand in the future. The productivity mystery, whatever its explanation, is certainly a major contributor to the underlying inflation in the economy. Unit costs are higher than they would be if productivity had been doing better, and higher unit costs sooner or later translate into higher prices.

One especially unpleasant fact about the economy, from an inflation-fighter's viewpoint, is that wages and prices are responding more sluggishly to conditions of economic slack than in the past. Up until the 1960's, business contractions brought a deceleration in wage increases. But in the economic slowdowns that began in 1969 and 1973, wages were actually rising faster six months after the trough of the recession than at the preceding cyclical peak. The consumer price index has lately followed a similar if less marked trend.

These developments to a large extent reflect structural changes in the economy. The rapid growth of the noncompetitive sectors—government, the regulated industries, and the nonprofit organizations—has tended to reduce the effect of the competitive forces that once served to slow wages and prices in a recession. Rigidity in wages has been increased by higher minimum wages, by various income-support measures for people who are not working, and by a huge increase in the number of workers with some kind of cost-of-living adjustment. Just since 1970, the number of workers whose union contracts provide such adjustments has risen from 25 to 60 percent of the total covered by major collective-bargaining agreements. "This development," says Schultze, "has taken some of the flexibility out of the economy."

It has also taken some of the flexibility out of economic policy. These days, Schultze says, an economic policymaker is in quite a bind. You can't do much about unemployment "without triggering new problems in productivity and prices." Arthur Okun, having been in Schultze's position himself, sympathizes with his plight: "If you can't forecast well enough to say speed up the economy or slow it down, then the whole notion of economic stabilization suffers."

That is certainly so in Congress. With the Administration having made major changes in fiscal policy to cope with unforeseen developments, Congress has come to feel that the White House doesn't know what it's doing. Many members, uncertain whether to step on the gas or the brakes, are turning to radical proposals. Some are urging that a new form of wage and price control, the so-called TIP, or Tax-Based Incomes Policy, be given a try. Senator William Roth of Delaware and Representative Jack Kemp of New York have gathered wide support for their proposal to cut federal taxes by 33 percent, or more than $100 billion, over a span of three years, without corresponding cuts in federal spending. Some conservative members want to put on a clenched-teeth demonstration of fiscal and monetary restraint to break inflation.

This economic free-for-all draws different reactions, depending upon where one sits. Greenspan welcomes the intellectual ferment as a valuable test of the theoretical framework on which economic policymaking rests. But Blumenthal, who has the pressing job of getting policy through Congress, fumes at the ready acceptance being given to the prescriptions of "know nothings," as he puts it. "Today's vacuum," he says, "has provided a happy hunting ground for amateur theorists, who always abound in economics." The rising level of confusion, Blumenthal adds, makes the pursuit of rational policies difficult. He, like many Congressmen, is looking for a "new Keynes" to lead policymakers out of their economic wilderness.

Puzzled and perplexed though they may be, Blumenthal and his colleagues do not have the option of sitting on the sidelines until the murk clears. The government is deeply involved in the economy whether the Administration has a coherent economic policy or not. Federal budget, tax, and monetary decisions, wise or foolish, have powerful and pervasive economic consequences. So the present perplexity in Washington is nothing to laugh about.

The fading of past illusions

There are, however, at least two silver linings in the cloud of perplexity. One is the possibility that dissatisfaction with the workings of the economy will lead to more tough-minded scrutiny of structural kinks and rigidities, and determined efforts to chop away at them. Another silver lining is the fading away of past illusions about the abilities of economists to manage the economy, fine-tune it, and make it behave according to their desires—or the desires of the politicians they serve.

To some extent, our present economic binds and stresses are consequences of such illusions. That sort of thing, at least, we probably don't have to worry about for a while. Whatever other adjectives may be applied to Washington economists over the next several years, it seems quite unlikely that anyone will be labeling them "overconfident."

10

Is Inflation All Due to Money?

ALBERT E. BURGER

INFLATION is an all-pervasive problem which affects everyone's decisions. Individuals must consider the outlook for prices when planning budgets or wage demands, when deciding whether to buy a house or in what form to hold savings, as well as a multitude of other economic decisions. Also, business is increasingly concerned about the outlook for inflation, especially as it relates to planning and capital investment.[1] It is not surprising, therefore, that persistent inflation has led to increased public demands that something be done to correct the problem.

The current Administration has responded to these demands by announcing an anti-inflation program which includes, among other aspects, a promise to intervene in individual price and wage decisions in an attempt to reduce inflationary pressures. But such an approach, at best, has only a very limited chance for success because it fails to distinguish between two key characteristics of the inflation process. First, there are increases (or decreases) in prices which result from nonmonetary factors that cover a gamut of influences such as the effects of weather on agriculture and actions of foreign oil producers. The basic characteristic of all these nonmonetary factors is that they have a transitory influence on inflation. They have their impact on the level of prices in selected periods, but their influence is either reversed in following periods or ceases to be a cause of period-after-period changes in prices in the same direction. It is the second aspect of inflation, the trend or persistent year-after-year increase of prices, that is really "public enemy number one." This is the aspect of inflation to which corrective economic policy must be directed. Otherwise, all other economic programs to stop inflation will end in frustration.

Contrasting Explanations of Inflation

The rate of change of prices can show considerable short-term fluctuation. For example, the implicit price deflator for gross national product rose at a 5 percent rate in the third and fourth quarters of 1977, accelerated to about a 7 percent rate in the first quarter of 1978, rose further to an 11 percent rate in the second quarter, only to recede back to a 7 percent rate in the third quarter of 1978.

In addition to this variation in the general price index, there are also frequent fluctuations in the prices of individual items included in the general price indexes. Since pronounced swings in the prices of specific goods or services sometimes coincide with fluctuations in the general index of prices, specific items are frequently cited as the cause of the current inflation. Also, because the magnitude and timing of price changes vary from item to item, the blame for inflation is often transferred, from period-to-period, from one item to another. Consequently, a number of explanations of the inflation process have been offered, involving at various times the behavior of such diverse items as steel prices, exchange rate movements, union wage demands, agricultural conditions, changes in minimum wages and even the behavior of the periodically elusive anchovy. Such an analysis provides an ever-changing array of inflation villains. The blame for inflation is shifted from Arabs to coffee producers to beef producers to steel producers to specific union leaders to large banks and so on.

Concentration on such short-term oscillations in the various elements of price indexes clouds the issue of the fundamental force behind the persistent increase in the general level of prices. The problem of inflation is much more than an unfortunate sequence of increases in the prices of particular items. Focusing attention on movements in the price of particular items or each wiggle in the general price indexes gives only a *description* of where and when the general inflationary pressures fall in the economy. The important issue is why prices, on average, *continue* to rise over an extended period of time.

An *explanation* of the fundamental source of a continued pressure on prices requires a broader, longer-run perspective that incorporates monetary developments. When the money stock grows too rapidly relative to the rate of increase of goods and services,

---
[1] John A. Tatom and James E. Turley, "Inflation and Taxes: Disincentives for Capital Formation," this *Review* (January 1978), pp. 2-8.

Reprinted from Federal Reserve Bank of St. Louis *Review*, December, 1978.

individuals find themselves holding more money than they demand, given existing income, prices, and yields (including interest rates) on other assets. In the process by which they attempt to pull their holdings of money in line with the quantity demanded, inflation results. To put the matter more simply, when "too much money is chasing too few goods" there will be *persistent* increases in prices. Consequently, analysis of persistent increases in the general level of prices requires consideration of the growth of the money stock. Such a monetary view contends that although prices can periodically rise or fall sharply due to nonmonetary factors, inflation continues only if these nonmonetary factors recur in succeeding periods, or if there is a continued excessive expansion of money.

The emphasis which is placed on the role of monetary actions in the fight against inflation depends very much on which of these two aspects of price changes is the center of attention. Concentration on movements in individual prices or short-term movements in the general price indexes typically leads to assignment of a limited role to monetary actions, a focus of attention on nonmonetary factors, and the recommendation of some form of direct controls on the prices of specific items. In contrast, consideration of why prices continue to increase period after period, pinpoints the rate of monetary expansion as the prime factor in the fight against inflation.

Money and Inflation

To illustrate the difference between inflation caused by monetary factors and short-term movements in price indexes caused by nonmonetary factors, consider the following simple monetary guide to inflation:[2]

> The rate of change of prices over the next year is equal to the average rate of growth of the money stock over the previous five years.

The results of using this shorthand representation of the driving force behind the inflation process and its long-run character are presented in Table I.[3] The information in this table shows that, over the period 1953-71, past or trend growth rates of money were a reasonably good guide to the year-to-year behavior of prices. During this nineteen-year period, the

---

[2]For other examples of the use of monetary guides to inflation, see Richard T. Selden, "Inflation: Are We Winning the Fight?," Morgan Guaranty *Survey* (October 1977), pp. 7-13, and Allan Meltzer, "It Takes Long-Range Planning to Lick Inflation," *Fortune* (December 1977), pp. 96-106.

[3]Annual data are calculated as to the average of the four quarters of data in a given year. For example, the growth rate of prices from 1976 to 1977 on an annual basis is computed by comparing the average of the four quarters in 1977 to the average of the four quarters in 1976.

Table I

Monetary Growth as an Indicator of Inflation

Period	(1) Growth Rate of Money	Period	(2) Growth Rate of Prices	(1)-(2)
1947-52	2.3%	1953	1.5%	0.8
1948-53	2.7	1954	1.4	1.3
1949-54	3.2	1955	2.2	1.0
1950-55	3.3	1956	3.1	0.2
1951-56	2.7	1957	3.4	-0.7
1952-57	1.8	1958	1.6	0.2
1953-58	1.5	1959	2.2	-0.7
1954-59	2.0	1960	1.7	0.3
1955-60	1.3	1961	0.9	0.4
1956-61	1.5	1962	1.8	-0.3
1957-62	1.8	1963	1.5	0.3
1958-63	2.2	1964	1.6	0.6
1959-64	2.2	1965	2.2	0.0
1960-65	3.1	1966	3.3	-0.2
1961-66	3.6	1967	2.9	0.7
1962-67	4.0	1968	4.5	-0.5
1963-68	4.8	1969	5.0	-0.2
1964-69	5.2	1970	5.4	-0.2
1965-70	5.1	1971	5.1	0.0
1966-71	5.5	1972	4.1	1.4
1967-72	6.1	1973	5.8	0.3
1968-73	6.2	1974	9.7	-3.5
1969-74	6.1	1975	9.6	-3.5
1970-75	6.2	1976	5.2	1.0
1971-76	6.0	1977	5.9	0.1

average difference between actual yearly inflation and that indicated by the past rate of monetary expansion was only 0.2 percentage point, and in two-thirds of the years the error was 0.5 percentage point or less. On a quarter-to-quarter basis, the rate of change of prices oscillated around the trend rate of inflation. However, the rate of change of prices returned consistently to that dictated by the rate of monetary expansion.

Also during this period, changes in the five-year trend growth of money accurately indicated changes in the year-to-year rate of inflation. As the trend growth of money slowed in the period 1958-63, inflation was reduced. Over the next eight years, the trend growth of money accelerated steadily from less than a 2 percent rate to a 5 percent rate, and inflation rose from less than 2 percent to 5 percent per year.

In contrast to the 1953-71 period, the last six years present some examples of abnormally large differences between changes in the price index and the inflation indicated by past growth rates of money. In particular, 1972 and 1974-75 stand out as glaring exceptions to the previous performance of the monetary guide to inflation. To understand the behavior of inflation since 1971, and how this experience fits into the general monetary explanation of inflation, it is crucial that one clearly understand the effect of nonmonetary factors on the behavior of prices. Specifically, it is very important to realize that, although the level of prices can change, sometimes even for a prolonged period, the rate of change of prices cannot continue to substantially deviate from the rate of monetary expansion.[4]

What special nonmonetary factors in 1972 and 1974-75 operated to cause such large deviations of actual changes in prices from those indicated by past growth rates of money?[5] First, 1972 was a year of price controls. By law, reported prices were not allowed to fully reflect market pressures, especially those pushing prices upward. Under such circumstances, the reported change in prices would be expected to be considerably less than inflation indicated by a monetary guide. From the perspective of a monetary interpretation of inflation, the gap in 1972 between price changes consistent with past money growth (about 5.5 percent) and those reported during wage and price controls (about 4 percent) indicates (1) an upsurge of prices when price controls were removed, and (2) an incentive for transactions to take place at prices above posted prices.

Other major differences between reported changes in prices and those indicated by past monetary expansion occur in the more recent period of 1974-75. Over this period, the level of prices was sharply and unexpectedly raised by the now well-known pricing actions of the major oil-producing nations and the nonmonetary effects of weather on agriculture. The actions of the Organization of Petroleum Exporting Countries (OPEC) resulted in a substantial, unexpected rise in the price of energy. Since energy is a basic input into most production processes, these

Table II

Growth Rates of Selected Components of Consumer Prices

Period	Food Prices	Energy Prices	All Items less Food and Energy	Monetary Rate of Inflation
II/71 — IV/72	3.9%	3.7%	3.1%	6.0%
IV/72 — I/74	19.6	22.3	4.6	6.0
I/74 — III/75	8.8	13.9	9.7	6.0
III/75 — II/78	6.2	6.9	6.6	6.0

OPEC actions had a widespread, and unexpected upward effect on costs of production. There was a decrease in the effective productive capacity of the economy. With aggregate demand affected to only a minor extent and real output reduced, the *level* of prices rose sharply.[6] Consequently, the rate of change of prices, computed over the period when these sharp upward adjustments in the level of prices took place, would be expected to be substantially, but temporarily, higher than that indicated by past monetary expansion. As their effect was absorbed in the economy, however, the *rate of change* of prices fell back to that dictated by the trend rate of money growth. Although in 1976-77 inflation returned to the rate dictated by monetary expansion, the *level* of prices remained about 4 percent higher, reflecting the effect of the OPEC actions.

Table II shows the movement of prices of selected groups of items during the period from mid-1971 to mid-1978. As shown in the table, price increases of all items other than food and energy were held to about a 3-4 percent rate while general price controls were in effect (August 1971 through April 1974). After controls were removed from most items, prices accelerated to about a 10 percent rate, as shown in the period I/74 — III/75. Table II also clearly shows that the sharp surge in prices from late 1973 into late 1975 was initially led by the sharp rise in agricultural and energy prices[7] and then was reinforced by the adjustment of prices of all other items resulting from the removal of price controls in early 1974. None of these components of consumer prices

---

[4]Even here, however, monetary factors still play a role, although indirectly. Autonomous events can have an effect on the demand for money, which, if not matched by a one-time change in the money supply, result in a one-time increase in the *level* of prices. In such instances, prices rise not because of an excessive increase in the money supply but because of excessive money balances created by a decrease in money demand.

[5]For a more complete technical discussion of the effects of special developments in 1972-74, see Denis S. Karnosky, "The Link Between Money and Prices — 1971-76," this *Review* (June 1976), pp. 17-23.

[6]For a technical discussion of the effect of the rise in energy prices, see Karnosky, "The Link Between Money and Prices — 1971-76," pp. 17-23; Robert H. Rasche and John A. Tatom, "The Effects of the New Energy Regime and Economic Capacity, Production, and Prices," this *Review* (May 1977), pp. 2-12; and "Energy Resources and Potential GNP," this *Review* (June 1977), pp. 10-24.

[7]Price controls on agricultural products were removed in September 1973. The initial OPEC rise in oil prices came in late 1973.

(food, energy, all other) continued the sustained double digit rate of increase. Since 1975 the average rate of increase of all these prices has fallen back into line with the sustainable rate indicated by the past rates of monetary expansion.

Implications for Monetary Actions

The above discussion has important implications for assessing the effects of past, current, and prospective monetary actions in the battle against inflation. The experience of the last six years makes it clear that it can be just as misleading to ascribe each and every reported increase in prices entirely to monetary factors as it is to ignore the effect of money on inflation. Consequently, failure to separate the monetary (trend) and nonmonetary (transitory) aspects of inflation can lead to confused demands on policymakers.

To illustrate the importance of this distinction, consider economic developments over the last six years. During the three-year period ended in the second quarter of 1971, the persistent rate of inflation was very much in line with the rate indicated by a monetary guide to inflation. Over the next six quarters, however, prices rose at about a 4 percent rate. Could this fall in inflation be attributed to monetary actions? The answer is no, the fall in *reported* inflation was strictly due to nonmonetary factors, that is, price controls that went into effect in August 1971.

From early 1973 through early 1975 prices rose very rapidly. From a 4 percent rate, inflation accelerated to about an 8 percent rate in the year ended first quarter 1974. Then, over the next four quarters inflation took another sharp leap upward, averaging 11.6 percent. If one attributes all of these increases in prices during this period to the cumulative effect of past monetary actions, then it appears that the Federal Reserve had let things get seriously out of hand. On the other hand, if the short-run influences of nonmonetary developments on prices are taken into consideration, quite a different conclusion emerges. Careful analysis of the effects on prices of weather, OPEC actions, and the removal of price controls would indicate a sharp rise in the level of prices beginning in late 1973 that was not the result of past monetary actions. The basic rate of inflation, the one determined by the cumulative effect of past monetary actions, remained at about 6 percent.

Early in 1975, inflation dropped sharply, and averaged 6.5 percent over the remainder of the year. Then inflation eased further to a 4.4 percent rate over the first three quarters of 1976. Was this substantial slowing in inflation the result of monetary policy actions? Again the answer is no. The slowing in the rate of change of prices from the double-digit pace of 1974 reflected only that the OPEC actions of late 1973 were not repeated in the following years, the general adjustment of other prices to the removal of price controls had been completed, and favorable agricultural conditions resulted in a sharp drop in the rate of increase of food prices. Did the basic inflation slow to a sustained 4.5 percent rate by late 1976? Again the answer is no. From late 1976 to the end of 1977 inflation returned to a 6 percent rate, the same as that indicated by the trend growth of money.

What was the effect of monetary actions, as measured by the growth of the money stock, on inflation over the six-year period 1972-77? In particular, what was the effect of allowing M1 to grow at about an 8 percent rate from late 1971 to early 1973, then cutting M1 growth to 6 percent for a year, further slashing it to 4 percent for a year, and then progressively reaccelerating M1 growth, first to 5 percent for six quarters, and then to almost 8 percent over the two-year period ended in the third quarter of 1978? Did these gyrations in money growth substantially change the basic rate of inflation? Using the past growth pattern of M1 as a guide to inflation, then again the answer is no. Money had grown at a 6 percent rate over the five years (20 quarters) ended in the fourth quarter of 1971, remained at 6 percent in the 20 quarters ended in early 1975 and by the end of the fourth quarter of 1977 the twenty-quarter growth rate of M1 was still essentially 6 percent.

Conclusions

In analyzing the inflationary process, one must be careful to avoid shortsightedness. In particular, short-run gyrations in prices must be distinguished from persistent changes in prices. Monetary policy cannot prevent the quarter-to-quarter fluctuations in the price level that naturally result from the dynamics of economic activity. However, concentrating on only these short-run fluctuations in the level of prices can result in falsely blaming nonmonetary factors for a persistent rise in prices. The analysis of inflation then tends to bounce, month-to-month, quarter-to-quarter from one item or sector of the economy to another. Such an approach diverts attention from the role of monetary actions, results in failure to permanently reduce inflation and ultimately means that inflation will return to plague the economy. The monetary actions of the government must be given a key position in any program to permanently reduce *persistent* inflation.

Over the first half of 1978, prices rose at about a 9 percent rate. Should inflation be expected to continue at this rate? The monetary guide presented in this paper, indicates a persistent inflation of about 6.2 percent for the period III/78 — III/79. Some economists would contend that individuals now adapt their expectations of inflation more rapidly than previously, hence, a five-year trend rate of growth for M1 is too long. If the period for calculating the trend rate of money is shortened to four years, the inflation indicated for III/78 — III/79 rises to 6.4 percent. Shortening the period further to three years, raises the basic inflation rate to 6.8 percent for the next year. Consequently, the lasting rate of inflation indicated by past monetary developments falls in a fairly narrow range of 6.2-7 percent, nowhere near a 9 percent rate.

However, just because a rough monetary guide to inflation, such as the one presented in this article, does not indicate that past monetary actions have yet cumulated into a 9 percent persistent inflation should not be taken as a cause for rejoicing. A persistent inflation of 6.5-7 percent is still at least three times as fast as any lasting inflation the U.S. economy experienced from the end of World War II through 1965. Furthermore, historical evidence indicates that the development of such a persistent inflation is a rather sluggish process that does not adjust immediately to accelerations or decelerations of the growth of money.[8]

Currently, the trend rate of money growth is being held down by the 5 percent growth rate that prevailed from the third quarter of 1973 to the third quarter of 1976. In sharp contrast, over the last two years (III/76 — III/78), the average rate of monetary expansion accelerated to 8 percent. As the effect of the 5 percent growth wears off, if money continues to grow at an 8 percent or faster rate, inflation will rise sharply to a persistent, year-after-year, 8-9 percent rate.

---

[8]For example, growth of money (M1) accelerated to about a 7 percent annual rate in 1968, after rising at an average rate of about 4 percent over the previous five years. Inflation did not rise to 7 percent in 1968, instead it was 4.5 percent, about in line with the 4 percent average growth of M1 over the previous five years. However, as the money stock continued to grow rapidly by past standards — at a 6 percent rate in 1969 — the five year average growth of M1 rose to 5.2 percent by the end of 1969 and the rate of inflation moved up to 5.4 percent in 1970. This increase in inflation took place even though the growth of M1 subsequently decreased to about a 4 percent rate in 1970.

11

IS THERE REALLY TOO MUCH MONEY?

"Public enemy number one" used to be a gangster with a tommy gun. Today, according to Administration press releases, it's inflation. The way to deal with the gangster, you may recall, was to surround his house with G-men, cut off his supplies, and wait for him to come out shooting. Many modern practitioners of economic war games are calling for a similar scenario to deal with inflation: surround the demon with financial controls, and cut off his access to money.

They base this strategy on a concept known to economists as "the money supply." And they point to the fact that, as prices rose by 9% in 1978, the amount of money in the economy rose by over 8%. We have inflation, the explanation goes, because the government has "printed" too much money. So, the way to fight inflation is for the government to restrict money's availability.

This explanation of inflation pops up quite regularly in the press. It has a reasonable ring: the more money there is, the more things cost. And the remedy sounds not only simple, but painless.

Unfortunately, the truth is quite the opposite. The analysis underlying the money-supply theory of inflation creates serious illusions about how the economy operates; and the function the theory serves, today, is to sell the public on the desirability of moving toward a new recession.

Surface Plausibility

Any economics book, whether it's by Karl Marx, Paul Samuelson, or Milton Friedman, will tell you that supply and demand determine the price of a commodity. If, for example, the supply of wheat available for sale rises more rapidly than demand, the price of wheat will fall.

With money, the situation is similar. Money is a commodity that gets used in the process of buying and selling other commodities. So the demand for money depends mainly on the amount of transactions that are being made by individuals, businesses and government.

(Continued on following page.)

Dollars & Sense magazine, 38 Union Sq., Room 14, Somerville, MA 02143 (monthly, $7.50/year).

The supply of money is usually defined as the amount of money which businesses and individuals can easily draw on to make purchases. This includes all the currency (bills and coins) in circulation. It also includes the far larger amount of funds deposited in banks.

The government has a certain degree of control over the amount of money. If the government acts to increase the supply of money more rapidly than the increase in the amount of buying and selling, then the supply will be greater than the demand. As would be the case with any other commodity, the price of money (measured in terms of the amount of goods money will buy) falls.

This falling price of money is what is meant by a "depreciation of the currency." But to say that the price of money is falling in terms of goods is the same as saying the price of goods is rising in terms of money — that is, inflation.

Inflation is thus "explained" as a result of government policy — a too rapid expansion of the supply of money. And indeed, throughout the inflationary 1970's, the money supply grew faster than production.

The particular culprit in the "money-supply explanation of inflation" is the Federal Reserve Board ("the Fed") which has responsibility for regulating the money supply. In previous issues (see "A New Head for the Fed," *D&S* #35) we've explained the details of this regulation. Two points are particularly important now:

First, the Fed doesn't control the money supply directly, but only tells banks what they can and can't do. Fed actions which allow banks to lend more money increase the money supply — for when a bank makes a new loan, someone acquires more cash or more money in their bank account.

Second, the Fed has other concerns in addition to the supply of money. In particular, it also has the task of regulating interest rates. And it cannot always achieve its money supply and interest rate goals at the same time.

Supply and Demand: Cause or Symptom?

Now, the Fed and its policies are often under attack by those who would explain inflation by the too rapid expansion of the money supply. The Fed's actions, however, are not well explained by either stupidity or evil intent. They are best understood as reactions, or symptoms, rather than causes.

Likewise, changes in supply and demand are not the explanation of inflation. These changes are but symptoms of more fundamental causes. In fact, supply and demand *never explain* anything — not the price of money, the price of wheat, nor the price of walnuts. Supply and demand are only useful categories in which we may place real explanations.

For example, to say the price of wheat fell because supply rose faster than demand is not an explanation. To explain the phenomenon we would need to know what caused the supply to rise. Were weather conditions good? Has technology been improved? Has the social organization of agriculture changed? Answers to these questions would uncover real causes.

With money and inflation, a similar approach is required. To say that inflation increased in 1978 because the money supply was increased inordinately is to obscure rather than reveal the cause of inflation. Why, it must be asked, did the Fed choose to expand the supply of money as fast as it did?

Most generally, the Fed was increasing the money supply during most of 1978 because it wanted to encourage expansion of investment. Throughout the economic growth that has been taking place since 1975, business investment in new plants and equipment has been abnormally low. The Fed, in the hopes of keeping the growth going, wanted to keep interest rates low so businesses would borrow and invest more.

(The interest rate may be thought of as the price of borrowing money. So increasing the supply of money which banks can lend should push down this "price." And in fact the "real" interest rate — the interest rate minus the rate of inflation — did not rise.)

The fact that the Fed decided to

encourage continued expansion did not mean that it was ignorant of the probable effect on inflation, or that it wanted inflation. The Fed's decision was a result of political realities. In early 1978 the unemployment rate had only recently dropped to 6%, and government policymakers were not willing to risk a new slowdown. The Carter Administration was not pushing strongly for budget cuts, and its counterparts on the Fed were not ready to keep the lid on the money supply.

By late in the year, however, political realities had changed. Rising inflation, a stable (though not particularly low) unemployment rate, and the international troubles of the dollar led to a different set of government policies. An austerity budget and slower growth of the money supply now seem to be the orders of the day, and forecasters talk more freely of a coming recession.

Are Policies Effective?

The changes in government policy during 1978 demonstrate the difficulties that the authorities have in manipulating the economy. Efforts to push growth tend to worsen inflation, and efforts to reduce inflation tend to create recession. It may be theoretically possible to steer a middle course, but political forces prevent the government from following the "ideal" policy.

Moreover, policies are often not as effective in reality as they look on paper. For instance, the Fed may allow banks to make more loans, but the banks may not find many more borrowers. Or, at the opposite extreme, banks may already have the capacity to make new loans when the Fed begins to follow a policy of monetary expansion, and the money supply may grow faster than desired.

Similar problems arise when the Fed tries to slow money growth. In any case, all this takes time. By the time Fed actions show results, they may be inappropriate because of changed conditions.

So, all in all, manipulating the economy through the money supply is a tough row to hoe. But it is no more difficult than the use of fiscal policy (adjusting taxes and government spending). And from the point of view of business interests, it has two political advantages: it requires no legislative action, and it is carried on with less public scrutiny or understanding.

Tightening the Screws

Right now, the Carter administration has chosen an economic policy of limiting economic growth — a policy which is likely to lead to recession by late 1979. This would raise unemployment and weaken the power of labor. It might also reduce inflation and improve the international position of the dollar. To get these favorable results, U.S. business seems willing — even happy — to risk the dangers which recession brings.

One side of Carter's recession policy is budget cuts. But pushing an austerity budget through Congress will require a lengthy fight. Not only will there be opposition from unions, organizations of Blacks and women, and other groups who have a lot to lose, but even conservative Congresspeople will try to defend their pet spending programs.

Therefore, monetary "restraint" by the Fed is an important second prong of the attack. Whether or not it affects inflation directly, by reducing the availability of credit it limits new investments and purchases by businesses and individuals. Less investment and buying mean less production and employment. The money-supply explanation of inflation can serve to obscure the real issues and build political support for this recessionary policy. ∎

12

The Realities of Inflation

By WALTER W. HELLER

It's not news that inflation is again Public Enemy Number One in national economic policy. On the rate of inflation hinges much of the fate of the dollar abroad and the course of monetary-fiscal policy, and with it the rate of unemployment and growth, at home. So far in the 1970s, in the face of one mild and one deep recession and of an unemployment rate averaging 6.3%, we have endured a 6% average rate of inflation.

More than ever, we are victims of the remorseless logic of the "uneasy triangle" or "unstable triad." Over 30 years ago, as modern policies of demand-management were putting the U.S. economy into peacetime orbit near full employment, Keynesian economists began to worry whether full employment, price stability and economic freedom of choice could co-exist.

In the face of strongly organized producer groups—powerful unions, oligopolistic business, and politically potent farmers—the economists' answer was a pessimistic one. With each group pushing for a larger slice of the economic pie, it seemed very doubtful that increasing productivity could satisfy those rising claims. Something had to give.

Either full employment had to give way to recession in order to maintain reasonable price stability; or price stability had to give way to inflation to maintain full employment; or economic freedom of choice had to give way to wage-price restraints or controls to reconcile reasonably full employment with reasonable price stability.

That insight of economists in the late 1940s — which said "no roses without thorns"—put its finger on the basic dilemma of modern economic policy, namely, how to achieve both high employment and low inflation without a controlled economy. What it did not foresee—especially after the happy experience of 1961-65, when recovery and rapid productivity advances satisfied both labor and business without inflation—was that high employment *and* high inflation would co-exist in the 1970s, that we would have the thorns without the roses.

For the monetarists, the answer to the dilemma is simplicity itself: too much money. Simply curb federal deficits and slow the increase in the money supply and inflation will wither away. What they fail to explain is (a) how it can be that three years of slack in the economy from early 1975 to early 1978—with the unemployment rate averaging 7½% and operating rates in manufacturing only averaging 79%—failed to dent the underlying rate of inflation; (b) how it is, in the face of careful studies showing that it takes a $200 billion loss of GNP to knock one percentage point off the inflation rate, that Spartan policies of tight money they advocate could subdue inflation without a "deep, deep depression" or years of economic slack; and (c) how it is that Germany—a favorite example of economic self-discipline—could achieve much lower inflation rates than the United States with *both* a faster growth in its money supply in the past four years *and* bigger deficits (for example, 4% of GNP in 1978 versus ½% in the U.S., federal, state and local combined).

The monetarists can run long-term correlations and regressions until they are blue in the face—and in the process prove, as Irving Fisher taught us years ago, that prices are bound to depend on the quantity of money in the long run—and still not come to grips with the institutional and political forces that breed and sustain inflation in the real world.

The Beginning of Wisdom

Those of us who are of a more institutional and pragmatic frame of mind—and hence less sure of ourselves—say instead, "Let's look at the anatomy of inflation and see how much of it is imbedded in our institutional structure or external forces largely beyond the reach of monetary policy and the grasp of the monetarists, and how much is truly responsive to a squeeze on demand via tight money." That may not yield anything like final answers, but it is at least the beginning of wisdom in shaping alternatives to a policy of putting the economy on a starvation diet of money.

A non-monetarist would notice that the Germans — because of past inflationary trauma; because the high-spending, low-saving 22- to 30-year-age group is only one-fifth of the German population against one-fourth of ours; because a rising D-mark means falling import prices; and because their "concerted action" strikes a rough annual bargain between business, labor and government—have strong structural and institutional defenses against inflation. Under the German circumstances, the conversion ratio—how much of a cutback in money translates into slower growth and how much into lower inflation—seems to be significantly more favorable than in the United States.

The Carter program is trying to improve the U.S. conversion ratio by coupling monetary-fiscal restraint to avoid demand-pull inflation with a vigorous policy of wage-price restraint to curb cost-push inflation. It seeks to cut into that relentless circular inflation of wages chasing prices and prices chasing wages that is so resistant to economic slack and recession.

We may gain a little better insight into the anatomy of our inflation by disentangling (1) the special factors that affect the level of prices for a limited period of time from (2) the underlying wage-price spiral (actually, more of a circle) that changes only gradually.

Starting with the latest available numbers for the Consumer Price Index in 1977 and 1978, we find the following:

—During 1977, prices rose 6.8%; during 1978, 8.9%, or roughly 2 percentage points more.

—The biggest price upswing was in three components of the CPI whose price behavior is largely unrelated to production costs and the underlying inflation: Food prices rose 3 percentage points faster in 1978 than in 1977 (11% versus 8%); the cost of homeowners' financing, taxes and insurance—moved mainly by rising mortgage rates—went up nearly 5 points faster (16% versus 11%); while used-car prices suffered a 15-point speedup.

—With those bad factors removed, the rest of the CPI rose at a 7.3% rate in 1978 versus 6.3% in 1977—this 1-point increase provides a first approximation of the step-up in the underlying wage-price or price-wage spiral.

An inspection of the behavior of indexes of wage increases and the GNP deflator leads one to similar conclusions about the basic inflation rate:

—The average hourly earnings index, a broad measure of hourly wage costs for production and non-supervisory workers, moved from a 7.5% increase, year-over-year, in 1977 to an 8.3% increase in 1978 (with 1978 levels estimated by averaging the second and the third quarter levels).

—Compensation per hour, covering all workers and including not just wages but private fringe benefits and the employers' share of payroll taxes, moved from an 8.1% rise in 1977 to a 9.1% rise in 1978.

—The private non-farm price deflator, a comprehensive index of prices of goods and services produced in the non-farm economy, moved from a 5.9% rise in 1977 to a 7.2% rise in 1978.

What accounts for this acceleration of roughly 1 point in the underlying price-wage spiral? Roughly one-half traces to the 15% increase in the minimum wage and the jump in payroll taxes during 1978. Tightening labor markets accounted for perhaps another third of the acceleration. And the rest can be largely ascribed to (a) the upward pressure on prices arising from devaluation of the dollar and (b) feedback of price increases into wage increases through formal and informal escalators in the wage-determination process.

Board of Contributors

Dissecting the inflation numbers does not establish any eternal verities. But it does warn us again that inflation is not a simple one-dimensional problem.

Reprinted by permission of Walter W. Heller from the *Wall Street Journal*, January 19, 1979.

What lies in store for us in 1979 on these wage and price fronts? Let's look first at the three indexes we have just reviewed:

—Last year, once the impact of the minimum-wage increase was absorbed, the underlying rate of wage inflation as measured by the hourly earnings index slowed down to about 7¾%. This year's boost in the minimum wage—9% versus last year's 15%—will add little to this underlying rate. When one factors in the wage-restraint program, aided by rising unemployment in the second half of the year, it seems reasonable to expect the increase in hourly earnings to slow down to 7½% during 1979 (fourth-quarter-to-fourth-quarter).

—Boosts in private fringes and payroll taxes will add nearly a point to the rise in hourly earnings, bringing the rise in hourly compensation to between 8¼% and 8½%.

—How does this translate into a figure for the private non-farm deflator? In the 1965-71 period, the percentage rise in the deflator was about 2½ points less than the rise in hourly compensation. In 1976-78, the difference averaged about 2 points. So an increase of about 6½% in the private non-farm deflator would be indicated by the projected behavior of hourly compensation. Allowing for some exceptional increases in domestic energy costs raises the projected fourth-quarter-to-fourth-quarter increase in the non-farm price deflator to around 6.8% (or nearly 7½% year-over-year).

When one turns back to the CPI, one has to add to the basic inflation rate reflected in the non-farm deflator such elements as the price of food, imported oil prices, and mortgage interest rates. The scheduled rise in imported oil prices would bring the CPI increase during the year to 7%. If food prices also rise 7%, they would add nothing further. Food prices are notoriously tough to predict and there is little basis today for predicting either a smaller or larger advance this year. If an end to the housing boom and a start of recession cool off mortgage interest rates and retard the rise in prices of homes, the increase in the CPI could be less than 7% during 1979 (though again, the year-over-year advance would be about half a point higher).

Optimistic Forecast

These price projections are at the optimistic end of the forecast range. They imply not only that some of the inflationary forces built into the early-1979 economy (rising minimum wages, payroll taxes, import prices, beef prices and mortgage-interest rates) will be ebbing later in the year but also that the Carter wage-price program will be making itself felt as the year wears on.

Dissecting the inflation numbers does not establish any eternal verities. But it does warn us again that inflation is not a simple one-dimensional problem. It reflects a multiplicity of forces, some persistent, some transitory. If we hope to subdue it without unconscionable costs in jobs and output, we will have to tackle it with a multiplicity of weapons.

That means wage-price restraint to zero in on our underlying circular inflation, monetary-fiscal restraint to curb demand, self-policing by government to minimize its costly and competition-stifling regulations, a rethinking of payroll tax and minimum wage hikes and farm price supports, measures to boost productivity and so on. And it also means resisting the simplistic siren songs of those who would have us believe that drum-tight money, or an end to federal deficits or mandatory controls provide a surefire answer to our anti-inflationary prayers.

Mr. Heller is Regents' Professor of Economics at the University of Minnesota, former chairman of the Council of Economic Advisers under Presidents Kennedy and Johnson and a member of the Journal's Board of Contributors.

Our Unmysterious Inflation

By Paul W. McCracken

What is to be made of this sharp acceleration in the rate of inflation?

Only three months ago the Eggert panel of economists was projecting an average rise in the price level (as measured by the GNP price index) from 1978 to 1979 of 7.8%. This was almost identical with the 7.7% rise projected by the President in his Budget Message and Economic Report. Projections disgorged by the complex econometric models were in the same range. The citizenry generally, as often happens, were a bit more realistic in their expectations. In January, the University of Michigan Survey Research Center found that the average expected price increase for the year ahead was 9.3%, and this has continued to rise.

If, in fact, prices continue to rise at rates that have prevailed so far in 1979, the year's price level will be about 11% above that for 1978, and during the year the price level will have risen something like 13%. And, if that pace were to continue, by the latter part of 1984 prices on the average would be double those confronting buyers today.

The more moderate earlier projections of 1979's rate of inflation may yet be realized. Two-thirds of the year still lies ahead. If, however, the January 1980 Economic Report to the President is able to record a rise in the price level for this year below 8%, the rise from here to the end of the year will have to be limited to something like a 5% to 6% per year pace. And short of draconian measures, the probability that such a deceleration will occur is low.

What has happened?

Oil prices have, of course, been rising, and they have particularly high visibility. In fact, a price index giving a weight of about 50% each to prices of hamburger and gasoline would be a reasonably good indicator of political pressures generated by inflation.

While prices of oil and gasoline are a subject about which our solons in Washington can generate a mighty rage, particularly if the television cameras are running at full throttle, oil prices do not explain the current inflation. Even the recent large rise in these prices leaves most of the current acceleration unexplained. (And it is not amiss to remind government that some prices for which it has quite direct responsibility have not behaved so impeccably—e.g., the 14% rise in postage prices during 1978.)

Nor is it just food—though the 20% per year rise in food prices has been a major source of the rise in both the rate of inflation and consumers' wrath. Even these sharp increases, however, leave in the statistical sense about three-quarters of the recent decline in the dollar's purchasing power unexplained.

Further Pyrotechnics Expected

While wage negotiations have occupied the center of the stage much of the time this year, there has as yet been no acceleration of wage inflation to parallel or explain the acceleration of price inflation. Further pyrotechnics can be expected here before the year is over, and Procrustes, the legendary Attica highwayman, would watch with awe as our wage-price managers simply lop off whatever of the incoming settlements do not fit.

The rise in average wage rates remains, however, consistent (assuming a continuation of negligible gains in productivity) with the 7% to 8% rate of inflation that had earlier been predicted. Naturally, if wage settlements break loose and move well into the double-digit zone, they will for the rest of the year mean more inflationary trouble, but they did not start us off on the current spiral.

While there is a tendency to resist the straight-forward analysis which points out that the king has no clothes on, a careful examination of the evidence leads ineluctably to the conclusion that the American economy is now simply in the throes of a classic inflation. Demand has been pushed too hard against the outer limits of our productive capacity. It would perhaps be less shattering to our sense of sophistication to believe that some mysterious new inflationary sickness has infected the economy, but the 1979 problem is an excessively rapid expansion in the demand for output relative to our productive capacity.

The evidence for this is clear. Exports of manufactured goods have been moving upward, since mid-1978, at a 25% per year

Board of Contributors

A careful examination of the evidence leads ineluctably to the conclusion that the American economy is now simply in the throes of a classic inflation.

rate. This, of course, was desirable in order to redress the imbalance in our external payments, but accommodating these large increases required appropriately moderated increases in the domestic demand for output. This moderation was not forthcoming. The result is that prices of raw materials, excluding fuel and foodstuffs, thus far in 1979 have been rising at a 30% per year rate.

Unfilled orders for durable goods have been exploding with annual rates of increases in the 40% zone. And unfilled orders for primary metals have been pushing upward at rates that would double the backlog by the year-end. (That this in some markets reflects multiple ordering is simply additional evidence of a tight economy.) The volume of advertising for help remains heavier relative to the size of the labor force than was true a year ago or before the 1974-75 recession. The proportion of companies reporting slower deliveries is at a level exceeded only by the brief spasm in 1966 and the overheated conditions of 1973 incident to that bout with double-digit inflation. These are all indicators of an economy under heavy demand pressures.

How, in a country with the best economic information system in the world, could this have come about?

For one thing, we have not yet really faced up to the implications of the fact that the capability of the U.S. economy to increase output has declined sharply as gains in productivity have been reduced to negligible proportions. In the five years from 1973 to 1978, output per hour (in the nonagricultural private economy) rose at the average rate of only 0.8% per year. We have, in short, been trying to activate with more demand an economy afflicted with arthritic tendencies.

The single most important explanation for this growing inability of the economy to deliver gains in productivity and real income is almost certainly the sluggish rates of capital formation that have prevailed during much of this decade. From 1975 to 1978 the amount of new plant and equipment put in place (in real terms) per person added to the work force has been about one-third below that for the 1955-1970 period, and the shortfall has been 50% for the amount put in place per person actually employed.

The figures would look even more grim if the considerable part of this capital formation required for purposes that do not improve measured productivity or capacity were excluded from the calculations.

This shortfall has had two quite predictable results. One is that we are running into shortages of plant capacity before the unemployment rate is down to anything like the 4.5% average that prevailed during the 1950s (largely "Republican years") or the 4.7% average for the 1960s (largely "Democratic years"). The casualties from this lack of investment activity are not economists or civil servants or corporate executives. And they are certainly not those who have gained affluence, influence and fame (and often all three) as professional opposers of new plants, new refineries, new generating equipment and the other requirements of an economy capable of opening up abundant job opportunities. The casualties of these activities are, of course, those still unemployed who now could be moving into regular employment if more plants, with their "Help Wanted" signs posted, had been built.

The Other 'Dividend'

The other "dividend" from this shortfall in capital formation is, of course, sluggish gains in productivity and real incomes. The operator of a large earthmover can rearrange more of the landscape in an hour than the operator of a small machine, but the larger one involves more capital formation (and saving). Moreover, it is with new equipment that the new and more advanced technology is actually put to work in production.

We may have here a perverse process at work. The reduced capability of the economy to deliver gains in real incomes has forced families, long accustomed to roughly a 30% increase in the real purchasing power of their paychecks each decade, to involve more of their numbers in employment. The spreading of our capital stock over more members, however, further adversely affects productivity, forcing yet more into employment, further limiting gains in productivity, etc.

There is, of course, no inherent reason why an economy with only a slowly growing capacity to produce cannot have a reasonably stable price level, and this leads to the immediate source of the current problem. The fact is that we have quite simply pursued overly expansive demand management policies—with adverse results compounded by these misjudgments about the upper limits in our capacity to produce. Budget policy in the conventional sense has its problems, and stronger constraints on the pressures forcing enlarged public outlays are needed.

The main source of excessive demands, however, is quite simply a monetary inflation—broadly defined to include the management of the economy's liquid assets generally. Throughout last year the supply of liquidity (the money supply, liquid Treasury obligations, CDs and other money market instruments) was growing at an 11% to 12% rate.

The current inflation will not be brought to heel until markets impose strong disciplines on wage and price increases. This means, it cannot too often be repeated, market conditions such that excessive price increases mean lost sales and outsized wage increases mean lost jobs. And these market conditions begin to emerge only when we find ways to assure that the creation of money and other liquid assets begins to match the slow pace at which the economy can now increase real output.

Mr. McCracken is Edmund Ezra Day University Professor of Business Administration at the University of Michigan, former chairman of the Council of Economic Advisers under President Nixon and a member of the Journal's Board of Contributors.

Reprinted by permission of Paul W. McCracken from the *Wall Street Journal*, April 23, 1979.

JOHN KENNETH GALBRAITH

On post Keynesian economics

Few contributions to a new economic journal could be less auspicious than one that attempted rigidly to define its field and to establish narrow or even specific parameters. Those concerned with the launching of this journal are, I believe, united in dissatisfaction with the present orthodoxy. All, I venture, would agree that present economic policy, derived as it is from present macroeconomic stereotypes, does not serve; and most would agree that our professional colleagues in Washington cannot survive indefinitely on explanations of past failure or predictions that all will be better in the future. Improved performance by the American economy will require a much more vigorously innovative tendency sustained by a much more innovative professional discussion than is the product of present professional habit with its associated comfort. It is such research and discussion over the widest possible range and at the most competent and responsible level that this journal will encourage.

Within the broad spectrum just specified, one can also hope for a sharp definition of individual positions. A journal should be eclectic. Its contributions should be definite. In keeping with this, I would like to offer a word on my own view of post Keynesian economics, although it is not a matter on which I have been unnaturally reticent in the past.

Post Keynesian economics, like the great Keynesian revision of forty years ago, is amendatory and not revolutionary. It holds that industrial society is in a process of continuous and organic change, that public policy must accommodate to such change, and that by such public action performance can, in fact, be improved. Its commitment is to reformist change, not revolution, but it does not consider this commitment any slight or passive thing.

The relevant historical change to which there must now be accommodation is in the nature of the industrial market. The market, with the maturing of industrial society and associated political institutions, loses and loses radically its authority as a regulatory force. Partly this is inherent in industrial development — in the institutions that modern large-scale production, technology, and planning require. Partly it is an expression of the democratic ethos, and, paradoxically, this is often much applauded by scholars of liberal view who are also, and inconsistently, defenders of the market.

Specifically, in the modern democratic context, people seek to gain greater control over their own lives. This extends to all of life's dimensions. They do not neglect the most obvious of all goals, which is greater control over their income. It would, indeed, be inconceivable were they to struggle for greater self-determination in all other aspects of life and leave this most vital of dimensions untouched.

The effort to control income takes one (or more) of three forms. By organization, assertion of some unique personal capacity, or recourse to the state people win the power to set or influence their wage, salary, or other return, or the price which is one dimension of their income. By such means they escape from the impersonal authority of the market or, at a

The author is Professor Emeritus, Harvard University.

minimum, reduce the authority of the market. Were it not that the market is a totem, the underpinning of all neoclassical orthodoxy, economists would long ago have reacted to this nearly universal effort, for they do not underestimate the desire for income and do not fail to appreciate its role as a liberating force. Their professional commitment to the market has, however, largely excluded from view this struggle to substitute greater self-determination of income for, as people of the modern industrial society see it, the impersonal tyranny of the market.

The instruments of escape — organizations, state action, personal qualification — are part of the everyday scenery of economic and political life. The most visible and, as I've long urged, the most important is the modern great corporation. It has extended the power over prices which the neoclassical orthodoxy still associates with the exceptional cases of monopoly and oligopoly to the production of some half of all private product in the advanced industrial economy.

The development of the modern corporation, in turn, extends a substantial authority over their own pay to all of those in its senior ranks. This is scrutinized by directors whom the executives in question have selected.

The modern economy also has a large demand for specialized technical, scientific, and professional talent. It sustains a large and growing artistic effort. These occupations convey some or much of the power over income that the classical economists once awarded to the painter, sculptor, or other producer of a unique commodity.

Where there are large corporations, there are strong unions. So for the corporate working force the market also gives way to the authority of organization. This organization is often cited as being remote from the individual, impersonal. But for the participant it is obviously regarded as far more benign, far more responsive, far less inimical than the impersonal authority of the market.

Where corporate or trade union organization does not provide escape from the market, the support of the state is sought for the effort. Farm support prices, the minimum wage, a complex and proliferating variety of industrial price and rate regulation all serve the same end.

As part of this broad thrust, such efforts as those of OPEC fall into place. They reflect a successful attempt at escape by raw material producers on whom the market was once thought to bear with particular rigor. Not even the most orthodox neoclassicist would now argue that oil, which costs a few cents to produce and sells for a hundred times cost, is a normal manifestation of the competitive market. And the large public planning apparatus now being created to adjust energy supply to demand is the predictable counterpart of the decline of the market.

Finally, there is the most rapidly growing sector of the modern industrial economy, that of the public services and transfer payments. Here, too, even devout neoclassicists speak of the nonmarket sector. Much of this sector, from housing to health care to welfare payments, owes its existence to an explicit recognition of the inadequate performance or the social unacceptability of the market economy. The replacement of the market is here extensively identified with a sensitive social conscience.

Post Keynesian economics, as I perceive it, is concerned with a world in which this escape from the market, this effort to gain control of price and income, is accepted. It reflects a much greater change than what is described as the Keynesian revolution. The Keynesian revolution accepted the need to manage aggregate demand. But this management, some problems of wage determination apart, did not invade or involve the role of the market. That was assumed to perform its function at a higher level of output and employment. The policy for achieving this higher level became the new macroeconomics. The traditional study of the market continued as microeconomics. The decline of the market is an infinitely more consequential development.

In particular, it has rendered nugatory the accepted techniques of macroeconomic management. Both monetary and fiscal policy, a vital point, depend for their effectiveness on the effectiveness of the market. When the market loses its authority, a restriction in aggregate demand does not arrest the upward movement in prices and incomes that reflects the successful escape from market power. Such restraints do, however, reduce output and employment. (They also can reduce prices in what remains of the market economy.) The failure of Keynesian macroeconomic policy to arrest the increase in industrial incomes and prices and its effect on output and employment leads to the combination of inflation and unemployment which is the most characteristic and unpleasant feature of the modern industrial scene.

The decline of the market, it will be evident, renders obsolete the distinction between macroeconomics and microeconomics. Keynesian macroeconomic policy fails because of the changes that have occurred in microeconomic market structure. The separation in economic instruction and thought between macroeconomics and microeconomics has become a truly unforgivable source of error.

Since neoclassical economics, in both its macroeconomic and microeconomic manifestations, depends on the market, its adherents are faced with a three-way choice. The first is to deny that anything much has happened to the market. In this way the validity of the existing market models is preserved in principle (and in the textbooks), though not, unhappily, in practice. The past is preserved at the price of increasing irrelevance. However, those so committed must on occasion wonder how long their convenient world will survive the evidence. Reality has a way of intruding even on the most useful of illusions.

The second choice is to accept that the market has declined but to believe that it can be retrieved. So, in accordance with personal predilection, economists urge the unwinding of government regulation, the abandonment of farm support prices, and the lowering or rejection of the minimum wage. And, of course, stronger enforcement of the antitrust laws is also demanded. This is, perhaps, the most compulsive act of piety. The disintegration of the unions is not urged, although, in all logic, it should be part of the obeisance. Even banality must be tempered by discretion.

With this reaction to the decline of the market goes an implicit and unexpressed confession of limited or negligible expectation. Genuflection is involved, not practical action. Proponents recognize, in effect, that a great organic movement, impinging powerfully on the public and its lawmakers, cannot be reversed by the same public and politicians in response to the hortatory urgings of economists. Still, this escape does not lead, professionally speaking, to our most rewarding posture. There is a measure of disrepute by association even with such a seemingly harmless figure as King Canute.

Neither the nonrecognition of the obvious nor the advocacy of the futile is a serviceable expedient. There remains the third choice, which I think is central to post Keynesian economics. That is to accept the decline of the market. Then one addresses oneself to considering how the resulting economic performance can be made socially acceptable to as many people as possible. That is my view as to what post Keynesian economics is about.

15

A Layman's Guide to the Keynesian-Monetarist Dispute

Peter D. McClelland

How curious it is that as the United States economy edges toward recession, one famous economist advocates a tightening of monetary policy,[1] while another equally famous economist opposes that tightening.[2] And why should the economics profession be so sharply divided on the merits of a tax-based incomes policy, or the merits of wage-price guidelines?[3]

The answer must surely lie in sharply differing views about the causal processes of our economy. Regrettably, the key areas of disagreement are almost impossible to detect in either the popular literature or the textbooks written by these men. The following brief survey attempts to remedy this defect.

The best place to begin is where Milton Friedman and other monetarists usually begin: with the quantity equation of exchange, or

$$MV \equiv PQ,$$

where M is the quantity of money in a society, V is its velocity of circulation (or the average number of times money changes hands in a year), Q is the quantity of real goods and services created and sold during that year,[4] and P is the average price of those goods. Every transaction in the marketplace is a two-way swap: the seller turns over goods or services valued at a price, and the buyer surrenders cash equal to that price. It must therefore *always* be true that the total value of cash turned over by buyers equals the value of goods and services received. That value, in turn, is nothing more than the sum of each commodity multiplied by its market price. This is why between the symbols MV and PQ one finds not an equals sign, but an equals sign plus a third line to indicate an identity. The relationship $MV \equiv PQ$ always holds.

A word of explanation concerning velocity. Economics has a long-standing tradition of illustrating complex mechanisms with oversimplified examples. Following in those footsteps, let us consider a medieval community in which the total sales in the village during a single year are as follows:

   4,000 pairs of shoes at $10 per pair = $40,000
   60,000 bushels of wheat at $1 per bushel = $60,000

The value of PQ is thus $100,000, or ($10 × 4,000) + ($1 × 60,000). Suppose that the total money supply in this community consists of 20,000 one-dollar bills. This is then the value of M. The implied velocity [5] is

$$V = \frac{PQ}{M} = \frac{\$100,000}{\$20,000} = 5.$$

Notice that V is calculated as a residual. We do not observe it directly in our medieval community (or anywhere else) but infer it from other data. If total transactions were $100,000 and the money supply was only 20,000 one-dollar bills, then on the average each dollar bill *must* have changed hands five times in the course of a year. All perfectly straightforward, one might think. Except that it is not. Lurking in this simple mathematics is a complicated problem that will become more apparent later on.

With the above equation in hand we can easily summarize the basic tenet of the monetarists. They make two assertions and one obvious inference. The assertions are (1) that V is "stable," and (2) that Q is not affected—or not affected very much—by M. (In more technical language this second point might be rephrased to read that Q is determined exogenously.) If these two assertions are granted, one can hardly deny what monetarists continually assert: that the main determinant of changes in the price level are previous changes in the stock of money. In the equation $MV = PQ$, if V is stable and Q is unaffected by M, then P will tend to vary with M. Our problem is therefore to understand what is meant by the two assertions noted. If we can also understand why Keynesians challenge those assertions, we shall be well on our way to understanding the Keynesian-monetarist dispute.

What is meant by the statement "Velocity is stable"? This variable could change for several reasons. The most obvious relate to improvements in the financial institutions of a community. The development of the telegraph, clearinghouses, or commercial banks can accelerate the rate at which the stock of money changes hands. Monetarists readily concede this point—they could hardly deny it—but emphasize that the evolution of financial institutions takes time. No *sudden and large* change in velocity should result from this development if the institutions themselves do not change suddenly.

The main threat to the monetarists' position lies elsewhere. Consider again the example of the medieval village. Suppose that half of those 20,000 dollar bills were actually hidden away in mattresses as a means of storing wealth. In that case, while total velocity was 5, the actual velocity of active money (i.e., the money that is not in mattresses but out in the marketplace) would be ($100,000 ÷ $10,000), or 10. No problems arise for monetarists as long as roughly half of the money supply is held idle in mattresses. But suppose for some reason that 40 percent of this idle money, or $4,000, suddenly becomes active *and* takes on the velocity of other active dollars. Then 14,000 dollar bills would change hands on the average of 10 times a year and the value of PQ would rise to ($14,000 × 10) or $140,000. Total velocity (that is, the V in $MV = PQ$), as noted previously, is calculated as a residual. Since the total money supply (M) is unchanged but the value of PQ has risen from $100,000 to $140,000, total velocity now becomes

$$V = \frac{PQ}{M} = \frac{\$140,000}{\$20,000} = 7.$$

How is this possible? In simplified terms, one can think of any community as having two "piles" of money, one idle and the other active. If some of the heretofore idle dollars are moved over into the active pile, then the supply of dollars bidding for goods and services increases, and the value of goods and services sold must also increase. In our example we achieved the seemingly odd result of an increase in total velocity (from 5 to 7) *not* because of an increase in the rate at which active dollar bills changed hands (that remained constant at 10), but rather because the proportion of the total money supply in active circulation increased [6] from 50 percent ($10,000 ÷ $20,000) to 70 percent ($14,000 ÷ $20,000).

The monetarists now have a problem. If large quantities of dollar bills jump back and forth between active and inactive piles, then clearly velocity will not be "stable." (In our example, when $4,000 moved over, V rose from 5 to 7.) Similarly, if the money supply were doubled *and* all of that extra money were added to the inactive pile, then prices would not tend to increase as the monetarists claim they should. The solution, as one might expect, is to argue that this does not happen. Monetarists usually make this point by claiming that the proportion of cash balances that people desire to hold is very stable.[7] This guarantees that the kind of jumping back and forth illustrated in the above example will not take place. It also means that when the money supply is dramatically increased, almost none of that new money will be held idle. If it is not held idle, it must be spent; if it is spent, it must increase the value of PQ; and if Q is relatively unaffected by changes in M, then the main impact must be to

Copyright 1975, © 1977, by Peter D. McClelland.

increase P. By this one assertion, then, the monetarists retrieve their central notion that changes in prices are largely determined by changes in the money supply.

Since the Keynesians challenge this conclusion, they must disagree with some of the premises in the above argument. One of the main premises in dispute is that the amount of money people want to hold idle cannot change significantly in the short run. Recall the speculative motive and the liquidity preference schedule of standard Keynesian analysis. The basic idea is that if the interest rate rises, the demand for idle cash by speculators will fall; if the interest rate falls, the demand for idle cash will rise.[8] In terms of the example used previously, this is equivalent to asserting that the movement of dollar bills between the two piles of active and inactive money is very sensitive—or at least quite sensitive—to changes in the rate of interest.

We have now clarified at least one major point of disagreement concerning how the economy actually works. The monetarists claim that the desire to hold idle cash is insensitive to interest rate changes (and to other factors as well); the Keynesians claim that the desire to hold idle cash is quite sensitive to interest rate changes. Notice two features. First, at the core of the debate is a question of fact concerning the responsiveness of certain decision makers: When interest rates fall, will the demand for idle cash balances increase by a lot or by a little? Second, when economists write about this dispute, the language chosen will usually include the phrase "the stability of velocity." What is seldom realized when the point is phrased this way is that the substantive issue is whether or not, over a short time period, large quantities of cash are moved between active and inactive balances in response to such changing economic variables as the rate of interest.

The second major puzzle is this: what is meant by the assertion that in the equation $MV=PQ$, Q is independent (or largely independent) of M; or to put the point in different words, that Q is determined exogenously? According to the monetarists, total real output (Q) in the long run is primarily determined by available technology and the supply of factors of production (usually lumped by economists into the four categories of land, labor, capital, and enterprise). Of negligible influence, they argue, is the supply of money. It follows that a large increase in the money supply—if it cannot affect Q, and if V is "stable"—must bring in its wake severe inflation.[9]

The Keynesians believe otherwise. The originator of this school of thought was puzzled by the existence of large-scale and sustained unemployment. Keynes knew only too well that according to classical price theory, if the supply of workers exceeds demand, then the price of workers—the wage rate—should fall until all those who want jobs at the prevailing wage rate can get them. Exit unemployment, one would think, except that it refused to exit in the 1930s. The most obvious answer to this puzzle became a central assumption of all Keynesian models. If wages are inflexible on the down side—if such economic forces as labor contracts and large unions prevent wages from being reduced—then whenever the demand for workers falls, the main effect will be rising unemployment rather than falling wages. How obvious the point appears in retrospect! In terms of elementary supply-and-demand analysis, if the demand curve falls and the adjustment cannot occur on the price (or wage) axis, then it must occur on the quantity (or employment) axis. The solution for unemployment is therefore to stimulate demand. An expansionary monetary policy can accomplish this through the conventional Keynesian mechanisms: an increase in the money supply should lower the interest rate; this lower interest rate should stimulate investment; the increased investment (through the multiplier) will stimulate income and consumption; and thus demand will be increased and unemployment reduced.

The monetarists refuse to accept the above as an adequate description of how our economy actually works. Leave the unemployment alone, they argue, and natural market forces will remove it.[10] If the demand for automobiles falls and workers are laid off in Detroit, the situation will be rectified by the forces of supply and demand. Some unemployed workers will find alternative jobs. Automobile producers will tend to cut prices or develop alternative devices to stimulate demand. If this unemployment is instead fought by an expansion of the money supply, the only result will be more inflation. Recall the point emphasized earlier: that newly created dollars, according to the monetarists, are like hot potatoes—no one is willing to hold them very long. If they are not held, they must be spent. An expansionary monetary policy is therefore viewed as setting in motion successive rounds of spending and respending that are sure to drive prices up even if, in the process, the demand for cars is stimulated and unemployment in Detroit falls. Finally, that reduction in unemployment would have occurred *sooner or later* through the forces of supply and demand. To put it harshly, the monetarists might say, why bother to feed the horses in order to feed the sparrows when the sparrows will be fed anyway?

The key phrase is "sooner or later." The Keynesian rebuttal is that existing market forces will remove unemployment, at best, very slowly. Equally important, they assert that the main impact of spending and respending dollars should be the bidding for resources that are currently idle rather than for those that are already employed. This in turn implies that the principal impact of injecting new dollars into the spending stream should be a reduction in unemployment rather than a bidding up of the price level.

We have now arrived at the second main bone of contention between these two competing schools. Once again the central issue is a question of fact: How rapidly do labor markets adjust when unemployment occurs? The monetarists reply, "Very rapidly"; the Keynesians, "Very slowly." Here too the language usually used by economists tends to obscure the substantive point. Few would guess that the question "In the equation $MV=PQ$, is Q determined exogenously?" boils down to a dispute over speeds of adjustment in labor markets.

In review, and on close inspection, the main points of disagreement are remarkably uncomplicated. When extra money is created, the monetarists argue that almost all of it is sure to be spent. The Keynesians claim that it is far from clear how much will be spent and how much will be held idle. During a recession, whenever new money is created—and however much of it is spent and respent—the Keynesians believe, the main impact will be the bidding for otherwise idle resources. The monetarists believe that the main impact will be the bidding up of prices.[11] If these are the arguments, why can they not be resolved? The answer is what one might expect: because we lack the tools to prove conclusively which view more accurately portrays how our economy actually works.

If we cannot resolve the debate, we can at least understand two further implications of these conflicting positions. The first concerns the question of whether or not inflation and unemployment are inversely related. When one goes down must the other necessarily go up? The monetarists answer no. Since they argue that changes in the money supply mainly affect prices and not output, it follows that efforts to control inflation by controlling the money supply should not affect total output or, by implication, total employment. The Keynesians believe otherwise. Why they believe that stable prices and full employment are conflicting goals is not always clear. Some concede that when aggregate demand is stimulated, at least some of the spending and respending will bid for employed resources rather than unemployed resources, thereby creating upward pressure on prices. Others suggest that (1) prices are determined partly by wage costs and (2) wage demands tend to be more moderate in periods of high unemployment.

The second implication of the above arguments concerns the effectiveness of fiscal policy as a countercyclical tool. The Keynesian position is so familiar as hardly to bear repeating. If unemployment is caused by inflexible wages and falling demand, the solution is to increase demand. This the federal government can accomplish either by spending more itself or by cutting taxes, thereby giving the public more to spend. In either case the resulting government deficit will have a multiplied effect upon consumption (and possibly a stimulating effect upon investment), causing demand to increase and unemployment to fall.

The monetarists' position is more subtle. They begin by noting that any increase in deficit spending must be financed.[12] That is, before the government can spend more dollars it must first acquire those dollars from somewhere. If it acquires them by expanding the money supply—if the dollars to be spent are newly created dollars—then the anticipated impact will be that outlined above: rising prices and little change in total output and employment. If instead the government finances its deficit by borrowing dollars from the public, the anticipated effects are that (1) increased borrowing will drive up interest rates, (2) the rise in interest rates (perhaps reinforced by rising prices) will cause a cutback in consumption and investment, and (3) this cutback in spending by the private sector *will exactly match* the increase in spending by the government. Fiscal policy therefore has no effect upon the size of the pie, only upon its division between the public and private sectors. But suppose that deficit is financed instead by the printing of new money, as noted above. The same answer applies, argue the monetarists. Total output will remain virtually unchanged but prices will rise as the government uses newly created dollars to bid away goods and services from the private sector. The resulting inflation will be a disguised form of taxation. The public must surrender part of the pie to the government, not because income taxes or sales taxes have increased, but because higher prices force them to relinquish part of the share they heretofore had.

The reader by now should be able to anticipate the Keynesian counterattack. In a world of inflexible wages and economic recession, they argue, the size of the pie can be expanded by an expansion of demand. If government deficits are financed by borrowing procedures that raise interest rates, there is no reason why the resulting cutback in public demand should *exactly* equal the increase in government spending. More to the point, in a recession the appropriate monetary policy is to expand the money supply and *lower* interest rates. But why, one might ask, do Keynesians expect that the spending and respending generated by an expansionary monetary and fiscal policy will have its main impact upon unemployment rather than upon prices? And why do monetarists expect exactly the opposite? The answer is no more complicated than referring to a point made previously. *The substantive issue mainly concerns the speed of adjustment in labor markets.* The Keynesians believe that without government stimulation of demand, unemployment can remain a serious problem for a long time; with that stimulation, it can be alleviated. The monetarists take the opposite view. Disequilibriums in product and factor markets, they argue, should be treated in the same manner as the sheep of Little Bo Peep: leave them alone. The implicit belief is that, if left alone, imbalances will correct themselves; if meddled with, they may become worse.

Notes

1. Paul A. Samuelson, "The Last Days of the Boom," *Newsweek*, April 30, 1979, p. 58. (In this book.)
2. Milton Friedman, "The Fed: At It Again," *Newsweek*, February 19, 1979, p. 65. (In this book.)
3. See, for example, the articles in this section by Weintraub and Jianakoplos, and in the section "Wage and Price Regulation."
4. The following analysis focuses exclusively on income velocity and ignores transactions velocity.
5. This assumes that all transactions involve an exchange of dollars and rules out the possibility of bartering with goods only.
6. Expressed in mathematical form, total velocity is the weighted average

$$V = \frac{MA(VA) + MI(VI)}{MA + MI},$$

where MA is active money, VA is the velocity of active money, MI is inactive money, and VI is the velocity of inactive money. Note that $MA + MI = M$ and $VI = 0$.

7. More correctly, what is assumed to be stable is the demand for real cash balances, or nominal cash balances adjusted for changes in the price level.
8. To review the behavioral premise, Keynesians assume that when interest rates are low (i.e., bond prices are high) many speculators will expect bond prices to fall and will therefore delay buying bonds, holding cash in the interim.
9. The key word here is "large." In the equation $MV = PQ$, if Q—or Gross National Product—increases gradually over time and P is to remain relatively stable, then the money supply should also increase at *roughly* the same rate as Q ("roughly" because gradual changes may also occur in V). This is why monetarists argue for a gradual expansion in M, rather than for a rigidly fixed money supply.
10. "Normal" unemployment, according to the monetarists, is determined by such factors as the interchangeability of job skills, the cost of labor market information, and the extent to which laws and organizations (such as unions) impede the free functioning of the labor market.
11. Notice the implied contrasting expectations concerning interest rate trends. If prices rise, interest rates should also rise to allow for expected inflation in the future. (A lender who normally receives 6 percent and now expects 10 percent annual inflation will demand 16 percent to compensate for being repaid in depreciated dollars.) Thus, if the main impact of an expansionary policy is on prices, interest rates will tend to go up as prices rise. If the main effect is lowered unemployed, then this kind of upward pressure on future interest rates should not occur, or at least not occur in any severe form.
12. Subsequent discussion focuses only upon deficits arising from increased spending. The arguments apply with equal force if that deficit is created by tax cuts.

16

Introduction and Summary

JOSEPH A. PECHMAN

This budget for fiscal year 1980 is lean and austere. It recommends a spending level well below that suggested by the recent momentum of Federal spending. It will disappoint those who seek expanded Federal efforts across the board. It meets my commitment to a deficit of $30 billion or less.

JIMMY CARTER, *The Budget of the United States Government, Fiscal Year 1980*, p. 3.

PRESIDENT CARTER'S "lean and austere" budget for 1980 was prepared at a time when the economy was expanding rapidly, inflation was running at an unacceptable rate, and politicians at all levels of government were still reacting to the approval of constitutional property tax limitations in California and other states. During its first two years in office, the administration pursued a policy of stimulating the economy in order to reduce the rate of unemployment. By the end of 1978, unemployment had in fact been reduced from 8 percent of the labor force to 5.8 percent and real gross national product was less than 2 percent below its potential. But the basic rate of inflation was rising—inflation, as measured by the consumer price index, rose 9 percent in 1978—and there was a clear need for a program to slow the economy. Thus economic and political objectives coincided. The President responded by making the reduction of inflation his top economic priority for 1979 and publicly committed himself both to sharply reducing the rate of growth of federal spending and to holding the 1980 budget deficit to $30 billion or less.

Coping with Inflation

Inflation has persisted for well over a decade, and there is universal agreement that steps must be taken to curb it. Inflation hurts those who must live on fixed or low incomes. It erodes the value of all fixed-value assets and interferes with the long-term planning of individuals and businesses. Proposition 13 and the proposed constitutional amendment to balance the budget are by-products of the social tension resulting from inflation.

The administration's anti-inflation strategy is to slow the rate of economic growth through tight fiscal and monetary policies so as to avoid placing excessive demands on the nation's resources. In addition, business and labor have been asked to voluntarily moderate the growth of prices and wages, and measures are planned to reduce the inflationary effects of government regulation.

Excerpted from Joseph A. Pechman, "Introduction and Summary," in Joseph A. Pechman, editor, *Setting National Priorities: The 1980 Budget.* Copyright © 1979 by the Brookings Institution.

The 1980 Budget

In beginning his planning for the 1980 budget, the President was faced with a rapid upward movement in federal spending. From fiscal 1976, the last full fiscal year before he assumed office, to fiscal 1979, total outlays have risen at an annual rate of about 11 percent. An increase of 8.7 percent would be needed in 1980 merely to maintain current service and activity levels without change; with such an increase in outlays, the deficit would exceed $30 billion if there were no change in the tax laws (table 1-1). Furthermore, the administration had made strong commitments to its NATO partners to participate fully in military weapons modernization and the improved combat-readiness of their armed forces. This meant that the President could meet his budget goals only by sharply reducing the rate of growth of nondefense spending.

The President's response to this tight situation was to hold the line on existing nondefense programs and on taxes. He kept his promise to raise real defense outlays by 3 percent but limited the annual pay increase of federal employees to 5.5 percent, repeated his 1978 proposal to contain the rise in hospital costs, cut spending for countercyclical programs, and recommended a number of reductions in low-priority social security benefits. The net effect of these decisions would be to hold the outlay increase in fiscal 1980 to 7.7 percent.

Table 1-1. Comparison of the Proposed Budget with the Current Service Budget, Fiscal Years 1978–80
Billions of dollars

Item	1978[a]	1979[b]	1980[b]
Outlays			
Current services	450.8	491.3	536.1
Proposed increases	...	1.9	7.0
Proposed decreases	...	0.1	−11.6
Proposed outlays	**450.8**	**493.4**	**531.6**
Receipts			
Current services	402.0	456.0	504.5
Proposed increases	...	...	−2.3
Proposed decreases	...	...	0.3
Proposed receipts	**402.0**	**456.0**	**502.6**
Deficit			
Current services	−48.8	−35.4	−31.6
Proposed	−48.8	−37.4	−29.0

Source: *The Budget of the United States Government, Fiscal Year 1980*, p. 16. Figures are rounded.
a. Actual.
b. Estimated.

On the receipts side of the budget, all general tax cuts for individuals and businesses were ruled out. The only major proposal was to provide real wage insurance for workers who are members of a group that conforms with the administration's 7 percent wage guideline for 1979. The estimated cost of the proposal is $2.5 billion, on the assumption that inflation will not exceed 7.5 percent during 1979. Tax increases were proposed to augment some existing trust fund receipts and to establish a new fund to clean up oil spills, but the amounts involved are small (roughly $200 million in 1980). With these changes, total receipts are estimated to increase 10.2 percent in fiscal 1980.

The 7.7 percent increase would bring outlays in 1980 to $531.6 billion and the 10.2 percent increase would raise receipts to $502.6 billion, leaving a deficit of $29.0 billion—one billion dollars below the President's ceiling (table 1-1).[1]

These estimates are based on a set of economic assumptions that are optimistic about both the growth of the economy and the rate of inflation. The administration expected the economy to slow down in 1979 but to avoid an actual recession (which is defined by many economists as at least two quarters of declining real output). It also forecast a reduction in the inflation rate from 9 percent in 1978 to 7.4 percent in 1979 and 6.3 percent in 1980. Prices in early 1979 were rising at a much faster rate than is consistent with the administration's projections, and many private forecasters believe that a recession will begin before the end of fiscal 1980.

An alternative set of budget estimates, based on a more pessimistic set of economic assumptions, has been prepared by the Congressional Budget Office. The CBO expects the economy to slow significantly in 1979, with a downturn beginning in the second half of the year and a mild recovery in 1980. It also projects higher inflation in both 1979 and 1980 than does the administration. On these assumptions, the CBO estimates that receipts in fiscal 1980 would be $499.4 billion, outlays would be $540.0 billion, and the deficit would be $40.6 billion—$11.6 billion higher than the President's proposed goal.

These figures are based on the budget program proposed by the President. But Congress is unlikely to approve the budget without making its usual substantial modifications. It may reject the hospital cost containment program, has already deferred action on most of the social security benefit reductions, and was being importuned by governors and mayors to restore at least some of the cuts in the grants-in-aid programs for state and local governments. Shortly after the budget was submitted, the administration withdrew its proposal to establish a national development bank, but at most this action will save only $200 million. On balance, after Congress gets through with the 1980 budget, outlays may be as much as $4 billion higher than the President's proposal unless defense spending is cut to make up the difference. This means that the 1980 deficit would amount to $33 billion with the administration's assumptions and about $45 billion with the CBO's less optimistic assumptions. Without real wage insurance, the deficits would be $30.5 billion and $42.5 billion.

In either case, the 1980 budget would represent a tighter federal fiscal policy than those of the last few years. If there were no change in the unemployment rate between fiscal 1979 and 1980, outlays

---

1. The analysis of the budget in this volume is based on the budget document transmitted to Congress in January 1979 (*The Budget of the United States Government, Fiscal Year 1980*). A revision of the estimates was released by the Office of Management and Budget in March ("Current Budget Estimates," March 1979), but the revised estimates are not incorporated in this volume because they did not change the budget outlook for fiscal years 1980–84 significantly and did not provide the detail needed to make a careful review of the budget. For fiscal 1979 the March estimates raised receipts by $5.8 billion and expenditures by $1.6 billion, thus reducing the estimated deficit by $4.2 billion (from $37.4 billion to $33.2 billion). For fiscal 1980 the estimated deficit was revised downward from $29.0 billion to $28.4 billion. None of the estimates in this volume reflect the President's April 1979 energy proposals.

would rise by 7.5 percent and receipts would rise by over 11 percent.[2] Even if Congress raised outlays $4 billion above those in the President's budget, the increase in outlays would be only 8.3 percent, making the budget less expansionary in 1980 than in 1979.

Monetary Policy

Monetary policy is also expected to contribute to the economic slowdown sought by the administration for 1979 and 1980. During 1978 private credit demands increased rapidly as the economy continued to expand. The money supply rose rapidly during the first nine months of the year, but interest rates went up as the Federal Reserve Board acted to restrain its growth.

A dramatic policy change was made on November 1, 1978, when it became apparent that foreign exchange traders were not satisfied with the steps that were being taken to control inflation in the United States. The new policy included a substantial tightening of monetary policy and a variety of special measures to support the dollar in foreign exchange markets. The growth of the money supply slowed significantly and interest rates reached their highest levels since their previous peaks in 1974. As a result, the federal funds rate (the rate at which banks borrow from one another to meet their reserve requirements) rose from 6.5 percent at the beginning of 1978 to 10 percent at the end of the year. The rate paid by the Treasury on three-month bills climbed from 6 percent to over 9 percent, and long-term federal bond yields rose from slightly less than 8 percent to about 9 percent.

Three major changes in financial markets have made the response of the economy to monetary policy uncertain. First, the regulations were changed to let commercial banks and other savings institutions issue new money market certificates of six-month maturity in minimum denominations of $10,000. Commercial banks were permitted to provide approximately the same yield on these certificates as the discount on Treasury bills, and the nonbank thrift institutions were allowed to pay an additional one-fourth of 1 percent. (In March 1979, the regulations were changed to prevent the compounding of interest rates during each six-month period and to limit the interest paid by the thrift institutions to the commercial bank rate when that is over 9 percent.) Second, commercial banks were permitted to transfer funds from a customer's saving account to cover a shortage in his checking account. Third, money market mutual funds, which started in the early 1970s, became attractive alternatives for holding short-term funds, and they grew rapidly in 1978. These innovations have significantly affected the forms in which people hold their liquid assets and hence growth rates of the monetary aggregates. But the rate of growth of the money supply in the last quarter of 1978 and in early 1979 remains low even after corrections are made for their estimated effects.

The new money market certificates played a critical role in cushioning the effect of tightening monetary policy on credit availability for home buying in 1978. In the past, when interest rates increased

---

2. These calculations are based on an assumed unemployment rate of 5.1 percent, which currently represents the level defined as "full employment" by the Council of Economic Advisers. (For an explanation of the full employment budget, see chapter 2.) The conclusion that planned receipts will rise much faster than planned outlays is valid regardless of the assumed level of unemployment.

sharply, funds would flow out of the thrift institutions into direct purchases of high-yielding securities because comparable yields were not available on deposits. This "disintermediation" would greatly restrict the supply of mortgage funds and lead to a reduction in residential construction. With the advent of the money market certificates, the thrift institutions held a major share of their deposits, and mortgage lending declined much less than in previous periods of high interest rates. The adjustment to credit restraint was much smoother in the home-building industry during this expansion, but the result is that interest rates must rise to even higher levels to achieve a given degree of restraint on aggregate demand.

The administration is prepared to accept high interest rates in order to "create a favorable climate for unwinding inflation," but it is impossible to predict how high they will have to go to meet this objective. If the economy slows down soon, the interest rates prevailing in early 1979 may turn out to be the peak for this cycle. On the other hand, further increases in interest rates could take place if the economy does not respond to the tighter monetary and fiscal policies already in effect.

Wage-Price Guidelines

In addition to restraining demand through monetary and fiscal policies, the administration is seeking to influence price and wage decisions directly. The mechanism is a system of voluntary price-wage guidelines. On the price side, the rules request that price setters decelerate their rate of price increases by half a percentage point relative to the increase they experienced in the base period 1976–77. Under this rule, a maximum increase of 9.5 percent is allowed and a minimum increase of 1.5 percent is accepted without challenge. Firms with cost increases that would push their prices above the 9.5 percent ceiling are permitted to apply a cost-justification rule involving profit markups.

The wage rules provide for a basic 7 percent increase (8 percent for the first year of union contracts, averaging 7 percent over the entire contract) with special rules for escalator clauses, fringe benefits, and other aspects of compensation.

As the program is voluntary, there are no court-enforced penalties for noncompliance. However, the government has stated that government contractors—especially large ones—may lose their existing contracts or the right to bid on new ones if they do not comply. The legal authority for such contract denials is questionable, and there has already been some litigation on the issue. In general, enforcement of the guidelines depends on moral suasion and public opinion. The harmful publicity—especially for large firms, which are the most visible—that would result from being branded a noncooperator is a strong incentive to comply.

As with previous efforts at direct intervention, the major focus of the guideline program is on the wage side, even though some of the most complicated rules involve prices. Wages are a major element of total costs; the premise of the program is that, if wage increases can be held to 7 percent, price increases will eventually fall below 7 percent because of rising productivity.

In theory, it is possible to imagine a guideline focused on prices and based on the assumption that wages would eventually follow prices. The problem is that, from an administrative point of view, controlling prices (or even setting rules for voluntary price restraint) is much more complicated than controlling wages because it is difficult to allow for the introduction of new products, changes in quality, changes in the prices of internationally traded goods and agricultural products, and differences in product mix. This is not to say that there are not many technical problems on the wage side, but the price side is much more complex.

Apart from the administrative aspect, a system of rules for wages is less likely to cause dislocations than rules geared to the absolute prices charged by a firm. Employers and workers tend to be tied together in long-term relationships. Within limits, wage restraints are unlikely to provoke labor shortages and the loss of valued workers. But product markets are more prone to shortages and distortions, because buyers and sellers are not often tightly linked.

The difficulty with a wage-centered program is that, even if prices are geared to wages over the long run, there are periods in which price movements reflect external influences. In early 1979, for example, upward pressure on prices came partly from the agricultural sector—where labor costs are only a minor factor—and partly from foreign oil prices. Bad news about prices makes it difficult for union leaders to sell wage restraint to their members. The Carter administration's initial solution to this dilemma was to propose real wage insurance, a potential tax rebate to workers in groups that accepted wage increases of 7 percent or less. Under this plan, workers in complying firms would receive a tax rebate proportional to the excess of price inflation above 7 percent, up to 10 percent.

While real wage insurance is a novel method of reconciling short spurts of price inflation with wage restraint, the plan had a number of drawbacks. It required the approval of Congress as a tax measure, a potentially prolonged process. Yet the plan needed to be put into effect quickly if it was to provide the desired incentive. Moreover, it is difficult to write guideline-type rules into the tax code and administer them. As a result, the actual plan did not include the details of the guidelines in such areas as fringe-benefit calculations, promotions, and low-wage workers. Congress was also concerned about the budgetary costs and the possibility of a large federal payout in a period of inflation. If the plan promoted wage restraint, the inflationary effects of the payout could be offset or more than offset by the reduced pressure on costs. There was no simple way of estimating the incentive effects, but it is clear that as time passed and the program was not adopted its incentive effects for the period it covered (October 1, 1978, to September 30, 1979) diminished. Wage setters had to make their decisions without knowing whether a tax rebate plan would be approved by Congress.

Apart from real wage insurance, a number of other problems will have to be resolved if the guideline program is to continue for an extended period. Nominally, the guidelines apply to firms and other units of all sizes, including governmental units. Yet the Council on Wage and Price Stability has a small staff and cannot monitor the entire economy. In principle, the council has established a system of appeals for exceptions from the wage and price standards, but it is not clear who will make such decisions or how timely access to the process can be provided. A price-wage program—especially a voluntary one—needs flexibility to adapt to changes in economic circumstances, such as a higher-than-expected level of inflationary pressure. In early 1979 it was unclear how such flexibility would be injected into the guidelines.

Regulatory Reform

The federal government affects costs and prices in many industries through its regulatory powers. Traditionally, regulation has been confined mainly to transportation, communications, energy, banking and finance, and agriculture. More recently, there has been an increase in health, safety, and environmental regulations, which affect a wide variety of businesses across the entire spectrum of industry and commerce.

The costs of regulation are reflected in the federal budget to only a small degree. Most of the costs are borne by business enterprises and are usually included in the prices paid by consumers. The benefits of regulation are significant, but they are difficult to measure. The unmeasured benefits of regulation must be balanced against the measured cost increases they may generate, but in a period of inflation it is particularly important to avoid adding to costs and prices unnecessarily.

The biggest success story in reducing prices through changes in regulation concerns the airline industry. The Civil Aeronautics Board permitted the airlines to charge lower fares and eased the restrictions on the use of air routes by the carriers. These actions markedly reduced fares, increased air travel, and raised airline earnings. In 1978 Congress enacted legislation to phase out entry and price regulation for domestic airlines by 1983. The new legislation should lower air fares even more (though fuel and other cost increases may affect them) and may also broaden the variety of services offered customers. Similar reforms in surface transportation have been proposed, but progress is likely to be slow because of the potential real income losses of truckers.

Regulatory reform in some of the newer agencies, such as the Occupational Safety and Health Administration and the Environmental Protection Agency, will also be difficult. While these agencies do not explicitly set prices, their decisions do affect costs and are therefore important for anti-inflation policy. Regulatory budgets that would limit the costs an agency could impose on the private sector have been suggested. However, measuring the costs of regulation is almost as complicated as measuring its benefits, and some agencies are not currently required to consider costs in many of their decisions. Thus though regulatory reform is vital, it will be slow in coming. In the meantime, the Carter administration has formed a regulatory analysis review group to encourage economic analysis of major regulations and a regulatory council to prepare a centralized calendar of proposed regulations.

Standard-setting regulation is not the only mechanism by which the government adds to costs without making budgetary outlays. Agricultural price supports and acreage set-asides are designed to increase the incomes of farmers by increasing cash prices for farm products. The principal beneficiaries of these policies are the most affluent farmers, not the poorest. Trade protection—especially for textiles, consumer electronics, steel, shoes, and sugar—is intended, without a visible government outlay, to raise the incomes of workers and businesses in industries subject to intense foreign competition. Minimum wages raise the incomes of some low-paid workers while reducing the employment prospects of others (often teenagers and members of minority groups). In each of these cases, the government could transfer income directly to alleviate hardship, but direct budget outlays would call attention to the irrational consequences of these policies; indirect, price-increasing methods are chosen because they are less conspicuous. Modification of any one of these policies would have only a slight effect on inflation in the near future, but a combination of several changes would help reduce the rate of price increases in the long run.

The Outlook for Inflation and Growth

The rate of inflation is likely to decline in the latter part of 1979, especially if a recession occurs. In that sense, there are grounds for optimism about inflation. However, since it is perpetuated by the price-wage spiral, a rapid reduction in the inflation rate should not be anticipated. The administration's wage guidelines may have to be relaxed to accommodate recent price developments, but it is important to retain a framework to encourage responsible behavior on the part of business and labor. Mandatory price and wage controls are another possibility, but controls lead to cumulative distortions of the economy, impose heavy burdens of compliance on business, and are expensive to administer.

The economy has been more buoyant despite monetary tightness and high interest rates than most forecasters expected. The pace slowed in the first quarter of 1979, but output was still growing. It is thus possible that the administration's relatively optimistic real growth assumptions will be realized and that the federal deficit in fiscal 1980 can be held in the vicinity of $30 billion. If a recession develops, the automatic stabilizers in the budget (unemployment compensation payments and reduced taxes) will raise the deficit. Efforts to prevent this, either through cuts in expenditures or increases in taxes, would exacerbate the recession.

The Humphrey-Hawkins Act passed in 1978 specified a goal of 3 percent inflation and 4 percent unemployment by the end of calendar year 1983. Thereafter, the inflation rate is supposed to be brought down to zero. However, the growth and employment objectives of the legislation cannot be reconciled with the need to reduce inflation. It would be self-defeating to overstimulate the economy just to reach the employment goals of the act in the time stipulated; the result would be an acceleration of inflation, which would then require measures to restrain the economy, and these, in turn, would lead to higher unemployment. In theory, it is possible to develop special programs for the structurally unemployed that could lower the measured rate of unemployment without intensifying inflationary pressure. But most employment programs have had mixed results; while they have provided temporary employment and income for some disadvantaged groups, they have not succeeded in training many workers for active participation in the economy at regular wages. The goals of the Humphrey-Hawkins Act are therefore unattainable with the present tools of economic policy.

The Domestic Budget

Nondefense outlays are scheduled to increase from $378.9 billion in fiscal 1979 to $405.7 billion in 1980. This 7.1 percent increase is only just enough to offset the rise in prices projected in the budget; in real terms, nondefense outlays will be virtually the same in 1980 as they were in 1979 and 1978. The composition of the nondefense budget does not remain the same, however. Despite proposed reductions in health care outlays and social security benefits, payments for individuals—social security benefits, federal employee retirement benefits, veterans' benefits, food stamps, public assistance, medicare, and medicaid—will continue to rise rapidly as the number of beneficiaries increases and medical prices rise. To keep the nondefense totals the same in real terms, it was necessary to cut outlays elsewhere, most notably in grants-in-aid to state and local governments. The major issues in the nondefense budget are the proposed reductions in health outlays, social security benefits, and grants-in-aid.

Health

The rise in health costs has become a large drain on the federal budget. Federal health outlays have more than doubled in the last five years and are expected to almost double again over the next five years if current policies continue. This is partly the result of the increasing demand for health care as incomes rise and the population ages, but it can also be attributed to the nation's health care financing system, which relies heavily on third-party reimbursement by private insurers and the federal government to pay doctors and hospital bills. Under this system, each health care decision is insulated from its financial consequences, with the result that there is little incentive for doctors or patients to economize in the prescription and use of medical services.

The Carter administration's ultimate objective in the health field is a comprehensive national health insurance system, but it recognizes that something must be done to slow the growth of hospital costs before such a system can be enacted. In 1977 it proposed to limit the annual increase in hospital revenues, but the proposal was rejected by Congress because of the determined opposition of the hospital lobby. The new budget contains an even more stringent version of hospital cost containment than the 1978 version. The average saving in federal outlays would amount to $1.7 billion in fiscal 1980, $4.9 billion in 1982, and $9.2 billion in 1984.

If Congress fails to enact any form of hospital cost containment, the administration may be forced to use the power it now has under the law to limit medicare and medicaid reimbursements. This would reduce the rate of growth of federal expenditures, but nothing would prevent hospitals from segregating medicare and medicaid patients and charging other patients more. The result would be a shift in costs from the federal government to private payers and a reduction in the quality of health care for the poor and the aged.

Social Security

The social security system, which will pay $115 billion in benefits to retired and disabled people and their dependents in fiscal 1980, is being examined carefully by at least four governmental commissions. This scrutiny of what is widely acknowledged to be the most successful federal program was undertaken partly because of the large increases in payroll taxes enacted in 1977 to put the system on a sound financial basis and partly because the character of the system has not changed even though basic economic and social changes have occurred since it was adopted. The administration is awaiting the results of the four studies before proposing fundamental changes in the system, but it feels that some reductions in low-priority benefits are called for in a period of budget stringency.

The administration proposes to set a limit on family disability benefits of 80 percent of predisability earnings; phase out benefits to students over the age of eighteen; terminate the $255 lump-sum death benefit; repeal the $122 minimum benefit (but retain the special minimum benefit of $11.50 a month for each year of covered employment above ten); and eliminate the widow's benefit for mothers after the youngest child reaches sixteen (instead of eighteen, as under present law). These changes would apply only to future beneficiaries, so that the immediate reduction in federal outlays would be small—only $700 million in fiscal 1980—but by 1984 the savings would amount to $4.4 billion.

Although the proposals are modest and leave the basic benefits intact, long-time supporters of social security have interpreted the administration's action as the beginning of an attack on the very structure of the system. In response to this pressure, the House Ways and Means Committee decided to consider early in 1979 only the suggested changes in disability benefits (which account for about 20 percent of the long-term savings from all the administration's proposals) and to defer action on the remainder of the program until late 1979.

Grants-in-Aid

Federal grants to state and local governments have risen sharply in the last decade—from $20.3 billion in fiscal 1969 to an estimated $82.1 billion in 1979. They rose from 17.4 percent of total state-local expenditures in fiscal 1969 to a peak of 26.7 percent in 1978, but they are now beginning to decline relative to both the size of the federal budget and state-local expenditures. The 1980 budget calls for $82.9 billion in federal grants-in-aid. This increase of $0.8 billion over 1979 outlays would amount to a reduction of more than 5 percent in real terms, even under the administration's optimistic inflation projections.

The largest proposed reductions in federal grants are in three programs that were introduced or expanded to speed economic recovery from the 1974–75 recession—local public works, public service employment, and countercyclical revenue sharing. Although these programs were intended to be temporary, the recipients have come to rely on them and the cutback is being resisted by representatives of the states, cities, and counties. Even if the grants enacted for purposes of economic stimulus are excluded, federal assistance to state and local governments will decline in 1980 by about 3 percent in real terms.

The allocation of federal budget funds in fiscal 1980 for grants-in-aid reflects no overall theme or principle other than the judgment that countercyclical aid should disappear when the economy reaches high levels of employment. The administration is putting the states and local governments on notice that the heyday of federal assistance has passed. The particular cuts proposed in the budget may not reflect congressional priorities, however, and a heated battle is likely to develop over the size and allocation of the cuts.

Prospects for Nondefense Spending

With defense outlays rising rapidly (see below), President Carter has responded to the public clamor for reducing the growth of federal spending by cutting the growth of nondefense outlays. The proposed cuts are being strongly resisted by the groups that benefit from the threatened programs. Other cuts are possible, but these would require even more unpalatable changes than those already proposed. The only other possibility is to offset increases in the nondefense budget by reductions in defense outlays, but this would also encounter strong opposition inside and outside Congress. Congress thus has little room to maneuver and will find it difficult to deviate very much from the President's proposed nondefense budget.

The Defense Budget

The President's budget proposes to raise national defense outlays from $114.5 billion in fiscal 1979 to $125.8 billion in 1980, an increase of $11.3 billion, or almost 10 percent. In real terms, this amounts to an increase of 3.1 percent, which corresponds to the commitment made by the President at the May 1977 meeting of NATO. Budget authority rises by 1.7 percent in real terms. The sharp increase in defense spending comes at a time when the growth in nondefense spending is being restrained. This reordering of priorities is in response to the widely shared perception that the Soviet Union is building up its military capability to dangerous levels and that U.S. leadership in world affairs is eroding.

The most significant issues in defense policy are to define the military purposes of U.S. forces and to allocate defense resources in a manner that will best achieve these purposes. The dispute over these issues raises serious questions about the effectiveness of current defense policy and may lead to basic changes that would alter the course of the current five-year defense plan.

. . .

The Budget Outlook

The budget outlook depends not only on spending and tax decisions but also on the state of the economy. The official five-year budget projections are based on the economic goals of the Humphrey-Hawkins Act. Under these unrealistic assumptions, federal spending would be reduced to 21 percent of GNP in fiscal 1981 and the budget would be nearly in balance that year. Thereafter, expenditures would decline to 19.3 percent of GNP and the margin of receipts over expenditures would increase rapidly until it reached $106.5 billion in fiscal 1984. This reflects the relatively austere spending program proposed by the President and the response of receipts to the assumed rapid growth of the economy.

An alternative set of projections based on more realistic economic assumptions has been prepared by the Congressional Budget Office. In these projections, the unemployment rate declines to 5.5 percent and the inflation rate to 6.0 percent in 1984. Receipts would not overtake outlays until 1982, but by 1984 the margin of receipts over outlays would amount to $126 billion (in a $3.9 trillion economy). The margin is greater in these alternative projections because receipts respond faster than outlays to the growth of nominal incomes at the higher inflation rate.

The $126 billion margin of receipts over expenditures also assumes that no new programs would be enacted and that there would be no tax reductions to offset the inflation-induced increases in receipts. In the past, Congress has not allowed individual income tax receipts to exceed 11 percent of personal income for very long. Without any changes in the tax law, individual income tax receipts in the five-year projections would rise to more than 14 percent of personal income in 1984. Reducing this percentage to 11 would require using up $103 billion of the 1984 margin.

Another claimant for part of the budget margin is the corporation income tax. In the past, when individual income taxes have been reduced, business taxes were also cut roughly in the ratio of 1:3. A cut of $103 billion in individual income taxes would thus generate a business tax cut of $34 billion if past practices were followed. In combination, the individual and corporation income tax cuts would amount to $137 billion, which is more than the estimated margin of receipts over expenditures in fiscal 1984. There is also pressure to roll back at least part of the payroll tax increases enacted in 1977, but any such action would reduce the margin available for income tax cuts.

One way of increasing the margin is to make cuts in existing programs beyond those proposed by the President in submitting the 1980 budget. For example, one proposal would restrict annual federal expenditure increases to the rate of inflation plus 1 percent. This limit would reduce federal spending to 18.5 percent of GNP, the lowest level since 1965, and would add $13 billion to the $126 billion margin, permitting some further tax cuts. To accomplish this objective, it would be necessary to reduce projected 1984 spending by about 2 percent, avoid all new spending, and confine inflation adjustments to the federal programs that have mandatory inflation adjustment features. Such large reductions in spending would require a political consensus that has not yet emerged.

Proposals are being made to adopt a constitutional amendment reducing the rate of growth of federal spending substantially below currently projected levels. One group of proposals would require a balanced budget every year; another would directly limit the growth of federal spending. Adding an amendment of either type to the Constitution would reduce fiscal flexibility and make it extremely difficult to use the federal budget to help stabilize the economy. A more appropriate method would be to require Congress to use its annual budget resolutions to limit spending and taxing. The amendment route would clutter up the Constitution and invite the use of techniques to circumvent the constitutional language.

17

PLAYING TO THE HAVES
Carter's Dangerous Budget Act
BY ROBERT LEKACHMAN

As POLITICAL documents, President Carter's new budget ("lean and austere") and soporific State of the Union message ("We cannot afford to live beyond our means") reflect an addiction to the latest public opinion polls. His utterances merit both the approval they received from William Safire and Alan Greenspan, chairman of the Council of Economic Advisers under President Ford, and the contempt they inspired from Arthur Schlesinger Jr.: "He's a Republican. He has the temperament of a small businessman who happened to become President."

Very likely Jerry Rafshoon, Pat Caddell, Ham Jordan, and other canny operators at 1600 Pennsylvania Avenue are pleased with the positioning of their patron. Jerry Brown's latest theme, a balanced budget forever, situates the shifty California governor far on the White House right; Senator Edward Kennedy's reiteration of traditional liberal Democratic positions speaks at the moment to a discountable minority on its left. The attractive scenario for Jimmy Carter is clear: Brown makes an unsuccessful run in the 1980 primaries, while Kennedy waits his turn in 1984. Occupying the cherished center is the President, thrifty but compassionate, eager to move forward toward a New Foundation "for our country and our world."

Faithful to the profuse preliminary advertisement, the budget blueprint for the New Foundation eliminates 158,000 Comprehensive Employment and Training Act (CETA) jobs, 250,000 summer slots for teenagers, 25,000 subsidized housing units, $400 million in school lunch subsidies, and $600 million in Social Security benefits. In addition, it cuts smaller sums from support for higher education, libraries, schools in Federally "impacted" areas, mass transit, farmers, and environmental protection.

The Pentagon is the one big winner. In redemption of his pledge to our NATO allies (whose reluctance to adequately finance their own defense has been mysteriously underwritten by successive administrations), Carter is asking for a 3 per cent hike in appropriations, after inflation. The increase is mostly for weapons procurement. If Congress approves, as is highly likely, appropriations for the next decade will automatically swell for tanks, infantry fighting vehicles, helicopters, fighter planes, missiles, and ships—SALT or no SALT.

To further reconcile more money for defense with a 1980 budget deficit of less than $30 billion—another of the numerical targets that enchant the President—it has been necessary to contract Federal grants to cities and states by 7 per cent in real terms. All that is left of last year's urban program is a National Development Bank whose jurisdiction, functions and organization remain undetermined.

Zero funds are being sought for wel-

Reprinted with permission from The New Leader, February 12, 1979. Copyright © The American Labor Conference on International Affairs, Inc.

fare reform, and even the $5.5 billion pencilled in for 1982 is a quarter of the cost of last year's Program for Better Jobs and Incomes. No numbers are attached to a national health initiative, presumably because no Administration program has yet been agreed upon.

The $29-billion deficit predicted for the fiscal year 1980 (beginning October 1, 1979 and ending September 30, 1980) is $8 billion below the estimated 1979 shortfall. Carter's dreambook prophesies a piddling $1.2 billion deficit in the 1981 accounts and surpluses of $37.8 billion, $72.7 billion, and $106.5 billion in the three following years.

The fate of his mean-spirited budget in Congress is as uncertain as the state of the economy and the mood of the voters. Republicans immediately muttered that the President had not cut enough. They were supported by the increasingly fatuous Senator William Proxmire (D.-Wis.), who grandly proposed balancing the budget right away—a mere matter of subtracting another $29 billion from nondefense allocations. Suspecting that Carter in a presidential election year will seduce the voters with another tax cut, Republicans are pushing a revised version of last session's unsuccessful bill sponsored by Representative Jack Kemp of New York and Senator William Roth Jr. of Delaware, designed to slash taxes along with spending.

When it comes to specific programs, conservatives and liberals of both parties are as likely to expand as to contract spending. Higher farm price supports are attractive to Senators Robert Dole (R.-Kansas) and George McGovern (D.-S.D.). Every President since Eisenhower has tried to shrink Federal aid to "impacted" areas, a number of them embarrassingly upper middle-income in composition. One can wish the President and his embattled Georgian budget director, James McIntyre, well without expecting them to succeed where more popular predecessors failed. Still another probable loser is the budget plan to reduce Social Security benefits for survivors and the handicapped. Aside from defense, the major new addition to expenditures is the $2.5 billion to finance wage insurance. In large measure because the White House has yet to present this potentially useful notion in credible form, it also appears to be going nowhere.

Budgets are as plausible as the economic assumptions that underlie price, revenue and expenditure forecasts. The Council of Economic Advisers last year forecast 6 per cent inflation and suffered the embarrassment of an actual 9 per cent. This time around it is predicting that by year's end inflation will simmer down to 7.4 per cent and unemployment, now a shade below 6 per cent, will rise no higher than 6.2 per cent. The fact that Charles Schultze, the Council chairman, was wrong last time does not mean he will be equally mistaken again. Still, it is worth more than passing mention that Alice Rivlin, head of the Congressional Budget Office (CBO), anticipates an actual recession; and Carter's very own Federal Reserve chairman, G. William Miller, took a cautiously gloomy line in his testimony to the Joint Economic Committee.

Recession or even zero growth will scramble all bets. For if unemployment soars to 7 per cent or higher, as the CBO expects, the deficit will swell from $29 billion to $41 billion because of diminished tax receipts and larger outlays for unemployment compensation, welfare, food stamps, and Medicaid. When unemployment verges on 7 per cent, it afflicts the white middle class families who are the pampered pets of the political season. At that point, Congress looks benignly at job-creation and tax-cutting devices that enlarge the deficit.

BUT HOWEVER transformed the President's budget may be by economic and political events, it remains a major statement of his intentions for the rest of his first term. And deliberately or otherwise, this budget injures several of the constituencies that united to push its author into the White House.

Take, for example, the relatively trivial $600-million cut in Social Security benefits. Some of the saving will be achieved by shifting widows and children between 16-18 years of age from the Social Security system to Supplemental Security Income (SSI). A combination of earlier schemes to aid the disabled, blind and elderly, this is widely regarded as another welfare program. Social Security is generally (albeit mistakenly) interpreted as an insurance protection, enjoys much higher public standing. Many of the affected families are black. Under the new arrangement, their stipends will be smaller. Moreover, the costs of SSI are shared by the states and localities. Thus at a stroke this minor economy insults and injures indigent blacks and women, and adds to the fiscal burdens of the communities where they are clustered. It is good luck that House Ways and Means Chairman Al Ullman (D.-Ore.) has declared his committee's agenda too clogged to take up the President's amiable suggestions.

In the case of cities suffering delicate health, the most disastrous feature of the New Foundation is its failure to lighten the burden of welfare and Medicaid, amounting to well over a billion dollars in recent municipal budgets. But nearly as harmful is the impact of revised and shrunken public job programs. For despite the Administration's own predictions of higher unemployment, the new budget proposes less to alleviate it than existing formulas offer at lower unemployment rates.

New York City's Mayor Edward Koch, who has cheerfully folded an additional $100 million of Federal aid into the city's financial plan, stands to receive not a dime. Instead, New York will lose between 5,000-6,000 CETA jobs, 16,000 summer positions for young workers, and several millions of dollars for local public works and subsidized housing. There will be fewer dollars for mass transit, environment protection, and Federal reimbursement of the cost of entertaining and protecting foreign dignitaries. Little things, but they add up. Detroit, Newark and Gary, cities that depend to a greater extent than New York on CETA funds to maintain essential public services, will be even more afflicted.

Overall, the 1980 budget is an exercise in redistributing the Gross National Product in a stagnant economy. Because 1978 wages rose only 5.5 per cent and prices jumped 9 per cent, an average blue- or white-collar worker lost 3.5 per cent of real income—a statistical fact closely related to the increasing number of women in the labor force. Last year's tax reduction quite deliberately shifted the fiscal burden from corporations and affluent individuals to the rest of the population. Social Security levies, highly regressive in their impact, are up. Personal income taxes, mildly progressive in application, are down. This budget continues the trend of redistribution from low and moderate income families to their more prosperous neighbors.

The point merits emphasis because the next decade is likely to be dominated by issues of distribution. The current *Economic Report* predicts annual productivity gains for the coming five years of a mere 1.5 per cent per capita, half the historic trend rate. The economics of growth are comparatively kind. Before Vietnam swallowed up all other issues, Lyndon Johnson was able simultaneously to reduce taxes in 1964 *and* fund the War on Poverty and the rest of the Great Society. Distribution is a more brutal matter. As the British economist Rudolf Klein has put it: "One man's prize is another man's loss. If the blacks want to improve their share of desirable goods, it can only be at the expense of whites. If the over-65s are to be given higher pensions or improved medical services, it can only be at the expense of the working population or the young."

The higher unemployment that accompanies slow growth also exacerbates group tensions. In the light of their communal histories, Jews and blacks were fated to split over affirmative action as the issue has registered first in education (Bakke) and now in a pending employment case. But what has embittered the conflict and virtually dissolved ancient alliances is the perception that desirable alternatives to professional training are much scarcer than they used to be. Layoffs pit unions against women's groups. When the Grey Panthers celebrated Congress' extension of mandatory retirement from age 65 to 70, the young were not seen dancing in the streets.

In alliance with the wage-price guidelines and higher interest rates, the 1980 budget threatens to continue the erosion of working class income. Much as AFL-CIO President George Meany warned, employers are doing their patriotic best to enforce the 7 per cent wage standard. The enforcers at the Council on Wages and Price Stability succeeded in keeping the settlement between the major oil companies and the Oil, Chemical, and Atomic Workers below 7 per cent. Although stronger unions will fare better, it is generally accepted in labor circles that contracts will come in smaller because of the guidelines.

The budget redistributes income among workers in a dubious fashion. Thus CETA employees and other moderately paid public job holders will be laid off, while a smaller number of better paid members of strong unions, like the International Association of Machinists (IAM), and the United Auto Workers (UAW), will be hired in defense plants. It is all the more to the credit of the IAM that its researchers have concluded there are more jobs for machinists in the civilian sector or in nondefense public employment than in weapons procurement. A billion dollars hires 59,000 men and women in private nondefense industry, 88,000 in government positions, and only 45,000 in defense work.

AMERICAN politics, thank heaven, are volatile. The current competition in beastliness between the major parties will seem politically profitable only so long as the losers are passive. They are showing signs of stirring. In January, for example, an organization formed by UAW President Douglas Fraser to counter the conservative drift, appropriately named the Progressive Alliance, collected representatives of 60 groups to work out a coalition strategy. Among those present were Fraser's own Auto Workers, the Machinists, the Communications Workers, the Urban League, and, interestingly, the AFL-CIO's Industrial Union Department. The side effects of the Proposition 13 virus may begin sooner than the Jerry Browns calculate.

Here we need to return to that champion tease, the senior senator from Massachusetts. When William ("Wimpy") Winpisinger introduced Kennedy at the IAM's legislative conference last month his opening comment was to the effect that he was happy to be sitting next to a president he could be proud of. Kennedys are intermittent social idealists and full-time politicians. If the omens are propitious, Teddy Kennedy may go in 1980, especially if Brown shows signs of stealing the nomination for himself.

Quite possibly, higher unemployment and inflation at the 8 per cent rate predicted by the CBO will compel a discredited Carter late this year to swallow still more of his words and ask Congress for mandatory controls. The budget, despite the actual and symbolic damage it inflicts on vulnerable constituencies, is unlikely to curtail an inflation solidly entrenched in the food, energy, health, and housing sectors of the economy. The polls now report Carter soundly whipping Ford and Reagan and losing to Kennedy. Should unemployment be higher by next Labor Day and inflation only slightly lower, the temptation among Democrats to take on the President may well be irresistible.

In 1960 I preferred Hubert Humphrey to Jack Kennedy. In 1968 I ran with clean Gene just as long as my sluggish contender showed signs of movement. In 1976 I wept with Fred Harris and Mo Udall. It is no doubt a sign of the flatness of the surrounding landscape that the current Kennedy stands tall. I could wish that my knight's coat of armor were shining white instead of tattle-tale gray, but in these bad days we must all take our champions where we find them.

Can Carter Reap a Windfall?

By Irving Kristol

President Carter is now doing so many things right in the area of economic policy that, if he continues along this path, he could easily be renominated and reelected in 1980. Ironically, he is doing them under the constraint of circumstance—against his will and, apparently, against his own best judgment. Call it providence, call it luck, the fact remains that he is being successful in spite of himself. His greatest danger at the moment derives from his own lack of assurance in all the right things he is doing.

True, the public opinion polls give Mr. Carter a very low rating for his economic policy. But this is hardly surprising. How can the American people feel any confidence in his economic statesmanship when he himself obviously lacks such confidence? He gives every appearance of being a man frustrated by events rather than in control of them, and he therewith evokes a spirit of frustration in the public that looks to him for leadership.

There are many reasons for this odd state of affairs. An important one, surely, is that the economic theories of his top advisers are no longer congruent—if ever they were—with economic reality. But more important, one feels, is the conception of the proper and only possible relation between politics and economics that dominates this administration, as it has—to one degree or another—dominated all post-New Deal administrations. This is the view that, since the American people are incapable of deferred gratification, it is the responsibility of politics to provide instant solutions to our economic problems. But while such a time frame may recommend itself to energetic politicians, it is worse than useless when applied to economic policy, which is only viable when a longer view can be sustained. For in economics we are always coping with the delayed effects of past events, while current policy in turn always takes time to yield its fruits. The cardinal sin in economic policy is impatience—but in the political process today, alas, patience seems to be one of the forgotten virtues.

Speaking to Americans as Adults

One suspects, however, that it is more forgotten by politicians than by the average citizen. What, one wonders, would the public mood be if President Carter felt it possible to speak to Americans as reasonable adults rather than as children to be manipulated by a mixture of promises and admonitions? Imagine him on television saying something like this:

"I certainly appreciate the anxiety we all feel, and the suffering we are experiencing, as a result of double-digit inflation. I want to assure you that the economic policies we are now following will bring down the rate of inflation—we are as certain of that as we are of the laws of arithmetic. But it will take time, and we do not expect to see any significant improvement until late this year or early in the next year. Governments cannot work miracles, any more than doctors can. There are some conditions that yield only to sustained treatment over time, and inflation is one such economic condition. Please be patient and let us grit our teeth and stick it out together. If we lack such patience, we shall only end up doing greater injury to ourselves."

He won't make any such speech, of course. To begin with, a substantial wing of his own party would promptly accuse him of "lacking compassion"—a favorite accusation of those who promise (and may actually believe in) instant solutions to social or economic problems. Moreover, he might think it politically inadvisable to speak candidly to the American people in this way—Mr. Rafshoon would doubtless inform him to this effect. And, in any case, he may not even believe that his hypothetical speech is true in substance—there are

Board of Contributors

Mr. Carter seems bent of doing the right things, while refusing to give the right reasons, and he may yet end up backing into the White House on the momentum of an economic program he never had any faith in.

plenty of liberal economists who would argue against it.

So Mr. Carter seems bent on doing the right things while refusing to give the right reasons, and he may yet end up backing into the White House on the momentum of an economic program he never had any faith in.

That program has two key points: a gradual slowing down in the rate of growth of the money supply, and a gradual narrowing of the budgetary deficit. There is room for disagreement as to the rate at which these processes should occur, but the precise rate is less important than the direction. Once the world's business and financial communities see "light at the end of the tunnel," they will quickly begin discounting a less inflationary future for the American economy. Inflation will then begin to subside, in step with inflationary expectations.

Mr. Carter was coerced into this program by the threatened collapse of the dollar in the international money markets, and it is this same alarming possibility that will make him stick to it. Like most politicians, he resents such involuntary servitude to economic reality—hence the sullenness of his acquiescence. But, whether he likes it or not, it is absolutely the right program—indeed, the only program—for coping with inflation. It will, however, take time to work its cure.

It is to buy such time that the administration instituted its "voluntary" wage and price controls—an absurd idea that was fated to unravel, as it is now doing. It will cause some unnecessary grief and distress before it utterly collapses, especially in its effect on collective bargaining. But here again Mr. Carter is in luck, if only he knew it. Congress's refusal to pass the administration's scheme for "real wage insurance" makes the whole "voluntary" program unworkable. And since Congress also shows no interest whatsoever in mandatory controls, the program as a whole will wither away, causing much bureaucratic anguish and little permanent damage.

OPEC (in its greed) has joined the Congress (in its wisdom) in forcing Mr. Carter to do the right thing about energy—i.e., decontrol and deregulate. It was bound to happen sooner or later, since there is no way any American government could permanently insulate our economy and our consumers from the prices prevailing in the world markets. Decontrol will, in the longer run, help keep those prices down, rather than up, since it will encourage the supply side of the energy equation. It will also, as Mr. Carter keeps lamenting, give "windfall profits" to some oil and gas producers. That is true enough—but, as Mr. Carter himself once observed, "life is unfair," and if an undeserved boon to the oil companies is also good for our longer-term economic health, then it is ridiculous to make too much of a fuss about it. There is, after all, something more than a little strange about an energy program—and ours has been such a program—whose overriding purpose is to keep such "windfall profits" out of the oil companies' hands. One doesn't have to be a partisan of the oil companies to see that this represents a perverted sense of economic priorities.

Two Dangers

Altogether, then, it is accurate to say that, though Mr. Carter gives the impression of a man whose back is to the wall, he is—if only he knew it—on the road to a healthier economy and (with a bit of luck on timing) probable re-election. But there are two dangers, both of which the White House may itself create.

The first—against which Milton Friedman has been warning—is an excessive constraint on the money supply, arising from political impatience with the time frame necessary to control inflation. This could provoke an unnecessary recession.

The second arises from the fact that a majority of our economists seem to be persuaded that a recession is inevitable anyhow. Behind this pessimistic view lie certain conventional economic theories about the relations among money supply, inflation, unemployment and economic growth. The fact that those theories are popular among economists does not mean that they are necessarily right. The stock market, which is the best leading indicator we have, seems to be saying that they are wrong.

The significance of these pessimistic predictions is that, at some point, they could cause Mr. Carter to feel prematurely that he can't just stand there but must do something. If he can manage to ignore them, and remain the prisoner of policies that are politically irksome and ideologically uncongenial, he may come out a hero. This would be a "windfall profit" for him—and the fact that many will think it "unfair" will not, one suspects, inhibit his glad acceptance of it.

Mr. Kristol is Henry Luce Professor of Urban Values at NYU, a Senior Fellow of the American Enterprise Institute and a member of the Journal's Board of Contributors.

Reprinted by permission of Irving Kristol from the *Wall Street Journal*, April 13, 1979.

19

Fed Plan to Slow Money Growth Further Is Signaled in Policy Report to Congress

By Richard J. Levine
Staff Reporter of The Wall Street Journal

WASHINGTON — The Federal Reserve Board delivered its new semiannual report on monetary policy to Congress yesterday in a snow-stricken capital that seemingly couldn't care less.

The 72-page report, required by the Humphrey-Hawkins Full Employment Act passed last year, signaled the Fed's intention to slow further the growth of the money supply in an effort to restrain inflation while avoiding recession.

"The objective of the Federal Reserve is to foster financial conditions conducive to a continued but more moderate economic expansion during 1979 that should permit a gradual winding down of inflation and the maintenance of the stronger position of the dollar," the report said. "At the same time, the current condition of general balance in the economy suggests that it should be possible to continue restraint to relieve inflationary pressures without triggering a recession."

This message was delivered to the Senate Banking Committee by Fed Chairman G. William Miller on a day when most of the federal government was closed because of the big weekend snowstorm. And committee chairman William Proxmire, the Wisconsin Democrat who proudly jogs to work, was the only one of the 15 members of the banking committee who was on hand to hear Mr. Miller's testimony. Also absent were the hordes of banking-industry lobbyists and journalists who usually gather when the Fed chief testifies on monetary policy.

Sen. Proxmire, who said afterwards that he held the hearing as scheduled because it was important and because nobody called and asked that it be postponed," told Mr. Miller he admired him for showing up. The central banker responded by declaring that the press could write that the hearing "took place in spite of the great snowstorm."

Major Disclosure

Aside from this exchange, however, Messrs. Miller and Proxmire were all business. The major disclosure in the report Mr. Miller gave was that the Federal Open Market Committee has lowered its targets for money-supply growth. For the year ahead, the Fed reduced the target range for growth of the narrowest money supply measure, or M1, which includes checking-account deposits plus cash in circulation, to 1½% to 4½% from the previous 2% to 6% range.

The target range for a broader money-supply measure, M2, which includes most bank savings and time deposits, was lowered to 5% to 8% from the previous 6½% to 9%. And the target for growth of a still broader measure, M3, which adds deposits at mutual savings banks and savings and loan institutions, was reduced to 6% to 9% from 7½% to 10%.

Chairman Miller told Sen. Proxmire the Open Market Committee believes these ranges "will bring to bear an appropriate degree of restraint in light of the current outlook for fiscal policy and the underlying strength of private demand in the economy."

Although the M1 growth range calls for "a marked deceleration" from the pace of recent years, the Fed chairman said, "this reflects in part an expectation that the shifting of funds to savings accounts in automatic transfer facilities and to NOW)negotiated order of withdrawal) accounts in New York State will continue to depress the growth" of checking-account deposits in 1979.

"Range of Uncertainty"

In fact, the Fed staff has projected that such switching around of money will dampen the growth of the narrowest money supply by "around three percentage points" this year, Mr. Miller said, though he conceded that "this projection carries a broad range of uncertainty." He also conceded that the central bank is puzzled by the recent shrinkage in the basic money supply and doesn't know if it is "a transitory phenomenon or one that is likely to persist for some time." This uncertainty, he added, is one reason why the M1 range is so broad.

The Fed has been reporting its long-term money supply targets to Congress on a quarterly basis since 1975. The Humphrey-Hawkins act requires only semiannual reports, but it requests a broader array of information.

Yesterday's Fed report was divided into three chapters: The first is a detailed discussion of recent economic and financial developments; the second covers the objectives and plans of the Fed, including the new money-growth targets, and the final chapter deals with the relationship of the Fed's plans to the Carter administration's economic goals.

The task of relating the Fed's plans to the administration's plans is a complicated one, the Fed said. But it insisted that "at this juncture, the monetary growth ranges and the administration's 1979 economic goals appear to be reasonably consistent."

Moreover, it said, "the output-price mix in the administration's 1979 forecast appears attainable if there is reasonable compliance with the wage-price standards and as long as there aren't any untoward shocks, such as an unanticipated surge in food or energy prices."

The Carter administration expects "real" gross national product, the total output of goods and services adjusted for inflation, to increase 3.3% this year after last year's 3.9% expansion. It has forecast that consumer prices will rise 7.4% this year after climbing 9% in 1978.

Assessing the economic outlook, the Fed said it foresees, as does the administration, "a moderation of economic growth in the year ahead." It said that the "absence of distortions and imbalances" in the economy indicates "that it should be possible to slow the pace of the expansion—and thereby relieve inflationary pressures — without prompting a recession." However, it warned, "any further acceleration of inflation or the occurrence of severe shortages of critical commodities, such as oil, would imperil this outcome."

As for specific sectors of the economy, the central bank expects a moderate decline in home building, a slower rate of growth in capital investment and less vigorous consumer spending in the year ahead.

Unemployment, the Fed said, should rise slightly from its current 5.8% level while inflation should slow somewhat. But the report indicated that the Fed's economists aren't at all confident that the wage-price spiral will slow. "Uncertainties will remain as a result of highly volatile and largely exogenous factors, such as farm prices and oil prices," it said.

Today Mr. Miller will make the same report on monetary policy and the economy to the House Banking Committee, where it's expected more lawmakers will be in attendance. In July, the Fed will issue a new monetary policy report that will include "preliminary ranges" for money-supply growth in 1980.

Reprinted by permission of the *Wall Street Journal.* © Dow Jones & Company, Inc., 1979. All Rights Reserved.

20
Can the Fed Stem the Tide?

By KAREN W. ARENSON

Tight money. That was the message the Federal Reserve Board was sending Nov. 1 when it jacked up the discount rate by a full point to a record 9½ percent. The foreign-exchange and stock markets here and abroad heard and responded, their rebound reflecting a belief that the Federal Government was finally going to curb inflation, whatever the cost.

Yet despite soaring interest rates, the economy remains stubbornly buoyant, and so does inflation. In the last week, the markets have had second thoughts about the program's potential for success. And there is a growing concern among some economists that monetary policy has become less effective, if not impotent, as a result of the Federal Reserve Board's own program to insulate one major segment of the economy — the housing market — from tight money.

"The Federal Reserve has adopted specific measures that impede its own effect," observes Henry Kaufman, economist and senior partner at Salomon Brothers.

As a result of changes in the money market, says Albert M. Wojnilower, managing director and economist at First Boston Corporation, "if you are looking for a rationing in credit, it can't be done around the present level of rates."

The Fed's now controversial program, unveiled in June, permitted savings institutions to offer six-month certificates of deposit with floating interest rates, pegged slightly above the rates on six-month Treasury bills. The higher rates have made the certificates more attractive to investors than T-bills and thus have drawn a flood of deposits back to the mortgage-making institutions.

Some economists, such as David A. Levine of Sanford C. Bernstein & Company, think that the implications of the changes in the financial system triggered by the savings certificate program could be so disastrous that Washington may have to ban it.

But most economists are more worried now about the impact of the new certificates on the Fed's ability to work a tight money strategy. If restrictive monetary policy is to slow economic growth — and thus curb inflation — tighter credit has to cause some segment of the economy to lessen its demand for funds and to cut its activity.

Traditionally, housing has been the fall guy in a period of tight credit. But housing activity is continuing at a strong pace, and no other segment of the economy appears to be as vulnerable to higher rates as construction and mortgages have been. Although, as Robert Solomon, a senior fellow at the Brookings Institution points out, "Just because the major impact has been on housing, doesn't mean there is zero effect elsewhere."

In the past, when the Fed tightened credit and sent interest rates up, every segment of the economy from the consumer to business and Government had to pay more for money. But where other borrowers appeared to be able to absorb higher rates without shutting down, the housing industry, which typically commands about one-quarter of available credit in the United States, got virtually knocked out of the capital markets.

This happened not because home buyers refused to pay higher rates for mortgages. Rather, savings institutions, which make most mortgages, were not allowed to pay high enough interest rates on deposits to hold and attract funds for making new mortgages; investors could obtain higher interest from Treasury bills and other market instruments. That withdrawal of funds from savings institutions in favor of high-yielding investments is a process called disintermediation.

To cushion the severe impact of disintermediation on housing, the Federal Reserve Bank, working with the Federal Home Loan Bank Board, devised the savings certificate plan by removing the artificial ceilings on the rates savings institutions could pay for deposits.

The certificates, which now account for about $22 billion in the savings banks, have apparently succeeded in keeping mortgage money flowing despite high interest rates, and that has been widely applauded. Deposit growth at savings institutions, which had slowed to less than 8 percent before the new certificates were introduced, has risen to 11 percent since then, according to a recent report by Bernstein & Company.

A gleeful Robert McKinney, chairman of the Federal Home Loan Bank Board, notes, "The housing market has not collapsed as it otherwise would have."

But if the certificates have successfully cushioned housing so far, no one can tell yet what the longer-term impact of those certificates will be, and concerns are beginning to surface.

As Mr. Kaufman puts it, "We are in uncharted waters. Our historical benchmarks have crumbled."

Publicly, some members of the Federal Reserve Board are expressing satisfaction that for the first time since World War II, housing is not bearing the full brunt of high interest rates.

Can the Fed Achieve Tight Money?

© 1978/79 by The New York Times Company. Reprinted by permission.

"This is an improvement, because the impact on the housing industry has been diminished and will be spread across the whole economy," says Henry C. Wallich, a governor of the Federal Reserve Board.

But sources close to the Fed say that Fed governors privately are expressing more concern, both over the inflationary impact of the strong housing industry and over the lessened impact of their own controls.

"The Fed does want to bring housing down," says one Washington economist with close contacts at the Fed. Housing is taking record amounts of money from the capital markets, he adds, at a time when the Fed would like to reduce total demand for capital.

However, if the Fed itself is not ready to express its doubts publicly, outside observers are. Among the questions they are asking are these:

● How high will the Federal Reserve Board have to push interest rates before there is any bite in economic growth? Says Mr. Kaufman, "In order for the Fed to slow credit creation, it must be willing to raise interest rates very high."

● How insulated is the housing industry really? Has the day of reckoning simply been postponed? Mr. Wojnilower of the First Boston Corporation, says, "If there is a squeezing out in the credit markets, housing will still carry a sizable share, though maybe not as much as in the past."

● If housing activity is not curtailed so severely by higher interest rates, what other sectors of the economy will suffer — and how much — in order to reduce economic growth? "Housing made it easy for the Fed to be tough guys in the past," says Paul Samuelson, Institute Professor at the Massachusetts Institute of Technology.

Although the housing industry itself amounts to only about 5 percent of gross national product, the decline in residential construction accounted for 40 to 60 percent of the decline in the G.N.P. in the last two recessions, according to the Bernstein report. The cutback in housing had a ripple effect that was enough to set off a slowdown in the general economy.

But today monetary restraint is apparently not taking hold. In recent weeks, the Federal Reserve has pushed interest rates up to record levels, with little indication that they are causing any real slowdown in the economy. With funds still available to all sectors of the economy, the Fed is now largely dependent on rates getting too high to be palatable, a point that apparently has not yet been reached. Nor will the high liquidity — a substantial amount of available cash — of corporate America make that sector likely to feel a pinch very quickly. No one knows where a crunch will come, since there is little experience from which to draw.

There is a profusion of views on what will happen next to the economy. Forecasts of the future course of the bank

In the past, higher interest rates hit housing hardest but they did the job; now the industry seems to be insulated.

certificates and the ebullience of the housing market help separate those economists forecasting strong growth ahead, from those looking for slower growth, or those anticipating a recession.

Mr. Wojnilower and Mr. Kaufman are among those who say the economy cannot be slowed without much higher interest rates. But others point to factors such as state usury laws that they believe should come into play to slow the growth of credit. And as before, it appears that mortgage money will be the first to dry up notwithstanding the new certificates.

Another potential obstacle to the continued health in housing could come where mortgage rates could rise too high for homebuyers. Mortgage rates soared to an unprecedented 10¾ percent in California last week. Surprisingly, even this rate appears to have deterred few borrowers, although savings and loan association executives including Alan Rothenberg, senior vice president at Citizens Savings and Loan Association in San Francisco, say they have begun to see the first signs of lower mortgage demand. Yet no matter how high mortgage rates may go, if people think that inflation and the price of a home will rise even faster, they will still be willing to pay the higher rates.

But even if home buyers remain willing to pay higher mortgage rates, lenders may find more and more of them unqualified to carry such expensive mortgages. Higher rates push up the monthly payments on a mortgage, and at some point borrowers may find they simply do not earn enough to meet such hefty monthly payments. The preponderance of the two-income family, however, has raised the amount of payments that a family can carry; this is one reason rates have been able to rise as far as they have. But Mr. Sumichrast estimates that each 1 percent rise in rates requires an extra $2,000 in income to support it, and knocks about 3 million potential borrowers out of the mortgage market. If this impact has not yet put a crimp in the market, many observers think it will eventually.

Yet another scenario is offered by Bernstein analysts. They predict that many of the savings banks issuing 30-year mortgages financed with high-priced six-month certificate funds will find their profit margins squeezed substantially. And some, particularly in states with usury laws that hold down the amounts that can be charged on mortgages, may face losses. Banking analysts anticipate that to prevent a crisis, the same regulatory authorities who created the certificates will ban them.

Of course, if the institutions who can not charge enough on mortgages either stop accepting six-month deposits, or take them but simply place the money in higher-yielding investments, they may not run into trouble.

But Mr. Levine of Bernstein points out that there are relatively few institutions following these strategies. "If even one-third of the less profitable institutions adopt the wrong strategy, there will be trouble," he says.

"In the past, the monetary brakes tended to lock when we used them, and it took the next 18 months to knock the dents out of our economic car," says Lyle E. Gramley, a member of the Council of Economic Advisers. "If the banks shave the rates they are paying on the certificates just a bit, rather than shutting off the certificates abruptly we might have a mild impact."

In fact, many of the housing start forecasts coming out now call for housing starts to drop somewhat next year. The Commerce Department this week estimated that there would be a rate of about 1.65 million new units next year, and George Hanc, chief economist and senior vice president of the National Association of Mutual Savings Banks is predicting a rate of about 1.7 million units. While this is clearly a drop from the 2 million rate forecast for this year, the decline is still well below the 700,000 unit drop in the 1973-1974 recession, and the certificates are considered a major factor in this.

Not everyone goes along with the soft landing theory. Mr. Kaufman of Salomon Brothers, for example, reasons that the speculative froth built into the California market could cause prices there to fall especially hard once the market turns.

21
INTEREST RATES: A BARGAIN AT 10%?

Throughout the fall, interest rates in the U.S. have been soaring. Banks and businesses are now borrowing money from each other at interest rates more than one and a half times as high as those of a year ago. Buyers of new homes are signing up for mortgage loans at a record average interest rate of just under 10%. Even the U.S. Treasury was forced to pay 9.36% in order to find purchasers for $2.7 billion of new two-year bonds issued in late November — the highest rate that the federal government has had to pay on any bond since the Civil War.

Journalists and economists seem to agree that the rapidly climbing rates have been caused by the policies adopted by "the Fed" — the Federal Reserve Board.

Critics of the Fed deplore the high costs imposed on borrowers and are especially concerned about potential cutbacks in housing construction. The Fed's supporters applaud the higher rates as an effective step to reduce the rate of inflation and to attract foreign money to the U.S. But both agree that Fed policy is primarily responsible for the soaring rates.

A careful look at what's actually going on, however, reveals quite a different set of conclusions: the record interest rates are mainly a reflection of the high level of inflation; they do not pose much of an additional burden for borrowers, beyond that caused by inflation; and they haven't come about as a result of intentional Fed policy.

In this area, as in others, it is a mistake to overestimate governmental control over what happens in a capitalist economy. In November,

President Carter did announce his intention to have the Fed raise interest rates as an anti-inflationary measure; if carried out, such a policy would increase the risk of recession. But it is too soon to see the results of those policies, and in any case, the administration's actions have been too small, so far, to

---

For borrowers, high inflation leads to a willingness to pay high interest rates; for lenders, it leads to an insistence on high interest rates.

---

have a dramatic effect on interest rates. Today's high rates result from longer-term, less planned, economic forces.

The Dual Nature of Interest Rates:

Interest rates are the price that borrowers pay for the use of money. Because there are many different kinds of borrowing, there are many different interest rates (see box, p. 5). For the most part, however, these rates move up and down together, so that it makes sense to talk about what is happening to the level of interest rates in general.

The level of interest rates results from the interactions of a wide range of factors. Anything that affects borrowers' desire to obtain funds or lenders' willingness to make funds available — that is, anything that affects either the demand for loans or the supply of money to lend — will affect the level of interest rates.

Interest rates are a cause as well as an effect of economic change. By making borrowing more or less expensive, and by making lending more or less rewarding, they influence how much borrowing people and businesses want to, and are able to, undertake.

The dual nature of interest rates is crucial to understanding their role in the economy. On the one hand, the level of interest rates is like a *thermometer* — it *registers* or measures what is happening in the economy. On the other hand, the interest rate level is like a *thermostat* — it *regulates* the amount of borrowing, and therefore to some extent the level of production and employment as well.

Thermostat for the Fed?

The most common explanation for the high level of interest rates focuses on their thermostatic function. According to this interpretation, interest rates are high because the Fed has taken steps to make them high. Why? Because higher interest rates will lead to less borrowing by consumers, by potential home-buyers, by businesses, and even by state and local governments — and therefore to less total spending in the economy, which should mean less inflation. Furthermore, high interest rates in the U.S. will encourage multinational corporations and rich individuals to move more of their money from bank ac-

---

Dollars & Sense magazine, 38 Union Sq., Room 14, Somerville, MA 02143 (monthly, $7.50/year).

counts overseas to bank accounts in this country, improving the U.S. balance of payments.

In short, the Fed is generally thought to have turned up the interest rate thermostat in order to help fight inflation and to aid in the defense of the dollar. But is this really what's behind the recent rise in interest rates? The Fed's policies are only one of numerous factors affecting the level of interest rates. And there are three good reasons for thinking that at the present, other factors are more important.

First, at least up through early November (for later periods, it's still too soon to tell), it appears that the Fed was not reducing the amount of money available to banks for lending, which is its primary method for making interest rates rise.

Second, the fact that something else was going on is indicated by the continuing expansion of every major kind of borrowing. In early November, the *Wall Street Journal* reported that in spite of mortgage rates exceeding 10% in many parts of the country, "bankers say they are still being bombarded with loan applications from long lines of eager home buyers."

A record amount of consumer credit ($25.9 billion) was extended in October, and at the end of that month consumer installment credit outstanding was up 20% from a year earlier. Meanwhile, corporate demand for bank loans seems to be, if anything, accelerating. If the Fed was trying to hold down borrowing by making credit too expensive, it was remarkably ineffective.

Third, a better explanation for high interest rates is readily available: the high and rising rate of inflation.

Or Thermometer for Inflation?

For borrowers, high inflation leads to a willingness to pay high interest rates. Consider families thinking of buying houses: if they expect that houses will be considerably more expensive next year, they will want to buy now, even if this means paying a high rate of interest to get mortages. Or consider a business thinking about borrowing to build a new plant: the plant will be built at today's costs, while the goods produced in it will be sold at next year's higher prices. Again, a high rate of inflation increases the willingness to borrow, even at high interest rates.

But why would banks or private investors lend money, if they expect that they will be repaid in future dollars worth considerably less than the dollars they loan? The answer is that lenders *will* be reluctant to lend — unless they obtain a rate of interest greater than the expected rate of inflation. Thus for lenders, high inflation leads to an insistence on high interest rates.

To determine the impact of interest rates on the amount of borrowing and spending in the economy, it is necessary to eliminate the effect of inflation. Doing this is simple in principle: just subtract the rate of inflation from the rate of interest; the difference is what economists call the "real" interest rate. Most economists agree that it is the "real" interest rate (the actual rate corrected for inflation) that affects the demand for borrowing.

A good rule of thumb is that the actual interest rate will normally be about two percentage points above the rate of inflation — that is, the real interest rate is usually about 2%. Lately, it has been lower than that: subtracting a 9% rate of inflation from a 10% rate of interest gives a real interest rate of only 1%. By this rough measure, borrowing money is now cheaper than usual, not more expensive.

From this angle of vision, it's easy to see that the current record levels of interest rates are primarily a thermometer, recording the high rate of inflation in the economy — not a thermostat that has been set by the Fed to reduce the amount of borrowing and spending.

The Fed's Dilemma

The analogy that we've been using suggests a simple solution: when you don't like the reading on the thermometer, you adjust the thermostat. Unfortunately for those who manage it, the U.S. economy isn't so easy to manipulate. The Fed has allowed inflation and, therefore, interest rates to increase to their present levels because serious measures to bring them under control would have led to even worse problems.

If the Fed had, in the last year, made a major adjustment of its interest-rate thermostat and pushed up the real interest rate, the result would almost certainly have been a recession. Not only is a recession costly and painful for workers, but it is also a risky proposition for business. There is always a chance that a recession will get out of hand, threatening the stability of both the domestic and international economic systems as borrowers become unable to repay the debts they have accumulated, and as intensifying trade wars among the competing capitalist nations leave everyone worse off.

In short, last autumn's high and rising interest rates reflected the high level of inflation which the Fed has been reluctant to try to control, for fear that the cure would be worse than the disease. As the symptoms have gotten more severe, however, pressure has been building for the Fed to do something about inflation.

Although the Fed hasn't announced its intentions (it rarely does), one thing can be predicted with confidence: interest rates won't go down and stay down until the rate of inflation does. ■

Sources: *Wall Street Journal*, 11/2, 11/10, 11/27, 12/8/78; *Barron's*, 12/14/78; *Business Week*, 10/12, 12/18/78.

TWO, THREE, MANY INTEREST RATES

There are a bewildering array of different interest rates in the U.S. economy. Only a few are of direct concern to working people and consumers. Most are for the numerous varieties of lending and borrowing that take place among banks, corporations, governments and rich individuals.

In addition to the overall economic conditions that affect the general level of interest rates, the rate of interest on any particular loan depends upon a number of more specific factors: the length of time until repayment; the risk that the loan won't be repaid at all; the size of the loan, and the cost of administering it; the ease with which the lender can sell the borrower's I.O.U. to a third party in order to obtain cash; and in some cases, government laws and regulations.

Money placed in an ordinary savings account at a commercial bank gets 5% interest. For a small, short-term personal loan from a consumer finance company, a borrower may have to pay interest at a rate of more than 30%. Most other interest rates fall somewhere between these two extremes.

Depositors get higher interest rates at savings & loan associations, savings banks, or credit unions. And they receive more if they deposit $1,000 or more and agree not to withdraw it for a year, or, even better, up to eight years. The maximum rates that various categories of banks can pay on different kinds of deposits are limited by the Federal Reserve's "Regulation Q" — an arrangement that clearly works against the interest (!) of small savers.

How Much Will It Cost?

The cheapest form of personal borrowing is generally for *home mortgages* — there is little risk for the bank (if you don't keep paying, they get the house!), and administrative costs are low compared to the size of the loan. The security that cars provide to banks isn't quite as good, and administrative costs are a larger percentage of the loan, so *auto loans* cost somewhat more. A bit more expensive are *personal loans from banks* (no collateral involved), and even worse is borrowing done with a *credit card*. The most expensive form of borrowing (leaving aside illegal loan sharks) is *personal loans from consumer finance companies* such as Household Finance or Beneficial Finance.

Among the most widely reported interest rates from the world of higher finance are: the *Federal Reserve discount rate*, which the Fed charges to banks that come to it in need of funds; the *federal funds rate*, which one bank charges another for the use of its money for a single day; and the *prime rate*, which the big banks charge their best corporate customers.

There are also a large number of more specialized I.O.U.'s such as: large ($100,000+) *certificates of deposit* sold by big banks; *commercial paper* (short-term I.O.U.'s from finance companies and other big corporations); *corporate bonds* (a major way that big companies raise money from pension funds and rich individuals); *U.S. government securities* (called bills, notes or bonds depending on the time between borrowing and repayment); and *state and local government bonds* (on which the interest is generally exempt from taxation).

Here are the latest values available in mid-December for a number of interest rates:

Savings account at a commercial bank	5.00%
Savings account at a savings & loan association	5.25%
U.S. government savings bond (Series E)	6.00%
Savings certificate at a savings & loan ($1,000+, 4-6 years)	7.50%
U.S. Treasury bond (30 year)	8.98%
Federal Reserve discount rate	9.50%
U.S. Treasury bill (90 day)	9.59%
Mortgage rate (average on new homes)	9.86%
Federal funds rate	9.88%
Certificates of deposit ($100,000, 180 day)	11.25%
Prime rate	11.50%
Mastercharge or Visa credit card loan ($500)	18.00%
Finance company (Massachusetts, $400 for six months)	30.44%

22
THE LAST DAYS OF THE BOOM

PAUL A. SAMUELSON

Where do we stand? On the verge of a slump? Or is the economy overheated, with even worse inflation still ahead?

There is no one view concerning all this. There never is. But I find the present lack of consensus remarkable. It requires close study.

Begin with the knowable facts. Last year ended with a bang, not a whimper. Real GNP grew at almost a 7 per cent annual rate at the year-end. Most experts had been expecting more like a 2 per cent rate.

The new year brought snow. No big deal in that. And no surprise that the first-quarter real GNP growth looked weak. In recent weeks, though, the pace seems to have quickened. From autos to machine tools, the word comes that sales are strong.

Prices are more than strong. And I speak not of oil and food alone. Firms find they can pass along all cost increases to the buyer.

Congressmen and voters act surprised. That shows how little thought they gave to what their own acts would do to push up prices. Payroll taxes were raised for 1979. So was the minimum wage. Since the Fed has in recent years created enough money for us to spend, and since we are learning how to turn over each unit of our money faster, the flame of cost rises meets with enough tinder to keep a pretty hot fire going.

MADE IN WASHINGTON: Why then do most economists see a recession just ahead? Some argue from strength to weakness. Things are just too good to last, they guess. Consumers have spent for so long, have gone so deeply into debt, that they surely will have to pull in their belts.

Firms now scramble for inventory. As each supplier becomes slow in filling orders, companies turn to other sources, engaging in multiple ordering that imparts a false sense of strength in over-all demand. The rosy hue on entrepreneurial cheeks is the flush of fever, not of sustainable good health.

I monitor some three dozen forecasters, those bank and research teams with past records worth watching. Most of them, I find, see considerable natural strength in the private American economy despite the fact that our present expansion is now a veritable Grandma Moses in age, if not a Methuselah.

The reason they expect a U.S. recession before Election Day 1980 lies mostly in

> *The rosy hue on entrepreneurial cheeks is the flush of fever, not of good health.*

their confidence that the government—the Administration, Congress and the Federal Reserve—will act to cool off the accelerating inflation now at work.

Loudest in singing this tune are the monetarists. What sex is to the single-minded Freudian, the money supply is to the monetarists. Why waste time with 36 experts and 57 sets of statistics when it is the drumbeat of Federal Reserve money creation that alone calls the tune?

If only Freud could deliver the goods he promises. My colleague Robert Solow has termed monetarism an advertising campaign still in search of its product. I must spend much of my time studying the many forces that alter the velocity of circulation of our money supply because sad experience has shown that predictions based solely on the money aggregates suffer needlessly large errors.

Money does matter. The fact that its growth has slowed down markedly since last fall is one of many factors to weigh. But how much weight? At this time there are several different schools of monetarists. Amen to that. There is more to learn from their disagreements than from their *simpliste* formulas.

Fed chairman G. William Miller is not a monetarist. Still, to explain why he has been as slow as he has been in putting on the credit brakes to fight inflation, one must take into account his perception—a correct one—that vocal monetarists will be blaming him for the next recession if it comes in the wake of a declining growth rate for the money supply.

Those who believe that a recession is too high a price to pay for a crusade against inflation are grateful to the monetarists. Like the sight of the piano soloist crossing hands at dramatic crescendos, we face the spectacle of Carter's Keynesian advisers putting pressure on the Fed to tighten up further on credit and money, at the same time that conservative monetarists and full-employment advocates are both opposing those moves.

ELECTION TIMING: Mr. Carter has a special problem—that of getting re-elected. Time is getting short for him to tuck in a mild recession, thereby damping down inflation, and be back in a vigorous recovery during the half year before November 1980.

I know the government has the powers to create a recession—a growth recession or a full-fledged one. I suspect it will find itself increasingly with the will to use those powers. So it is my guess that the natural vigor of the private economy will yield in the end.

Though that needn't be fatal to his cause, it won't be good for Candidate Carter. It will be good for the Republicans—and not bad for Teddy Kennedy.

Copyright 1979 by Newsweek, Inc. All Rights reserved. Reprinted by permission.

23

By Milton Friedman

The Fed: At It Again

The Federal Reserve System's propensity to swing from one extreme to the other has produced a cyclical pattern in my columns on monetary policy. Most of the time, I criticize the Fed for increasing the quantity of money too rapidly and thereby promoting inflation. But once during every cycle, the Fed shifts course. When it does, it steps on the brake too hard, and I find myself criticizing the Fed for increasing the quantity of money too slowly. That time has arrived in this cycle.

THE INFLATION PHASE

From April 1975 to September 1978, the quantity of money (as measured by M_2, currency plus all deposits at commercial banks other than large CD's) grew at the rate of 10 per cent per year.* Since the end of World War II, M_2 grew that fast during only one prior period of equal length—from February 1970 to July 1973, when it grew at the annual rate of 10.4 per cent. By no coincidence, an inflationary explosion followed the earlier period of rapid growth and did not reach its peak until a year and a half later, in December 1974, when the consumer price index was more than 12 per cent higher than in December 1973.

Similarly, by no coincidence, an inflationary explosion followed the recent period of rapid monetary growth. In December 1978, prices were 9 per cent higher than in December 1977. Though inflation has not reached the earlier peak, it is still accelerating. Even if rapid monetary growth does not resume, the current inflation is not likely to reach its peak until late 1979 or early 1980, by which time it may well challenge the earlier record.

In 1973, the Fed finally slowed monetary growth, at first mildly, then, in 1974, sharply—that was the most recent occasion on which I criticized the Fed for overdoing it.

In October 1978, the Fed finally slowed monetary growth, this time sharply from the outset. M_2 has grown at the annual rate of 3.3 per cent from September 1978 to January, the latest month for which data are available.

That rate is fine as an ultimate target, but it reflects too steep a decline. So low a rate for a few months may do no harm, but it would be a major mistake to keep monetary growth that low very much longer.

THE PRESENT DANGER

Past history demonstrates that the danger of unduly restrictive policy is not an idle one. That is exactly what occurred in 1974, as it has, repeatedly, during the whole of the Fed's history. The golden mean has had a way of escaping the Fed, which has tended to be extremist—either pumping up the money supply too rapidly, or holding it down too rigidly.

An overly restrictive policy that produced a severe recession would, after a delay, drive inflation down more than a moderate policy. However, that result would be bad, not good, for two reasons. First, past inflation and the long-term commitments most of us have entered into make it desirable to unwind inflation gradually, not abruptly. Second, any favorable effect on inflation would probably be temporary—as it was after the restrictive monetary policy of 1973-1975. Sooner or later—and with a 1980 election looming, no doubt sooner—the recession would produce a sharp reversal of policy, another swing to the opposite extreme, and we would be off on the inflationary road again.

WHERE DO WE GO FROM HERE?

Hope springs eternal. Perhaps this time the Fed will promptly end its overrestrictive policy, without going to the other extreme. Perhaps it will foster moderate monetary growth and keep at it long enough finally to get rid of inflation and provide the basis for sound growth. That would call for a gradual and steady reduction of monetary growth over something like a five-year period to a rate of about 3 to 5 per cent per year.

Unfortunately such an eminently desirable outcome is not likely. The patience, perseverance and foresight required to initiate and maintain any such policy are hard to come by in the political atmosphere of Washington.

A more likely outcome is that the Fed will repeat its past performance: maintain an unduly restrictive monetary policy too long, then swing sharply to an overexpansionary policy. That would produce some slowing of inflation as a delayed reaction to initial restriction. It would then be followed by another inflationary explosion—perhaps in 1981 or 1982.

---

*For reasons given in my column, "Money Watchers Beware" (Newsweek, Oct. 30), I use only M_2 and omit reference to the other most widely watched monetary aggregate, M_1, currency plus demand deposits.

Copyright 1979 by Newsweek, Inc. All Rights Reserved. Reprinted by permission.

24

Proposal for an Anti-Inflation Package

Sidney Weintraub

A spillover from Proposition 13 in California has been a revival of the old-time religion of slashing government expenditures and banishing inflation from the land. This is a monstrous delusion. Incomes policy will be imperative even under Spartan budgets.

Suppose we succumbed to the present fervor for curtailing government spending? With current pay trends, any prospective cutback would be dwarfed in a short time by the income bulge. Economy-wide, employee compensation is running about $1.3 trillion per annum. An 8 percent annual pay hike will add $100 billion. At 10 percent the figure is $130 billion. In five years the pay balloon will compound to $600-$800 billion—about half the current aggregate and well above projected federal outlays of $500 billion for fiscal 1979.

Support has materialized for a tax-based incomes policy (TIP), as originally proposed by Dr. Henry Wallich and myself, and for the variants of Drs. Okun and Seidman. Public awareness of the ideas has widened. In the United Kingdom a version of the concept is on the parliamentary docket for enactment.

On the premise that the "carrot" and the "stick" will both influence conduct, the following package reflects my own concept of the proper legislative design for TIP.

1. *Amend the Davis-Bacon Act.* According to law, prevailing wages must be paid on current government or government-assisted construction. The government is thus already operating an incomes policy. Labor and business now lobby for contracts which create jobs, and shortly thereafter there are strikes for higher pay, involving raids on the public purse. A new clause, however, can require that, over the life of the contract, average pay increases for all personnel are not to exceed 5 percent per annum.

A construction authorization incomes policy (CAIP), should help hold the line on construction excesses. Penalties can include disallowing overpayments on the corporate income tax form, and remanding sums equal to the excess above 5 percent to the government.

2. *Amend government procurement contracts.* CAIP can be applied to government procurement generally, especially to defense contracts, where pay increases are paid for by the public.

3. *Reduce personal income taxes.* Reduce the personal income tax by a credit of 2 percent on employee compensation, with a minimum tax reduction of $200 and a maximum of $300 on all incomes rising by 5 percent or less per annum. This borrows from the original Okun proposal. Largest percentage benefits would redound to wage earners' advantage and help induce wage restraint.

4. *The (modified) Wallich-Weintraub TIP.* All business firms employing 500 or more employees or having an annual wage and salary bill of five million or more, are subject to the following tax provisos:

a. For average employee wages that increase by not less than 3 percent nor more than 5 percent per annum, the firm's tax rate will be lowered by (at least) 2 percent below the standard corporate tax rate.

b. If the average annual pay increase exceeds 5 percent, the firm will be subject to progressive penalty tax rates.

Essentially, (b) is the original Wallich-Weintraub TIP. Proviso (a) is inserted (from Dr. Seidman) with the 3 percent floor intended to preclude greater rewards to firms that beat down pay levels; it dispels any possible allegation that TIP is a plan to "create slave labor." It should also encourage pay moderation to foster price stability. Restriction to large firms should render the proposal administratively feasible. Others may prefer to include only firms that are even larger in size.

5. *TIP-CAP: A productivity bonus.* Firms reporting average value-added per employee surpassing the economywide 2-3 percent trend of the past might be

SIDNEY WEINTRAUB is Professor of Economics, University of Pennsylvania, and co-editor of the *Journal of Post Keynesian Economics.*

© 1978. Reprinted from *Challenge:* The Magazine of Economic Affairs by permission of M. E. Sharpe, Inc., White Plains, New York.

granted a pay prerogative above the 5 percent norm. Calculations would have to be made for average product corrected for price level inflation (CAP, or Corrected Average Product). This would be a bit more complicated than TIP calculations, but would involve only simple subtractions (of cost of materials from sales receipts) and applying standard price level indexes as a deflator.

This would be a productivity bonus. Perhaps one-third of the superior productivity increase above 6 percent might be added to the 5 percent standard increase. Not all of the productivity gain should be commanded by employees, however, for the firms should be motivated to reduce prices.

6. *TIP supplements*. Various supplements can be attached to TIP-CAP to assure compliance. For example, certain firms might be in cash-flow financial straits if their 5 percent settlement offer were rejected by labor, resulting in a strike. Such firms might be cleared for a government-guaranteed loan to meet fixed charges. Clearly, loan availability would have to be monitored to prevent collusion.

Labor, in rejecting a settlement at 5 percent (or a trifle more) might be subject to penalties ranging from mild to stringent, depending on strike duration and the (vague) national interest. Labor specialists should promote this discussion.

7. *Amending the anti-trust laws*. To allay objections that prices are absolved from sanctions, the Federal Trade Commission (FTC) might be mandated to report quarterly on trends and profit margins, especially among the 2,000 largest firms, measured in terms of sales or employment.

Firms reporting extra productivity improvement should be expected to lower prices. Where there is evidence that they are not doing so, the FTC might be empowered to report and to seek remedial policies.

Profit margins have been declining. Until contrary evidence emerges, further action can be deferred.

8. *Government employees*. Average pay increases for federal employees would be limited to 5 percent per annum, with corrections every two or three years if the private sector trend exceeds this norm. State and local employees would be brought under the same 5 percent tent through the leverage of federal grants or other federal aid programs.

Conclusions

These appear to be the essential legislative provisos to accomplish a firmer match-up of money, wage and salary trends to the productivity norms. None of them does violence to the market economy; mostly, they invoke the tax laws and, confining them to the largest firms, they spell only minor complications. They are modest by way of intervention in the market system. If successful, they ought to capture the big prize of full employment without inflation. Over the past decade a workable policy of price level stabilization would have enhanced GNP by $50 to $150 billion per annum. Inflation drift will inflict equal or greater annual losses in the future.

Chancellor of the Exchequer Healey, in the United Kingdom, is reported to advocate a 5 percent ceiling on annual pay hikes. Sanctions involve denying government loans to firms that puncture the norm, and refraining from government purchases from violators.

The Healey program is a cousin of TIP, more attuned to the widespread nationalization of industry and capital market structure in the United Kingdom. The Healey program, if enacted, should practically subdue their rapid inflation. The recent 10 percent inflation rate under 10 percent pay hikes speaks volumes compared to the 25 percent rates under the 25 percent pay explosion of recent memory. England has learned some concrete incomes policy lessons from its hard knocks. We should not wait for catastrophic price bursts to complete our own education.

25

Can Tax-Based Incomes Policies Work?

As inflation has grown more and more serious, it has become fashionable to talk about a tax-based incomes policy (TIP) as a possible device to moderate it. I am very sympathetic to the idea of an incomes policy, but I find it difficult to see how TIP can be implemented. The following are the most difficult problems, as I view them. (The issues are thoroughly explored in *Curing Chronic Inflation*, Arthur M. Okun and George L. Perry, eds., Brookings Institution, 1978.)

Coverage. About 13 million firms filed federal tax returns in 1975, including 10.9 million sole proprietorships, 1.1 million partnerships, and 2.0 million corporations. In addition, there were 0.5 million returns of nonprofit organizations and over 78,000 governmental units. Most of the business firms have no employees, many report no net income, and only a relatively small number of large businesses keep personnel records. Yet, if a tax penalty (for firms that grant too high a wage increase) or a tax subsidy (for firms that hold wage increases down) is to be designed, the law must be explicit about how every one of these units is to be treated.

A penalty would be easier to administer than a subsidy, because it could be limited to large firms. But as I shall indicate below, I am not persuaded that it is feasible to measure average wage changes for all economic units in a manner that would be satisfactory for a tax-based wage penalty or subsidy.

As for the subsidy approach, I assume that we would not ask the average farmer, or the average corner drugstore owner, or most self-employed professionals who have a few employees, to report manhours on a tax return. Moreover, many firms with only a few employees might be denied a subsidy if they happened to shift to higher-paid workers. To avoid the problems that the small firms would have, the wage subsidy would probably be given to all employees in such establishments and to the owners as well. This is not fatal for the wage subsidy plan on administrative grounds, but it would mean that a substantial fraction, if not a majority, of all workers would get the subsidy whether they conformed with the wage guideline or not.

The economic unit. The unit for tax accounting purposes is a legal entity which, in our complex economy, often bears little relationship to the unit which enters into wage bargains with its employees. Large corporations generally file consolidated returns that include the operating results of many, but not necessarily all, of their subsidiaries. So far as wages are concerned, the branches or subsidiaries of a large firm in this country often bear no relationship to one another or to the parent firm. Accordingly, the rules would have to be flexible enough to permit the unit of calculation to be relevant to the wage-setting process. Under wage controls, the business firms themselves made this decision and I assume the control agency could modify the decision if it was deemed necessary. But for purposes of a wage subsidy or penalty, definite rules would have to be set out either in the legislation or in the regulations so that labor and management knew exactly what wage bargains they were dealing with. However, I am not aware of any usable guides to the writing of such rules.

It would be necessary to prescribe other rules to make inter-year wage comparisons for new firms, mergers, spinoffs, sales of facilities, changes in product mix, and other types of abnormal situations in which the wage data would not accurately reflect changes in average wages. This is what is referred to in tax language as "the excess profits tax problem": that is, the problem of estimating the tax base when it depends upon events and conditions in two or more adjacent years. The decisions made for the excess profits taxes in the United States were the subject of extensive and time-consuming litigation every time the tax was used, and no one on the government or the business side was ever satisfied. I can imagine a set of arbitrary rules that economists or tax administrators might agree to, but Congress would find it difficult to accept such rules. (One example: it has been suggested that, for new firms, a base year wage structure might be constructed from averages for other firms in the same industry. But the only data of this type that do exist are those of the Bureau of Labor Statistics and they could not possibly be applied to a particular firm.) In the end, the legislation would be complex and, like the excess profits tax, would impose unforeseen costs on business which would lead to further legislation and litigation to moderate those costs.

Timing of penalty or subsidy. From an administrative or compliance standpoint, it would be much easier to impose a penalty or provide a subsidy after the end of the accounting period. If the proposal is for a penalty based on profits, it should be possible to rely on the business firm to take the penalty into account in its wage decisions.

Just the opposite is true for a subsidy to workers accepting a wage increase below the guideline percentage. To appeal to workers to accept the constraint, the subsidy must be prospective and must be incorporated into the current tax withholding tables so that the workers will have immediate

© 1978. Reprinted from *Challenge:* The Magazine of Economic Affairs by permission of M. E. Sharpe, Inc., White Plains, New York.

tangible evidence that their disposable income will not be impaired by the policy. (Two sets of withholding tables would be required, but this is only a minor complication compared to the others.)

The basic problem is that labor and management would find it extremely difficult to incorporate a prospective subsidy into their wage bargaining and, incidentally, to come to an agreement in a few weeks before the beginning of each year. Unless the bargaining unit were coterminous with the unit for determining the subsidy, no worker or group of workers would know whether the deal they made would actually trigger the subsidy until negotiations were completed with the other bargaining units in the same firm. Management would have the same problems: how could it be sure that the construction workers would accept a wage increase that, together with the agreement with coal miners, would trigger a subsidy to both groups?

I conclude that a retrospective penalty on profits based on wage changes is feasible. For prospective subsidies to workers, there are numerous pitfalls and I frankly do not see how they can be overcome to the satisfaction of labor and management.

Prices. The original tax-based incomes policies were to increase profits taxes of firms with excessive wage increases, so that prices were not involved at all. Others have suggested that, to be even-handed, it would be necessary to provide penalties against firms with above-average price increases. Unfortunately, any kind of tax penalty or subsidy that depends upon a change in average prices of particular firms is simply impractical. All the problems of constructing price indexes would emerge—treatment of new products, quality change, measurement of costs to be passed through, etc.—and there is really no solution to most of them. I leave it to the reader to judge whether a tax-based incomes policy can be applied to wages and not to prices.

Controls versus tax-based incomes policies. I believe it is not productive to argue whether tax-based incomes policies are another form of controls or not. The question is which approach is feasible, and what are their relative costs.

It is true that a tax-based incomes policy can be disregarded by any firm and its workers if they wish. But the rules and regulations must be written so that all economic units in the country understand them and make their decisions accordingly. Even if it is agreed that some of the rules must be arbitrary, I doubt that it will be possible to arrive at such arbitrary rules through the tax legislative process as we know it today.

Under controls, Congress avoids the hard decisions and lets the controlling agency make the arbitrary rules. One reason why controls seem to be more acceptable than tax penalties or subsidies is that relatively few firms are ever involved in disputes under controls, whereas a tax penalty or a subsidy would apply to all or a large number of firms and the perceived hardships and disputes would be numerous. Both devices lead to capricious results, but I am at a loss to understand why their proponents believe that tax-based incomes policies would be more acceptable to labor, management, the public, and Congress.

JOSEPH A. PECHMAN
Director of Economic Studies, The Brookings Institution. The views expressed are the author's and do not reflect those of the officers, trustees, and other staff members of The Brookings Institution.

A Tax-Based Incomes Policy (TIP): What's It All About?

NANCY AMMON JIANAKOPLOS

SUBJECT corporations to higher corporate income tax rates if they give pay raises which are too large. This is the essence of a plan devised by Governor Henry C. Wallich of the Federal Reserve Board and Sidney Weintraub of the University of Pennsylvania.[1] Their proposal to use the tax system to curb inflation is called "TIP," an acronym for tax-based incomes policy. As inflation continues to plague the economy, many economists feel that the traditional tools of monetary and fiscal policy are inadequate to handle the situation and have recommended direct measures to stop wage and price increases.[2] The Wallich-Weintraub plan has received considerable attention as a policy measure which might be capable of dealing with the problem of inflation.[3]

Before adopting a program such as TIP, it is important to understand clearly how the proposal would operate and, more importantly, whether it would achieve the desired results. The first part of this article describes the functioning of TIP and the rationale for such a program as envisioned by Wallich and Weintraub. The rest of the article is devoted to an assessment of whether TIP would accomplish its stated objectives.

HOW WOULD TIP OPERATE?

According to the plan presented by Wallich and Weintraub, TIP would be centered on a single wage guidepost established by the Government.[4] The acceptable percentage wage increase could be set somewhere between the average increase in productivity throughout the economy (asserted to be around 3 percent) and some larger figure which incorporates all or part of the current rate of inflation. The ultimate aim of the guidepost is to bring wage increases in line with nationwide productivity increases.

The TIP guidepost is directed at wages only, although the tax is levied on corporate profits. The basic assumption behind TIP is that monetary and fiscal policies have been ineffective because they have not been able to prevent labor from obtaining wage increases in excess of productivity gains, even when there is significant unemployment in the economy. Furthermore, Wallich and Weintraub contend that empirical evidence supports the view that price in-

---

[1] Wallich and Weintraub first collaborated on this idea in Henry C. Wallich and Sidney Weintraub, "A Tax-Based Incomes Policy," *Journal of Economic Issues* (June 1971), pp. 1-19.

[2] See, for example, "Another Weapon Against Inflation: Tax Policy," *Business Week,* October 3, 1977, pp. 94-96; "Debate: How to Stop Inflation," *Fortune* (April 1977), pp. 116-20; Lindley H. Clark, Jr., "Uneasy Seers: More Analysts Predict New Inflation Spiral or Recession in 1978," *Wall Street Journal,* December 2, 1977.

[3] See, for example, U. S. Congress, Congressional Budget Office, *Recovery With Inflation,* July 1977, p. 40; U. S. Congress, Joint Economic Committee, *The 1977 Midyear Review of the Economy,* 95th Cong., 1st sess., September 26, 1977, p. 76; "Well-Cut Taxes Should Be Tailored," *New York Times,* December 21, 1977.

[4] Unless otherwise noted, all descriptions of TIP in this article are based on Wallich and Weintraub, "A Tax-Based Incomes Policy"; Henry C. Wallich, "Alternative Strategies for Price and Wage Controls," *Journal of Economic Issues* (December 1972), pp. 89-104; Henry C. Wallich, "A Plan for Dealing With Inflation in the U.S.," *Washington Post,* August 21, 1977; Sidney Weintraub, "An Incomes Policy to Stop Inflation," *Lloyds Bank Review* (January 1971), pp. 1-12; and Sidney Weintraub, "Incomes Policy: Completing the Stabilization Triangle," *Journal of Economic Issues* (December 1972), pp. 105-22.

Reprinted from Federal Reserve Bank of St. Louis *Review*, February, 1978.

creases have been a constant markup over unit wage increases. Therefore, if wage increases can be kept down, price increases will also be held down.

The corporate income tax system would be employed to enforce the TIP guidepost. Corporations which grant wage increases in excess of the guidepost would be subject to higher corporate income tax rates based on the amount that wage increases exceed the guidepost.

In order to understand how TIP would operate, consider the following example. Suppose the guidepost for wage increases is set at, say, 5 percent for a particular year. In the base year, Corporation A had a total wage bill of $100,000 and in the following year granted increases which brought its total wage bill to $108,000 — an 8 percent increase. Assuming no change in either the number or composition of the employees, this 8 percent increase is 3 percentage points above the guidepost. This excess would then be multiplied by a penalty number. If, for instance, the penalty was set at 2, the corporate tax rate of Corporation A would be increased by 6 percentage points (3 percentage point excess times penalty number of 2). Thus, instead of paying 48 percent of its profits in taxes, the existing corporate tax rate, Corporation A would have to pay 54 percent of its profits, as a penalty for acceding to "excessive" wage demands.

Wallich and Weintraub argue that because of competitive forces this additional tax could not be shifted forward to prices.[5] They, therefore, believe that such a tax penalty would cause corporations to deal more firmly with labor. In their view the penalty would ultimately restrain the rate of wage increases and, hence, reduce the rate of inflation.[6] Since wage increases would be curbed, corporations would not have higher costs to pass through in the form of price increases, thereby eliminating a major "cost-push" element of inflation. Furthermore, since the increases in incomes of workers would more closely approximate increases in productivity, there would be smaller increases in spending, reducing the "demand-pull" aspect of inflation.

Wallich and Weintraub acknowledge certain difficulties in computing the corporation's wage bill. One method which they believe would overcome many of these difficulties would be to construct an index of wages, rather than using the gross dollar figure. Using this method, wages, fringe benefits, and other related payments would be computed for each job classification and skill level and divided by the hours worked at each level. These wage figures would then be combined into an index weighted by the proportion of each of these classifications in the entire corporation. Changes in this index would then be compared to the guidepost in order to assess whether the corporation would be penalized.

Administrative problems are not neglected by Wallich and Weintraub. They recognize that the tax laws must be specific and "airtight" in order to avoid loopholes. However, it is argued that TIP would not involve establishing a new bureaucracy. Most of the data necessary to administer TIP are already collected for corporate income tax and employee payroll tax purposes.

One of the principal merits of TIP, in the view of Wallich and Weintraub, is that it would not interfere with the functioning of the market system. They argue that there would be no direct controls or distortions to the pricing mechanism. Firms would still be free to grant large wage demands, but would face the penalty of a higher corporate tax rate.

Rather than a short-term plan to curb inflation, TIP is envisioned to be a long-term means of reducing the rate of price increase. However, TIP is not intended to function by itself. Both Wallich and Weintraub see it as a supplement to "appropriate" monetary and fiscal policies. In addition, if labor contends that TIP would hold down wages while allowing profits to increase, Wallich proposes the implementation of an excess profits tax. This could be accomplished by increasing the basic corporate tax rate to keep the share of profits in national income constant.[7]

WOULD TIP WORK?

The TIP proposal has two principal objectives:

(1) to curb inflation, and

---

[5] See Richard A. Musgrave and Peggy B. Musgrave, *Public Finance In Theory and Practice* (New York: McGraw-Hill Book Company, 1973), Chapter 18, pp. 415-29, who contend that empirical evidence is inconclusive in determining whether the corporate income tax is shifted.

[6] Studies by Yehuda Kotowitz and Richard Portes, "The 'Tax on Wage Increases': A Theoretical Analysis," *Journal of Public Economics* (May 1974), pp. 113-32, and Peter Isard, "The Effectiveness of Using the Tax System to Curb Inflationary Collective Bargains: An Analysis of the Wallich-Weintraub Plan," *Journal of Political Economy* (May-June 1973), pp. 729-40, analyze the effect of TIP on an individual firm and conclude that theoretically TIP should lead to lower wage settlements for an individual firm.

[7] Other adjuncts proposed for TIP include a payroll tax credit designed to entice workers to accept lower wages. See Lawrence S. Seidman, "A Payroll Tax-Credit to Restrain Inflation," *National Tax Journal* (December 1976), pp. 398-412.

(2) to avoid interfering with the functioning of the market.

Given these aims of TIP, one can analyze whether TIP will, in fact, be able to accomplish its goals. Other issues raised by TIP, such as the costs of implementation and the ability of firms to avoid the tax penalty of TIP, will not be discussed here.[8]

Would TIP Curb Inflation?

TIP is based on the assumption that most of the inflation in the economy is of a "cost-push" nature. Inflation occurs, according to this framework, because labor is able to attain wage increases in excess of increases in productivity. Business is not capable of resisting, or finds it does not pay to resist, labor's demands. Faced with higher costs, businesses pass these costs through in the form of higher product prices. As prices rise, further wage increases are granted, forming the basis of a wage-price spiral. TIP is proposed as a measure which will intervene in this process and bring inflation to a halt.

As the Congressional Budget Office stated in a recent study, the assumption that inflation is the result of "cost-push" is "a conjectural notion at best."[9] A major challenge to the concept of "cost-push" rests on empirical evidence supporting an alternative theory of the cause of inflation. According to this other view, ongoing increases in the general price level (inflation) are primarily the result of excessive increases in the rate of monetary expansion.[10] Lags exist between the time when the money stock is increased and when prices rise. In this framework, the observed relationship between the rate of wage increase and the rate of price increase is explained as part of the adjustment process through which prices increase in response to increases in the money stock. This view does not deny the "cost-push" phenomenon, but contends that it is consistent with the view that inflation is ultimately caused by money growth.[11]

When the stock of money is increased faster than the rate of increase in production, people find themselves with larger cash balances than they desire to hold. In order to bring their cash balances down to desired levels, they will spend the money, thereby bidding up prices on goods and services, and the general price level will rise. As long as the stock of money increases faster than the demand for money, inflation will persist, even if TIP manages to hold down wages temporarily.

Conversely, just as inflation is caused by excessive growth of the money stock, the only way to stop inflation is to reduce the growth of the money stock. As the rate of monetary expansion is reduced, people will have cash balances below their desired levels. They will reduce their rate of spending in order to build up these balances. As spending (demand) falls, the rate of inflation will decrease. Prices are "sticky," and just as it took several years to build up the current rate of inflation, it will take several years for inflation to wind down. One of the by-products of reducing inflation is a temporary idling of resources, since prices do not tend to be flexible in the short run. This is a cost of reducing inflation which must be borne, just as there are costs imposed on society as inflation mounts.

The idea that there are certain "key" wages in society, such as union wages, to which other wages and prices adjust, confuses the *motivation* for increasing the money stock with the *cause* of inflation.[12] If certain unions are able to attain large wage increases, even in the face of falling demand, the prices of the products produced by this labor will increase. As prices increase, less of this product will be demanded and the use of the resources (labor and capital) which produce this product will be decreased. Unemployment will rise as resources are freed to work in the production of other products whose prices are lower. The relative prices of products will change, but the average price level will be unchanged.

---

[8]For a discussion of implementation problems, see Gardner Ackley, "Okun's New Tax-Based Incomes-Policy Proposal," Survey Research Center, Institute for Social Research, The University of Michigan, *Economic Outlook USA* (Winter 1978), pp. 8-9. Although Ackley deals with the anti-inflation proposal put forward by Arthur Okun, he notes that the critique also applies to the Wallich-Weintraub proposal.

[9]Congressional Budget Office, "Recovery With Inflation," p. 41.

[10]Empirical support of this view for the period 1955 to 1971 is presented by Leonall C. Andersen and Denis S. Karnosky, "The Appropriate Time Frame for Controlling Monetary Aggregates: The St. Louis Evidence," *Controlling Monetary Aggregates II: The Implementation*, Federal Reserve Bank of Boston, Conference Series No. 9, September 1972, pp. 147-77. Additional evidence for the period 1971 to 1976 is found in Denis S. Karnosky, "The Link Between Money and Prices — 1971-76," this *Review* (June 1976), pp. 17-23.

[11]See Leonall C. Andersen and Denis S. Karnosky, "A Monetary Interpretation of Inflation" in Joel Popkin, ed., *Analysis of Inflation: 1965-1974*, Studies in Income and Wealth, Vol. 42, National Bureau of Economic Research, Inc. (Cambridge, Massachusetts: Ballinger Publishing Company, 1977), pp. 11-26.

[12]This argument draws on Armen A. Alchian and William R. Allen, *University Economics: Elements of Inquiry* (Belmont, California: Wadsworth Publishing Company, Inc., 1972), pp. 684-85.

However, if the Federal Reserve policymakers keep a close watch on these "key" industries and see an increase in idle resources (unemployment) in these industries, they may take actions to alleviate the unemployment by increasing the money stock. The increases in spending resulting from monetary expansion will bid up average prices and return relative prices to a position similar to that prior to the granting of the wage demands. It was as a consequence of the excessive wage demands that policy actions were *motivated*, but it was monetary expansion which *caused* the subsequent inflation.

Some proponents of TIP base their support on the belief that TIP will reduce *expectations* of inflation. Lower expectations of inflation in the future, according to this view, will lead to lower demands for wage increases and eventually lower prices. However, expectations of inflation do not cause inflation.[13] It is ongoing inflationary forces in the economy, excessive rates of monetary expansion, which lead to expectations of future inflation. Curbing inflationary expectations requires curbing the underlying forces which cause them.

Wallich and Weintraub agree that TIP is a supplement to, not a substitute for, "appropriate" monetary and fiscal policy. However, the character of their "appropriate" monetary policy is questionable. In the basic article which outlined TIP, Wallich and Weintraub stated, ". . . the proposal is conceived as a supplement to the familiar monetary-fiscal policies so that the economy might operate closer to full employment without the inflationary danger of excess demand and 'overheating.' "[14] Indeed, in a later article Weintraub is more specific: "Given a suitable incomes policy to align wages (and salaries) to productivity, monetary policy would be released to make its contribution to full employment. . . Full employment requires ample money supplies for its sustenance."[15] Thus, it appears that "appropriate" monetary policy, in the view of Wallich and Weintraub, is expansionary; however, a restrictive monetary policy is necessary to curb inflation.

This disparity in determining the appropriate character of monetary policy points out another problem with TIP. Given the lag time involved in the functioning of monetary policy, it might appear in the short run that TIP is, at least temporarily, holding down prices. If, at the same time, the Federal Reserve increases the rate of monetary expansion, inflationary pressures will actually be augmented. An incomes policy, such as TIP, gives policymakers the illusion of taking corrective measures against inflation when, in fact, reducing the rate of monetary expansion is the only way to accomplish that goal. In summary, it appears that TIP would not be effective in reducing inflation and could make matters worse by fostering inappropriate monetary policy.

Would TIP Interfere With the Market?

Wallich and Weintraub argue that TIP would not interfere with market pricing because no ceilings are placed on any wages or prices. TIP operates through the tax system, yet it is based on a *single* guidepost for every firm and industry. They contend that a single guidepost is appropriate because in competition all comparable workers would earn the same wage. TIP, therefore, is only imposing what competition would achieve.

The problem with this argument is that it is only true if all industries are in equilibrium and remain there. In a growing, changing economy, equilibrium prices and wage rates are changing. Prices and wages are constantly moving toward new equilibria; hence, there is no reason to believe that each sector in the economy would be at equilibrium when TIP was imposed or would remain there afterward. In the U. S. economy, demands and tastes of consumers are constantly shifting and the technology and products offered by business are also changing. As a consequence, the equilibrium prices of some goods are rising (houses, for example) while others are falling (electronic calculators). In addition, some firms are growing, making large profits, and seeking additional labor, while others are declining, earning very little profit, and contracting their labor forces.

Imposing a single wage guidepost would distort the price system. It does not matter whether the guidepost is imposed through the tax system or by direct fines and penalties. Those firms which are growing or are adapting to changing consumer tastes have an incentive to hire scarce resources (capital and labor) away from other firms, but they would be penalized either through a lower rate of return, if they grant "excess" wage demands, or by a barrier to growth if they adhere to the guidepost. Consequently, in some instances labor would not be compensated in accord

---

[13] Weintraub supports this contention in Weintraub, "Incomes Policy: Completing the Stabilization Triangle," p. 116.

[14] Wallich and Weintraub, "A Tax-Based Incomes Policy," p. 1.

[15] Weintraub, "Incomes Policy: Completing the Stabilization Triangle," p. 110.

with the demand for its services. In other cases, firms would not be able to attract all the labor they desired. Relative prices would, therefore, be distorted by the establishment of a single guidepost for all firms and industries.

The TIP proposal would lead to a misallocation of resources. Prices, when allowed to operate freely, offer signals of where demand is increasing and where demand is falling. Resources move to those industries or firms where they will receive the highest compensation. The TIP proposal would obscure these price signals and, hence, resources would not move to where they would be used most efficiently. The economy would suffer since production would be lower than it would be otherwise.

The distortions in the economy caused by TIP could have a very long lasting effect. Capital (plant and equipment) is allocated by the market to those firms which have the highest rate of return. The TIP proposal would reduce the rates of return of those firms which are growing, and capital would not be adequately allocated to them. Capital generally tends to have a relatively long life. Once it is misallocated, as a result of TIP, it would not be easy to reallocate it to a more efficient use. Thus, TIP could have serious long-term consequences, as a result of the distortions it would cause in the price system.

CONCLUSION

TIP is an incomes policy designed to reduce inflation without interfering with the market system. The essence of the proposal is to subject corporations to higher corporate income tax rates if they granted pay increases in excess of a single Government-mandated guidepost.

TIP would not be successful in reducing the rate of inflation because it is based on the premise that inflation is largely a "cost-push" phenomenon — higher wages leading to higher prices, which lead to still higher wages. Inflation, however, is caused primarily by excessive growth of the money stock. The TIP proposal, therefore, deals only with the symptoms of inflation, rather than attacking inflation at its root.

TIP would distort the market pricing system because the imposition of a single wage guidepost would not allow relative prices to adjust fully to change. This would lead to inefficiencies and a lower level of production than would be otherwise attainable.

Inflation is a serious problem, and there are no magic solutions. There may be a temporary reduction in the apparent rate of inflation with TIP, but eventually leaks will develop in the system and prices will rise anyway. The only way to stop inflation is to reduce the rate of monetary expansion.

27

Disintermediation: An Old Disorder With A New Remedy

R. ALTON GILBERT and JEAN M. LOVATI

IN the summer of 1977, yields on short-term U.S. Treasury bills rose above the maximum interest rates that commercial banks and most thrift institutions are legally permitted to pay on passbook savings deposits.[1] By the end of that year, interest rates on U.S. Treasury securities had risen above ceiling interest rates on time deposits with longer maturities. In the past, when market interest rates have risen above legal ceiling rates on time and savings deposits by similar margins, the growth of these deposits has slowed sharply. This is called *disintermediation*.

Thrift institutions provide a major source of residential construction and mortgage credit, and thus, disintermediation tends to reduce the supply of credit available to the housing market. Since residential construction is a major industry, and since the stabilization of housing construction has a high priority in public policy, disintermediation at thrift institutions is of special concern to policymakers.

In an attempt to reduce the extent of disintermediation, Federal regulators of depository institutions authorized a new category of six-month time deposits called money market certificates (MMCs), which commercial banks, savings and loan associations, and mutual savings banks were permitted to offer after June 1, 1978. This paper analyzes the role of MMCs in preventing disintermediation and the implications of continued growth of deposits through MMCs for expansion of mortgage lending and residential construction activity.

CHARACTERISTICS AND GROWTH OF MMCs

The ceiling rate on MMCs at commercial banks is equal to the current discount yield on six-month Treasury bills; at thrift institutions, the ceiling rate is one-quarter of a percentage point higher.[2] The rate for *new* MMCs is adjusted weekly to the yield on six-month bills at the most recent bill auction. For previously issued MMCs, the ceiling rate remains unchanged until maturity. The minimum denomination in which MMCs are issued is $10,000, the same as that for Treasury bills.

Around 11,700 commercial banks — approximately 79 percent of all insured commercial banks — are estimated to have been offering MMCs at the end of last year (Table I). These banks recorded an out-

---

[1] Thrift institutions are savings and loan associations, mutual savings banks, and credit unions. The maximum interest rates which federally-regulated credit unions are allowed to offer on time and savings deposits are slightly higher than the ceiling rates at commercial banks, savings and loan associations, and mutual savings banks.

[2] A Treasury bill has a face value which is payable by the U.S. Treasury at maturity. Investors pay various fractions of the face value of Treasury bills, the fractions reflecting maturity and discount yield of the bills. To illustrate the calculation of discount yield, consider a one-year bill for which an investor pays 90 percent of face value. The discount yield on that bill is 10 percent. For a discussion of how discount yields may be converted to a bond equivalent basis, see footnote 4.

Reprinted from Federal Reserve Bank of St. Louis *Review*, January, 1979.

Table I

Growth of Money Market Certificates

	Interest Rate on 6-month Treasury Bills[1]	Commercial Banks[2] Number of Offering Institutions	Commercial Banks[2] Amount Outstanding ($ millions)	Mutual Savings Banks[3] Number of Offering Institutions	Mutual Savings Banks[3] Amount Outstanding ($ millions)	Savings & Loan Associations[4] Amount Outstanding ($ millions)
June 7	7.16%	6,455	$ 774	224	$ 847	$ —
June 28	7.23	7,963	2,055	258	1,596	5,400
July 26	7.50	8,961	5,470	273	3,504	11,790
August 30	7.47	9,825	7,792	331	5,009	15,080
September 27	7.98	9,886	9,679	364	6,136	19,338
October 25	8.56	10,552	13,858	319	8,908	26,660[5]
November 29	9.00	11,065	19,729	349	10,841	34,630[5]
December 27	9.52	11,658	22,956	431	12,822	not available

[1] New issue rate, for week ending Saturday four days earlier than date shown.
[2] Based on a sample of 527 commercial banks.
[3] Based on a sample of 95 mutual savings banks.
[4] Data for end of month.
[5] Estimated figures; FSLIC - insured associations.
SOURCE: Federal Reserve releases G.13, H.6 and Federal Home Loan Bank Board *News*.

standing balance in MMCs of $23 billion in December, representing 4.5 percent of their net time and savings deposits (not seasonally adjusted).[3]

Thrifts have experienced even larger growth in MMCs. Mutual savings banks are estimated to have had about $12.8 billion of these certificates outstanding at the end of the year. At the end of November, MMCs represented 7.7 percent of total mutual savings bank deposits. Total MMCs outstanding at insured savings and loan associations is estimated to have been about $34.6 billion in late November, or 8.3 percent of savings capital.

Growth of MMCs has had a substantial effect on deposit growth at commercial banks and thrift institutions and, thus, has enabled the institutions to avert major disintermediation. Conditions for disintermediation began to develop in 1977 when the interest rate on three-month Treasury bills (bond equivalent yield) rose above the ceiling rate on savings deposits at commercial banks in May, and above the ceiling rate on savings deposits at savings and loan associations and mutual savings banks in July (see Chart I).[4] By the end of 1977, market interest rates on U.S. Treasury securities were above ceiling rates on time deposits of all maturity classes at commercial banks and thrifts, and in 1978, market interest rates rose even higher relative to ceiling rates.

As a result of increases in interest rates, growth of net time and savings deposits at commercial banks slowed gradually from July 1977 through May 1978 (Table II). In contrast, growth of net time and savings deposits at commercial banks began to accelerate in June 1978, the month that MMCs became available. Deposits at thrift institutions have followed a similar pattern, with growth rates slowing from August 1977 through May 1978 and accelerating thereafter.

COMPARISON TO PAST PERIODS OF DISINTERMEDIATION

Comparison of the growth rates of deposits before and after June 1978 underestimates the full effect of MMCs in preventing disintermediation. Market interest rates have risen substantially since June 1978,

---

[3] Net time and savings deposits of commercial banks exclude large ($100,000 and over) negotiable certificates of deposit at large commercial banks.

[4] Yields on Treasury bills must be converted to a bond equivalent basis in order to compare them to interest rates on deposits. To illustrate the difference between discount and bond equivalent yields, consider a one-year Treasury bill with a face value of $10,000 which is sold at a discount yield of 8 percent. The buyer would pay $9,200 for the bill and receive $10,000 at maturity one year later. The bill is sold on a discount basis, meaning that the buyer pays less than the face amount, and the discount yield is determined by calculating the difference between the purchase price and the face amount as a percentage of the *face amount* (i.e., $800 as a percentage of $10,000). Converting the discount yield to a bond equivalent yield involves calculating the difference between the purchase price and the face amount as a percentage of the *purchase price*. For the Treasury bill described above, the bond equivalent yield is 8.70 percent ($800 as a percentage of $9,200).

Table II
Annual Rates of Deposit Growth

Month	Net Time and Savings Deposits at Commercial Banks	Deposits at Nonbank Thrift Institutions
1977 Jan.	13.4%	16.1%
Feb.	12.6	13.7
Mar.	11.6	12.2
Apr.	8.8	11.8
May	8.7	12.5
June	11.0	13.1
July	16.0	15.8
Aug.	8.8	19.0
Sept.	9.3	18.4
Oct.	9.2	15.6
Nov.	10.0	11.8
Dec.	4.7	11.0
1978 Jan.	8.7	9.0
Feb.	7.9	7.2
Mar.	6.2	8.0
Apr.	5.4	7.5
May	6.9	7.5
June	8.5	9.6
July	10.8	11.8
Aug.	12.1	14.8
Sept.	12.5	17.2
Oct.	9.5	14.5
Nov.	11.0	10.4
Dec.	2.4	9.7

and thus the differentials between market interest rates and fixed ceiling rates on time and savings deposits have widened in recent months. Therefore, without authorization of MMCs, and with all other ceiling rates unchanged, deposit growth would have been expected to slow substantially after June 1978.

The appropriate method of analyzing the role of MMCs in preventing disintermediation is to compare the rates of deposit growth in recent months to those of past periods when the differentials between market interest rates and fixed ceiling rates on time and saving deposits were comparable to current differentials. The historical patterns of differentials between ceiling interest rates on three categories of time and savings deposits at thrifts and market interest rates on U.S. Treasury securities of comparable maturities are presented in Charts I and II. These differentials during recent months have been similar to the prevailing differentials during parts of 1969, 1973, and 1974, when the three-month Treasury bill rate rose to more than 3 percentage points above the ceiling rate on passbook savings accounts at thrift institutions, and yields on one-year Treasury bills rose to about 2.50 percentage points above the ceiling rate on one- to two-year time deposits.

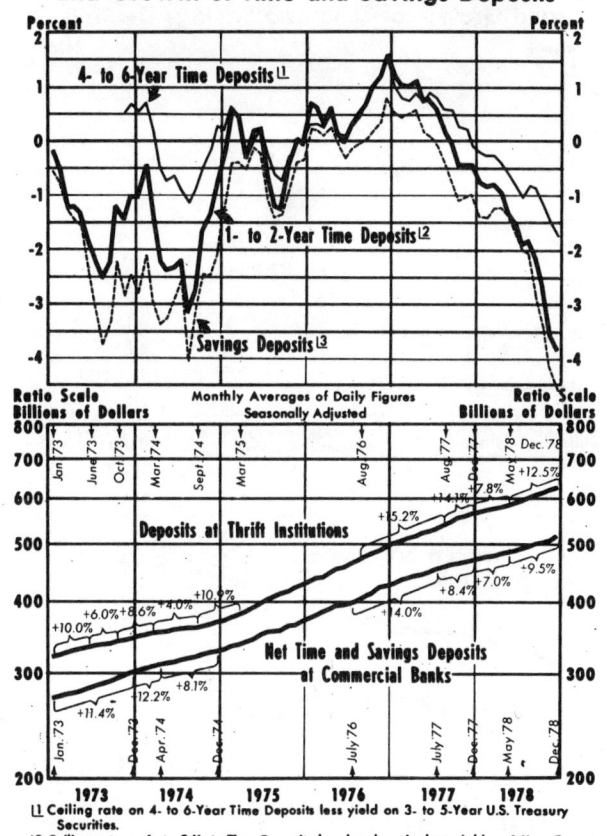

Disintermediation in 1969

Economic activity during 1969 is comparable in several ways to economic activity in 1978. The economy had been expanding for several years prior to 1969, and real disposable personal income rose throughout that year. Therefore, to the extent that deposit growth slowed as market interest rates rose above ceiling rates on time and savings deposits, depositors reacted to relative yields, and not to a decline in personal savings.

By early 1969 the differentials between market rates and ceiling rates were having a marked impact on deposit growth. Net time and savings deposits at com-

Chart II
Ceiling Interest Rates on Deposits at Thrift Institutions Less Market Interest Rates, and Growth of Time and Savings Deposits

/1 Ceiling rate on Savings Deposits less bond equivalent yield on 3-Month Treasury Bills.
/2 Ceiling rate on 1- to 2-Year Time Deposits less bond equivalent yield on 1-Year Treasury Bills.
Percentages are annual rates of change for periods indicated.
Latest data plotted: December

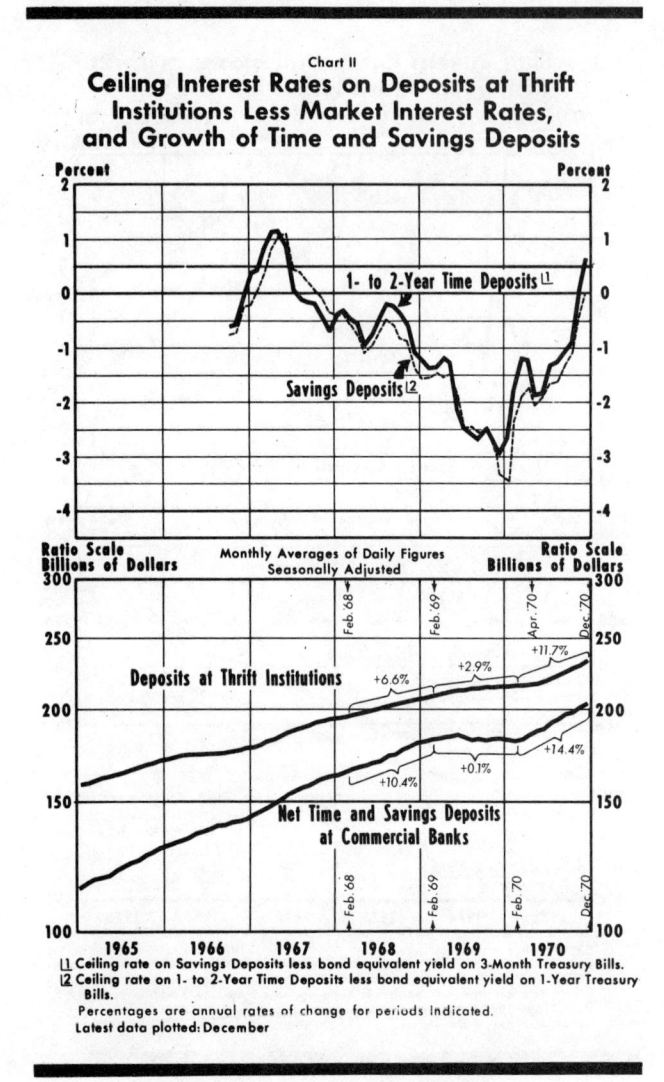

mercial banks were essentially unchanged from February 1969 to February 1970, compared to a 10 percent increase in the previous year. However, as short-term interest rates declined in 1970, net time and savings deposits resumed rapid growth.

Growth of deposits at thrift institutions also was affected by the rise of short-term market interest rates relative to ceiling rates. From February 1969 to April 1970, deposits at nonbank thrift institutions rose at a 3 percent rate. As market interest rates declined in 1970, growth of deposits at thrifts increased, rising at a 12 percent rate from April to December 1970.

Disintermediation in 1973

Economic activity in 1978 also was similar to that in 1973. The economy again had been expanding for several years prior to 1973, with real disposable personal income rising throughout the year. However, interest ceiling rates were changed during several months in 1973, having a significant effect on growth of deposits. The ceiling rates on time deposits of $1,000 or more with maturities of at least four years were suspended in July 1973, thus permitting commercial banks and thrift institutions to offer competitive rates of interest on these deposits (commonly called "wild card" deposits). The ceiling rates were reinstated in November 1973.

Commercial banks were able to maintain rapid growth of net time and savings deposits during 1973 because of the significant growth in long-term time deposits, even though market interest rates were substantially above ceiling rates on savings deposits and time deposits with maturities of less than four years. Thrift institutions experienced relatively slow deposit growth for four months in 1973, possibly as a result of competition with commercial banks for "wild card" deposits. Deposits of thrifts grew at a 6 percent rate from June through October 1973, compared to a 14 percent increase in the previous year.

Disintermediation in 1974

It is difficult to compare the influence of deposit interest ceilings on growth of deposits in 1978 to that in 1974 because some of the factors which influence deposit growth were different in the two years. For example, growth of personal savings, an important determinant of deposit growth at financial institutions, was slowed by the recession in 1974.[5] Nevertheless, deposit interest rate ceilings also appear to have influenced the pattern of deposit growth during 1974. This effect was more pronounced at thrifts than at commercial banks.

Deposits at thrifts grew at a 4 percent rate from March through September 1974, compared to an 8.6 percent rate of increase in the previous five months. Market interest rates began declining sharply in the fall of 1974, and deposit growth increased at a 10.9 percent rate from September 1974 through March 1975, the trough month of the past recession. Thus, the rate of deposit growth increased as market interest rates declined relative to ceiling rates on time and savings deposits, even though economic activity was still declining. This observation indicates that the slow deposit growth at thrifts during the six months

---
[5]For a survey of empirical studies on the determinants of deposits at financial institutions, see Edward F. McKelvey, *Interest Rate Ceilings and Disintermediation*, Staff Economic Studies, Board of Governors of the Federal Reserve System (April 1978).

ending in September 1974 was influenced not only by the effects of the recession on personal savings, but also significantly by the ceilings on deposit interest rates.

Comparison to 1978

In contrast to past experience, deposit growth at commercial banks and thrifts has accelerated in recent months, even though the margins between market interest rates and ceiling rates on categories of time and saving deposits other than MMCs have been about the same as during past periods of disintermediation. The differences between growth rates of deposits in recent months and in other periods analyzed above indicate that MMCs have had a significant role in preventing disintermediation.

SIGNIFICANCE OF MMCs FOR THE HOUSING MARKET

The availability of credit from thrift institutions is essential for financing residential construction. Since thrift institutions provide a major portion of both residential construction credit and residential mortgages, a reduction in deposit growth at thrifts limits the credit available to the housing market, and substantially reduces residential construction activity.

Authorization of MMCs has enabled thrift institutions to remain competitive for deposits during a period when market interest rates have been above ceiling rates on other categories of time and savings deposits. Thus, permission to offer MMCs has allowed thrift institutions to remain potential suppliers of mortgage credit, and thrifts have increased their residential mortgages substantially. During the year ending October 1978, residential mortgages held by savings and loan associations increased 14.4 percent, and mutual savings banks increased their residential mortgages 8.2 percent.

The significance of MMCs to the continuing high rate of housing starts in the current expansion can be analyzed by examining Chart III. The shaded areas represent periods when yields on three-month Treasury bills were 100 basis points or more above ceiling rates on savings deposits at thrift institutions. In 1969-70 and 1973-74, the shaded areas correspond closely to periods of declining housing starts. In contrast, yields on three-month Treasury bills have been 100 basis points or more above the ceiling rate on

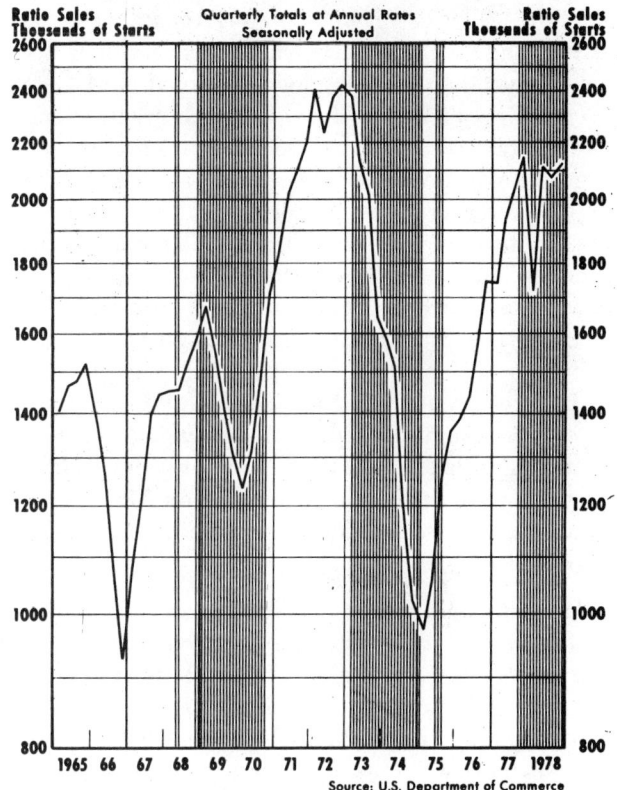

Chart III
New Privately Owned Housing Units Started

Shaded areas indicate periods when bond equivalent yield on Three-Month Treasury Bills is greater than thrift institution passbook rate by 100 or more basis points.
Latest data plotted: 4th quarter
Source: U.S. Department of Commerce

savings deposits since the fall of 1977, yet the pace of residential construction activity remains relatively strong.

Housing starts have averaged an annual rate of about 2.1 million units in recent months, just below the highest rate of housing starts in the current expansion. This relatively high level of housing starts continues after almost four years into the current expansion. For comparison, housing starts in early 1969 peaked after a little over two years of expanding residential construction, and similarly, housing starts in late 1972 peaked two years after the previous recession trough.

However, permission for thrifts to offer MMCs does not assure a continued flow of mortgage credit. The ceiling interest rate on MMCs at thrifts is currently about 9.75 percent which, under daily compounding, is adjusted to about 10.25 percent. That rate is at or above the usury ceilings on residential mortgages in several states. Even in states with no usury ceilings or with usury ceilings above prevailing interest rates, the spread between rates being paid on new MMCs and the yields on new residential mortgages is relatively narrow.

With the yields on MMCs approximately the same as mortgage yields, thrifts which increase their mortgages outstanding by issuing additional MMCs may eventually experience losses on such transactions if interest rates continue to rise. Most residential mortgages remain outstanding for several years and have fixed interest rates. Deposits attracted by issuing MMCs must be reissued at prevailing interest rates every six months as they mature to avoid deposit outflows. Thrifts which make additional mortgage loans face the risk that the interest rates on their deposit liabilities will continue to rise while the yields on their assets remain fixed. Therefore, thrifts cannot determine the profitability of increasing their residential mortgages solely by comparing the yields on mortgages to current interest rates on MMCs. They must consider, in addition, the possibility that interest rates will continue to rise.

Thrifts which attract additional deposits through MMCs may find investments other than residential mortgages more profitable. Although thrifts keep a relatively high proportion of their assets in residential mortgages to maintain special tax benefits, they have some margin within which they can change the mix of their assets without altering their tax status. Some thrift institutions reportedly are issuing MMCs and using those funds to buy large short-term certificates of deposit of commercial banks.[6] A shift of investments by thrifts from residential mortgages to short-term securities, however, is not yet indicated by aggregate information. In recent months, thrifts have increased their holdings of mortgages at about the same rate as the increase in their deposits.[7]

CONCLUSIONS

Deposit growth at commercial banks and thrift institutions has slowed in past periods when market interest rates rose above ceiling interest rates on time and savings deposits, a reaction called *disintermediation*. During the current phase of rising interest rates, Federal regulators have dealt with the threat of disintermediation by permitting commercial banks and thrift institutions to offer money market certificates, with ceiling interest rates which change weekly in line with discount yields on six-month Treasury bills. Growth rates of net time and savings deposits at commercial banks and deposits at thrifts have increased substantially since this new category of time deposits was authorized.

Growth of deposits at thrift institutions in recent months has facilitated the rapid expansion of mortgage lending, and residential construction activity has remained at a relatively high level, especially for a period with such high interest rates. However, the continued expansion of mortgage lending and residential construction is not assured by permission for thrifts to offer MMCs. Even if thrift institutions continue to have rapid deposit growth, they will not necessarily invest these funds in residential mortgages, since other types of investment may be more profitable.

---

[6]"A Surprisingly Simple CD Rollover," *Business Week*, December 4, 1978, pp. 84-85, and "Money Market Certificates Are Selling Well, But Most Proceeds Aren't Going to Mortgages," *Wall Street Journal*, December 7, 1978.

[7]From May 1978 (the month before MMCs were authorized) to November, the rate of increase in mortgages outstanding at savings and loan associations was slightly higher than the rate of increase in their deposits (a 6.8 percent increase in mortgages and a 5.8 percent increase in deposits). Mortgages held by mutual savings banks (MSBs) increased 3.9 percent from May to November 1978 (the latest month for which data are available), while deposits of MSBs rose 2.8 percent.

Automatic transfers: Evolution of the service and impact on money

Randall C. Merris

Commercial banks began offering automatic transfers from consumer savings to checking accounts November 1. With transfers made automatically through prior arrangements with their banks, consumers can keep more of their bank balances in interest-bearing savings accounts. Automatic transfers also are intended to reduce the volume of checks returned for insufficient funds—a costly inconvenience for everybody concerned. They are also expected to make it easier for consumers to meet the minimum balance requirements of their checking agreements.

The authorization extends only to consumer accounts. Corporations, partnerships, and other organizations, including units of government, are excluded from use of the service under plans approved last May by the Federal Reserve and the Federal Deposit Insurance Corporation. A majority of mutual savings banks can also offer automatic transfers.

Voluntary for both banks and consumers, automatic transfers can be made only on written authorization of the customer. The authorization must be given when the customer signs up for the transfer program. Arrangements can be made for banks to transfer funds automatically from interest-bearing accounts at thrift institutions, such as savings and loan associations. In that case, all three parties, of course, have to agree to the transfers in advance.

Although ordinarily waived, banks have the right to require 30 days' notice for withdrawals from savings accounts. Regulations governing automatic transfers require that banks prominently disclose the information that they reserve this right for automatic transfer accounts, just like any other savings plans.

Banks must also keep monthly records on the dollar volumes of savings subject to automatic transfer, the number and volume of transfers, and any service charges or interest forfeitures that result from transfers.

As with other innovations in banking, the advent of automatic transfers has created uncertainties, for both banks and the monetary authorities, about the pricing and packaging patterns that will emerge. There are also uncertainties about the effects of this new service on the money supply and the conduct of monetary policy.

Impact on money

With consumers able to keep more of their bank balances in savings accounts, there will be a tendency for automatic transfers to reduce the money supply, as conventionally defined. The shift, therefore, has implications for monetary policy.

The money supply, defined most commonly as currency plus demand deposits held by the public, excludes savings deposits. This definition, called M1, is one of the measures of the money supply the Federal Reserve uses in conducting monetary policy. Money supply figures based on this definition will reflect any reductions in consumer checking balances resulting from the introduction of the automatic transfer service. And there will be no indication of the offsetting increase in savings deposits.

Although the Federal Reserve does not control M1 directly or completely, it sets target ranges for growth of M1. And efforts are made to meet the M1 targets through policy actions that directly affect the reserve holdings of member banks and indirectly influencing all financial markets. To gauge the

---

Excerpted from Federal Reserve Bank of Chicago *Economic Perspectives,* November–December, 1978.

effectiveness of monetary policy, the Federal Reserve monitors movements in M1 along with other changes in economic data.

As automatic transfers allow consumers to transact the same volume of business with smaller balances in their checking accounts, the income velocity of M1 can be expected to rise. This velocity, called V1, is GNP divided by M1. Because both GNP and M1 are expressed in dollars, V1 is a pure number rather than a dollar or percentage figure.

Although the income velocity of M1 tends to vary with economic conditions, rising with expansions and falling with contractions, the trend has been essentially upward since the Second World War. Calculated from seasonally adjusted data, V1 nearly tripled in just over three decades, rising from 2.0 in early 1947 to 5.9 in early 1978. Reflected in this trend is better economizing on M1 holdings as interest rates have risen and improvements in the techniques of money management that have opened up for both consumers and businesses.

Automatic transfers are just another in a series of innovations that, like bank credit cards, have allowed consumers to make more effective use of their money and, like savings certificates, have provided attractive alternatives to holding money.

Consumers held almost $93 billion in demand deposits last June.[1] That was over a third of the demand deposits counted in M1. It was over a fourth of the $352.8 billion seasonally adjusted M1 total.

Consumer demand deposits at weekly reporting banks—which include the large banks that are most likely to introduce automatic transfers—totaled almost $37 billion. These deposits accounted for close to 15 percent of the demand deposit component of M1 and about 10 percent of total M1.

If reductions in consumer demand deposits even approach the amounts that could eventually be shifted into savings accounts, the increase in the income velocity of M1 could be substantial. How much V1 increases, and how soon, depends on the number of banks that introduced automatic transfers and the success of the pricing and promotion schemes they employ.

* * *

Impact on monetary policy

Considerations of pricing and packaging create uncertainties about the extent of shifts that can be expected from checking to savings deposits. But while these uncertainties complicate the use of M1 targets in the conduct of monetary policy, two factors are working in favor of the monetary authorities.

One is that the shift will not come all at once. Automatic transfers are expected to bring only a gradual downward shift in the demand for M1 and, therefore, a fairly slow increase in the income velocity of M1. Many banks indicate they have no immediate plans for introducing automatic transfers. Many customers will not sign up at first. For many, automatic transfers are simply priced out of their reach for now. Also, some of the plans that have been announced require that customers still maintain some checking balances.

---

[1] The consumer deposit figures are estimates of gross demand deposits. They are slightly larger than the adjusted demand deposits used in calculating M1.

As automatic transfer services become more widely available, the Federal Reserve will have already been monitoring its use, studying the effects on M1, and adjusting its M1 targets as needed.

The other is that M1 is not the only definition the Federal Reserve uses in making monetary policy. A more broadly defined monetary aggregate is M2, which includes the currency and demand deposits in M1 plus time and savings deposits at commercial banks, excluding large negotiable CDs (those of $100,000 or more). This measure is not affected directly by shifts from consumer checking accounts to savings accounts. It includes both.

Although dollar-for-dollar shifts from checking to savings balances do not affect M2 directly, this measure is influenced indirectly by the declines in the average reserves member banks are required to hold against their deposits. Reserve requirements for banks belonging to the Federal Reserve System are stated in terms of non-interest-bearing reserves as a proportion of deposits of a particular type.

Requirements for demand deposits vary from 7 percent to 16.25 percent, graduated by the deposit holdings of the banks. Requirements for savings deposits are 3 percent, regardless of the dollar holdings of a particular bank.

Shifts into savings deposits reduce the average reserve requirement as a proportion of total deposits. Without offsetting action by the Federal Reserve, lowering the ratio of required reserves to deposits can lead to expansion of bank credit, and consequently, M2.

The introduction of automatic transfers is expected to take long enough that the Federal Reserve will not need to engage in sudden large-scale moves to absorb member bank reserves. Reserves released through growing acceptance of automatic transfers can be neutralized by the Federal Reserve through its day-to-day dealings in government securities.

Through open-market operations, the Fed can sell government securities, reducing total reserves in the banking system. The volume of sales arising from the introduction of automatic transfers will probably be small, comparable certainly to the operations used in connection with earlier revisions in average reserve requirements and occasionally to offset Treasury financing activities.

A fall in average reserve requirements resulting from automatic transfers will be consistent with the secular decline in member bank reserve requirements since the Second World War. Having to hold reserves in the form of non-interest-earning assets is a burden on member banks that is not shared by the many state-chartered banks that have elected not to become members of the Federal Reserve System.

With no change in the current structure of reserve requirements, automatic transfers will reduce the implied costs of membership in the Federal Reserve through the reduction in average reserve requirements.

By making bank savings accounts more attractive, automatic transfers could bring savings flows that amount to more than mere shifts from checking balances. Not only will bank savings accounts be made more attractive compared with other interest-earning assets consumers may hold, but depositors may in some instances need to switch funds from other sources to meet the minimum balance requirements of automatic transfer plans. Unexpected changes in M2 arising from these shifts are not apt to be large.

Introduction of automatic transfers may also increase the general acceptance of M2 as a definition of money. By making bank savings deposits more readily available for consumer purchases and payments, automatic transfers can enhance inclusion of these deposits in the money supply. From the standpoint of policy, M2 will certainly be easier to follow during the transition than M1.

Crucial to policy makers, of course, are linkages between the money supply and economic activity. As always, the Federal Reserve will be watching both M1 and M2 and their relationships to movements in the real economy.

29

Automatic transfers and NOW accounts compared

Automatic transfers from savings have been compared—too closely in some cases—with NOW accounts. NOW is an acronym for a check-type draft called a *negotiable order of withdrawal*. NOW accounts pay explicit interest and offer their owners the privilege of writing orders of withdrawal that, like checks, can be made payable to third parties.

Savings banks in Massachusetts and New Hampshire began offering NOW accounts in 1972. Under special authorization by Congress, these accounts are available today at savings banks, savings and loan associations, and commercial banks throughout New England. And despite approval of automatic transfers by the Federal Reserve and the FDIC, congressional authorization of NOW accounts has recently been extended to federally chartered banks and thrift institutions in New York State.

Although acceptance of NOW accounts was slow at first, even by some banks and thrift institutions, they have become widely used as a form of savings and payments in all six New England states. Over 70 percent of the commercial banks in New England were offering NOW accounts at the beginning of 1978. Altogether, that was 682,855 accounts worth $1.8 billion. They earned over $7.3 million in interest in December 1977. An average of 13 NOW drafts were written that month on each account.

Automatic transfers from savings can be viewed to some extent as a substitute for authorization of NOW accounts nationwide—an idea that was considered in 1976 and 1977. The two, however, are very different, and comparisons between NOW accounts in New England and automatic transfers should be drawn with caution.

The experiment in New England, where banks and thrift institutions offer NOW accounts on the same terms, differs sharply from the automatic transfer services that are becoming available at many of the nation's largest and most innovative banks, without the direct participation of savings and loan associations.

The experience in New England has been of some help to banks in providing an initial guide to pricing transfers and tailoring them to customer needs. But NOW accounts are imperfect as a guide to longer-range planning for automatic transfers, which will surely show their own patterns of consumer demand, account activity, and bank operating costs.

Experience with NOW accounts is apt to be of little use either in predicting how long it will take automatic transfers to become widely accepted as a banking service or in estimating initial and long-run deposit shifts from checking to savings balances.

Reprinted from Federal Reserve Bank of Chicago *Economic Perspectives*, November–December, 1978.

RECENT DEVELOPMENTS ENABLING DEPOSITORS TO USE INTEREST-EARNING BALANCES FOR PURPOSES PREVIOUSLY REQUIRING NON-INTEREST-EARNING DEMAND BALANCES

30

September 1970 The Federal Home Loan Bank Board permitted federally chartered savings and loan associations to make preauthorized nonnegotiable transfers from savings accounts to third parties for household-related expenditures.

June 1972 State-chartered mutual savings banks in Massachusetts began offering NOW accounts following a favorable ruling of the Massachusetts Supreme Court. NOW accounts are functionally equivalent to interest-bearing checking accounts.

September 1972 State-chartered mutual savings banks in New Hampshire began offering NOW accounts.

January 1974 Federal legislation authorized all depository institutions except credit unions in Massachusetts and New Hampshire to offer NOW accounts.

January 1974 First Federal Savings and Loan of Lincoln, Nebraska, installed customer-bank communications terminals in two supermarkets enabling customers to withdraw funds from their savings accounts to pay for items purchased from the stores.

Early 1974 Money market mutual funds became widespread. These funds permit shareholders to redeem shares either by checks drawn on designated commercial bank accounts, by wire transfer, by telephone or by mail.

August 1974 The National Credit Union Administration permitted Federal credit unions to issue share drafts which, like NOW accounts, are functionally equivalent to interest-bearing checking accounts.

November 1974 Commercial banks were authorized to accept savings deposits from state and local governments.

April 1975 Commercial banks were authorized to transfer funds from a savings deposit to a checking account upon receipt of a depositor's telephone order.

April 1975 The Federal Home Loan Bank Board extended its 1970 action by permitting federally chartered savings and loan associations to make preauthorized transfers from savings accounts to third parties for any purpose.

September 1975 Commercial banks were permitted to make preauthorized nonnegotiable transfers from savings accounts to third parties for any purpose.

November 1975 Commercial banks were authorized to accept savings deposits from partnerships and corporations operated for profit, limited to $150,000 per customer per bank. In conjunction with telephone-ordered transfers, this authority made it possible for small businesses to earn interest on funds that can be readily used for transactions.

February 1976 Federal legislation extended NOW account authority to all New England States.

October 1978 Federal legislation extended NOW account authority to New York State.

November 1978 Commercial banks were authorized to offer automatic transfers from savings deposits to demand deposits.

Reprinted from Federal Reserve Bank of Richmond *Economic Review*, November–December, 1978.

Behavior of the income velocity of money

... consideration of the stock of money alone is not sufficient for assessment of the adequacy of the economy's liquidity. Money has a second dimension, namely, velocity, or—in common parlance—the intensity with which it is being used.[1]

Monetary policy decisions are based on the likely impact future money supply growth will have on the nation's economic activity. How much of an increase in the volume of money is needed to achieve the desired level of activity depends, however, on how intensively the stock of money is used—its velocity. If the rate of money use is expected to change from what it has been in the past, a different quantity of money will be needed to maintain the past level of economic activity. As each dollar is used more often, fewer dollars are needed to facilitate the same amount of transactions. As a first step in determining future velocity movements, it is useful to analyze the past.

Postwar behavior of velocity

Of the several measures of the velocity of money, the one most commonly used is the income velocity of M-1 (V-1) defined as the ratio of GNP to M-1[2]. Since the end of World War II the income velocity of M-1 has been on a generally rising trend. Over the past 30 years V-1 has risen at a 3.5 percent average annual rate—from a ratio of 2.05 in the first quarter of 1947 to 5.82 in the second quarter of 1977.

Quarter-to-quarter rates of change in V-1, however, have been quite volatile. They have ranged, in compounded annual rates, from a 5.9 percent decline in the first quarter of 1949 to a 22.4 percent gain in the third quarter of 1950. Over the past decade quarter-to-quarter rates of change in V-1 ranged between extremes of –3.7 percent in the fourth quarter of 1970 to 11.5 percent in the third quarter of 1975.

During the postwar period movements in V-1 have had a discernible cyclical pattern. From the peak to the trough in the first five of the six postwar recessions, V-1 declined. In the 1973-75 recession the average annual rate of change in V-1 slowed to 1.5 percent from the 3.4 percent average gain in the 1971-73 expansion.

During the recovery phases of the six business expansions since 1947, V-1 has generally risen at a rapid rate. From the first quarter of 1975 to the first quarter of 1976, the first year of the current expansion, V-1 rose at a rate of 8.3 percent, faster than in any other first year of recovery since the 1950-53 expansion. As the economy moves from recovery to expansion, the rate of increase in V-1 tends to slow and then to pick up again as the expansion proceeds. In the second year of the current expansion, V-1 grew at a rate of 3.5 percent, somewhat above the 3.1 percent rate observed in the second year of both the 1961-69 and 1971-73 expansions but below the 4.0 percent average second-year pace of the five previous expansions.

The seemingly erratic short-term movements in measured velocity and its pro-

---

[1] Arthur F. Burns, Chairman, Board of Governors of the Federal Reserve System, statement before the Committee on Banking, Housing and Urban Affairs, U.S. Senate, May 3, 1977.

[2] GNP represents the current value of annual spending on final goods and services. M-1 is defined as currency and demand deposits held by the public. While the income velocity of M-1 is most commonly used, similar income velocity measures exist for other measures of income and/or money.

Reprinted from Federal Reserve Bank of Chicago *Economic Perspectives*, September–October, 1977.

Velocity has been on a rising trend over the postwar period

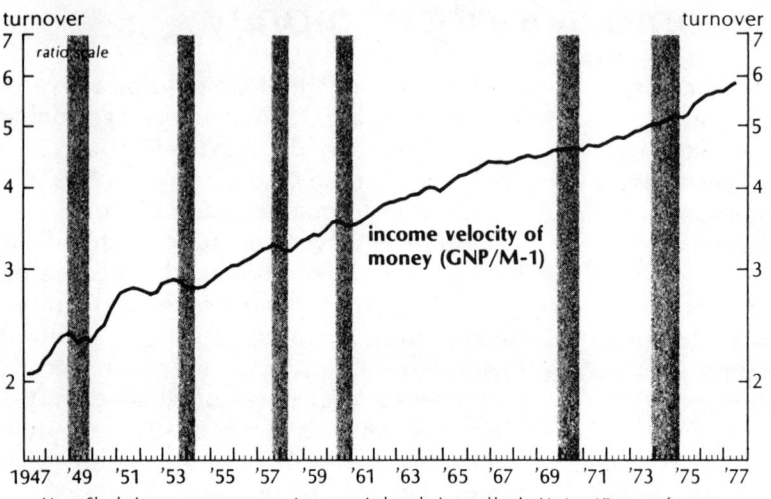

income velocity of money (GNP/M-1)

Note: Shaded areas represent recessionary periods as designated by the National Bureau of Economic Research.
SOURCES: M-1—Board of Governors, Federal Reserve System; GNP—U.S. Department of Commerce.

nounced cyclical pattern may suggest that the relationship between monetary growth and GNP is extremely loose and unpredictable. However, it is generally recognized that there are substantial lags between changes in money and changes in GNP. Indeed, most studies indicate that the primary impact of a monetary change on GNP is not felt for six months to a year, with the total effect being distributed over an even longer period. When this lagged relationship is taken into account, the money-GNP relationship—though far from perfect—is much tighter than the variable behavior of measured velocity would suggest. Nevertheless, the relationship is subject to gradual modification over time, as payments habits and basic economic conditions change, and these changes show up as secular, or longer-term, trends in velocity.

Factors affecting velocity

The postwar rise in V-1 indicates that the public has been reducing its holdings of M-1 balances relative to GNP. This economization of cash balances has been influenced by economic, institutional, and technical factors.

A major economic factor influencing the postwar rise in velocity is the general rise in interest rates that has occurred. Individuals, businesses, and state and local governmental units hold checking account balances and currency primarily to facilitate expenditures. As interest rates rise, the opportunity cost of holding noninterest-earning M-1 balances increases. To the extent that highly liquid interest-earning investment alternatives are available, money-holders have an incentive to shift funds in excess of transactions needs out of M-1 balances into earning assets.

Over the postwar period investment alternatives have been greatly expanded. For example, the increased desire of corporations to reduce cash balances led to the expansion of existing market alternatives—such as commercial paper—and the development of new instruments—such as certificates of deposit. The introduction by thrift institutions of a wider variety of consumer-type time and savings accounts and the development of money market mutual funds enhanced individuals' access to interest-bearing substitutes for M-1 balances. More recently, regulatory changes permitting businesses and state and local governments to hold savings accounts at commercial banks and the development of NOW (negotiable orders of withdrawal) accounts in New England have induced smaller businesses, state and local governments, and individuals to shift additional funds out of M-1 balances.

An increase in the technical efficiency with which funds can be transferred is another factor tending to increase velocity. Thus, such developments as wider use of wire transfer of funds and, more recently,

Rates of change in velocity differ over the business cycle

Recessions		Expansions				
				Rate of change in V-1		
Period	Rate of change in V-1	Period	Trough-to-peak	First year	Second year	Third year
(Peak-to-trough)	(percent)	(Trough-to-peak)		(percent)		
48-IV to 49-IV	-2.7	49-IV to 53-III	5.9	14.2	5.2	1.8
53-III to 54-II	-2.9	54-II to 57-III	5.0	5.3	4.3	4.9
57-III to 58-II	-3.1	58-II to 60-II	5.4	6.6	4.1	—
60-II to 61-I	-1.7	61-I to 69-IV	3.1	5.9	3.1	3.5
69-IV to 70-IV	-0.3	70-IV to 73-IV	3.4	2.7	3.1	4.6
73-IV to 75-I	1.5	75-I to 77-II*	5.7*	8.3	3.5	4.6**

Average annual rates of change in the income velocity of M-1 (V-1 = GNP/M-1).
*Current expansion continuing.
**Rate of change in V-1 in 77-II, the first quarter of the third year of expansion.
SOURCE: M-1 data—Board of Governors, Federal Reserve System; GNP data—U.S. Department of Commerce; Business cycle turning points—National Bureau of Economic Research.

telephonic transfer of funds between savings and checking accounts at commercial banks also help explain the postwar rise in velocity.

Since M-1 balances are held primarily to facilitate expenditures, the increasing availability of overdraft facilities and the more widespread use of credit cards have probably reduced the average amount of M-1 needed for transactions purposes and thus influenced the rise in velocity.

Prospects for future velocity movements

These factors in different combinations affect velocity in a complex fashion. Over the first two years of the current expansion, rates of change in the income velocity of M-1, though unaccompanied by the rise in interest rates observed in previous expansions, have generally been consistent with past patterns. Technical and institutional factors, however, have increased the ability of individuals, businesses, and state and local governments to reduce M-1 balances without sacrificing liquidity. In addition, cash management techniques once implemented are likely to be continued even though interest rates fall.

History suggests that, as the economy proceeds through the third year of expansion, velocity will continue on an upward trend at perhaps a faster pace than observed in the second year of expansion. The expectation of continued real economic growth, together with the likelihood that interest rates may rise as credit demands strengthen later in 1977, tends to reinforce this conclusion.

Anne Marie Laporte

Anti-Inflation Program

VOLUNTARY WAGE AND PRICE GUIDELINES

By JIMMY CARTER, *President of the United States*

Delivered to the Nation over National Radio and Television, Washington, D.C., October 24, 1978

GOOD EVENING. I want to have a frank talk with you tonight about our most serious domestic problem. That problem is inflation. Inflation can threaten all the economic gains we've made, and it can stand in the way of what we want to achieve in the future.

This has been a long-time threat. For the last 10 years, the annual inflation rate in the United States has averaged 6½ percent. And during the 3 years before my Inauguration, it had increased to an average of 8 percent.

Inflation has, therefore, been a serious problem for me ever since I became President. We've tried to control it, but we have not been successful. It's time for all of us to make a greater and a more coordinated effort.

If inflation gets worse, several things will happen. Your purchasing power will continue to decline, and most of the burden will fall on those who can least afford it. Our national productivity will suffer. The value of our dollar will continue to fall in world trade.

We've made good progress in putting our people back to work over the past 21 months. We've created more than 6 million new jobs for American workers. We've reduced the unemployment rate by about 25 percent, and we will continue our efforts to reduce unemployment further, especially among our young people and minorities.

But I must tell you tonight that inflation threatens this progress. If we do not get inflation under control, we will not be able to reduce unemployment further, and we may even slide backward.

Inflation is obviously a serious problem. What is the solution?

I do not have all the answers. Nobody does. Perhaps there is no complete and adequate answer. But I want to let you know that fighting inflation will be a central preoccupation of mine during the months ahead, and I want to arouse our Nation to join me in this effort.

There are two simplistic and familiar answers which are sometimes proposed—simple, familiar, and too extreme. One of these answers is to impose a complicated scheme of Federal Government wage and price controls on our entire free economic system. The other is a deliberate recession, which would throw millions of people out of work. Both of these extreme proposals would not work, and they must be rejected.

I've spent many hours in the last few months reviewing, with my own advisers and with a number of outside experts, every proposal, every suggestion, every possibility for eliminating inflation. If there's one thing I have learned beyond any doubt, it is that there is no single solution for inflation.

What we have, instead, is a number of partial remedies. Some of them will help; others may not. But we have no choice but to use the best approaches we have and to maintain a constant search for additional steps which may be effective.

I want to discuss with you tonight some of the approaches we have been able to develop. They involve action by Government, business, labor, and every other sector of our economy. Some of these factors are under my control as President—especially Government actions—and I will insist that the Government does its part of the job.

But whether our efforts are successful will finally depend on you as much as on me. Your decisions—made every day at your service station or your grocery store, in your business, in your union meetings—will determine our Nation's answer to inflation as much as decisions made here in the White House or by the Congress on Capitol Hill.

I cannot guarantee that our joint effort will succeed. In fact, it is almost certain not to succeed if success means quick or dramatic changes. Every free government on Earth is wrestling with this problem of inflation, and every one of them knows that a long-term disease requires long-term treatment. It's up to us to make the improvements we can, even at the risk of partial failure, rather than to ensure failure by not trying at all.

I will concentrate my efforts within the Government. We know that Government is not the only cause of inflation. But it is one of the causes, and Government does set an example. Therefore, it must take the lead in fiscal restraint.

We are going to hold down Government spending, reduce the budget deficit, and eliminate Government waste.

We will slash Federal hiring and cut the Federal work force.

We will eliminate needless regulations.

We will bring more competition back to our economy.

And we will oppose any further reduction in Federal income taxes until we have convincing prospects that inflation will be controlled.

Let me explain what each one of these steps means.

The Federal deficit is too high. Our people are simply sick and tired of wasteful Federal spending and the inflation it brings with it.

We have already had some success. We've brought the deficit down by one-third since I ran for President—from more than $66 billion in fiscal year 1976 to about $40 billion in fiscal year 1979—a reduction of more than $25 billion in the Federal deficit in just 3 years.

It will keep going down. Next year, with tough restraints on Federal spending and moderate economic growth in prospect, I plan to reduce the budget deficit to less than one-half what it was when I ran for office—to $30 billion or less.

The Government has been spending too great a portion of what our Nation produces. During my campaign I promised to cut the Government's share of our total national spending from 23 percent, which it was then, to 21 percent in fiscal year 1981. We now plan to meet that goal 1 year earlier.

Reducing the deficit will require difficult and unpleasant decisions. We must face a time of national austerity. Hard choices are necessary if we want to avoid consequences that are even worse.

I intend to make those hard choices. I have already vetoed bills that would undermine our fight against inflation, and the Congress has sustained those vetoes. I know that the Congress will continue to cooperate in the effort to meet our needs in responsible, noninflationary ways.

I will use the administrative and the budgetary powers of my office, including the veto, if necessary, to keep our Nation firmly on the path of fiscal restraint.

Restraint involves tax policy as well as spending decisions. Tax reduction has never been more politically popular than it is today. But if future tax cuts are made rashly, with no eye on the budget deficits, they will hurt us all by causing more inflation.

There are tax cuts which could directly lower costs and prices and help in the fight against inflation. I may consider ways to reduce those particular taxes while still cutting the budget deficit, but until we have a convincing prospect of controlling inflation, I will oppose any further reductions in Federal income taxes.

To keep the Government to a manageable size, I'm ordering tonight a cut in Federal hiring. This order will mean a reduction of more than 20,000 in the number of permanent Federal employees already budgeted for this fiscal year and will cut the total size of the Federal work force.

I've already placed a 5½-percent cap on the pay increase for Federal employees, and Federal executive officers are receiving no pay increases at all.

It's not enough just to control Government deficits, spending, and hiring. We must also control the costs of Government regulations.

In recent years, Congress has passed a number of landmark statutes to improve social and environmental conditions. We must and we will continue progress toward protecting the health and safety of the American people. But we must also realize that everything has a price and that consumers eventually pick up the tab. Where regulations are essential, they must be efficient. Where they fight inflation, they should be encouraged. Where they are unnecessary, they should be removed.

Early this year, I directed Federal agencies to eliminate unnecessary regulations and to analyze the costs and benefits of new ones. Today, for instance, the Occupational Safety and Health Administration, sometimes called OSHA, eliminated nearly 1,000 unnecessary regulations.

Now, we can build on this progress. I've directed a council of my regulatory departments and agencies to coordinate their regulations, to prevent overlapping and duplication. Most important, the council will develop a unified calendar of planned major regulations. The calendar will give us, for the first time, a comprehensive list of regulations the Federal Government is proposing, with their costs and objectives.

As President, I will personally use my authority to ensure that regulations are issued only when needed and that they meet their goals at the lowest possible cost.

We are also cutting away the regulatory thicket that has grown up around us and giving our competitive free enterprise system a chance to grow up in its place.

Last year we gave the airline industry a fresh shot of competition. Regulations were removed. Free market forces drove prices down, record numbers of passengers traveled, and profits went up. Our new airline deregulation bill will make these benefits permanent. For the first time in decades, we have actually deregulated a major industry.

Next year we will work with Congress to bring more competition to others, such as the railroad and trucking industries.

Of all our weapons against inflation, competition is the most powerful. Without real competition, prices and wages go up, even when demand is going down. We must therefore work to allow more competition wherever possible so that powerful groups—government, business, labor—must think twice before abusing their economic power. We will redouble our efforts to put competition back into the American free enterprise system.

Another reason for inflation is the slow-down in productivity growth. More efficient production is essential if we are to control inflation, make American goods more competitive in world markets, add new jobs, and increase the real incomes of our people.

We've made a start toward improving productivity. The tax bill just passed by the Congress includes many of the investment incentives that I recommended last January. Federal support for research and development will continue to increase, especially for basic research. We will coordinate and strengthen Federal programs that support productivity improvements throughout our economy.

Our Government efforts will attack the inflation that hurts most, inflation in the essentials—food, housing, and medical care.

We will continue to use our agricultural policies to sustain farm production, to maintain stable prices, and to keep inflation down.

Rising interest rates have always accompanied inflation. They add further to the costs of business expansion and to what consumers must pay when they buy houses and other consumer items.

The burden of controlling inflation cannot be left to monetary policy alone, which must deal with the problem through tight restrictions on money and credit that push interest rates up. I will work for a balanced, concerted, and sustained program under which tight budget restraint, private wage and price moderation, and responsible monetary policy support each other. If succesful, we should expect lower inflation and lower interest rates for consumers and businesses alike.

As for medical care, where costs have gone up much faster than the general inflation rate, the most important step we can take is to pass a strong bill to control hospital costs. This year the Senate passed one. Next year I will try again, and I believe the whole Congress will act to hold down hospital costs—if your own Members of Congress hear from you.

Between now and January, when the new Congress convenes, I will be preparing a package of specific legislative proposals to help fight inflation.

The Government will do its part, but in a country like ours, Government cannot do the job alone. In the end, the success or failure of this effort will also rest on whether the private sector will accept—and act on—the voluntary wage and price standards I am announcing tonight.

These standards are fair. They are standards that everyone can follow. If we do follow them, they will slow prices down so that wages will not have to chase prices just to stay even. And they point the way toward an eventual cure for inflation, by removing the pressures that cause it in the first place.

In the last 10 years, in our attempts to protect ourselves from inflation, we've developed attitudes and habits that actually keep inflation going once it has begun. Most companies raise their prices because they expect costs to rise. Unions call for large wage settlements because they expect it to happen, it does happen; and once it's started, wages and prices chase each other up and up. It's like a crowd standing at a football stadium. No one can see any better than when everyone is sitting down, but no one is willing to be the first to sit down.

Except for our lowest paid workers, I'm asking all employees in this country to limit total wage increases to a maximum of 7 percent per year. From tonight on, every contract signed and every pay raise granted should meet this standard.

My price limitation will be equally strict. Our basic target for economy-wide price increases is 5¾ percent. To reach this goal, I'm tonight setting a standard for each firm in the Nation to hold its price increases at least one-half of one percentage point below what they averaged during 1976 and 1977.

Of course, we have to take into account binding commitments already in effect, which will prevent an absolute adherence to these standards. But this price standard is much lower than this year's inflation rate, and more important, it's less than the standard for wage increases. That difference is accounted for by rising productivity, and it will allow the income of America's workers to stay ahead of inflation.

This is a standard for everyone to follow—everyone. As far as I'm concerned, every business, every union, every professional group, every individual in this country has no excuse not to adhere to these standards. If we meet these standards, the real buying power of your paycheck will rise.

The difficulty with a voluntary program is that workers fear that if they cooperate with the standards while others do not, then they will suffer if inflation continues.

To deal with this concern, I will ask the Congress next January to enact a program that workers who observe the standards would be eligible for a tax rebate if the inflation rate is more than 7 percent. In other words, they would have a real wage insurance policy against inflation which might be caused by others. This will give our workers an additional incentive to observe the program and will remove their only legitimate reason not to cooperate.

Because this is not a mandatory control plan, I cannot stop an irresponsible corporation from rising its prices or a selfish group of employees from using its power to demand excessive wages. But then if that happens, the Government will respond, using the tools of Government authority and public opinion.

Soon after they raise prices or demand pay increases that are excessive, the company or the union will feel the pressure that the public can exert, through new competition to drive prices down or removal of Government protections and privileges which they now enjoy.

We will also make better use of the $80 billion worth of purchases the Government makes from private industry each year. We must be prudent buyers. If costs rise too fast, we can delay those purchases, as your family would, or switch to another supplier. We may not buy a fleet of cars this year, for example, if cars cost too much, or we may channel our purchases to suppliers who have observed our wage and price standards rather than to buy from those who have not.

We will require firms that supply goods and services to the Government to certify their compliance with the wage and price standards. We will make every effort, within legal limits, to deny Government contracts to companies that fail to meet our wage and price standards. We will use our buying power more effectively to make price restraint and competition a reality.

The Government now extends economic privileges to

many parts of the private economy—special franchises, protected wages and prices, subsidies, protection from foreign competition. If wages or prices rise too fast in some industry, we will take that as a sign that those privileges are no longer needed and that this protection should be removed. We will make sure that no part of our economy is able to use its special privilege or its concentrated power to victimize the rest of us.

This approach I've outlined will not end inflation. It simply improves our chances of making it better rather than worse. To summarize the plan I'm announcing tonight:

We will cut the budget deficit.

We will slash Federal hiring and reduce the Federal work force.

We will restrain Federal pay.

We will delay further tax cuts.

We will remove needless regulations.

We will use Federal policy to encourage more competition.

We will set specific standards for both wages and prices throughout the economy.

We will use all the powers at our disposal to make this program work.

And we will submit new anti-inflation proposals to the Congress next January, including the real wage insurance proposal I've discussed tonight.

I've said many times that these steps will be tough—and they are. But I also said they will be fair—and they are. They apply equally to all groups. They give all of us an equal chance to move ahead.

And these proposals, which give us a chance, also deserve a chance. If, tomorrow or next week or next month, you ridicule them, ignore them, pick them apart before they have a chance to work, then you will have reduced their chance of succeeding.

These steps can work, but that will take time, and you are the ones who can give them that time. If there's one thing I'm asking of every American tonight, it is to give this plan a chance to work—a chance to work for us.

You can help give it that chance by using your influence. Business and labor must know that you will not tolerate irresponsible price and wage increases. Your elected officials must know how you feel as they make difficult choices.

Too often the only voices they hear are those of special interests, supporting their own narrow cause. If you want Government officials to cut inflation, you have to make sure that they hear your voice. I have heard you with unmistakable clarity.

Nearly 40 years ago, when the world watched to see whether his nation would survive, Winston Churchill defied those who thought Britain would fall to the Nazi threat. Churchill replied by asking his countrymen, "What kind of people do they think we are?"

There are those today who say that a free economy cannot cope with inflation and that we've lost our ability to act as a nation rather than as a collection of special interests. And I reply, "What kind of people do they think we are?"

I believe that our people, our economic system, and our Government are equal to this task. I hope that you will prove me right.

Thank you, and good night.

33
Those Mystifying Guidelines

Executives struggle with the paper chase in never-never land

"The program-year rate of price change is the sales-weighted average of the percentage changes of a company's product prices measured from the last calendar or fiscal quarter completed prior to October 2, 1978, through the same quarter of 1979."

Anyone who is an expert at deciphering gobbledygook might lend a hand to C. Milton Allen, senior vice president of Houston's Panhandle Eastern Pipe Line Co. For the past two months, he and 15 aides have been waging a bleary-eyed battle to make sense out of not just that mumbo-jumbo masterpiece but plenty of others like it. The language is from the pricing regulations drawn up by the Council on Wage and Price Stability (COWPS) to enforce Jimmy Carter's Stage II guidelines. The rules were supposed to put some muscle into the White House's campaign against inflation, but they have become a source of bafflement for lawyers, accountants and businessmen everywhere.

Under the plan, labor and management would cooperate through a system of voluntary restraints in which both sides would make sacrifices. With some exceptions, price rises would be held to less than the average of the past two years, while wages and most benefits would go up no more than 7% annually. All companies, no matter how large or small, would be expected to follow the guidelines. Firms with sales of $250 million or more annually would have to file reports to COWPS showing that their price rises were being kept within the prescribed limits. Offenders would first be warned privately by COWPS. If that did not work, they would be publicly denounced—in extreme cases by Alfred Kahn, who is Carter's chief spear carrier against inflation.

Carter's inflation fighters did score early success in persuading unions to restrain wage demands, but last week the AFL-CIO announced plans to challenge the program in court. The federation argues that the National Labor Relations Act requires employers to bargain "in good faith" with unions, and claims that doing so is impossible if companies know they can lose federal contracts by agreeing to excessive wage increases.

The hardest struggle has been to police prices. In the U.S.'s trillion-dollar economy, no single formula could be fair to every company. COWPS' 45-page booklet of basic regulations is so loaded with well-intentioned but confusing caveats, qualifications and exceptions that not even lawyers seem able to understand it. Meanwhile, fresh legalese spews forth almost daily from COWPS in an effort to clarify, amplify or refine earlier regulations and procedures.

This has placed a staggering burden on COWPS' 130-member staff. Though it is growing by 10 to 15 a week, the staff has a budget for only 230 employees, vs. the more than 4,500 that administered wage-price controls during the Nixon years.

Even a cast of thousands seems barely adequate. Every day more than 1,200 phone calls come in from corporate comptrollers and finance officers anxious to learn what the regulations actually mean. Tidal waves of paper work arrive in the mail from companies disgorging themselves of pricing data in an effort to prove compliance or plead for exemptions, or just beat back the bureaucrats with a statistical deluge. Example: when Carter complained that Hershey Foods was raising the price of its candy bars by a nickel (to 25¢) in November, Hershey fought back by barraging COWPS Director Barry Bosworth with data on such minutiae as how many times a year the company prints candy wrappers. The answer: once.

More data may soon be pouring in. Responding to a personal telephone plea by Carter to help COWPS monitor price rises around the country, AFL-CIO President George Meany last week urged union members to jot down the cost of goods in stores. Labor will gather the data and mail them to Washington. That, of course, will simply overload the already groaning machinery.

It is doubtful that COWPS can even keep track of, let alone digest, the data that it is already collecting. Early in February it published a list of 207 of the nation's largest corporations that had replied favorably to President Carter's appeal to cooperate. This promptly brought protests from officers of 200 more companies, who said that their firms had also pledged to help. The companies charged that bureaucratic oversight, which in some cases resulted from actually losing the compliance letters, created the false impression that the firms did not intend to play ball at all.

Whether or not his staff catches up with the paper chase, Bosworth is encouraged by the reception that businessmen are at least publicly giving the program. Says he: "They come in saying they want to be in compliance and asking how to do it. They're grudgingly going along. Philosophically, they don't like the guidelines, but they want to comply."

Tough as it is, compliance is easier for giant corporations than for companies that have sales of $250 million to $500 million. These middle-size companies often lack the in-house legal and accounting expertise, let alone Washington law firm contacts, necessary to figure out COWPS' demands or to protest if they seem excessive. Says Bosworth: "We're getting cooperation from large corporations but not from the small ones. The smaller firms look at the regulations and sometimes say, 'My God, I can't even read them.'"

Even so, executives seem willing to give Stage II a chance. They fear a groundswell of support for mandatory controls if Carter's voluntary approach fails. Says Justin Dart, chairman of Dart Industries of Los Angeles (Tupperware, Duracell batteries): "I have a lot of doubt about whether the guidelines will work, but no doubt at all about doing everything we can to make them work."

One difficulty is that many firms failed to keep track of all the prices they have charged over the past two years. Now they have to go back and try to gather every price on every product. Edmund Pratt Jr., chairman of Pfizer Inc., the pharmaceuticals maker, says that it has taken his staff "many, many hours" to dig up such data and that the expense to the company was "very, very high."

Managers in high-technology industries complain that the guidelines may boomerang because limits on wage increases could cause some companies to lose efficiency and thus force them to raise prices. The dilemma is severe in the microelectronics industry, where rapidly rising salaries have attracted top engineers, pushed up productivity dramatically, and enabled companies to slash prices year after year. Data General Corp. has already filed for exemptions, and Digital Equipment Inc., another leading electronics firm, is also complaining about the impact the guidelines could have on it.

The guidelines are riddled with uncertainties. It is unclear whether companies can raise prices to cover increased costs brought on by Government regulations, such as Washington's antipollution and stiffer mileage standards for the auto industry. What to do about rising prices of raw materials is equally vague. Companies are supposed to be able to pass them along, but under the guidelines materials suppliers should keep the prices from going up in the first place. In theory that is fine, but prices for many of the most essential commodities—oil, aluminum, copper—are partly or wholly set

Reprinted by permission from TIME, The Weekly Newsmagazine; Copyright Time Inc. 1979.

by foreign producers and cartels, like OPEC, that care nothing at all for the niceties of Stage II.

Some executives worry about the possibility of stockholder suits. Says George Kneeland, chairman of St. Regis Paper Co.: "Within legal limits, companies are in business to maximize profits. But if the guidelines are simply voluntary and not actual law, why should a company comply with a program that limits profits? You're in never-never land."

In an effort to get executives back on a firmer footing, COWPS is drafting what amounts to a translation of the pricing regulations into plain English. This, Bosworth hopes, will help smaller corporations to comprehend and comply. There will also be much more public pillorying of greedy companies and unions in the coming weeks. Explains Bosworth: "These firms are spending millions of dollars on p.r. that could be wiped out if the finger is pointed at them. They don't want the image of being unpatriotic."

In winning compliance with the guidelines, public criticism may be more effective than the threat of cutting off Government contracts. It is, of course, true that many powerful corporations depend on federal projects. Says Norman Roberts, a Litton Industries vice president: "You're damned right I take the warnings seriously. I have to. It's a very crucial part of our sales." But there is a real question about whether or not an attempt to withhold a contract could be made to stick. The precedents are unclear, and lawyers for the General Accounting Office, which watches over contract awards, have testified that denying a contract to the lowest bidder would be illegal.

Ultimately, the best hope for beating inflation is not to browbeat industry and unions but to deal with the inflationary plague that is spread by the Government. Certainly wage and price restraint is important, and Stage II is better than outright controls. But excessive Government spending, towering deficits and ever multiplying regulations are also fundamental causes of the price spiral. Says Pfizer's Pratt: "We have told the President, as most companies have, that we will abide by the guidelines. But what the Government itself is doing is a big part of the problem." In short, the nation would benefit tremendously if Washington were to adopt and obey some price guidelines of its own. ∎

34

Braking the Spiral?
Wage-Price Guidelines Just May Help a Bit, Many Executives Say

Most Big Firms Seen Likely To Comply; U.S. Deficit, Teamster Pact Hold Key

Pressure Put on Suppliers

By RALPH E. WINTER
Staff Reporter of THE WALL STREET JOURNAL

Don't give up on President Carter's wage-price guidelines yet. Many executives making key wage and price decisions at big companies haven't.

In the first place, the executives say, the "voluntary" program isn't voluntary for the nation's 500 largest companies; they have little choice but basically to comply, although they may bend the standards a bit. And while the executives don't view the program as any panacea, they expect it to hold wages and prices somewhat below levels that would be reached without such guidelines.

Their optimism is tempered with many qualifications. They are well aware of how strongly the inflationary current is running. The Labor Department has just announced, for example, that last month producer prices for finished goods—products ready to be shipped to retailers—rose at a 15.6% annual rate, the highest in more than four years. One government analyst observed that the "increase pervaded the entire spectrum of goods at all stages," and Alfred Kahn, chairman of the Council on Wage and Price Stability, called it a "catastrophe."

The optimistic executives also acknowledge that the four-month-old guidelines program has had little effect so far and even that it still is so undeveloped that its eventual impact is highly uncertain. Moreover, inflation may worsen for a while because of the Iranian oil cutoff and soaring prices of basic commodities. And above all, the executives emphasize that if the federal government fails to do its part, the guidelines program will wither and die.

Teamsters in Spotlight

First, the executives say, the Carter administration has to force the huge Teamsters union to accept a contract that at least appears to meet the guidelines. But one skeptical company president says, "Frankly, I'm not convinced Carter has the backbone to stand up to the Teamsters. And if the Teamsters get 10% a year, we're not going to take long strikes trying to get our employes to take 7%."

And then, the executives add, Congress has to adhere to President Carter's pledge to reduce the federal budget deficit. But many doubt that Congress has the backbone to stand up to the political pressures generated by budget-cutting.

So, some observers are pessimistic. "The wage and price guidelines are all cosmetic," says David M. Zarnoch, a Cleveland Trust Co. economist. He says the inflation rate will be determined by the money supply and the size of the federal deficit—both decided politically and not by companies and unions subject to the guidelines.

Cost-Push Theory

However, many company officials are more optimistic about the guidelines than some recent public assessments would seem to indicate. "Prices are high and rising because of cost-push inflation," says A. J. Ashe, senior vice president of B.F. Goodrich Co., who is overseeing compliance at the big manufacturing concern. He expects the guidelines to limit the rise in labor costs and to force companies to try to hold down other costs as well. "Some people may be surprised at how effective the program is," Mr. Ashe says.

Many purchasing agents agree. A survey of the National Association of Purchasing Management found that 62% of members responding expect the wage-price guidelines to work "moderately" well in curbing inflation.

What's more, top executives of leading companies say they are supporting the program. They cite three reasons: The government has too many levers, such as regulatory actions, import policies, contracts and tax rulings, for them to risk ignoring the guidelines. Second, although profits probably will be hurt a bit for some companies and paper work will expand for all, the guidelines aren't expected to be particularly painful; holding down wage increases, for instance, doesn't irk companies. Finally, corporate officials are extremely concerned about inflation and fear much-harsher mandatory controls if the present effort fails.

Impact of Compliance

The executives say their compliance with the guidelines will affect prices and wages in several ways:

—It will delay and limit price increases by the major companies themselves. Most concerns say they will comply on a company-wide basis, by limiting average price increases on all their products during the 12 months begun last Oct. 1 to 0.5 percentage point below their average annual rate of increase during 1976 and 1977.

—Major companies won't allow suppliers to raise prices at will. The guidelines give purchasing agents a little more determination and muscle in the unending shoving match with suppliers.

—Monitored companies will shell out a little less in pay increases. Many expect to grant more than 7% a year in combined wage and benefit improvements, "but we can wrap ourselves in the flag and get a little more leverage at the bargaining table," says one industrial-relations vice president.

One survey of 634 big companies found that 73% have cut budgets for salary increases and that the average boost will be 7.1%, instead of the 8.5% previously planned.

And companies will work harder to control other costs. More capital spending will be aimed at cost-cutting rather than expansion, for instance, and plant managers will come under intense pressure to save money.

Unfortunately, consumers won't notice much change in the price spiral for some months, at least. Because the currently surging producer prices haven't been passed along at the retail level yet, the 9% rise in consumer prices last year won't moderate quickly. In addition, producer prices themselves are still being pushed up by price and wage increases effected before the guidelines program was begun.

And other inflationary forces are at work. U.S. demand remains strong for most products, and economic expansion in Europe and Japan is helping push up prices of internationally traded commodities such as pulp, steel scrap, hides and textile fibers. The guidelines can't fend off higher prices for imported products—the most-pointed example of which is oil. The guidelines also are severely limited because they don't apply to many inflation-prone consumer goods and services, such as meat and produce, mortgage interest rates, utility bills and auto-repair charges; in fact, many of the monitored companies have been raising prices far less than the overall increase in consumer prices. And an inflationary psychology has been building up among Americans, with everyone trying to raise his own income and prices as fast as possible to avoid being left behind.

The upshot of all these forces, economists and corporate executives say, is an inflationary momentum that only a rigidly enforced wage and price freeze could halt quickly.

Moreover, federal inflation-fighters, beset by many sticky problems, haven't been able to institute quickly even their "voluntary" guidelines. Bureaucratic confusion also apparently has taken its toll. Mr. Kahn, chairman of the Council on Wage and Price Stability, said recently that only 207 of the top 500 companies had pledged that they "intend" to follow the guidelines, but many of the companies omitted from his list complained that they had indeed announced similar intentions. Mr. Kahn himself said that "the overwhelming majority of the remaining responses expressed support for the guidelines program but asserted they needed to await further clarification" of the standards. Standards still haven't even been set for the banking industry.

The council will get a further indication today of companies' willingness to cooperate. About 1,000 of the biggest concerns are due to submit data on how they are organized for purposes of complying with the guidelines; involved will be such information as how subsidiaries or various lines of business will be handled in reporting price increases. In addition, approximately the

Reprinted by permission of the *Wall Street Journal.* © Dow Jones & Company, Inc., 1979. All Rights Reserved.

500 largest companies are supposed to file financial data showing their prices and profit margins during a base period.

Despite the many problems, optimistic corporate officials think that the guidelines will gradually brake the inflationary spiral —if the program is accompanied by prudent government fiscal and monetary policies and if the Teamsters are whipped into line.

"Other than the Mafia, there's nobody less popular than the Teamsters," one executive says, "so the administration could make some real points by standing up to them."

According to key corporate officials, here is the outlook:

BIG COMPANIES' PRICES: Few companies are bumping into ceilings yet. Most went into the program with a good price-cost relationship, partly because they anticipated controls. Auto makers, for instance, got a big 1979-model price increase early. Executives expect fewer price increases in February and March, a little spurt in April and May and then another period of more-stable prices. The reason: Corporations are allowed to make half their price increases for the current fiscal year before March 31 and the other half in the six months to Sept. 30. So some companies are posting most increases in the first few months of each half-year to obtain maximum benefit.

Guidelines are limiting price increases on some items, such as steel, that purchasing agents think otherwise would go higher. But some companies, such as Dow Chemical Co., expect competition to prevent them from raising prices anywhere near the ceilings. And in other cases, the guidelines may delay routine price increases, and such delays in themselves slow inflation, says Frank C. Roberts, a vice president of Eaton Corp., a diversified manufacturing company.

Overall, the impact is expected to be modest. Some companies may switch to the alternative method of compliance—limiting profit margins on sales to the average of the best two of the past three years—if unexpected cost increases force them to raise prices above guideline levels. But most hope to avoid conceding that they can't comply with the price test.

SUPPLIER PRICES: Many monitored companies say they expect their suppliers to obey the rules, too. "Most of our vendors were prompt in saying they intend to comply," says George A. Harris, vice president, materiel, at TRW Inc., a big manufacturer. "In a few instances, we've told suppliers making increases that appeared to be out of line to show us in writing how they are in compliance. Only one supplier took an arbitrary position of 'pay up or we'll take you out of the delivery schedule,'" Mr. Harris says.

Pitney-Bowes Inc. wrote to more than 2,000 suppliers, including publications in which it advertises, and asked them to comply. So far, "well over a third" have responded, all favorably, says the office-equipment concern, adding that the guidelines are "bound to have a trickle-down effect." Other companies say they will use the guidelines to put pressure on hospitals, doctors and others providing services under fringe-benefit plans. Goodrich's Mr. Ashe says he was instrumental in scaling back a 15% rise in room charges at an Akron hospital where he serves on the board.

WAGES AND SALARIES: Companies think the guidelines will have real impact on labor costs, if the Teamsters comply. "We have settled four contracts that do comply with the guidelines, and we have taken a strike at another location" to obtain such a contract, says the president of a large industrial-products company. "They weren't big unions that could expect 10% a year, but we were able to use the guidelines to pull down their expectations from 8½% or 9% to about 7% a year."

Corporate officials cite the recent oil-industry settlements, which comply with the guidelines, as evidence that the program is moderating contracts. But the 60,000 refinery workers have limited bargaining power because supervisors can run the highly automated refiners for months.

However, only about 20% of the nation's work force is unionized, executives note, and the other 80% is even more vulnerable to the pay limits. A big consumer-products company, for instance, gave non-union employes a 5% general pay raise this year, down from the 6% granted a year ago when the cost of living was rising more slowly. Some will get merit raises on top of that, but the total pay-out will comply, the company says.

Nonetheless, salaried employes at many big companies probably will get average pay increases exceeding 7%. Retirements usually remove higher-paid people from the payroll and allow others to be promoted to higher brackets. Some concerns say they can give increases averaging about 9% without pushing total salaried payroll through the 7% ceiling. Raises granted under cost-of-living escalators, which are calculated for guideline purposes as if consumer prices were rising at a 6% annual rate, also will help push some pay increases over 7% a year, employers add.

OTHER COSTS AND PROFITS: Monitored companies will sharpen their already-effective cost-control systems, but some expect the guidelines to drag down profits a bit. "We'll have to work together harder than ever on worker productivity and efficient use of our resources," says Ruben F. Mettler, TRW chairman and chief executive. "If we did nothing extra, the guidlines program would cost us something in earnings. I would guess that there will be a modest negative impact anyway, but we'll minimize it through improved cost-effectiveness."

Many executives expect the guidelines to help gradually slow down cost increases across much of the economy. If, for example, big companies grant smaller pay boosts, everyone's labor costs—the largest element in the cost of goods and services—will begin rising more slowly, the executives say. To the extent that the guidelines reduce inflation and help strengthen the dollar in world markets, import prices may climb more gradually. Interest rates may drop. And, with price increases limited, the guidelines may spur suppliers to try to maintain profits by improving efficiency.

However, nearly all corporate executives say the guidelines will be useful only on a short-term basis, by helping slow the inflationary spiral while more-fundamental policy changes start attacking its basic causes.

"We are complying with the guidelines, with the spirit as well as the letter, because we know it is in our best long-range interest to do so," Eaton's Mr. Roberts says. "But the more rules they write, the more difficult it is to live with the program. And the longer it lasts, the more apparent its weaknesses will become."

35

Most prices are already controlled but not by the government.

The Case for Controls

by Robert Lekachman

Last month in *The Wall Street Journal*, Herbert Stein, the conservative economist who reluctantly presided over Nixon price and wage controls in 1971 and afterwards, warned President Carter that he was poised upon the slippery downward path toward the same destination. Stein sketched a strong story line. Jawboning *a la* Robert Strauss will be a palpable fiasco, leading to "voluntary" guideposts or—in Carter administration newspeak—"standards" for allowable wage and price hikes. As the standards predictably become items of hooting and derision, various politicians eat their previous statements in the national interest and opt for mandatory powers over refractory corporations and unions. All that separates 1978 from 1971, Stein said, is a new control gimmick. This is TIP, short for tax-based incentive schemes which either promise rewards for good behavior (the Arthur Okun model) or impose tax penalties for inflationary conduct (the Henry Wallich-Sidney Weintraub variant). Otherwise, *plus ca change, plus c'est la meme chose*. As expected, Stein's moral is: stop right here and turn back before it is too late.

I agree with Stein that controls are in our near future. Unlike him, I consider them potentially benign, if they are appropriately designed and judiciously applied. What follows then is a minority case for controls which, the pollsters report, are favored by a majority of the public, but opposed by business, labor, and most of my colleagues. It is well to start with a practical consideration. In the absence of credible executive action against inflation, the Federal Reserve will do its thing by raising interest rates so high and reducing monetary growth so severely that our aging business cycle recovery will sputter to a halt and give way to another recession. Ominous signs are numerous that the Fed has already embarked on just such a course. Although G. William Miller is younger, brisker, and shorter of wind than the canonized Arthur Burns, he is as much imprisoned by the anti-inflation ideology of central banking as any other Federal Reserve chairman.

The latest Congressional budget resolution, it is true, can be interpreted as a sign of fiscal restraint and an excuse for the Fed to control its anti-inflationary zeal. The projected 1979 fiscal year deficit, a mere $38.7 billion, is smaller both than the current deficit and the administration's projections for the coming year. Unfortunately today's inflation has more to do with cost-push pressures and external events than with excessive total demands for goods and services. It is simply not true that too many dollars (created by federal profligates) are chasing too few goods and services. Notwithstanding popular mythology about the inevitable connection between federal deficits and inflation, a truly balanced federal budget would moderate inflation only slightly. But it certainly would precipitate a sharp contraction and sickening unemployment rates.

Still something must be done about inflation. The omniscient pollsters, once more, report that it is the most pressing of public issues. Its impact resonates in the defeat of "big-spenders" like Representative Donald Fraser in Minnesota and "big taxers" like

Massachusetts's Governor Michael Dukakis. Continuing inflation is certain to cause the defeat in November of more liberals and more liberal legislation. Humphrey-Hawkins has become the victim of the new conservative mood stimulated by inflation.

The outlook is anything but cheerful. The second-quarter jump in the cost of living exceeded an annual rate of 10 pecent. Price increases seem to have moderated since then, but the pause is likely to be temporary. In 1979, a series of major labor contracts come up for renewal—petroleum refining in January, construction beginning in February, trucking at the end of March, rubber in April, clothing in May, electrical products in July, meatpacking in August, and autos and farm implements in September. These agreements cover nearly two million workers and exert a strong influence upon labor costs in the non-union sector. The outcome of teamster negotiations, applicable to over a half a million truck drivers, is especially important. There is not a hope in hell that any union would be allowed by its members to settle for an increase smaller than the current inflation rate plus something extra for gains, real or conjectural, in productivity.

As everybody including the Carter administration and the Fed fully realizes, unless the cost of living is somehow controlled in the next few months, a series of 1979 labor contracts will be negotiated at highly inflationary rates. In the waning months of 1978, the grim choices before the White House are a credible anti-inflation program or a presidential reelection campaign in the middle of a recession. Congressional fiscal restraint and Federal Reserve monetary policy manifestly are inadequate. All that is left is controls.

Are controls even worse than unemployment and inflation? Ask almost any economist and he or she will enthusiastically itemize the trade's bill of particulars against controls. The familiar litany goes like this. Controls rudely interfere with market haggling which generates prices and wage rates consistent with the intensity of consumer demand and the eagerness of sellers to fill it. When the customers are in an acquisitive mood, prices rise—as they should. When the merchants are hungry for sales, they slash prices and run legitimate sales—as they should. Shifting consumer tastes, changing relationships between the demand for and the supply of various skills and frequent innovations by profit-seeking business types all guarantee constant flux in myriads of individual prices. Nobody sets either prices or wage rates. They emerge from the interplay of consumers seeking to maximize their satisfactions and producers equally intent on maximizing profit, just as your introductory textbook explained these matters.

When the process works well, sellers respond alertly to the signals their customers emit. The latter evoke more supply when they buy unexpectedly large quantities. When consumers unexpectedly buy less than sellers hoped, retailers, wholesalers, and processors all reduce orders or output. The consumer is king or queen, caster of the dollar votes which enrich some businessmen and bankrupt others.

Into this competitive Eden enter the controllers equipped with a barrel of apples of discord. To set prices, wages or both is to design a multitude of regulations. As ever, hordes of bureaucrats are mobilized to compose, administer and interpret them. All bureaucracy is slow, cumbersome, inflexible and unimaginative, and public bureaucracies are the most club-footed of all. Before long, inequities begin to multiply. Evasion and black markets proliferate. At some point, controls break down as the inevitable consequence of public resentment, intolerable interferences in private decisions and sheer unworkability. The economy is set free, wages and prices explode and the net impact of the economy's temporary captivity is some alteration of the chronology of inflation—a bit less during the controls phase and a great deal more in its aftermath. In retrospect the Nixon controls were just successful enough in 1971 and 1972 to aid the reelection of their perpetrator. When they were drastically weakened, early in 1973, inflation resumed as though nothing had happened. Thus it has been since the days of Diocletian, that pioneer Roman price controller. Never has it been possible for very long, major wars alone excepted, to maintain effective controls in market economies.

If by chance controls do persist for years or decades, they defeat their own aims. In New York City, it is frequently claimed, the net effect of rent controls is rapid housing abandonment, sluggish construction of new apartments and inadequate maintenance of existing structures. Furthermore, rent control provides inadvertent subsidies to many lucky but unneedy middle-class tenants, among them the writer of this article, the mother of a former editor of this journal and others of our like. As I shall shortly suggest, there is another side to this story.

The case for controls is much stronger than the cynical argument that presidents, contemplating the next election in fear and trembling, tend to resort to them in preference to executive inaction which opens the door to recession and involuntary retirement to civilian life. The case *against* controls is premised on the prevalence of free competition. Only when prices and wages are the genuine product of individual preferences, competitively exerted by buyers and sellers, do markets really operate to widen individual choice, encourage innovation, reward efficiency, and punish sluggards.

But genuine price competition occurs only when sellers are too numerous to collude tacitly or overtly to avoid such rivalry. Unhappily a very large part of the American economy is otherwise arranged. In most branches of manufacturing members of the *Fortune* honor roll—the mighty 500 largest corporations—play dominant roles. In 1977 the auto big three registered sales respectively of $55 billion, $19.2 billion and $7.7 billion. The tidy total, $81.9 billion, is about five percent of GNP. Who believes that General Motors, Ford, and Chrysler engage in classic price competition? As the universe is aware, General Motors has traditionally acted as the industry's price leader. Price leadership is commonplace in industries organized in large units.

These industries are numerous and important. The seven sisters of the energy industry—Exxon, Texaco, Mobil, Standard Oil of California, Gulf, Standard Oil of Indiana, and Shell are majestic presences not only in oil extraction, transportation, refining and marketing, but also in coal, shale, solar research and a variety of activities unrelated to energy. These "rivals" are intricately associated with each other in dozens of joint ventures.

IBM of course dominates computer technology and sales. General Electric and Westinghouse lead in consumer appliances and industrial equipment. Reynolds and Kaiser share the market for light metals. General Mills, Beatrice Foods, Ralston Purina, Borden, Coca Cola and General Foods are the princes of processed foods. And so on.

Market power is concentrated in finance as well as manufacturing. In 1977 our 50 largest commercial banks enjoyed deposits of $521.2 billion and loans of $380.7 billion. By themselves, the five leaders—Bank of America, Citicorp, Chase Manhattan, Manufacturers Hanover and J. P. Morgan—presided over deposits of $219.2 billion and loans of $162.3 billion.

As those who lack the green stuff need not be reminded, money is political as well as economic power. In 1974, when New York's big banks stopped marketing municipal bonds and notes, the city teetered on the edge of default. In 1978 New Yorkers continue to live with the consequences of this financial decision, among them several levels of supervision of city affairs exercised variously by the Secretary of the Treasury, the governor of the state, the Municipal Assistance Corporation and the Emergency Financial Control Board. Services are fewer, the streets are dirtier and treatment of the poor is meaner as a consequence of essentially private decisions by those who wield great power. In its reluctant approval last summer of loan guarantees, Congress extended outside supervision of the New York budget for as long as 19 years.

Huge assets are similarly concentrated in the coffers of the larger life insurance companies. Last year the assets of the top fifty totaled $278.1 billion. As usual, in the land of giants, the tallest half dozen tower over their fellows. Prudential, Metropolitan, Equitable, New York Life, John Hancock and Aetna registered balance-sheet assets of $155.2 billion, substantially more than half of the sum for the 50 leaders. These massive organizations (dare I call them bureaucracies?) make investment decisions of tremendous community import. A discreet policy of redlining "changing" neighborhoods (read increasingly black and Hispanic) accelerates deterioration, discourages local merchants and white residents and brings to pass the prophecy of decline implicit in the original redlining decision.

At the risk of becoming tedious, I must add a word about public utilities. ATT is seven times the size of General Telephone & Electronics, number two. Blessed as it is by profits of $4.5 billion, assets in excess of $94 billion and nearly a million employees, no wonder that ATT has won most of its contests with state and federal regulators. Even New York's warmly despised Con Ed ranked seventh in 1977 with assets of $6.8 billion and profits of $323.6 billion, blackout or no blackout.

I recite these dreary statistics in reiteration of a single, simple point. Over a broad expanse of the American economy, price competition is a myth. In 1974 and 1975, two bad years for auto sales, GM and its friendly rivals *raised* prices about $1000 per chariot. This year when the appreciation of the mark and the yen substantially increased the dollar prices of Volkswagens, Toyotas, Datsuns and Hondas, the American companies did not gratefully seize a chance to enlarge the domestic share of the rapidly growing subcompact market. Instead in the wake of each German or Japanese price advance, domestic producers raised their own prices. Somewhat similar events have occurred in steel. Over the years the companies have raised prices, lost customers to foreign producers and substitute materials, and screamed successfully for federal help. The Carter administration's trigger price system, welfare for the mighty, has allowed domestic prices and profits to rise and thus done its bit to exacerbate inflation.

These market strategies may be either intelligent or stupid from the standpoint of managers and stockholders. Here the relevant, crucial fact is the sheer capacity of a very few human beings at the head of a small number of huge private enterprises to choose pricing policies capable of either promoting or diminishing inflation. GM's Thomas Murphy might have decided to sell more units at lower average prices and unit profits. He opted for fewer units at higher prices. For all I know (or Mr. Murphy knows), this was the right way to maximize long-run profits. No one can be sure. But the process of decision is far removed from textbook expositions of how prices emerge from the interplay of supply and demand. These prices "emerge" from the deliberate meditations of a very few people. Even the textbooks concede that the normal effects of oligopoly include higher prices, smaller output and larger marketing and advertising expenditures than their parallels in competitive markets.

In passing, I should properly salute another sacred cow. Americans revere both the oldest antitrust statutes in the universe *and* the large corporations whose conduct they ostensibly monitor. As Thurman Arnold persuasively argued four decades ago, the major function of the Sherman and Clayton Acts is the rendition of occasional ceremonial exorcisms of monopoly that reassure the gullible and allow conglomerates to spread and multinationals to proliferate. The antitrust division of the Department of Justice celebrated a famous triumph over the oil trust—in 1911. Things have not gone so well since then.

If antitrust is a farce, inflation is a permanent menace, fiscal and monetary policy are demonstrably incapable of combining reasonably full employment with acceptable price behavior and deep recession is politically and socially unacceptable therapy, there isn't much left except some kind of incomes policy. No wonder then that so many countries on so many occasions have ignored their economists and installed social contracts (Great Britain), price controls (Sweden), combinations of wage and price controls (the usual American preference) or national wage settlements implicitly combined with price restraint (the Netherlands and West Germany).

Our choice in 1978 and 1979 is between a good and a bad set of controls. Good controls begin with recognition that concentration of economic power, an apparently permanent characteristic of advanced industrial societies, requires an equally durable political response. President Carter ought to seek and Congress ought to grant power in appropriate circumstances to impose price controls, wage controls or both. In a democracy government can appropriately refrain from regulation of the private sector only in those industries where competition genuinely disperses economic power. In the 50 percent or more of the economy dominated by large units, substitution of public price standards for private ones is a gain in political accountability. Voters routinely evict politicians who bungle. Against private price controllers they have no practical recourse.

Controls must be equitable if widespread resistance, evasion and active sabotage are to be averted. In current conditions, there is an excellent case for accepting George Meany's challenge. Still brooding over the injustices of Nixon controls, Mr. Meany has consistently insisted that before unions can fairly be expected to restrain their demands for wage improvement, sellers must first display appropriate price discipline. Despite much political propaganda to the contrary, union settlements up to now have been generally moderate, the special case of the miners aside. Even strong unions have done little more than keep abreast of the cost of living. The Carter administration, whose relations with the unions are strained, could do worse than opt for price controls and proceed to wage controls only if price controls fail to evoke good union behavior.

Sensible controls are selective, not universal. Nixon's efforts to regulate retail prices were ill-advised on at least three grounds. They required a huge bureaucracy for effective enforcement. They generated much resentment, especially in the hearts of small merchants, crushed by new paperwork. Worst of all, they were unnecessary. With only a few exceptions, retailing is a genuinely competitive activity. Here the general case in favor of free markets and against controls contains merit. Controls ought to be applied to the concentrated sectors in which very large private bureaucracies operate major economic units. The numbers of such units are small enough to be supervised by a control bureaucracy quite modest in size.

Here it is appropriate to return briefly to rent controls. If the New York experience of them has been one of exemplary horror, why are an increasing number of other communities reimposing or thinking of reimposing these dreadful devices? For partisans of "free" markets, the explanation is unpleasant. It is the fact that the construction industry has lamentably failed to provide anything like the needed quantities of low and moderate price housing, privately owned or rental. The average price of a home today is $63,000, and it is rising one percent monthly. This means only the top fifth of the income distribution can really afford to buy a home. Now, a combination of cash allowances for low-income families and publicly financed modestly priced apartments and homes is certainly preferable to controls on grounds of both equity and efficiency. But with all their inequities and inefficiencies, controls seem preferable to a "free market" in real estate without these added elements which do not seem to be in prospect. Thus the cry for controls is likely to increase in intensity wherever—as in health and housing—markets fail to deliver the goods.

Ours is an inflationary world. Controls over concentrated industries, and activities like construction and health where market failure is glaring will drain only some inflation out of the American or any other economy. Harvest failures enlarge farm exports to the Russians, the Chinese and the Africans. Supermarket prices rise. Frost destroys the coffee harvest in Brazil. OPEC plans to respond to the inflation which it helped mightily to stimulate by raising 1979 prices. We are increasingly entangled in a world economy and affected by our currency and trading connections with friends, enemies and neutrals.

Controls are no panacea. Nevertheless, some restraint of inflation is preferable to none or very little. In the modern world, the giant corporation, usually global in scope, is the successor to the Holy Roman Church of the Middle Ages and the national state which followed it. Corporate decisions affect all of us far too intimately to allow of private autonomy.

Candidate Carter had it right when he opted for standby controls. President Carter has it wrong in opposing such controls now. He should make a meal of his more recent instead of his earlier utterances.

The Economic Consequences of Wage-Price Guidelines

MICHAEL E. TREBING

VOLUNTARY wage and price guidelines have now been adopted as a major element in the Government's anti-inflation program. The pricing behavior of firms and wage demands of labor are considered by a large portion of the population to be incompatible with the social objective of reducing inflation. Restraint in wage and price movements is believed to be necessary. Monetary and fiscal restraint alone apparently have been judged as either not being able to accomplish this objective or as carrying too high a cost, in terms of lost output and employment.[1]

Although the guideline approach is popular with the public, remarkably little discussion has been directed toward its implications.[2] In particular, the probable efficiency and distributional consequences of the program have received little public attention.

THE DECELERATION PLAN

Wage and Price Arithmetic

The Administration has set explicit numerical standards for wage and price increases.[3] The basic guidelines specify that annual increases in wage and fringe benefits be held below 7 percent and that price increases be limited to 0.5 percent less than their annual rate of increase during 1976-77.[4] An alternative test for firms is to apply a "profit-test." If a firm cannot meet the price standard, it is requested to limit its pre-tax profit margin on sales to the average of the best two of the past three years. In addition, total profit increases must be below a 6.5 percent ceiling, unless accounted for by volume increases.

The program requires that deceleration of prices be achieved in each market, purportedly with individual firms sharing equally in the burden of lowering inflation.[5] The target for inflation is 6 to 6.5 percent over the first year of the program. In order to reach these objectives, the program's aim is to have prices rise at the same rate as unit labor costs, with average wage increases of 7 percent minus 1.75 percentage points for projected productivity growth yielding an inflation rate of 5.25 percent. The Administration allows an additional 0.5 percent for "legislatively mandated payroll costs" and arrives at a rate of 5.75 percent.[6] The Administration states: "The wage/price standards are designed to serve as guides for the behavior of decision-making agents who have *discretionary power over the prices and the wages* that they receive."[7] [emphasis added]

While the guidelines are "voluntary," the Administration has emphasized its intention to compel firms to comply by manipulating both Federal procurement policy and the Government's broad regulatory authority. The program also encourages that the force of public exhortation be directed at those large firms which exhibit "excessive" price increases.

The Administration has requested that Congress pass a "real wage insurance" program. Under this scheme, workers who meet the pay standard will receive a tax rebate if the rate of inflation exceeds 7 percent. The purpose of the rebate is to reduce workers' fear of cooperation by insuring that they will not have their purchasing power reduced if the rate of inflation is not held to less than 7 percent.[8]

---

[1]This conclusion is clearly stated in *White Paper: The President's Anti-Inflation Program* (accompanied the President's announcement of the guideline program on October 24, 1978) pp. 1-4.

[2]A recent public opinion poll demonstrates the popularity of the adopted guideline policy. In a November 1978 Harris Poll 63 percent of the respondents supported the program. See Louis Harris, "Americans Support Anti-Inflation Plan," *St. Louis Globe-Democrat*, October 20, 1978.

[3]In this article the word "standards" is used interchangeably with guidelines and guideposts. For details of the program see U.S. Council on Wage and Price Stability, *Fact Book: Wage and Price Standards* issued October 31, 1978.

[4]Ibid. pp. 20-40. The pay standard applies not to individual workers but to average pay increases for "groups" of workers.

The price standards are directed at individual firms and apply to an "overall average price" and not to specific products.

[5]See *White Paper*, p. 7.

[6]*Fact Book*, pp. 15-16. Even with widespread compliance, the Administration concedes that prices will probably rise within the range of 6 to 6.5 percent. This would represent, however, an improvement over the first six months of 1978 when prices rose at a 10 percent annual rate.

[7]Ibid. p. 16. The paragraph continues: "Thus, standards are not directly relevant to pricing behavior in those markets in which prices are determined by the impersonal workings of supply and demand." The program exempts raw materials and auction type markets which include (1) prices of agricultural and industrial raw materials, (2) interest rates, and (3) prices which historically have moved in tandem with an organized open exchange market.

[8]Note that a 7 percent pay increase and a 7 percent inflation rate gives zero increase in real income *before* taxes — even if productivity rises 1.75 percent. Given the progression in the income tax structure, real income (after taxes) declines. See Nancy Jianakopolos, "Paying More Taxes and Affording It Less," this *Review* (July 1975), pp. 9-13.

Reprinted from Federal Reserve Bank of St. Louis *Review*, December, 1978.

Incomes Policy and Inflation

Voluntary wage and price standards can be classified as an "incomes policy". This generic term, loosely defined, includes all of those actions taken by a government to affect the level of money incomes or prices by actively participating in wage and price decisionmaking.

Although more popular in European countries, a wide range of incomes policies have been tried in the United States in recent years.[9] Included have been relatively weak attempts to persuade or "jawbone" specific firms and workers to hold down wage or price increases in the spirit of social responsibility.[10] Such a program was adopted during the Kennedy Administration and carried over into the early years of the Johnson Administration. At the other extreme, incomes policies have included former President Nixon's rigid program of mandatory criteria for wage and price behavior throughout the entire economy. Guidelines represent an attempt to achieve a compromise between the two extremes. By strengthening the persuasive element used under the jawboning method while attempting to avoid the harsh consequences of strict wage and price controls, guidelines represent a politically tempting route.

WHAT "CAUSES" INFLATION?

The "Cost-Push" View

The acceptance of voluntary wage and price standards as an alternative prescription for reducing the general rate of inflation stems from the idea that inflation is generated by "cost-push" factors. This view describes how rising wages, the largest component of business costs, continually force prices upward. The resulting inflation is known to the public as a wage-price spiral. A similar version of this view concludes that inflation is the consequence of increases in the market power of firms and labor over the prices they charge. According to this analysis, prices and wages are "administered" by large firms and trade unions without regard to competitive market forces.

The cost-push view has great popular appeal since it depicts the inflation process as a struggle for income shares between capitalists and workers. However, economic theory reveals that many implications of this view of inflation are illogical or, at best, questionable.[11] It is argued that monopoly power exists in the market place and that firms have the ability to push prices above competitive levels and raise the average price level. But this analysis ignores the question of why the monopolies had been charging less than the high monopoly price.

The theory of monopoly pricing predicts that firms which have protection from the entry of competitors into their markets are able to receive prices above those of competitive markets. Once the monopoly price has been achieved, however, further increases are limited to the opportunities provided by the market. If monopoly power is now causing prices to rise, either monopoly power is increasing or monopolists had been behaving irrationally and have just discovered their market advantage. There is little evidence to support either alternative.[12]

Undeniably, many economic groups exhibit enough market power to influence the level of certain prices and wages. These monopoly prices are higher than they would be if the specific market were competitive. But, except for a slight rise due to the resource misallocation, the overall level of prices and wages will remain substantially unchanged.[13] For example, if wages in a particular industry are pushed up above competitive levels less employment will result. Labor will then be released for use in other sectors where a downward pressure on wages will result until a new equilibrium is reached. More importantly, however, this analysis is unable to explain persistent increases in prices, month after month, year after year.

A Monetary View

An alternative theory is that inflation is a monetary phenomenon. This view holds that changes in money

---

[9]For historical surveys of incomes policy in the United States and abroad see U.S. Congress, Congressional Budget Office, *Incomes Policies in the United States: Historical Review and Some Issues*, May 1977; Lloyd Ulman and Robert J. Flanagan, *Wage Restraint: A Study of Incomes Policies in Western Europe* (Berkeley, California: University of California Press, 1971); Walter Galenson, ed., *Incomes Policy: What Can We Learn From Europe?* (Ithaca, New York: New York State School of Industrial and Labor Relations, Cornell University, 1973); and Craufurd D. Goodwin, ed., *Exhortation and Controls: The Search for Wage-Price Policy, 1945-1971* (Washington, D.C.: The Brookings Institution, 1975).

[10]These efforts are sometimes referred to as "moral suasion."

[11]See George J. Stigler, *The Organization of Industry* (Homewood, Illinois: Richard D. Irwin, Inc., 1968), pp. 244-45 and Milton Friedman, "What Price Guideposts?", *Guidelines: Informal Controls and the Market Place*, ed., George P. Shultz and Robert Z. Aliber (Chicago: University of Chicago Press, 1966), pp. 17-39.

[12]For a survey of the evidence regarding the relationship between market concentration and price changes see Steven Lustgarten, *Industrial Concentration and Inflation* (Washington, D.C.: American Enterprise Institute for Public Policy Research, 1975).

[13]One purpose of a union monopoly, for example, might be to gain real wage benefits for its rank and file. To accomplish this objective the union has several alternatives available to it. It may try to reduce the supply of labor through restrictive licensing practices or by not allowing non-union workers

growth exert a strong influence on total spending in the economy. When people find that they are holding cash balances which are greater than desired, they spend the excess money on real and financial assets and bid up their prices.

The monetary view does not deny the existence of a wage-price spiral, but interprets the cost-push analysis as a confusion of the cause and effect relationships of the inflation process. According to the monetary view, the observed patterns of wage and price adjustments are normal responses to excessive money growth. For inflation to persist, the higher prices, *no matter where they originate*, must be validated by increases in the money supply. With money growth held constant, price increases can be maintained only through reduced production and employment. For such a situation to persist, businesses would have to willingly accept lower profits and labor would voluntarily remain unemployed and refuse to accept employment at lower wages. The empirical evidence does not support such irrational behavior.[14] Only when monetary authorities actively ensure that the spiral is fully augmented through increases in the money supply, will inflation result.

WILL VOLUNTARISM SUCCEED?

The underlying requirement for a successful guideline policy is that firms and wage-earners restrain themselves from acting economically as *individuals*. In a market economy the motive of individual self-interest is crucial. Consumer preferences are revealed through the market by nonrestricted opportunities and/or purchases of goods and services at their market price. These prices reflect not only the costs of production, but also the nature of demand for the good in question. The free movement of prices and the consequent incentives and disincentives that are created assure that resources in the economy will move toward satisfying these individual demands.

An appeal for individual restraint conflicts with a very basic economic observation about human behavior — consumers naturally strive to maximize their individual well-being. Economic self-interest is the major motivating factor behind economic activity. Guidelines, on the other hand, represent rules that substitute "social responsibility" for self-interest. The conflict between the two views is glaring. Economic incentives argue against *individual* compliance with the social motives and wealth is transferred to those who stand apart from the program.

The Kennedy Administration guideposts of 1962-67 represent a prime example of these conflicts. This voluntary program established upper wage limits which were equal to overall productivity gains for the economy.[15] The problem which resulted in the demise of the productivity rule was that the guideline principles did not take into account the fundamental pressure created by accelerated money growth. When the productivity guidelines were initially adopted, the trend of productivity growth was substantially above the rise in consumer prices. Wages based on the productivity rule thus provided for growth in real wages (money wages adjusted for price changes). As money growth accelerated and inflationary pressures intensified in 1965 and 1966, the wage standard became viewed as unfair. Labor, discovering that the purchasing power of their wages was falling, found the argument for holding down wages unacceptable. As key settlements began to exceed the guideposts, the program was abandoned.

The degree of compliance with price guidelines will be associated with the severity of the penalties against those who choose to ignore them. If the controls are truly voluntary and involve no costs for violation, there is little chance that they will succeed since gains from noncompliance can be realized without costs. If economic sanctions are used against violators, however, each firm will weigh the expected costs and benefits involved. If the expected costs of noncompliance are less than the benefits, the firm will choose to ignore the guidelines.[16] Avoidance can also take the form of "black-market" transactions above the controlled price or product quality changes.

Though the burden of the program is intended to be equally shared, this will not be the case. Government penalties through procurement policy will not affect private decisions in a uniform fashion. Some firms are dependent upon either government purchases of their output or are directly influenced by government policies. Other firms, however, may be outside the range of government sanction. Holding down the price of particular goods by penalties benefits the purchasers of these goods and the sellers of unaffected competitive goods. The losers are the sellers of the controlled goods, those prospective buyers of the controlled goods who can no longer

---

to obtain jobs. Secondly, the union might seek a higher wage through collective bargaining and thus accept the unemployment forthcoming at this higher wage.

[14] See Denis S. Karnosky, "The Effect of Market Expectations on Employment, Wages and Prices," Working Paper #17, Federal Reserve Bank of St. Louis.

[15] The Council of Economic Advisers, *Economic Report of the President* (Washington, D.C.: United States Government Printing Office, 1962), pp. 185-90.

[16] The same type of "cost-benefit analysis" will occur when labor contemplates compliance with wage guidelines and the rebate scheme which supplement them.

Table I

Productivity Changes for Selected Industries, 1971-76
(Annual Rates of Change)

	Output per Employee-hour[1]
Hosiery	11.1%
Synthetic Fibers	7.4
Wet Corn Milling	7.2*
Aluminum Rolling & Drawing	5.5
Pharmaceutical Preparations	4.3
Paper, Paperboard, & Pulp Mills	2.5
Petroleum Refining	2.1
Steel	1.8
Concrete Products	0.8*
Primary Aluminum	−1.4
Hydraulic Cement	−1.5
Copper Rolling & Drawing	−1.7
Coal Mining	−4.3

*1971-75

[1]The output per employee-hour figure is computed by dividing an output index by an index of aggregate employee-hours for production workers.

Source: U.S. Department of Labor, *Productivity Indexes For Selected Industries*, 1977 edition, p. 5.

Table II

Wages, Prices and Employment by Industry (1971-77)
(Annual Rates of Change)

	Prices[1]	Employment[2]	Wages[3]
Manufacturing	6.0%	1.0%	7.7%
Construction	8.2	1.1	5.7
Services	7.3	3.8	7.7
Trade	6.5	3.1	6.4
Finance	4.9	2.8	6.6
Communications	3.4	0.9	9.9
Transportation	5.9	0.8	7.7
Utilities	8.9	1.1	7.8
Mining	18.2	5.1	9.6
Agriculture	9.5	2.7	6.5

[1]Changes in implicit GNP price deflator by industry.
[2]Full-time and part-time employees.
[3]Labor compensation per full-time equivalent employee.
Source: *Survey of Current Business.*

obtain them, and the purchasers of the competitive goods. The losses exceed the gains because of the misallocation of resources.

The proposed "real wage insurance" plan which would supplement the guidelines, if enacted, serves to shift the burden of compliance among economic groups. If certain workers are guaranteed a constant real wage, the forthcoming rebates could reduce real incomes to the rest of the nation provided there is an increase in the federal deficit. To the extent that these larger deficits are "monetized", inflationary pressures will be supplemented, thereby reducing the wealth of all holders of money and monetary instruments.[17]

The real-wage insurance program is said to be capable of breaking inflationary psychology and be able to bring about more rapidly the achievement of price stability. Lower expectations of inflation in the future, according to this view, would translate into lower demands for wage increases and eventually lower prices. This viewpoint, however, confuses how inflation expectations develop. Expectations *per se* do not cause inflation. Curbing expectations will require controlling of the underlying force which causes them to prevail. If price controls only delay the upward thrust of prices caused by expansive money growth, expectations of future inflation will not be reduced.

If inflation expectations are not reduced by slower monetary growth, the longer-run objective of reaching price stability will be abandoned. For example, since market pressures will eventually push prices upward, reaching the objectives of wage stabilization in the future will be made more difficult. Following a period of controls, a stable wage structure is far more likely to allow a resumption of moderate rates of wage increase than a structure in which distortions, perpetuated by public policies, require rapid readjustment at the bargaining table. Experience with this type of "wage-price explosion" is well documented from European experience with control programs.[18]

MARKET DISTORTIONS AND CONTROLS

Most economists agree that, for the sake of efficiency, *relative* wages and prices should remain flexible. Relations among the wages of workers of different skills and of workers in different localities, industries or even firms should be allowed to vary according to changes in demand and supply. For example, firms which are growing have an incentive to hire scarce resources (labor and capital) away from other firms. Consequently, if upper limits are imposed upon the payments that can be offered to attract scarce inputs, the firms will not be able to meet the demand for their output. Relative prices, therefore, should be allowed to move in order to allocate resources into their most productive uses.

The dynamic character of the U.S. economy is evident from Tables I and II. The tables display that changes in employment and prices have varied across industries. Some industries have experienced rapid productivity growth; others have not. Employment growth has varied from industry to industry and generally reflects underlying demand conditions. The application of a single price and wage standard to all situations ignores this ongoing adjustment process

---

[17]For an analysis of the administrative problem with the "real-wage insurance" program, see Gardner Ackley, "Okun's New Tax-Based Incomes Policy Proposal," *Economic Outlook USA* (Winter 1978), pp. 8-9.

[18]Ulman and Flanagan, *Wage Restraint,* p. 223.

and confuses movements in relative prices (shifts of resources between economic groups) and the general level of prices. To minimize efficiency losses, it would be necessary to keep a watchful eye on individual wage and price relationships and make exceptions based on individual market situations. A tradeoff is therefore faced by the policymaker. The more stringent the guideline (less exceptions) the greater the efficiency losses. On the other hand, "weak" guidelines are not likely to gain the acceptance of the populace who judge the probable success of the guidelines by the strictness of the program. The program is therefore unlikely to reduce inflation expectations.

Implicit in the decision of who should be covered by guidelines are important judgments regarding the distribution of income among industries and between the factors of production. In other words, control programs politicize questions of income distribution. In a market economy, relative prices are signals that allocate society's resources into their most productive uses. Reflecting changing market conditions, these relative prices are always in motion and are independent of political criteria for distributing income between economic groups. Any guideline based on a simple percentage price increase for all individual firms, however, is implicitly centered on an acceptance of wage and price relationships (at the time of policy implementation) as stable ones and assumes that the relationships will remain fixed throughout the period of the guidelines.

Direct government controls, therefore, offer little inducement for the efficient development and use of resources, and contain no automatic mechanism for resource adjustments and the alleviation of shortages or excesses in production. Rather than being an aid to growth and vitality, they lead to retardation of economic resiliency and replace market forces by political ones.

The U.S. experience with control programs demonstrates these market misallocations. Price controls during World War II resulted in the substitution of low-quality goods for higher quality goods and black markets were commonplace as individuals developed lack of respect for the law. In later years, subsidies to producers became an increasing part of the control program as fixed prices were insufficient to provide the necessary incentives for production. Recent voluntary programs were also unable to avoid selective scarcities. For example, the Kennedy guideposts were blamed for shortfalls in supply of aluminum and sulfur and potential users were forced into using costly substitutes. Similarly, under the Nixon Administration controls, shortages developed for zinc, lead, steel, fertilizer, petrochemical products and a long list of other products.

Table III

The 1962-66 Guideposts Period

Annual Percentage Changes

	M1[1]	WPI[2]	CPI[3]
1962	2.2%	0.3%	1.1%
1963	2.9	−0.3	1.2
1964	4.0	0.2	1.3
1965	4.3	2.0	1.7
1966	4.7	3.3	2.9

[1]Demand deposits plus currency and coin held by the nonbank public.
[2]Wholesale Price Index.
[3]Consumer Price Index.
Source: Department of Commerce.

THE ROLE OF MONETARY ACTIONS

The program is further complicated by the timing of monetary action. In order to validate decelerating inflationary pressures, it will be necessary to supplement the program by tighter monetary action — reducing growth in the money supply. But a problem exists in the timing of monetary actions and the control policy. Relations observed in the past indicate that previous changes in the money supply have effects on current variables — the pattern of aggregate spending is determined by past monetary actions.[19] A perfectly timed effort by monetary and price control authorities will be difficult to achieve.

The apparent failure of the Kennedy and Nixon control programs to reduce inflation can be interpreted in a monetary framework. A monetary explanation for the failure of the 1962 guideposts is evident in Table III. When the guidelines were adopted, consumer prices were rising at a moderate 0.7 percent rate. (The average change in the Wholesale Price Index between 1958 and 1964 was near zero.) Throughout the life of the guideposts (1962-66), however, money growth increased steadily each year. The money stock grew 1 percent per year from 1959 to 1961, but increased steadily each year of the program.[20] Correspondingly, prices and wages moved upward reacting to the more rapid growth of spending. When the program was abandoned in 1966, consumer prices were rising at the rate of 3 percent.

During the Nixon price control period (1971-74), money growth data reveals that the controls camou-

---

[19]One study which provides a more detailed statement of the theory and evidence supporting these conclusions is Leonall C. Andersen and Keith M. Carlson, "A Monetarist Model for Economic Stabilization," this *Review* (April 1970), pp. 7-25.

[20]Empirical support for the money-price relationship for the period 1955 to 1971 is presented by Denis S. Karnosky's, "The Link Between Money and Prices — 1971-76," this *Review* (June 1976), pp. 17-23.

flage a period of overly expansive monetary policy during the 1970's. Although non-monetary factors (the oil embargo and the shock of controls) temporarily influenced the money-price relationship, the growth of the price level by 1975 paralleled that rate predicted by the trend growth of money.[21]

Movements in the rate of inflation have been closely associated with movements in the trend growth of the money stock. The accompanying chart shows that both U.S. control periods since World War II have been marked by money growth above its long-run trend. Correspondingly, in both cases rates of change in prices eventually moved upward reflecting this long-run trend.

Without curtailing aggregate spending, individual demands will be simply shifted among controlled and uncontrolled goods.[22] Holding prices below their market clearing levels will increase the quantity demanded of controlled goods. If total spending is not reduced through monetary or fiscal actions, those who are unlucky and do not receive the goods that would have been supplied without controls, will shift their spending to other products which represent, in most cases, close substitutes. The increased demand in uncontrolled markets will put upward pressure on these prices.

CONCLUSION

"Voluntary" wage and price guidelines have recently been adopted as an accompanying policy alongside the more traditional economic stabilization tools of monetary and fiscal policy. By establishing rules for pricing behavior, the Administration hopes to dampen a wage-price spiral that appears to be self-sustaining.

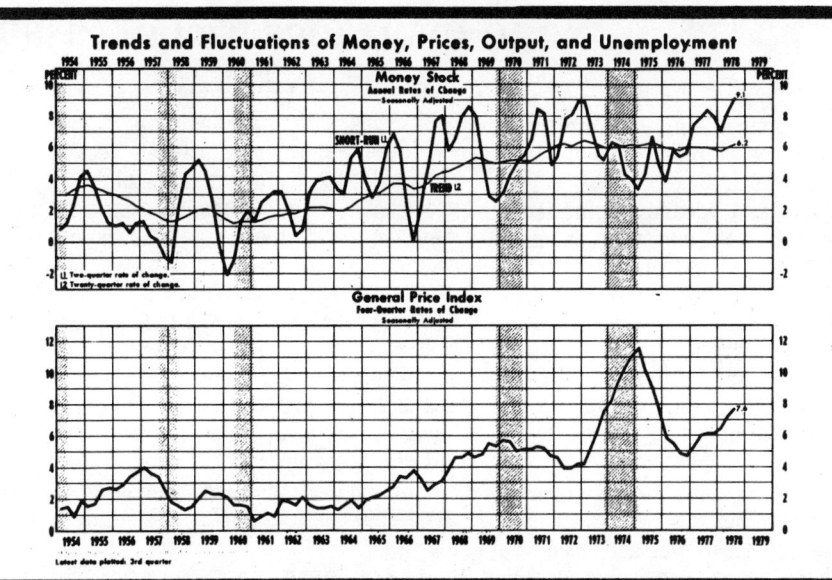

According to the monetary view of inflation, the logical foundation of the control program confuses the results and causes of inflation. According to this view, inflation results when money growth persistently exceeds growth in the amount of money demanded. The observed wage and price adjustment (the so-called wage-price spiral) are but parts of the general response in the economy to excessive money growth. Inflation expectations, which are generated by excessive money growth, will be reduced only when the growth rate of money is slowed.

Any short-term benefits received from strict compliance with the guidelines will be costly. The unconstrained market system provides an efficient signaling system for moving resources between alternative uses. Any control framework will probably conflict with these price signals and will cause distortions which reduce the resiliency of the market system to changing market conditions. The emergence of black-markets and disguised price increases through reduced product quality are two examples of devices that have arisen in response to previous programs and may arise in the current program to circumvent the controls.

Past incomes policies in the U.S. have been unable to reduce inflationary pressure because monetary actions remained expansive. If monetary actions remain expansive throughout the current program, accelerated inflation appears inevitable. The fundamental forces of supply and demand cannot be repealed through *any* type of control program.

---

[21] Ibid.
[22] The word "controlled" refers equally to those "voluntary" responses that are reactions to government sanctions.

37

Wage Insurance Embarrassment

As the Congress reconvenes, it finds itself facing a major problem: how to save the administration's face on its wage insurance proposal. The House Ways and Means Committee, which was to hold hearings on the President's wage insurance proposal on January 22, has had to postpone the hearings because of a lack of credible witnesses to testify in its behalf. And Treasury Secretary Blumenthal has apparently advised the President not to press the proposal and suffer another defeat.

The problem is that the wage insurance proposal, as we remarked the first time we saw it, was scribbled on the back of an envelope. One would have hoped that the administration would have learned something from its experience with the $50 rebate, "comprehensive" tax reform and the crude oil equalization tax. But scrutiny of the wage insurance proposal shows that President Carter has once again committed the prestige of his office to a gimmick.

The administration's anti-inflation program is based on the idea that wage increases determine the rate of inflation. If wages rise, say 7% faster than productivity does, then inflation is expected to be 7%. In this view, the way to prevent inflation from rising is to get agreement on a 7% cap on wages and salaries. Since few believe the administration's theory of inflation and fewer still want to be held to a 7% increase if inflation is higher, agreement has been hard to get. To secure agreement, the White House proposed to insure people against inflation in excess of 7%. If inflation turned out to be 10% after all, each person would receive 3% of his wages as a (taxable) tax credit.

If this seemingly simple idea had been staffed out, the administration would have discovered a whole series of problems. If money continues to grow faster than output, inflation will continue, and the wage insurance scheme will be far from costless. Indeed, with wage and salary disbursements running at over $1.1 trillion, the cost could be as high as $11 billion for every percentage point of inflation above 7%—a big gamble to take on a bad theory. If everyone is covered and inflation ends up at 10% anyhow, the $30 billion budget deficit becomes a $63 billion deficit, further escalating inflation.

The administration claims the proposal would be costless, but its own lack of confidence in this assertion is shown by its proposal to limit the potential revenue loss by insuring only the first $20,000 of a worker's wages against only 3 percentage points of inflation above 7%. The administration's own doubts have not reassured the unions.

Other problems arise with inequities of coverage. Farmers and the self-employed are not eligible for the insurance, while workers whose wages wouldn't have gone up by more than 7% anyway are rewarded if inflation is higher.

And there is the matter of fringe benefits. If they are not included in the 7% cap, unions can force high-cost compensation packages on employers and then collect on the wage insurance. If fringes are included, some way must be found to value them—not always an easy task. The current cost of future pension benefits depends on the method of funding, for example, and their value to the worker depends on his longevity. The most likely outcome amounts to fighting inflation with mountains of paperwork.

What strikes us as the biggest problem of all, however, seems to have escaped everyone's attention. A worker who agrees to a 7% pay increase instead of a 10% increase has not just given up 3% for one year only. He has given it up for every future year as well. A 35-year-old worker earning $20,000 who forgoes a 10% raise for a 7% one has given up $600 in each of the next 30 years. He is out $18,000, and is not compensated by a one-shot $600 tax credit.

To truly compensate the worker, the tax credit has to be given for every year of his working life. That mounts up rapidly. If only half of the $1.1 trillion wage and salary disbursements are covered and inflation is 10% instead of 7%, $16.5 billion must be added each year to the government's budget for a period equal to the average life expectancy of the current work force. In the second year of the program, the 7% raises get compounded into the insured wage base, so if 10% inflation continues the government has to shell out a new $17.7 billion plus repeating the first year's $16.5 billion. Even if inflation thereupon stopped, to keep the work force whole it would be committed to $34.2 billion each year for a long time to come.

The wage insurance proposal is so sloppy that it raises, yet again, questions about the administration's competency. As in the case of the $50 rebate, we will credit the President when he eventually recognizes a bad proposal, bites the bullet, and withdraws it. But we would much rather credit him with the ability to learn to test the water before he jumps in.

Reprinted by permission of the *Wall Street Journal*. © Dow Jones & Company, Inc., 1979. All Rights Reserved.

38

The minimum wage: a perspective

The Federal minimum wage was established in the depression conditions that gripped the United States economy in the late 1930's. Aimed at bolstering the paychecks of low-wage workers, the law not only has continued but has been expanded. Now, forty years after the initial legislation, the minimum wage provisions cover nearly two thirds of the nation's employees. More than 4½ million workers, or about one in every twenty workers, were directly affected by the 15 percent jump in the Federal minimum wage to $2.65 on January 1, 1978. While such increases in the legal wage floor have the beneficial effect of raising the earnings of particular segments of the working poor, they also entail certain social costs as well. Increases in the minimum wage contribute to raising the underlying rate of inflation. At the same time, because laws cannot mandate increases in worker productivity, a higher wage floor can exceed some employees' productivity so that employers cut back on their payrolls, creating unemployment for some. Recent research suggests that increases in the minimum wage serve to raise the joblessness of teenagers, particularly minority youths.

The minimum wage forty years later
The Fair Labor Standards Act (FLSA) of 1938 was designed to improve the working conditions of American labor. Among other features, the legislation introduced a minimum wage of 25 cents per hour that would serve as "a floor under wages". At first, the minimum wage was limited to employees in industries engaged in the production of goods for interstate commerce. It is estimated that initially the legislation covered about 11 million workers, or about 25 percent of total employment.

Over the ensuing forty years, various amendments and revisions raised the minimum wage (table). As a result of the 1977 amendments, the legal wage floor rose to $2.65 per hour and, on January 1, 1979, the wage floor is legislated to rise to $2.90 per hour. Subsequent increases are slated to bring it to $3.35 per hour at the beginning of 1981.

As the wage rate was raised over the years, the coverage of the legislation has been broadened to the point that coverage has expanded markedly in low-wage industries.[1] By 1976, some 56 million workers, or close to two thirds of total employment, were covered by Federal minimum wage legislation. The continued expansion of coverage of the minimum wage provision of the FLSA was reversed by a 1976 Supreme Court decision. In a ruling, referred to as the National League of Cities decision, the Court held that state and local government employees who are engaged in traditional governmental functions are not subject to the minimum wage provisions. As a consequence, an estimated 5 million workers were removed from the coverage of the legislation.

From the start, the FLSA allowed employers to apply the value of board, lodging, and other facilities traditionally furnished to employees toward meeting minimum wage requirements. In 1966, when the coverage of the minimum wage was extended to many workers whose compensation depended importantly on tips, the amendment permitted employers to count employees' tips as meeting up to one half of the minimum wage. In addition to raising the minimum wage, the 1977 amendment provided for a step-by-step reduction in this "tip credit" from the current 50 percent to 40 percent by 1980.

Coverage of the FLSA's minimum wage provisions

---

[1] As the coverage of the minimum wage has been expanded, the pay of newly covered workers has not been immediately brought into parity with the wages of those already covered. Instead, wage schedules have been established to bring the newly covered workers gradually into equality with the general minimum wage over a period of several years.

Reprinted from Federal Reserve Bank of New York *Quarterly Review*, Autumn, 1978.

Chronology of Federal Minimum Wage and Worker Coverage, 1938-81

Effective date	Minimum wage ($ per hour)	Worker coverage (in thousands)
October 24, 1938	.25	11,000
October 24, 1939	.30	12,500
October 24, 1945	.40	20,000
January 25, 1950	.75	20,900
March 1, 1956	1.00	24,000
September 3, 1961	1.15	27,500
September 3, 1963	1.25	27,500
February 1, 1967	1.40	40,400
February 1, 1968	1.60	41,600
May 1, 1974	2.00	56,100
January 1, 1975	2.10	57,400
January 1, 1976	2.30	56,100
January 1, 1978	2.65	51,900*
January 1, 1979	2.90	†
January 1, 1980	3.10	†
January 1, 1981	3.35	†

* National League of Cities decision eliminated most state and local government coverage.

† Not available.

Source: United States Department of Labor, Employment Standards Administration.

has always varied with respect to industry and occupational groups. In many industries, such as manufacturing and transportation, the coverage is nearly complete. Institutions of higher education, as well as certain other employers of full-time students on a part-time basis, may offer wage scales at special rates below the minimum. In addition, in order not to burden small businesses, the Congress exempted retail and service firms with annual sales of less than $250,000 from the minimum wage. As a result of the 1977 FLSA amendments, this sales level was raised to $275,000 on July 1, 1978 and is scheduled to rise further, ultimately reaching $365,500 on December 31, 1981. With respect to occupations, executive, administrative, professional, and outside sales jobs, as well as casual baby-sitting and serving as a companion for the aged and infirm, are exempt from minimum wage legislation.

Hurting some it aims to help

Concern for the well-being of low-income Americans led the Congress to enact and to expand the minimum wage legislation. Underlying these Congressional actions was the view that any employed American should be able to enjoy a standard of living above the poverty level. There is little question that, for the majority of workers whose wages are close to the minimum, an increase in the minimum wage increases their paychecks and they are better off than they would be otherwise. But that is only one effect of an increase in the minimum wage. While lawmakers can raise *wage rates*, incomes may not necessarily increase since the higher wage will result in some workers being unable to find jobs or working fewer hours. The central problem is that laws cannot mandate increased worker productivity.

If the minimum wage is raised above the pay level consistent with a worker's productivity, employers respond by reducing their payrolls. Who will bear the burden of the higher minimum? It will be the least productive, low-skilled workers—those whose productivity is below the hourly wage floor. In the jargon of economists, they are the "marginally productive" workers, many of whom are teenagers and minorities, who lack experience and suffer handicaps that lower their productivity.

For the most part, economic theory has always recognized that imposing a wage floor creates unemployment for some. What economists were unable to answer was whether the unemployment effects were large or small. For many years, numerous studies tried to evaluate the impact of the legislated wage on unemployment, but the results were inconclusive. The problem centered on isolating the effects associated with the minimum wage from the myriad of influences that affect unemployment. More recently, however, the inconclusive evidence of the past has given way to research that has established a clear link between unemployment among youths, especially minority youths, and increases in the minimum wage. The econometric evidence offered by Gramlich, Ragan, and Mincer, among others, has clearly established that teenagers' employment is adversely affected by the minimum wage legislation.[2] Establishing this relationship meant using advanced statistical tools that were designed to distinguish between the effects of the minimum wage and the influence of other factors, such as economic activity.

Why does the minimum wage affect teenagers? The answer is simple: most young people are low-wage earners and, as a result, raising the minimum wage can be expected to have a more pronounced impact on them than on other workers. In mid-1977, the average

---

[2] Edward M. Gramlich, "Impact of Minimum Wages on Other Wages, Employment, and Family Incomes", *Brookings Papers on Economic Activity* (II, 1976); James F. Ragan, Jr., "Minimum Wages and the Youth Labor Market", *Review of Economics and Statistics* (May 1977); Jacob Mincer, "Unemployment Effects of Minimum Wages", *Journal of Political Economy* (August 1976).

teenager was paid $2.58 per hour, some 28 cents above the 1977 minimum and 7 cents below the 1978 minimum. Black youths were paid even less, on average.

Although the estimates of the effect of a raise in the minimum wage on youth joblessness differ, a reasonable estimate suggests that by itself raising the minimum wage to $2.65 per hour added about 1 percentage point to the unemployment rate of all teenagers and 3 to 4 percentage points to the jobless rate of black youths. In addition, on the basis of historical experience, the increase in the minimum wage may be expected to reduce substantially full-time employment of teenagers and to force many of them into part-time employment.[3] Although these youths will be denied full-time employment, they will be employed on a part-time basis and will not be included among the jobless.

With increases in the minimum wage serving to reduce job gains, teenage joblessness, especially among minorities, remains an important social problem. In September 1978, the teenage unemployment rate stood at 16.6 percent, remaining unrelentingly high. Among black and other minority youths, the official rate of joblessness hovered close to 35 percent in September 1978. Moreover, the official rate of unemployment probably *understates* the actual unemployment of youths, particularly among blacks and other minorities. This understatement is because many minority youths, faced with such limited prospects of finding employment, simply withdraw from the labor force by ceasing to look for work, and thus are no longer counted among the unemployed. The result is that a much smaller proportion of minority youths are in the labor market. For example, the participation rate of young black males is around 40 percent, compared with some 65 percent of white youths who are in the labor force.[4]

A high rate of joblessness among youths is not new, nor is it unique to the United States.[5] The rate of unemployment among young people should be expected to be greater than for adults. In part, this is because youths are not closely tied to the labor market and are also searching alternative job opportunities.

But the current rate of joblessness is unacceptably high. What is particularly distressing is that early experiences in the labor market are likely to affect lifetime earnings and employment behavior. Thus, the lack of jobs means failing to gain on-the-job training, work experience, and the opportunity to develop work habits. Government programs such as the minimum wage inhibit the efficient functioning of the markets, tending to raise the rate of unemployment.

The "need" to limit low-paying jobs

One point made by some in support of the Federal minimum wage is that increasing the legal wage floor is a way of eliminating menial, or so-called "dead-end", jobs. Employers respond to the increase in wages by substituting capital for labor inputs. Such capital outlays serve to raise productivity, or output per man-hour, which means a higher standard of living for the nation. Advances in the nation's potential to produce are to be desired, but the unemployment associated with such changes as the replacement of manually operated elevators by automatic elevators is not necessarily welcome. Many of today's high school seniors, let alone the large number of dropouts from school, lack the basic reading, writing, or computational ability necessary to obtain entry to skilled jobs. In view of these realities, there is clearly a need for jobs to accommodate the many youths who have but limited skills.

In any case, labeling jobs as dead-end positions is unwarranted. Jobs that are so labeled can be an important opportunity for many disadvantaged youths. Unskilled jobs are entry-level jobs, positions from which individuals can progress and advance. These jobs offer a chance for many of the nation's disadvantaged youths to obtain some of the rudimentary skills that many lack.

Inflation and the minimum wage

In addition to affecting employment, increases in the minimum wage also increase prices, since the rise in the wage floor represents an important rise in employers' wage costs. The Department of Labor estimates that the 1978 increase directly added more than $2 billion to the annual wage bill of the economy. In addition to the nearly 5 million workers whose wages were directly affected, the minimum wage can also lead to a rise in the wages of others as the entire pay structure of many firms or industries is adjusted to the higher base pay.[6] With labor productivity growth unlikely to be affected in the near term, these higher wage costs mean increased unit labor costs. This, in turn, leads to

---

[3] On this point, see Edward M. Gramlich, "Impact of Minimum Wages on Other Wages, Employment, and Family Incomes", *Brookings Papers on Economic Activity* (II, 1976).

[4] The labor force participation rate is the proportion of the noninstitutionalized population 16 years of age and above in the labor force, *i.e.*, the proportion of the population of working age who are either employed or seeking employment. The participation rate can be determined separately for the population as a whole or for any particular demographic group. For more on this topic, see "The Changing Composition of the Labor Force" in this Bank's *Quarterly Review* (Winter 1976).

[5] For an overview of this important social ill, see Walter E. Williams, *Youth and Minority Unemployment,* a study prepared for the Joint Economic Committee, July 6, 1977.

[6] To some extent, this indirect effect could be offset by a lowering of wages in those sectors of the economy not covered by the legal minimum. This would be due to an inflow into those sectors of workers who were displaced by the higher wage.

increased pressure on prices as businesses act to pass on these higher costs to customers.

How much have prices risen? While precise estimates are beyond economists' abilities, the M.I.T.-Penn-Social Science Research Council econometric model provides a rough measure. This large econometric model contains about 200 equations that attempt to capture the behavior of various economic sectors. Based on historical relationships embodied in the model, the measurable direct and indirect effects of the 1978 increase in the wage floor resulted in an increase in the overall level of prices of about ⅓ percent. Price pressures are, of course, relatively greater in those sectors that make greater use of low-wage labor. Thus, for example, prices of food away from home show larger increases since reportedly 30 percent of the food service industry's payroll is composed of low-wage teenagers.

In addition to these inflationary impacts, the minimum wage legislation also works against reducing inflation in other ways. By helping to cement inflationary expectations into the wage structure, it reinforces the persistence of inflation. The legislated wage increases through 1981 represent close to a 10 percent annual rate of increase, well above the 7 percent private sector wage growth posted in recent years. By confirming the prospects of continued wage hikes, it becomes increasingly difficult to reduce the rate of inflation, as inflation is a dynamic problem in which the conditions inherited from the past feed the inflation process. The process becomes sustained when the expectations are deeply ingrained in society's thinking—in its contracts and laws.

The jump in the legal minimum is only one of several governmental influences that have exacerbated the rising cost pressures on businesses. The 1978 rise came at a time when important payroll taxes—namely, social security and unemployment insurance—were also increased. While the impact on prices of each of these increases separately may be small, taken together these government-mandated increases are likely to have added as much as 1 percent to labor costs, thus widening the gap between compensation and productivity. Looking ahead, the 9.4 percent increase scheduled for 1979, which will raise the wage floor to $2.90 per hour, appears to be less inflationary than this year's 15 percent hike. However, after taking into account the level of wages of affected workers in relation to the minimum wage floor, the impact on the aggregate wage bill in 1979 will be about the same as this year.

Conclusion

The Federal minimum wage law raises the income of millions of marginally productive workers. But the benefits of the minimum wage are not without social costs. Among these costs are higher rates of youth joblessness and greater inflation. The price of ignoring these negative influences is high—both for the economy and for society. Unquestionably, people who lack the ability to earn a decent living must be helped. The issue is whether the minimum wage is an effective tool with which to alleviate poverty. While research may never be able to provide a definitive answer, it seems that increases in the legal wage floor offer at best an imperfect solution to important social concerns, since remedying the ills of some poor people comes at the expense of others who are equally impoverished. Clearly, alternatives need to be explored in greater depth. Attempting to ameliorate some of the harmful effects of the minimum wage legislation by allowing a subminimum differential for teenagers or newly hired workers is one possible solution. Another alternative might be a wage subsidy program, whereby the government pays part of the wages of low productivity workers. In any case, efforts to raise the level of marketable skills by improving and expanding training and educational programs should be intensified.

Robert T. Falconer

Proposition 13
and its Aftermath

*By Anita A. Summers**

In the first phase of the great tax reform flurry that began sweeping across the country last year, the banner headlines went to California's Proposition 13. Now they're going to a state-initiated Constitutional amendment to limit the Federal budget; and many states are on the lookout for ways to respond to tax protests in their own capitals. Clearly, the accelerated pressure to reform reflects a general discontent.

---

*Anita A. Summers is Research Officer and Economist at the Philadelphia Fed, where she has served since 1971. Trained in economics at Hunter College, the University of Chicago, and Columbia University, she is well known for her studies of urban public finance and education.

This article is adapted from an address presented before four meetings of the Pennsylvania Bar Association in fall 1978—in Harrisburg (October 17), King of Prussia (October 27), Pittsburgh (November 1), and Scranton (November 9).

While proposals for tax capping at the Federal level introduce a complex of issues connected with the use of Federal fiscal policy for economic stabilization, issues are far from being resolved even at the state and local level. Proposition 13 and several of its progeny reflect a confusion of the objectives of budget capping with those of fiscal reform. Restraining the size of government (and its associated tax burden), reducing government inefficiency, and reforming state and local taxes are distinct objectives. Each of them has an agenda that is appropriate to it alone and not to the others. But Proposition 13 and its variants have failed to keep them separate.

In practice, the size of state and local budgets will not be controlled best by any one constitutional or legislative action, and the fairness of the property tax will not be improved simply by lowering it. Responsible

Reprinted from Federal Reserve Bank of Philadelphia *Business Review,* March/April, 1979.

reformers who share the concerns of the taxpayers will want to consider many measures.

WHAT UNDERLIES THE CURRENT DISCONTENT?

Why have the past few years seen so much concern with reform of state and local government fiscal affairs? In part because growth rates of real income have been declining while the tax burden has been increasing. This combination of trends has focused attention on the total tax burden, on efficiency in government, and on the incidence of the major taxes. More particularly, it has led to protests against having government spend as large a portion of total income as it does and against the very visible property tax.

Income, Taxes, and Big Government. Recent assaults on the size of government and the level of taxation undoubtedly reflect the squeeze on family budgets. Real personal disposable income increased about 50 percent from 1957 to 1967 but only about 32 percent from 1967 to 1977. People have perceived and reacted to this shift in trends but without fully appreciating that it arises from different factors. The slower growth of real income in recent years reflects a combination of escalating inflation, a substantial number of recession years, and sluggish growth in productivity.

Against this background of slow growth in real income, the more rapid real tax growth—51 percent from 1957 to 1967 and 38 percent from 1967 to 1977—stands out sharply. This tax growth reflects several factors. First, the United States has become increasingly concerned about social justice since World War II. Legislation and major court decisions, for example, reflect the increased emphasis on income redistribution as a policy criterion in the public sector. And this emphasis has translated into growth in Social Security, unemployment compensation, welfare, medical care, education, and many other income transfers and public services—or, in other words, into growth in government expenditures, which are supported from tax revenues. Second, those who want certain government expenditures can lobby more easily than those who want lower taxes: those who want ramps for the handicapped on street corners, for example, can coalesce to lobby for the budget allocation, but those who don't want to pay the, say, 10 cents extra in taxes needed to finance these accommodations, are too diffused to resist them effectively. Third, government decisionmaking, which in principle is based on cost-benefit calculations, often underestimates the cost of new programs.[1] And fourth, rewards in the public sector tend to favor those who manage larger entities over those who produce more services with less resource input.

For all these reasons, government expenditures, and the taxes associated with them, have expanded. As the growth in real income has declined, the protest against this expansion has become more urgent.

Distaste for the Property Tax. A good deal of protest lights on the very visible property tax. In a period of rapidly rising property values, the property tax is a conspicuous target. The rising property value is not very visible (unless the property is sold), but the rise in the property tax bill has to be faced every year. Moreover, though the property tax has diminished from about 80 percent of all state and local taxes at the turn of the century to about 45 percent in the 1960s and about 35 percent now, it remains a major tax in the United States. Out of every $1 thousand of personal income, $123 goes to state and local taxes, $45 of which is paid in property taxes. The property tax is a perennial target.

---

[1] The reason is that there's a downward bias on the cost side: the efficiency losses involved in engaging in an activity in a noncompetitive market are not included in the calculations. For a fuller discussion of this issue see Anthony M. Rufolo, "Upward Biases in Government Spending?" *Business Review*, Federal Reserve Bank of Philadelphia, November/December 1978, pp. 15-23.

Public finance texts criticize it, the urban poor rail against it, Center City businessmen condemm it, and those who have retired on fixed incomes abhor it. Why so much criticism?

In a nonagricultural economy such as ours, *the property tax does not closely reflect the value of public services received by the property owner* (there is no evident relation of the value of fire protection services to the value of property, for example); and *the value of property is not a very good indicator of the owner's ability to pay*. A match-up of tax payments with value of services and ability to pay is a standard criterion for a good tax. So the property tax might appropriately be faulted on these grounds.

The property tax has been attacked also for its *regressivity*—its tendency to take a smaller percentage of income from those whose incomes are higher. And it can be regressive, but not for the reasons traditionally cited.

Until recently, people argued that since an increase in the property tax increases the cost of housing, and since lower income persons spend a larger portion of their income on housing, the burden of the property tax is heavier on them. In recent years, however, economists have become more sophisticated at tracking through the real incidence of taxes.[2] They now recognize more fully that taxes may not fall only on homeowners who write checks to the tax collector and that, in the case of the property tax, part of the burden will be borne by all those who own interest-earning capital. Since the rich own more such capital than the poor, the tax incidence has some progressive portion. And, further, when economists look at the ratio of the value of housing to lifetime income, rather than to a single year's income, they find that this ratio is about the same for all income groups. While there is more evidence still to be gathered on the incidence of the property tax, the notion that the property tax is regressive seems highly questionable— provided, of course, that it's administered properly.

The property tax, however, generally is *not* administered properly.[3] In most places, *assessments are not levied uniformly and are not kept up to date*. Assessment lag has the effect of producing higher assessment ratios in areas where market values have declined (inner city sections, for example) and lower assessment ratios in areas where market values have risen (affluent residential sections). So, while the property tax doesn't have to be regressive, in certain places it turns out to be so. The protests of the poor may not be supported in the public finance text, but they are supported in the urban assessor's records.

The plight of the *fixed-income owner* also has received a good deal of attention. The classic case is that of the person who retires to live on a fixed income in a house whose value has risen substantially since the time of purchase. The capital appreciation can't be realized unless the house is sold, but the property taxes rise to reflect that appreciation. The individual's current income doesn't allow for living in the house, but the value of the asset does. Should such a person have to sell his house? The view of fixed-income homeowners, and of others whose income is temporarily depressed, is really one of vocal and strong opposition to rising tax bills in relation to unrealized gains in housing value. But the opposition lights on the property tax as a whole rather than on any of its remediable defects.

The property tax, then, has been the most conspicuous target of anger in the tax protest

---

[2] An excellent presentation of current perspectives on the property tax is given in Henry J. Aaron, *Who Pays the Property Tax? A New View* (Washington: Brookings Institution, 1975).

[3] See Nonna A. Noto, "Uniformity in Assessment: High on the List of Property Tax Reforms," *Business Review*, Federal Reserve Bank of Philadelphia, May/June 1978, pp. 13-23, for an analysis and documentation of the issue.

because of its visibility and because of the accessibility to the taxpayers of those who levy it. Further, it doesn't bear a close relation to services received, it is administered in a way which converts it into a regressive tax, and it falls harshly on the fixed-income homeowner.

Mixed in with these concerns about the incidence of this major local tax are political concerns about the size and efficiency of government and more generalized concerns about the burden of taxation at a time when growth rates of real income are declining. The confluence of these factors produced Proposition 13 and its progeny—state and local budget reform initiatives throughout the country.

PROPOSITION 13 AND ITS PROGENY

'Proposition 13' has become almost a generic term for any legislative proposal designed to hold down expenditures, restrain revenues, or reduce the property tax. Actually, of course, Proposition 13 is a tax-capping amendment to the California constitution which was passed overwhelmingly by almost 65 percent of the voters. Variants of this proposal appeared on ballots in a number of states last November, and though none has reached the voting stage in Pennsylvania, several are being considered here. All in all, very few states have accepted Proposition 13's variety of assault on the property tax, but some have opted for considerably broader types of restraint.

California. Although the rhetoric of the Proposition 13 campaign reflected a desire to respond to all the underlying issues—a government become too big and operating too inefficiently, a total tax burden grown too heavy, and an allocation of the tax burden become too inequitable—the weight of the amendment itself fell on the much-maligned property tax.

The concern about the size of government and its associated tax burden was reflected in the restraints imposed on state and local tax increases. As a result of the amendment, state increases are permitted only on a two-thirds vote of the state legislature, and enactments of new taxes by local governments require a two-thirds vote of the electorate. The absence of any automatic growth allowance makes it virtually certain that some enactments will occur. But, most important, it imposes no criteria for selecting which services will be curtailed. And it suggests no incentives to achieve restraint by operating with greater efficiency. The concern that government has gotten too big does not mean that every service is regarded as too big. Yet Proposition 13 does nothing to identify which services should be axed. Indeed, the only attempt to be specific is the targeting of, not an expenditure item, but a tax: the legislature is prohibited from enacting any new property taxes (new ad valorem or sales taxes, for example).

The property tax is hit forcefully in the California amendment, reflecting, in addition to the notion that taxes are too high, the notion that property taxes allocate the burden inequitably: Proposition 13 places a ceiling on property taxes at 1 percent of market value as of March 1, 1975, with a few exceptions; it limits increases in assessed valuation to 2 percent per year, unless two-thirds of the voters subsequently decide otherwise; and it prohibits full reassessment except when property is sold. Every which way, the property tax as a source of revenue is checked.

The problems with legislating such a severe attack on one form of taxation are many, and they are only beginning to unfold. For one thing, rolling the tax base back three years means that current taxes do not reflect the relative shifts in market values that have occurred since the base date. If, for example, the demand for housing in one area has become much greater than the demand in another, the increase in the market value in the high-demand area will escape capture arbitrarily. Placing a fixed ceiling on the percentage annual increase in assessed valuation from a prior base period implies a continuation of this distortion into the indefinite future. Also, allowing full reassessment only at time of sale sets up a direct financial inducement to stay put, though no one suggested during the campaign that limiting residential mobility was included in the amendment's intent or that it ought to be a policy objective at any level of government. And it means that residential property owners will pay a higher percentage of the property tax than businesses, since businesses move less often—again, not part of the original intent of the amendment. Finally, and ironically, the same taxpayers whose vote for Proposition 13 was a vote against Big Government now have demanded rent controls (already set up in Los Angeles and Beverly Hills) because their rents have continued to rise even with the enactment of Proposition 13!

What has happened in California is that the full force of taxpayer discontent has fallen on the property tax. Proposition 13's broad restraints on raising taxes do attack the issue of the total burden. But its other provisions fail to address the property tax incidence issues that people are really concerned with.

Other States. A few states, notably Nevada and Idaho, adopted proposals very similar to Proposition 13; and Alabama, Missouri, and Massachusetts placed strong restraints on the property tax. These states are likely to develop the same set of problems that California has experienced since last July. Fortunately, though, most other states that voted on budget capping did not mix it up with property tax reform. They registered their distaste for large governments and high taxes, but they also recognized the need for some growth factor and did not single out one tax as a target. Arizona passed an amendment to limit state expenditures to 7 percent of personal income; Hawaii and Texas tied growth in state expenditures to economic growth in the state; and Prince George's County in Maryland, along with the states of Michigan, North Dakota, South Dakota, and Illinois all moved in a similar direction. None of the legislative initiatives, however, took on the issues of government productivity and selection criteria for curtailing expenditures.

Pennsylvania. Pennsylvania differs from California in many ways, so that the buildup of pressures about the size of the total tax burden and the incidence of the property tax has not been as intense. The market value of housing has not risen as much as in California; the property tax is not relied on as heavily ($62.71 per $1 thousand of personal income in California, in contrast with $29.95 in Pennsylvania); for some time, local governments have been able to use nonproperty taxes in Pennsylvania; and there is a circuit breaker law here which refunds property tax payments to those with low incomes and to the elderly. In addition, the Pennsylvania state government is not sitting on a budgetary surplus, and its constitution, unlike California's, does not permit the use of the initiative process for putting questions on the ballot.

Many proposals have been made in this state that address one or another of the underlying concerns. Some try to provide more tax relief to the elderly and those with low incomes. Some try to limit property tax revenue á la Proposition 13. And some try to limit the total amount of state and local spending (which would require a constitutional amendment).

Thus the pressure to pass capping legislation or property tax reform is weaker in Pennsylvania than in many other places because the property tax is relatively low, other more elastic local taxes are used more extensively, and the procedures involved in placing ceilings on revenues and expenditures are more intricate. When and if Pennsylvanians cap or reform taxes, or do both, they should be able to benefit from the experience of other states and be able to choose legislation which attacks the problems surrounding the property tax and the size of state and local budgets more satisfactorily than does Proposition 13.

SENSIBLE APPROACHES TO CAPPING AND REFORM

To control the size of government, to improve government efficiency, and to reform the property tax are clearly expressed concerns of the American taxpayer. But no one agenda will meet all three of these. Responsible action involves considering several policies to meet the several concerns.

Controlling the Size of State and Local Government Budgets. The most rational approach to budget control would involve careful cost-benefit analyses of all expenditure lines to develop appropriate selection criteria for the services to be curtailed most severely or eliminated entirely. In recent years, cost-benefit analyses have become much more common at the Federal level, but they still are relatively rare at the state and local level. Even where they are done, the political process does much to alter what the calculations suggest. The result is that all across the country we are feeling a dissatisfaction with the size of the total burden and, therefore, a desire to limit that total burden.

If, indeed, the total is what is to be limited, then the expenditure side of the budget is the one to focus on. Overspending is the objectionable activity; revenue collection only provides the means to carry out spending plans. By concentrating on the expenditure side, the major causes of increased spending can be eliminated and the real choices can be emphasized. And those choices have to do mainly with services provided by government. At the state and local levels, taxes go almost entirely for public services. Limiting expenditures means limiting those services, and this tradeoff should be spelled out explicitly in tax limitation proposals.

Clearly, if a decision is made to cap expenditures, the use of *some sort of broad measure of economic activity as the anchor seems appropriate* in calculating the level of the cap. Growth in personal income in a state and growth in gross state product have been suggested as measures. (In some states, limiting growth in expenditures to inflationary growth has been proposed. This, of course, would not allow any growth in the economic base of the state to be translated into growth in public services). In addition to tying expenditure growth to a broad measure, *consideration should be given to using an average over several years of the measure.* Few citizens would want state and local expenditures to fluctuate as sharply, as rapidly, and in the same direction as annual fluctuations in economic activity.

But, beyond adopting an overall ceiling, *rational control of expenditures involves improving productivity in the public sector.* Everyone is for it, but it doesn't happen. And it is unlikely to happen without merit rewards, in the form of merit salary increments, for clear evidence of improved output from the same input. Awareness that a Streets Commissioner has received a merit increase because his department has taken care of more potholes this year with the same number of men and trucks as last year, for example, is likely to do much more for public-sector productivity than exhortation would. Use of the many anlytical tools available to improve service delivery probably would be stimulated by the likelihood of tangible rewards. As it stands now, the tools are available but not the rewards for using them.

The desire to limit the size of state and local budgets has been expressed clearly in this country over the last few years. It is to be hoped that this expressed voter preference will not be confused with concern for property tax reform, but that it will be met by a combination of responsible measures—relating expenditure growth to a several-year average of a broad measure of economic growth for the region and providing real incentives to improve productivity in the public sector.

Reforming the Property Tax. Inner city residents, business, and the elderly all complain about overly high property taxes. But the property tax would be made much more palatable if a number of new procedures were adopted. *Maintaining uniform assessments through frequent and regular revaluation of property* would eliminate the relatively high assessment ratios borne by those who live in areas where property values are growing relatively smaller and would meet much of the concern with the tax on the part of the urban poor. *Reducing the extensive amount of property exempted from the property tax,* much of which clearly is not being used for the public interest, would reduce the percentage of the tax that business has to pay. The concerns of the elderly, those on fixed incomes, and those who are suffering from temporary income squeezes might be met best by *allowing deferral of tax liabilities* until a later date—date of sale for the elderly and for those on fixed incomes, a set date in the future for other homeowners. Circuit breaker laws give relief, but they give relief to the rich as well as the poor, which is costly in terms of tax revenues.

All of these changes could help relieve concerns about the inequities of the property tax and redeem its much-maligned reputation. Simply rolling back the assessed valuations, California style, does not alter these inequities, which arise from defects in the procedures used to administer the property tax. Altering the procedures is the right medicine for the illness.

SUMMARY

The taxpayer malaise that has reached to all levels of American government in the last few years reflects several overlapping concerns. People have a generalized dissatisfaction with the size of government, with its associated tax burden, and with its waste and inefficiency; and they are concentrating their dissatisfaction in a frontal attack on the highly visible property tax. But meeting these several concerns will require a menu of policy approaches. Controlling the overall magnitude of state and local budgets calls for broad-based ceilings and productivity incentives. Reshaping the distributional effects of the property tax calls for making assessments uniform, for regularizing revaluations, and for reviewing exemptions and deferrals of tax liabilities.

If, in this state, we confuse these issues, we may put a cap on our state and local budgets, but the way those budget dollars are raised and spent will not reflect attainable levels of efficiency and equity for fiscal management. In brief, Proposition 13 should not be Pennsylvania's role model. H.L. Mencken once said that "for every human problem there is a solution which is simple, neat, and wrong." This dictum applies to fiscal reforms as well as to other human affairs!

Shades of the Founding Fathers

The drive for a new Constitutional Convention

Wanted: statesmanlike figure bearing close resemblance to James Madison (or someone who at least has read him) to direct possible second Constitutional Convention devoted to balancing budget and perhaps other matters. No Keynesians need apply. Address: Box 1787, c/o U.S. Congress.

The ad has not yet been placed, and the convention has not yet been called, but much of official Washington is beginning to be afraid that it might be. Since the one and only Constitutional Convention of 1787, there has rarely been such a determined effort to convene another. Altogether 27 state legislatures have voted to call a convention to approve an amendment requiring a balanced federal budget. The National Taxpayers Union,* which is leading the drive, estimates that the necessary 34 states will be reached by summer.

The issue has already been injected into 1980 presidential politics. Staking out political ground to the right of Jimmy Carter, California Governor Jerry Brown has supported the movement for a convention. Over the indignant opposition of many fellow Democrats in his state, he has arranged for speaking engagements around the country to promote the convention.

The prospect of a Constitutional Convention is unnerving for most members of Congress. They fear they will be moving into a constitutional no man's land uncharted by the founding fathers. Article V of the Constitution simply provides that a convention will be called when two-thirds of the state legislatures petition Congress for one. Any amendments adopted by the convention must be ratified by three-quarters of the states before taking effect. There is no evading the clarity of the text. As Alexander Hamilton wrote in Federalist Paper No. 85, "The words of the article are peremptory. Congress *shall* call a convention. Nothing in this particular is left to the discretion of that body."

Congress, however, must attend to all the not-so-trivial details of such a convention. How will the delegates be chosen? Will the states have equal representation, as in the U.S. Senate, or will their votes be weighted according to population? How long can the convention go on? Above all, must it stick to the issue for which it was called, or is it free to consider other matters as well? The convention can certainly be restricted, declares U.S. Attorney General Griffin Bell. "Limits can be set," he says. "Congress has a duty to do so." Paul Freund of the Harvard Law School agrees: "Since the Constitution is silent on details, the details become a political question. Since Congress issues the call, it can define the jurisdiction of the convention."

Others are not so sure. They cite the example of the first Constitutional Convention, which was called to amend the Articles of Confederation and ended up forming a completely new government. Barber Conable, a conservative Republican Congressman from upstate New York, warns against "constitutional Russian roulette." Such a convention, says Constitutional Scholar Raoul Berger, would be "the town meeting of town meetings." Inevitably, he feels, delegates would press for such causes as making affirmative action mandatory, outlawing abortion, banning school busing, reducing the power of the judiciary. Says Howard Jarvis, apostle of California Proposition 13 but no fan of the convention route to achieve his goals: "A convention would give every crackpot a chance to write the supreme law of the land."

As some liberals contemplate this approaching forum, they fantasize a runaway mob repealing the entire Bill of Rights. Others are less anxious about such a possibility. Says Jerry Brown: "The idea that the American people want to junk the Bill of Rights is absurd. I think the American people believe in the Bill of Rights, and they also believe in a balanced budget. The idea that all the giants lived in the 18th century shows the same lack of confidence that is troubling this country in other respects." Senate Minority Leader Howard Baker is also unperturbed. A Constitutional Convention, he feels, would "limit itself. I have a fundamental confidence in the people who would attend."

Many conservatives and liberals alike doubt the wisdom of requiring an annual balanced federal budget. In a period of recession, they argue, a deficit may be necessary to stimulate the faltering economy. Says Senate Majority Leader Robert Byrd: "At the very time when flexibility is needed to deal with serious economic fluctuations, an absolute requirement to balance the budget would tie the hands of Congress."

Conservatives fear that the Government would be tempted to balance the budget by raising taxes rather than cutting spending. Many of them favor an amendment proposed by, among others, Economist Milton Friedman. Instead of a flat requirement that the budget be balanced, Friedman urges limiting any increase in annual spending to the amount of growth in the gross national product; if the rate of inflation exceeded 3%, however, the spending increase would be trimmed. In times of emergency a two-thirds vote of Congress could authorize additional outlays. "In a sense, the Government has always balanced its budget,"

---

*Founded in 1969, the union is a nonpartisan group of more than 100,000 members who fight for less government spending and lower taxes.

Reprinted by permission from TIME, The Weekly Newsmagazine; Copyright Time Inc. 1979.

says Friedman, "if not by what we call taxes, then by the hidden tax of inflation." Alan Greenspan, chairman of the Council of Economic Advisers under President Ford, agrees. There is no way of writing an amendment to ensure a balanced budget, he believes. The complexities are insuperable. He favors an amendment that would require all money bills to be passed by a two-thirds vote in both Houses of Congress, instead of the present simple majority.

A balanced budget is traditional Republican Party doctrine, but the G.O.P. is split on the issue. At a meeting of party officeholders last week in Easton, Md., a constitutional amendment to balance the budget was rejected in favor of one to limit spending. Supporting the balanced-budget amendment were such presidential aspirants as Ronald Reagan, Howard Baker, Robert Dole and John Connally. Baker favors a proposal to require a balanced budget unless overruled by a two-thirds vote of both houses. "This formula," he says, "satisfies the principal concerns about a balanced budget by permitting enough flexibility for Congress to approve a deficit in time of economic or military emergency."

Other leading Republicans, including National Party Chairman Bill Brock and House Minority Leader John Rhodes, were opposed. Said Rhodes, who objects to any kind of amendment involving fiscal policy: "I don't like constitutional gimmickry. If the American people want a balanced budget, they should elect a Republican Congress." Rhodes echoes other authorities who believe that the Constitution should not be encumbered with specific policies that can be settled by the normal political process. But the House minority leader was challenged by Congressman Bud Shuster, chairman of the House Republican Policy Committee. Pointing out that 103 of the 159 House Republicans had sponsored some kind of constitutional amendment to achieve a balanced budget, Shuster said of Rhodes: "I think he is wrong. He is obviously speaking for himself and not for a majority of Republicans." Dole warned that if the Republicans do not soon reach a consensus on the subject, they may forfeit the issue to the Democrats. "I'm concerned that this be a Republican issue," said Dole. "But we're about to lose it."

About 65 versions of a budget-balancing amendment have been introduced in Congress. Within a month, the Judiciary Committee in each house will begin hearings with a lengthy list of economists and lawyers, most of whom will warn of the enormous complexities in convening a Constitutional Convention, or in drafting an amendment to balance the budget. Says House Judiciary Committee Chairman Peter Rodino: "I would hope that the people in the states would pause, knowing that a responsible committee of Congress is looking at the matter." Delaying tactics have already begun. Senator Birch Bayh, chairman of the subcommittee on the Constitution, claims that only 16 of the 27 states voting for a Constitutional Convention have submitted valid petitions. In the case of the other states, he contends, petitions have not been received or have been improperly filed.

Judging by past attempts to call a convention, Congress feels it is justified in reacting slowly. Of three major efforts by the states this century to amend the Constitution by convention, one succeeded in forcing Congress to act; the other two eventually collapsed. At first, Congress resisted petitions from the states for a convention to require the direct election of U.S. Senators, who were then chosen by the state legislatures. But by 1912 enough petitions had arrived to persuade Congress to yield to public pressure and approve the 17th Amendment, providing for the popular election of Senators. A quarter of a century later, a movement began to put a 25% ceiling on the federal income tax rate in peacetime. Because of confusion over petitions, it was never clear exactly how many states had voted for the resolution, so Congress procrastinated until support waned for what was called by its foes the "millionaire's amendment." In 1964 the U.S. Supreme Court's one-man, one-vote ruling provoked an almost one-man crusade by Illinois Republican Senator Everett Dirksen to overturn the decision by constitutional amendment. Five years later only one additional state was needed to call a convention, and Wisconsin became the battleground. The amendment was rejected by the Wisconsin legislature, and the movement died out.

Congress cannot count on the current drive subsiding any time soon. Even if Congress manages to block the budget-balancing amendment, the demand for cost cutting will continue. As Jarvis says, "The people don't want a convention. They want tax reduction." In the end Congress will have to take some action to appease public opinion. The whole Constitutional Convention movement would not have started in the first place if Congress and the Carter Administration had been more responsive to the public outcry for tax relief during a time of rapidly rising inflation. Congress has all the power it needs to curb spending; all it may lack is the will and the courage.

Realists to the core, the framers of the Constitution knew that there would be times when even the best of governments would resist the will of the people it claims to serve. The effect of Article V is that without actually being used, it can pressure Congress to make the kind of change that is desired by a substantial majority of the American people. ■

CLAMOR FOR A CONSTITUTIONAL CONVENTION

TIME Map by Paul J. Pugliese   Source: National Taxpayers Union

- Passed resolution calling for a convention
- Passed in one house of legislature
- Bills filed and awaiting action
- No bills filed

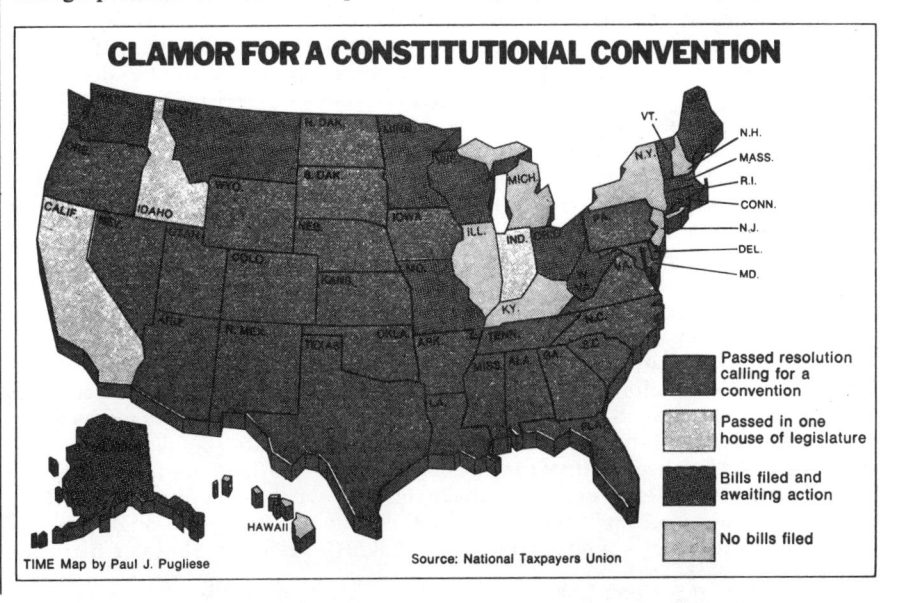

41
Pro and Con
A Constitutional Ban on Red Ink?

Yes—The U.S. must "balance what it produces with what it spends"

Interview With
Edmund G. Brown, Jr.
Governor
Of California

Q Governor Brown, why do you favor a constitutional amendment prohibiting deficits in the federal budget?

A I believe that the time has come for this nation to balance what it produces with what it spends.

Q Many economists argue that such a ban would impose a straitjacket on government. How do you answer that?

A The resolution pending before the California Legislature provides for exceptions in the event of national emergency such as war, a national disaster or a serious condition of unemployment. Those are matters that can be worked out as the concept is developed and refined.

My own judgment is that governments have great difficulty in controlling spending. An external force is necessary. I would point out, as an example, Proposition 13, which passed in California last June. Prior to its passage, the whole spectrum of conventional opinion in the business world, the political world, the bureaucratic world and the union world—all concluded that Proposition 13 was such a disaster that the state could not endure after its passage.

But we are enduring. We have scaled back 3 billion dollars in proposed state spending, and our programs are functioning effectively.

Q Which proves what?

A This strongly suggests that, with the aid of an external limit, state and local governments can increase their productivity and limit excessive spending.

What happened in California can certainly happen at the national level. The magnitude of the reductions forced by Proposition 13 is greater than the reductions that would be required under a balanced-budget constitutional amendment.

Q What about a time when—with no national emergency or unusual unemployment—the economy is poised on the brink of recession? Would spending cuts required by such an amendment bring on recession?

A Many economists think the economy is now headed for a recession after years of deficit spending. So I would turn the question around and ask those who propose that we deficit-spend year in and year out, even at the peak of the business cycle: What is the explanation for the recurring recessions that are sweeping this country and harming those least able to afford recessions—the poor, minorities, the elderly and people on fixed incomes?

I'm not unaware of the need for appropriate stimulus. But I believe that a balanced budget can be constructed in such a way that the investments required to make this a great country can be made—and will be made—by the people. The problem is that, instead of borrowing for capital investment

NO—"There are many occasions in which deficits are appropriate and necessary"

Interview With
Gardner Ackley
Chairman, President's
Council of Economic
Advisers, 1964-68; Now,
Professor of Economics,
University of Michigan

Q Professor Ackley, why do you oppose a constitutional amendment requiring a balanced federal budget?

A First, because there are many occasions in which deficits are appropriate and necessary; and, second, because there are many occasions in which deficits are unavoidable.

Q Many people say that printing money to finance deficit spending has been a major factor in inflation. Isn't drastic action needed to remedy that?

A Printing money to finance a deficit is not a necessary consequence of a deficit. A deficit will add to the money supply only if the Fed chooses to let it.

I think that fairly drastic actions may be needed to deal with some of our problems, but I regard a constitutional amendment as an inappropriate action. I'm sure many people think something needs to be done about inflation, as I do. But simply because some people think deficits are the main cause of inflation doesn't make it so.

Q You don't believe that deficit spending has been a major cause of our inflation?

A There have been many occasions when deficits were inappropriate and did contribute to inflation. There are many other occasions in which deficits were appropriate and had no inflationary consequences.

Q If there are times when deficits cause inflation, why not have a constitutional ban on them?

A Because under some circumstances the attempt to eliminate deficits—through cutting expenditures or raising taxes—would only aggravate the unsatisfactory circumstances of the economy and might not succeed in eliminating the deficit.

Think about the middle 1930s, for example, or about 1975. If we had tried to avoid a deficit by raising taxes or cutting expenditures or both, we would mainly have further depressed the economy, but we probably would not have been able to eliminate the deficit.

Q Why?

A Simply because the effect of cutting expenditures or raising taxes is to reduce the level of economic activity and reduce tax collections. In such cases, efforts to balance the budget would not merely be self-defeating but disastrous to the economic well-being of the entire country.

Q Do you believe government spending can be brought under control without a constitutional amendment?

A I don't know what "bringing government spending under control" means. As a percentage of gross national product—GNP—federal spending shows no rise over any reasonable period. It fluctuates when the growth of output slows or increases as a result of recessions and booms, but

Reprinted from "U.S. News & World Report."

Interview With Governor Brown (continued)

in productive assets, we are borrowing to pay current expenses. No state or corporation can long do that.

I would also point out that California is in the forefront across the broad spectrum of social and labor programs, and yet we've been able to do it with a balanced budget.

Q Critics of the balanced-budget plan argue that cutting spending or increasing taxes when the economy is weak simply slows the economy, reduces revenues and widens deficits—

A That's the conventional wisdom. It deserves consideration in the drafting of a constitutional amendment. But what concerns me is that this theory has been so distorted that deficit spending continues in periods of great economic boom and high job creation, which is where we are today.

Q Who would declare a national emergency?

A The Congress.

Q And under what set of standards?

A The California resolution calls for Congress to exercise that authority by a majority vote. There may be other ways to do it. These are matters that should be fully debated.

I am trying to get the United States to face the fact that the controlling economic theories are bankrupt, that our productive assets are not being renewed in a way to sustain historical rates of growth, that our position in the world is declining, that the spirit of our people is discouraged, and that any individual, any state, any nation must come to a balancing of accounts.

Q We've been having frequent economic slumps. Wouldn't it be pretty unstabilizing to have to declare a national emergency to cope with recession every few years?

A Hopefully, if we would balance our budget, we wouldn't have as many recessions, which often follow inflationary excess. The 1974-75 recession followed on the heels of some of the worst inflation we've seen in the history of our country, and also followed on the heels of heavy deficit spending. So the argument that balancing the budget creates recession flies right in the face of the fact that we've been continuously printing money—deficit spending—and the result has been recurring recessions, a dramatic drop in our dollar, a dramatic slowdown in investment and a loss of confidence on the part of the American people.

Q It is argued that a restriction like this in the Constitution is a vote of "no confidence" in representative government. Do you believe that our elected representatives are no longer to be trusted with our tax dollars?

A That's a specious argument. The Constitution, in Article V, contains a provision that looks to the states for convening constitutional conventions or stimulating amendment proposals by Congress. I am only following the mandates of Thomas Jefferson and James Madison. What was good enough for them is certainly good enough for me and, I have a hunch, good enough for the American people.

The scare tactics and the false alarms that are being raised miss the point. Instead of fighting this movement, I suggest that the economists in Washington sit down and figure out a way that we can achieve our objectives with a balanced budget.

Today, we are not building for the future. We are stealing from it. That is cause for alarm. □

Checking over charts for the 532-billion-dollar budget for 1980 proposed by President Carter.

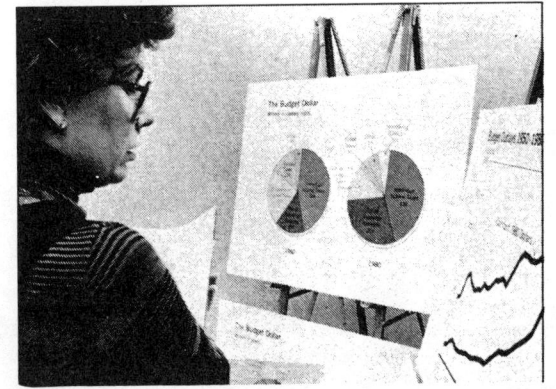

Interview With Mr. Ackley (continued)

there's been no trend in it in recent years. Also, it's a lot lower than in other countries whose economic health seems to be admired by the promoters of this idea.

May I also add that those other countries have considerably larger deficits than ours—repeatedly. Any hope that merely eliminating deficits will improve our economic performance is just a dream.

Q Most plans for a constitutional amendment call for a suspension of the ban on deficits in a national emergency. Wouldn't such a provision provide the needed flexibility?

A I don't know exactly how a national emergency might be defined. If a constitutional ban on deficits could be suspended merely by presidential proclamation, then it would seem both harmless and meaningless.

Q But do you think that an exception for emergencies might make the constitutional amendment workable?

A It wouldn't make it wise. It might make it workable but meaningless. If a deficit can be had whenever a President declares a need, what's the point of the exercise?

I think this kind of amendment doesn't belong in the Constitution at all. It's a legislative matter. The Constitution ought to deal with matters of fundamental principle. This is not a fundamental matter. It may be that Congress and the Presidents have often unwisely formulated budgets—with bad consequences—but they've also made unwise decisions about foreign policy and about everything else. You can't prevent that by just cluttering up the Constitution with ad hoc limitations on the powers of government.

Q What is a better way to curb government spending and taxing—if that's desired?

A If the problem is regarded as government spending rather than deficits, then it ought to be defined in terms of a limit on government spending as a percentage of national income or gross national product.

Q Would you accept a constitutional curb on spending as a percentage of GNP, with an exception for emergencies?

A I would oppose it because, once again, it seems to me we tie our hands by an arbitrary rule in an effort to make ourselves wise. It would be better just to become wise and act wisely, taking account of all the circumstances, rather than resorting to a blind prohibition.

Q The arguments for this constitutional amendment are much like those for Proposition 13 in California—both are popular actions forcing government to cut spending. Has the result of Proposition 13 been good or bad?

A If people want to limit the extent to which they tax themselves for local purposes, I suppose they have the right to do so.

That's quite different from amending the federal Constitution. State fiscal policy doesn't really affect the national economy, but the national fiscal policy does. It's an important tool of economic management, and it ought not to be arbitrarily limited.

I understand people's frustration and their desire to strike out at something that promises to solve their problems. A few months ago, some of the same people who are now advocating a constitutional amendment were advocating as a solution to all our problems a 30 percent tax cut with no reduction in expenditures. I regarded that as a disastrous and irresponsible proposal, and I regard the amendment as another disastrous and irresponsible proposal. □

42

THE BALANCED BUDGET MANIA

Twenty-eight state legislatures have now asked Congress to call a Constitutional Convention to consider an amendment requiring the federal government to balance its budget. The Constitution provides for calling such a convention when thirty-four state legislatures act (two-thirds of the total).

While the movement for a balanced budget had previously grown without much fanfare, it has now begun to receive a great deal of attention. Also, since California's "liberal" governor Jerry Brown joined the campaign for a balanced budget amendment in January, considerable confusion has developed around what had been seen as a "conservative" movement. *Dollars & Sense* offers the following dialogue as our contribution to the fanfare:

Why has the "balanced budget" become such a big issue recently?

The effort to force the federal government to operate with a balanced budget is part of the movement to slash government spending. It's one way in which the Proposition 13 forces have gone national.

What exactly does it mean for the budget to be "balanced"?

The budget is balanced when the amount that the government takes in as taxes during the course of a year equals what it spends. When expenditures are greater than tax revenues, there is a budget *deficit* (and when tax revenues are greater than expenditures, there is a budget *surplus*).

How can the government spend more than it takes in? I have to balance my personal budget, private corporations go out of business if they lose money, and state and local governments are required to operate with balanced budgets.

You're making two mistakes. First, it's not quite right to say that the government is spending more than it takes in. It is spending more than it takes in from *taxes*, but makes up the difference by borrowing.

Second, you're wrong about families, corporations, and state and local governments. They all borrow a lot in order to make major purchases (homes, factories, schools). They repay each individual loan over time, but they keep on borrowing more as well. It's amazing, but true, that federal government debt has grown much more slowly than that of the other major categories, and is now the second smallest of the four (see table, p. 5).

But didn't the government always manage to balance the budget when I was a kid?

Only if you grew up in the 1920s. Federal government deficits have been a pretty steady fact of life ever since. If we consider the fifty-year period that ends with the budget Carter sent to Congress in January, there was only one stretch (1947-60) when surpluses and deficits were even equally common (seven of each). Of the other 36 years, only one (1969) saw a surplus.

I can see why the opponents of deficits think it would take a constitutional amendment to wipe them out. But *why* does the government over-spend so frequently?

Since the Great Depression, the federal government has taken on the role of trying to handle the very serious problems continually being created by the normal operation of the economy. One of the most important and recurrent of these is that business, left to its own devices, often won't invest enough to keep the economy growing. This isn't a

Dollars & Sense magazine, 38 Union Square, Room 14, Somerville, MA 02143 (monthly, $7.50/year).

question of not having enough profits to re-invest (as those who claim business is being taxed to death maintain). It's a question of not being sure that the additional output made possible by investing could be sold to yield still more profits.

In the 1970s, business investment in new plants and machinery has been consistently low, and the danger of economic stagnation keeps reappearing. By providing extra demand for goods and services, deficit spending has helped keep things going.

You mean it doesn't matter *what* the government spends on — just that it has to spend?

Not entirely. The government also has become the instrument for resolving (or, more often, papering over) all sorts of conflicts in the society. In the normal operation of a private enterprise system, lots of people end up poor. In order for there to be some winners, there must be a lot of losers. But losers cause trouble. They can vote, they can organize, and sometimes they get downright ornery and disrupt things with strikes, demonstrations, even riots.

So the government steps in with programs of social services and social control. That costs money. The same thing happens on an international level, providing the impetus to a lot of military spending.

So the problem isn't with the government itself, even though the government is getting all the blame?

Right. The problems have originated in the economic system, which the government is attempting to manage. In the process, the government is changing the form of the social crisis. Instead of people rebelling against business and the way it works, they are rebelling against the government. The crisis has been displaced from the private sector to the public sector.

This is not to say that government spending has *solved* the economy's problems. While the deficit spending policy appeared to work in the 1960s, the huge deficits of the 1970s (over $40 billion in four different years) have been accompanied by soaring prices and taxes, slower growth, and declines in the international position of the U.S. And many of the liberal social programs of the 1960s have fallen far short of fulfilling their goals.

What the forces pushing the budget-balancing amendment have been doing quite successfully is convincing people that budget deficits have somehow been the *cause* of all these problems.

Well, what about the claim that balancing the budget would bring about lower taxes?

False. What's been happening is that increases in government spending have led to tax hikes — but because higher taxes are so unpopular, the government hasn't been able to raise them as much as it would like. It would be perfectly possible to bring the budget into balance by *increasing* taxes rather than by reducing spending.

Certainly the balanced budget people aren't calling for higher taxes!

No, of course not. And this demonstrates that their real goal isn't ending deficits so much as cutting spending. They figure that, because of the political risks to officials who raise taxes, the actual effect of a balanced budget requirement would be lowered spending.

What about inflation? Haven't budget deficits been responsible for that?

They contribute to inflation, but the connection is not automatic. It depends on the state of the economy. The first half of the 1960s saw an average inflation rate of just over 1%, despite the continual budget deficits.

The connection with inflation also depends on the form of government borrowing — specifically on whether the Federal Reserve Board expands the supply of money at the same time.

It makes much more sense to regard all of the disturbing economic developments of the 1970s as manifestations of the deeper problems of the economic system: the problems of stagnation and class conflict. High levels of government spending, including deficits, have been an attempt — obviously only partly successful, but nevertheless more promising to those in control than any available alternative — to ward off the consequences of these underlying problems.

Does this explain why many big business interests are not in favor of the balanced budget amendment movement?

Partly. The point is, they want the government to maintain flexibility. They believe, for example, that budget deficits are needed to get out of deep recessions, as in 1975, or when there are very serious domestic and international conflicts, as in the late 1960s. The chief economist for the Conference Board (a leading policy-planning organization for business, formerly headed by current Federal Reserve chairman G. William Miller) recently explained, "While we remain committed in principle to a balanced budget, we have gradually accepted the results of cyclical behavior of the budget." Which means, in English, they're in favor of deficits to get out of recessions.

Even the National Association of Manufacturers, the most conservative and provincial of the big business groups, has refrained from taking a position in favor of the amendment.

Still, big business interests are interested now in holding down government spending. They would like to reverse some of the real gains made by the social struggles demanding better government programs. They would like lower taxes for themselves. And even if lower spending leads to a recession, they understand that periodic recessions are (as we've discussed in other reviews) good for profits in the long run.

Federal government borrowing has grown more slowly than that of other major sectors of the economy.

Debt Outstanding
(in billions)

	1950	1978	% Increase
Consumers & Homeowners	$67	$1031	1440%
Non-Financial Corporations	$71	$834	1070%
State & Local Governments	$22	$390	1220%
Federal Government	$217	$611	180%

Note: For comparison, the Gross National Product grew by 640% in the same period. Source: *Wall Street Journal*, 2/15/79.

The more cautious big business position may be seen in an alternative constitutional amendment that the corporate-backed National Tax Limitation Committee (see "Economy in Review," *D&S* #40) proposed in February. This amendment would link government spending levels to the overall growth of the economy and the rate of inflation, but would permit Congress to exceed this ceiling with a two-thirds vote. Among the drafters of this proposal are conservative economist Milton Friedman and Ford Motor Company chief economist William Niskanen.

So where is the big push for a balance budget coming from? And why now?

First the when. This isn't a new idea. Franklin Roosevelt got elected on a platform that criticised Herbert Hoover's budget deficits. Truman and Eisenhower — and even Kennedy until almost two years after his election — also strongly endorsed the conventional wisdom that balanced budgets were a good thing. Only in the 1960s did it become fashionable for politicians to support the idea of deficit spending to aid the economy. The balanced budget rallying cry has reappeared now as part of the conservative reaction against the failure of liberal economic policies to deal successfully with the system's problems.

Its backers are the same people who pushed Proposition 13 and the more extreme tax cutting proposals. In particular, many businesses that operate on a local, rather than national or international level tend to see high government spending as an unmitigated evil. The outlook of people that run such businesses is often rather narrow, and it is not greatly affected by concern for the functioning of the system as a whole.

It is not surprising that these smaller business interests have built support through state legislatures. Locally based anti-spending groups are able to gain a good deal of popular support. Many people who have attained some degree of security and well-being are frightened by inflation and taxes. Big-government becomes an easy focus of "middle class" discontent.

But what about Jerry Brown and his argument that by forcing a balanced budget liberals can force cutbacks of military spending?

This argument is unconvincing to say the least. The whole movement for cutting government spending has been directed at social programs. While Brown may be able to ride the movement, he is not going to change it into something else.

The movement to cut government spending is inherently a politically conservative one. It is based on the idea that our social system in general and our capitalist economy in particular are basically sound and will work well if left to themselves. People who recognize the fallaciousness of that idea can hardly support the effort to have the federal budget always balanced. ■

43
WHAT DECONTROL OF OIL WILL MEAN

The directors of the American Petroleum Institute had just started dinner at their semiannual meeting in New Orleans last week when the television sets were turned on. They applauded when Jimmy Carter acknowledged early on that the Federal red tape governing U.S. oil production had become "so complicated it's almost unbelievable." But that was the last cheer Carter got. Scattered boos rang out as the President attacked "undeserved windfall profits" of oil companies. Groans greeted his warning that the powerful oil lobby would do everything it could to quash a tax on those profits. And when Carter suggested a new tax credit for Americans who use wood-burning stoves, the nation's top oil executives laughed aloud.

But the substance of Carter's new energy program—decontrol of domestic oil prices—was quite pleasing to oilmen. Though they were plainly upset at the prospect of a windfall-profits tax, they seemed to understand and reluctantly accept Carter's basic calculation. "If it is politically essential that there be an excess-profits tax to accomplish decontrol, then so be it," Thornton F. Bradshaw, president of the Atlantic Richfield Co., said in Los Angeles. "Decontrol is worth anything." Congress must now pass the tax, and a special-interest fight over what to do with the proceeds could delay—or even kill—the measure.

Altogether, the Administration predicts the new program could save the U.S. nearly 1 million barrels a day of imported oil and cut $6 billion from the U.S. import bill by the mid-1980s. But the benefits won't come cheaply. The higher prices for crude that Carter seeks will inevitably affect the cost of every refined-petroleum product, from jet fuel and kerosene to home-heating oil and gasoline. According to the Department of Energy, decontrol will add perhaps 5 cents to the price of gasoline at the pump—now an average of 70 cents per gallon. But DOE's figures are already in dispute. A day after Carter's speech, Democrat Henry Jackson of Washington, chairman of the Senate Energy Committee, said that decontrol would actually push up the pump price by as much as 20 cents a gallon by 1981.

RIPPLE EFFECT: Whatever the precise impact on fuel prices, there seemed little doubt that the Carter plan would send ripples through the entire economy, cutting the nation's potential growth rate a bit and eating into real income. By Administration calculations, which many private economists consider conservative, decontrol will tack on perhaps three-tenths of a percentage point to a national inflation rate that is already alarmingly high (page 74). But in the long run, the President's men argue, decontrol will prove to be anti-inflationary by spurring new supply and by reducing oil imports, thus steadying the dollar in the foreign-exchange markets.

In public, the reaction of business and financial experts at home and abroad was generally favorable. The money markets were steady in the wake of the speech, and in Bonn, the dollar climbed to a 1979 high against the Deutsche mark. European leaders, in particular, were relieved that Carter was finally planning to fulfill his pledge to bring U.S. oil prices to world levels.

BYZANTINE SYSTEM: Carter's authority to remove controls on oil stems from the Energy Policy and Conservation Act of 1975 (EPCA), which enshrined a Byzantine system of price limits that had been evolving since 1971. Under the current system, about two-thirds of all U.S. oil falls into one of two categories: "old" oil, which is defined as production equal to the amount an existing field was pumping in 1972, and "new" oil—production from old fields that exceeds the 1972 level or oil from wells drilled after 1972. Both have been held well below the world price set by OPEC—now

Offshore rig: Higher prices for Big Oil

RAISING THE LID

After OPEC quadrupled prices, the U.S. strengthened controls on oil, allowing higher prices for newly discovered oil but limiting the price of "old" oil from existing wells. Decontrol will now let all U.S. oil rise in price to the world level set by OPEC. The result: higher gasoline and heating-oil prices.

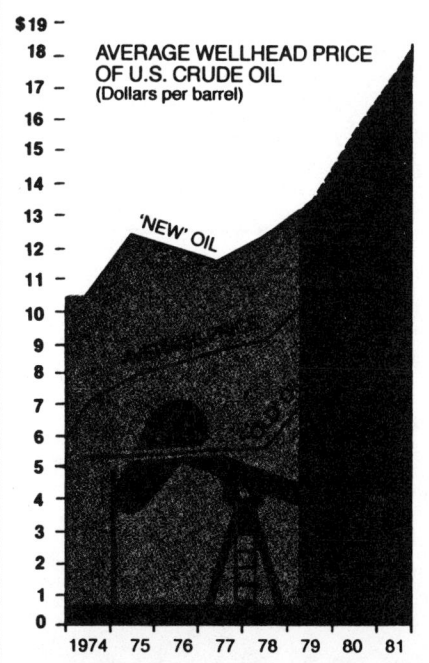

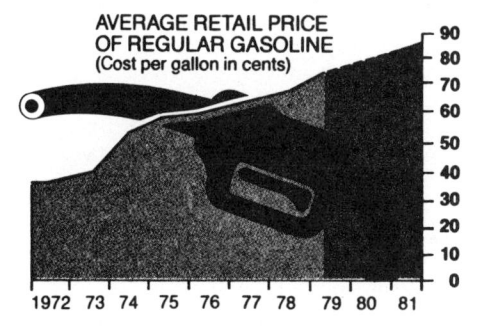

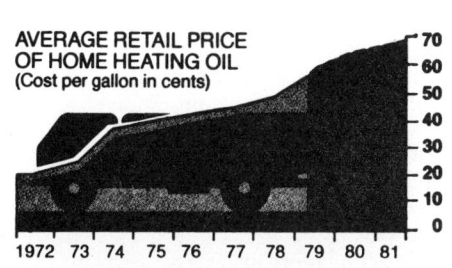

AVERAGE WELLHEAD PRICE OF U.S. CRUDE OIL (Dollars per barrel)

AVERAGE RETAIL PRICE OF REGULAR GASOLINE (Cost per gallon in cents)

AVERAGE RETAIL PRICE OF HOME HEATING OIL (Cost per gallon in cents)

PROJECTIONS ASSUME OPEC PRICE BOOSTS TOTALING 23.9 PER CENT BY 1982
Sources: American Petroleum Institute; projections by Chase Econometric Associates, Inc.

Copyright 1979 by Newsweek, Inc. All Rights Reserved. Reprinted by permission.

$14.54 a barrel—with old domestic oil now selling for roughly $6 a barrel and new oil going for about $13. Only the oil from Alaska's North Slope and output from "stripper" wells that yield fewer than ten barrels a day can sell at the world price.

One result of the system is that some old wells have been capped even though they have not run dry—simply because oil companies find that the controlled price is barely enough to cover their production costs. At the same time, the cost of exploration has risen much more rapidly than controlled prices. As a result, production has inevitably declined. In 1978, total domestic oil production was 11 million barrels lower than it was in 1972. Finally, since the EPCA tried to cushion the U.S. from the price shock of imports by averaging the cost of foreign oil into the domestic price mix, it has provided little incentive to wean the U.S. from them. "While we object to OPEC decisions to raise prices," says Energy Secretary James Schlesinger, "retaining the low prices on U.S. oil subsidizes imports."

But the EPCA also decreed that the controls would expire automatically in October 1981—and it gave the President room for discretionary action. On June 1, 1979, he has the authority to dispose of the controls any way he sees fit: he could extend them until they run out, for instance, or he could drop them immediately.

THREE STEPS: Carter has chosen a middle course—decontrol in three distinct stages—to minimize the shock to the economy that would result from lifting the lid in a single step. Starting June 1, old oil will be permitted to rise toward the world price at a rate of 1.5 per cent a month. All oil discovered after June 1 will immediately be permitted to fetch the world price. Then, on Jan. 1, 1980, old oil will start moving toward the world price at a faster rate—3 per cent a month. And the price of controlled new oil will start increasing in monthly increments as well. On Oct. 1, 1981, all oil will be decontrolled, with the various categories converging at whatever price then holds sway in world markets—by one estimate, roughly $18 per barrel (chart).

According to Department of Energy calculations, lifting the controls would quickly boost production from older U.S. fields, bring on a new round of exploration and add to supplies. By 1985, DOE estimates, 750,000 additional barrels of oil will be gushing through American pipelines each day as a result of decontrol. DOE strategists also predict that the higher prices will persuade many oil-users to switch to other sources of energy, such as coal or nuclear power—provided, of course, the accident at Three Mile Island doesn't deter the nation from building more nuclear power plants.

Higher oil prices will certainly fatten the profits of oil companies, already at an all-time high and the subject of heated criticism (page 27). In his speech, Carter repeatedly stressed his intention to prevent profiteering as a result of decontrol. "As surely as the sun will rise tomorrow," he said, "the oil companies can be expected to fight to keep the profits which they have not earned."

To avoid handing over such windfalls to the oil companies, Carter will ask Congress to pass a new tax, specifically aimed at keeping the profits down. Under the Administration proposal, fully half the windfall profit oil companies gain from rising prices would go to the Federal government. The new tax, added to existing state and Federal levies, would leave the companies with only about 30 per cent of the price bonanza—about $4.2 billion in 1981. What's more, even after domestic oil reaches the world price, the tax would continue to operate: every time OPEC imposed a new price boost and domestic oil moved up to meet it, 50 per cent of the added take would go to the U.S. Treasury.

The new tax would produce an estimated $1.6 billion in 1980, $4 billion in 1981 and $5.8 billion in 1982—even more if OPEC raised prices sharply in those years. The Treasury would then transfer the proceeds to a new Energy Security Fund, which would recycle the money into a variety of projects. In the first year, approximately one-third would be rebated to poor families with yearly incomes below $7,800 to help them cope with the rising cost of energy; the rebate would come to about $100 per four-member family. About $200 million would be channeled into mass transportation in the form of aid to localities and rehabilitation of railroads.

NEW STOCKPILES: What is left—about $900 million from the first year's take and between $3 and $5 billion in 1981 and 1982—would nearly double Federal investments in energy. Much of the money would be earmarked for specific U.S. regions. In the Northeast, for example, a 10 million-barrel stockpile of residual fuel oil—used by utilities and in-

Gasohol in Iowa: A call for some unconventional sources of energy

Louisiana driller, Schlesinger: 'Low prices tend to subsidize oil imports'

dustrial corporations—would be established to cushion against shortages. In other areas, funds would bolster research and the development of new energy technologies such as coal gasification and the extraction of shale oil.

In a bid to placate critics of decontrol, Carter included a hodgepodge of tax credits for less traditional energy sources. His plan provides write-offs for builders who use "passive solar design"—architectural tricks to make maximum use of the sun's power. It would also make permanent the current Federal-sales-tax exemption for gasohol, a mixture of 90 per cent gasoline and 10 per cent alcohol that is increasingly used for automobile fuel in the Midwest.

'CHEAPEST SOURCE': Carter also stressed conservation—what he called "our cheapest and cleanest energy source." To encourage fuel savings, his new plan proposes a variety of voluntary measures, from strict adherence to the 55-mile-an-hour speed limit to a request that state governments set goals for gasoline savings. Carter also asked commuters to use car pools and mass transit and homeowners to keep thermostats to 65 degrees in winter and 80 or above in summer. And he exhorted Americans to take advantage of existing tax credits for insulating houses and using solar energy. Altogether, the DOE estimates, such actions could save the U.S. 250,000 barrels of oil a day by 1985.

But if voluntary conservation does not take hold, Carter said that he would seek mandatory measures to ensure a cut in oil consumption. He has already asked Congress for the authority to order weekend closings of service stations if state plans do not achieve adequate savings of gasoline. He would also like to require commercial-building owners to match the thermostat settings he is asking of homeowners—a measure DOE statisticians figure would save at least 195,000 barrels of oil a day. Meanwhile, Carter has already ordered executive agencies of the Federal Government to cut general energy use by 5 per cent—and he has started phasing out free parking spaces for Federal employees.

Carter is also relaxing environmental standards a bit. He has postponed for one year a regulation requiring U.S. refiners to reduce the lead content in gasoline. Since some refineries are not fully equipped to produce lower-lead gasoline, they would have had to close down if the rule went into effect next October as originally scheduled, thus reducing gas supplies by an estimated 350,000 barrels a day. Finally, Carter has ruled that the Environmental Protection Agency may consider large price gaps between low- and high-sulfur fuel oil when states ask for temporary suspensions of the clean-air standards. This would permit emergency use of high-sulfur fuel when the prices of low-sulfur oil soar.

Many energy experts doubt that Americans will willingly sport long johns in winter and forgo summer air conditioning. Nor will higher prices at the pump necessarily force motorists to drive less; in Europe, for example, where the price of gasoline has soared to more than $2 a gallon, driving is just as heavy as ever. "Only when there are Sunday closings and mandatory conservation measures will people react," says Norman Stein of the New England Energy Congress, a research group.

LONG-TERM BOON: Decontrol is much more likely to work than appeals for voluntary conservation. And the long-term benefits could be considerable. According to James Osten, an economist at Data Resources, Inc., the U.S. could save $4 billion a year on oil imports—and the saving may rise to as much as $40 billion annually by 1990. That would help correct the huge U.S. balance-of-payments deficit and strengthen the dollar in the currency markets. What's more, Arnold Safer, energy economist for the Irving Trust Co., argues that money spent on domestic oil is more likely to be pumped back into the U.S. economy. "The OPEC nations get the dollars and they can't spend them," says Safer. "The sheiks can buy only so many Cadillacs."

It will take time, of course, for the longer-term pluses of decontrol to outweigh the short-term minuses of higher inflation and a somewhat lower growth rate. At a minimum, oilmen admit, it will be at least two years before there is a visible boost in domestic production and a cut in oil imports. But long before then, Carter's plan will face serious difficulties. All of the package's tax and mandatory-conservation proposals must pass Congress. And recent history suggests that Congress will find it hard to agree. Already, special-interest groups are bombarding their congressmen with complaints and requests. Oil-state representatives, for instance, are unhappy about the size of the proposed tax. And oil-industry critics would prefer a confiscatory measure—leaving no excess profits at all.

DRIVER'S SEAT: But Carter has one thing going for him: if Congress fails to pass a windfall-profits tax, it would bear the brunt of the criticism for allowing Big Oil to keep 100 per cent of the proceeds of decontrol.

Carter now finds himself in the driver's seat—and a bit more popular with oilmen. "The thought went through my mind as the speech unfolded that this is a very courageous action," says Shell Oil Co. president John F. Bookout, who watched Carter's speech at the New Orleans meeting. "He didn't have to do this." But the truth is that Carter probably had little choice. It was five years ago that OPEC served notice on the world that the era of cheap energy had ended. The day had to come when Americans would fully pay the new price.

MERRILL SHEILS with RICH THOMAS and GLORIA BORGER in Washington, LEA DONOSKY in New Orleans, RONALD HENKOFF in New York and bureau reports

The Nature and Origins of the U.S. Energy Crisis

JAI-HOON YANG

AGGREGATIVE economic policy is designed to stabilize the general price level and the growth in output and employment. Monetary policy, as a general tool of aggregate demand management, seeks to achieve these goals by affecting the volume of total spending in the economy. Whether ultimate goals of this policy are achieved depends to a large extent upon the external shocks to which the economy is subjected. Regardless of the sources of these shocks — weather, foreign actions, or changes in institutional conditions — they must be taken into consideration in the process of monetary policy planning and execution. One of the recent shocks has been the sudden and dramatic increase in the relative price of energy, which has significantly affected U.S. productive capacity.[1] This article traces and analyzes the underlying factors which were instrumental in rendering the U.S. economy vulnerable to the energy shock.

In the wake of the Arab oil embargo in 1973-74 and the weather-induced natural gas crisis in the winter just passed, concern about an energy crisis has spread across the U.S. The crisis often has been identified as an *energy gap* manifested as shortages of gasoline in 1974, and of heating oil and natural gas last winter. The emergence and the prospective persistence of such an energy gap often have been diagnosed as being the result of rising demand for energy and dwindling supplies of oil and natural gas. However, such a perception of the nature and the roots of the energy crisis is based on an uncritical acceptance of the "lump-of-energy" conception and on a denial of the laws of demand.

An alternate view of the energy crisis rejects the identification of the energy problem as a growing imbalance between the absolute quantity of energy demanded and supplied. Rather, the energy problem is diagnosed as the apparent "failure" of the energy market to accommodate the amount of energy demanded at policy-mandated prices, and the seemingly progressive deterioration in the capacity of the energy market to adjust to man-made and weather-induced shocks.

The history of U.S. energy markets reveals that the roots of the current crisis have been nurtured by past public policy measures. These policies were adopted in response to demands by segments of the energy industry for protection from the rigors of market competition. The crisis is rooted in the supplanting of the market mode of competition by the political mode. From this perspective, it is difficult to avoid the conclusion that past public policies (pursued to shelter some segments of the energy industry) have been, in large measure, responsible for the energy crisis.

THE NATURE AND ROOTS OF THE U.S. ENERGY CRISIS: TWO VIEWS

A Prevalent View

A widely accepted diagnosis of the nature of the U.S. energy crisis is one of growing imbalance in the nation's energy budget. Such a diagnosis is based on the premise that the amount of energy demanded will continue to increase, while the amount of oil and natural gas supplied will diminish.[2] The "crisis" the U.S. faces is often said to be a grave threat to the nation's economic security and the American way of life.

This conception of the energy crisis is, thus, that of an inexorable emergence and worsening of an *energy gap*, unless dependence on nonrenewable fossil fuel in general, and on oil and natural gas in particular, is not reduced. In estimating the length of the "grace period" during which plans for an oilless future must be made, the projections of energy "demands" are based upon alternative assumptions of the rate of growth in energy usage in the form of oil consumption. Such projections are typically made by extrapolating the historical

---

[1]Robert H. Rasche and John A. Tatom, "The Effects of the New Energy Regime on Economic Capacity, Production, and Prices," this *Review* (May 1977), pp. 2-12 and "Energy Resources and Potential GNP," this *Review* (June 1977), pp. 10-24.

[2]S. David Freeman, Director, *A Time to Choose*, Final Report by the Energy Policy Project of the Ford Foundation (Cambridge: Ballinger Publishing Co., 1974).

Reprinted from Federal Reserve Bank of St. Louis *Review*, July, 1977.

rates of growth in energy usage and by assuming different (lower) rates of growth under alternative conservation plans.[3] Then, given geological estimates of potentially recoverable oil reserves, the computation of the grace period becomes routine.

For example, some estimates of the grace period use as a benchmark the estimate of about 2 trillion barrels of total world recoverable oil. Even using a "conservative" projection of a 3 percent rate of growth in oil demand, as contrasted to the 8 percent rate of growth in the 1960s, the world's presently estimated recoverable oil resources would be exhausted before 2020. The arithmetic is unassailable and, hence, the spectre of freezing in the dark arises if the U.S. is not weaned away from its dependency on oil in time.[4]

The policy prescriptions that often follow from such a view of the energy problem are mandated conservation and the pursuit of technical energy efficiency during the transition into a new energy regime.[5] Such a transition is deemed to be facilitated by a mix of standby and regular excise and consumption taxes on energy, subsidies, tax credits, "reform" of the utility rate-making procedures, a system of incentive pricing for *new* oil and natural gas, and by a set of mandatory allocations and conversions to coal — the more plentiful "interim" fuel.

An Alternate Market-Based View

The essence of the energy problem from the alternate view is that the problem is one of apparent (or potential) "malfunction" in the market for energy. This view focuses squarely on the capacity of the energy market to respond to unforeseen shocks, such as the recent oil embargo and severe weather, and to accommodate foreseeable changes in the quantity of energy demanded. When the energy problem is framed in this manner,[6] the accumulated stock of knowledge regarding the functioning of markets can be used to diagnose the nature and the origins of the energy problem.

Despite its importance, energy must be viewed as a commodity not unlike any other commodity that competes for a share of limited budgets. Hence, the amounts of energy demanded and supplied are both determined by laws that govern consumer and producer behavior.

According to the *first law of demand*, the lower the price (that is, the lower the sacrifice incurred in terms of other goods that have to be given up to purchase energy), the higher is the quantity demanded, other things being equal.[7] And, according to the *second law of demand*, the longer the elapsed time after a price fall, the greater will be the extent of substitution toward the commodity which has become cheaper. As prices fall, increases in the quantity demanded occur, first, because more is demanded by the *present* users and, second, because *new* users enter the market.

Such an adaptive behavior on the part of consumers is mirrored in a similar behavior on the part of producers in an exchange system organized within a general private property framework. Thus, a greater quantity of energy will be supplied as prices rise because more energy will be supplied by the *present* producers and *new* (higher-cost) producers will be enticed to enter the market.

The nature of the energy problem from the market view is the "inadequate capacity" of the energy market to adjust to unexpected shocks, such as the man-made oil embargo and nature-induced severe weather conditions. Such a conception of the nature of the energy problem leads one to heed Santayana's dictum that, "those who do not learn from history are condemned to repeat it," and to study the history of energy markets in the U.S. for a clue to the roots of the current energy crisis.

Such a study of the history of energy markets, especially the markets for oil and natural gas, reveals some general characteristics of the energy market which have circumscribed its adjustment capacity, such as the exceptionally long (three-to five-year) lead

---

[3] Ibid., pp. 19-25.

[4] For a graphic illustration of the apocalytic vision of the dismal energy future evoked by the recent discussions of the energy crisis, see Isaac Asimov, "Essay," *Time* (April 25, 1977), p. 33.

[5] Such a regime is characterized by renewable and essentially inexhaustible energy sources, such as solar and wind energy, and viable nuclear fusion technology.

[6] For a statement of this approach, see Armen A. Alchian, "An Introduction to Confusion," in *No Time to Confuse* (San Francisco: Institute for Contemporary Studies, 1975). Also see Edward J. Mitchell, *U.S. Energy Policy: A Primer*

(Washington, D.C.: American Enterprise Institute (AEI), 1974); Hendrick S. Houthakker, *The World Price of Oil* (Washington, D.C.: AEI, 1976), Washington, D.C.; and Douglas R. Bohi, Milton Russel, and Nancy McCarthy Snyder, U.S. Congress, House of Representatives, Committee on Banking, Currency, and Housing, *The Economics of Energy and Natural Resource Pricing*, A Compilation of Reports and Hearings, 94th Congress, 1st Session, Parts 1 and 2, March 1975, pp. 1-230.

[7] Armen A. Alchian and William R. Allen, *University Economics*, 3rd. ed. (Belmont, California: Wadsworth Publishing Company, 1972), pp. 60-66.

times for end-use delivery and the common pool problem.[8] More importantly, a historical inquiry, which will be discussed in greater detail in later sections, also reveals that deep government involvement in the past has greatly attenuated the adjustment capacities of the energy market.

For example, the legacy of the demand prorationing system,[9] which arose in the 1920s, and the subsequent voluntary and mandatory import quotas on oil products (on national security grounds) in the 1950s, is evident in the current problem. Indeed, the formation of the oil producers' cartel (OPEC) in 1960 was proximately caused by the imposition of mandatory import quotas in the U.S. in 1959.[10] The Supreme Court's ruling on the Phillip's case in 1954 also was one of the roots of the current energy problem.[11] The more recent price controls on energy imposed in mid-1971 also have had adverse effects.

The unifying thread in the apparently disparate set of causes of the energy problem, is the replacement of the market mode of competition by the political mode of advocacy politics. The more successful were those who sought relief from the rigors of competition through political means, the less robust became the adjustment capacity of the energy markets to unforeseen shocks.

Comparison of the Two Views

The market-based view of the energy crisis denies the usefulness of the prevalent conception of the energy crisis as that of an ever accelerating shortfall in the amount of BTUs (British Thermal Units) embodied in finite and nonrenewable oil and natural gas. The fatal flaw in the prevalent view is the failure to perceive the fundamental distinction between (1) rising prices in response to changes in underlying schedules of demand and supply, and (2) the phenomenon of rising shortages in quantity supplied relative to quantity demanded, because prices *do not* or *are not allowed* to adjust fast enough to equate the quantity demanded to quantity supplied.

According to the market view, the adherents of the prevalent view, in advancing their various scenarios of impending disaster, ignore adaptive human behavior under perceived changes in scarcity and opportunities. They base their scenarios instead on the arbitrary projections of quantity demanded relative to estimates of fixed "recoverable" reserves of oil and gas.[12] Such a mechanistic conception of the problem neglects the roles which changes in price and technology play in inducing revisions in the estimates of recoverable reserves, as well as in altering the quantity demanded of oil and gas *and* the quantity supplied of alternate sources of energy. Such neglect reflects two underlying false premises.

The first premise is that energy is an "essential resource." According to this premise, the demand for energy is insensitive to changes in its price. The premise, in essence, denies the fundamental laws of demand. This premise is falsified by the available evidence which indicates that the quantity demanded of energy is sensitive to both its price and consumer income.[13] More importantly, the price sensitivity of demand for energy is greater in the long run than in the short run.

---

[8]The common pool problem is similar to the fishery problem in that both arise due to the ill-defined property rights over the common resource at issue. Typically, the applicable law with regard to property rights is the rule of capture. That is, the exclusive property rights are created at the instant of capturing fish or drawing oil from the pool. There exist, therefore, incentives for co-owners of the pool to extract as much of the oil as they singly can. Such an unrestrained behavior on their part, however, tends to reduce the ultimate amount of oil recoverable by drilling, relative to the more paced rate of drilling known as the "maximum efficient rate of production (MER)." Hence, the logic of joint maximization would call for a rate of production not to exceed MER. The problem involved in striking an agreement to promote joint maximization is similar to the one in forming a cartel of producers to coordinate production decisions. See U.S. Congress, Senate, Committee on the Judiciary, *Governmental Intervention in the Market Mechanism: The Petroleum Industry*, Hearings before the Subcommittee on Antitrust and Monopoly, 91st Congress, 1st Session, Part 2, 1969, pp. 1070-71.

[9]Market demand prorationing refers to the system of allocating production quotas to individual oil producers. It arose in response to the common pool problem in the production of crude oil. Since the transaction costs (inclusive of negotiation and enforcement costs of agreed upon output shares) involved in determining the oil to be drawn from a common pool by co-owners are substantial, such determination was done through the mediation of various state regulatory commissions. Rationing of the quota was specified in terms of the allowable percentage of MER (maximum efficient rate of production), with a view to controlling total production such that the targeted market price of oil could be sustained. Ibid., pp. 1069-73.

[10]See Kenneth W. Dam, "Implementation of Import Quotas: The Case of Oil," *The Journal of Law and Economics* (April 1971), pp. 1-60.

[11]The Supreme Court ruled that the Federal Power Commission *must* regulate the wellhead price of natural gas flowing in interstate commerce. Phillips Petroleum Company V. Wisconsin, 347 U.S. 622, 1954. See Edmund W. Kitch, "Regulation of the Field Market for Natural Gas by the Federal Power Commission," *The Journal of Law and Economics* (October 1968), pp. 243-80.

[12]For a discussion of various concepts of (mineral) reserves and the problems in estimating them, see U.S. Congress, House of Representatives and Senate, Joint Economic Committee, *Adequacy of U.S. Oil and Gas Reserves*, 94th Congress, 1st Session, 1975, pp. 14-27.

[13]Dale W. Jorgenson, ed., *Econometric Studies of U.S. Energy Policy* (Amsterdam: North-Holland, 1976); Also Houthakker, *The World Price of Oil*, p. 8.

The second premise is that the reserves of oil and gas in particular, and other nonrenewable energy resources in general, are a predetermined, fixed "lump" which is independent of both price and technology. This premise ignores the fact that reserves are essentially adjustable inventories which the energy producers hold in order to safeguard their market positions. The amount of reserves (inventories) producers want to hold, then, is dependent upon the perceived cost of holding them relative to the expected returns from such holdings.

The prevalent view of the nature and origins of the energy crisis is, thus, based on twin fallacies: the lump of energy fallacy and the denial of the fundamental laws of demand. Such a view tends to ignore the following facts: (1) that the demand for energy is a derived demand,[14] (2) that energy produces valued output in conjunction with other scarce factors of production (such as labor and capital), (3) that other factors are substitutable for energy in the production process (hence other factors are valuable, as is energy), and (4) that the substitution of one form of energy for another depends on the relative cost of alternative forms of energy.[15]

Underlying the prevalent view is a concept that could be characterized as the "BTU theory of value." A strict BTU theory of value would hold that energy is the *only* scarce resource and, as such, is as fallacious as the Marxian labor theory of value, which holds that labor is the sole source of value. If the issue is presented so starkly, one would be hard put to find an advocate of such a BTU theory of value. However, the theory, at least in its applied forms, appears to have substantial adherents.

A variant of the BTU theory of value imputes an inherent, independent value to a specific source of BTUs, such as oil or natural gas. This variant denies the proposition that a dollar's worth of energy (in whatever form) is equal in value to a dollar's worth of labor or capital. Therefore, a question regarding the cost of conserving energy in terms of non-energy factors of production is seldom raised explicitly in assessing the comparative merits of various energy programs.

For example, some proposals to conserve the BTUs embodied in natural gas would use taxation and other measures to induce conversion to coal of electric power and industrial plants, designed to operate on natural gas. The question of cost-effectiveness in terms of the *total* resource use, relative to the desired output forthcoming from the production process, is seldom fully addressed. Implicit in this view is either a belief in the inherent value of the BTUs embodied in natural gas and the denial of the scarcity value of other cooperating factors, *or* a lingering belief that the price of natural gas does not, or will not be permitted to, reflect its true scarcity value.[16]

The market-based interpretation of the energy problem implies that the urgent task of public policy is to make the energy market *more* responsive to *unexpected* shocks and *expected* changes in market demand and supply conditions. Such a goal is likely to be achieved only if tinkering in the energy market by self-serving domestic power groups, acting through the government, is effectively curtailed.[17] Public pol-

---

[14]Demand for energy is a derived demand in the sense that an energy resource is not wanted for its own sake but for the output of the objects of more immediate consumption, such as comfortable temperatures and transportation services, which energy helps to produce.

[15]For recent articles which document the "abundant" availability of energy at higher market prices (from such sources as untapped natural gas reservoirs, Devonian shale and geopressured methane), see *The Wall Street Journal* editorial pages, 27 April 1977 and 14 June 1977. For an account of a series of substitutions of alternate fuels used for illuminants as the price of whale oil (the dominant lighting fuel in the U.S. in the early 1800s) rose drastically, see Murray L. Weidenbaum and Reno Harnish, *Government Credit Subsidies for Energy Development* (Washington, D.C.: American Enterprise Institute, 1976), pp. 4-5.

[16]Should the price indeed reflect the true scarcity value of natural gas, and, even given that, should some industrial users decide to use natural gas in conjunction with the natural gas powered capital goods already put in place (presumably because the total resource cost is lower than the alternative of enforced capital replacement), the only basis for questioning such a decision appears to be a BTU theory of value.

[17]In case of a discrepancy between direct private costs and total social cost of using energy resources in the presence of pollution externalities, an intervention through excise taxes could be appropriate. It may also be appropriate to attempt to induce changes in the discount rate that market participants use to optimize the time distribution of extraction and consumption of energy resources, if a demonstrable basis exists for a bias in the market interest rate. For a classic discussion of the problem of social cost, see Ronald H. Coase, "The Problem of Social Cost," *The Journal of Law and Economics* (October 1960), pp. 1-44. For a voluminous literature inspired by the Coase work, see William J. Baumol, "On Taxation and the Control of Externalities," *The American Economic Review* 62 no. 3 (June 1972), pp. 307-322 and various comments on the article together with "Reply," *The American Economic Review* 64 no. 3 (June 1974), pp. 462-92. For a discussion of the "proper" social discount rate for capital deepening decisions, see Kenneth J. Arrow, "Discounting and Public Investment Criteria," in *Water Research*, A. V. Kneese and S. C. Smith, eds. (Baltimore: Johns Hopkins Press, 1966), pp. 28-30; Jack Hirshleifer, James C. DeHaven, and Jerome W. Milliman, *Water Supply* (Chicago, The University of Chicago Press, 1960), pp. 139-41; Stephen A. Marglin, "The Social Rate of Discount and the Optimal Rate of Investment," *The Quarterly Journal of Economics* 77 no. 1 (February 1963), pp. 95-111; Gordon Tullock, "The Social Rate of Discount and the Optimal Rate of Investment: Comment," *The Quarterly Journal of Economics*, 78 no. 2 (May 1964), pp. 336-45.

icy becomes questionable if it is based exclusively on conserving particular forms of energy, such as oil and natural gas, without an explicit regard to the total cost of that policy, including the capital cost, relative to the demonstrable total benefits.

PAST PUBLIC POLICIES AS THE ROOTS OF THE ENERGY CRISIS

The Natural Gas Market

The controls on the wellhead price of natural gas, which were imposed in the 1960s, were below the market clearing level in the 1960s. According to the first law of demand, mentioned above, the expected result was an increase in the quantity of natural gas demanded by existing users of natural gas. According to the second law of demand, as the lower price persisted, there entered a new class of users, such as electric utilities. At first glance, it would appear that there should have been a "shortage" of natural gas, as the quantity demanded outstripped the quantity supplied when prices are held down artificially. This was not the case, however.

It appears paradoxical that an "artificially" low price of natural gas led to an *actual* increase in consumption, rather than to a mere increase in *attempted* consumption. Why did producers supply enough gas to accommodate the increase in quantity demanded at the artificially low price? The resolution of this puzzle holds a key to unravelling the nature of the fallacy imbedded in the prevalent view of the energy problem.

The technological nature of the natural gas (and oil) industry is such that the industry maintains a relatively high inventory-to-sales ratio.[18] The inventories are held in the form of *proved reserves*. The existence of inventories helps to dampen fluctuations in the current price and facilitates quantity adjustments to fluctuations in demand. The amount of reserves (inventories) sellers want to hold is systematically related (1) to the expected future market price relative to the current price, and (2) to the cost of holding inventories.

To understand what we observed in the 1960s — (1) the simultaneous lowering of the regulated price of natural gas below the market clearing level *and* increased consumption and production of natural gas, and (2) the conversion to natural gas by utilities and industrial users — it is necessary to review the history of regulatory control on the wellhead price of natural gas since the Phillips case of 1954.

The Federal Power Commission (FPC) approached its Supreme Court mandated task of regulating the wellhead price of natural gas on a case by case basis until the early 1960s. The case by case approach, however, put such a strain on the FPC's resources that the commission itself estimated that its 1960 case load would not be completed until the year 2043.[19] Faced with such a backlog of case load, the FPC introduced in 1961, the Permian Basin method of area-wide rate-making.[20]

Under the Permian Basin methodology, the FPC would establish a "just and reasonable" ceiling price for all natural gas produced within a broadly defined producing area such as the Permian Basin in Texas or Southern Louisiana. This method of price control resulted in the practice of basing the permitted price on the historical cost of a low cost producer in a given area. Therefore, the new method was instrumental in inducing a downward revision in the expected *future* price of natural gas.

Chart I indicates that the hypothesized downward revision in the expected price was in fact borne out by the actual price behavior. The relative price of natural gas declined on balance in the post-Permian 1960s, in sharp contrast to its rising trend between the late 1940s and the early 1960s. Chart I also shows that the actual thrust of regulation after the Phillips case of 1954 and prior to the Permian Basin proceedings, was such that the price of natural gas was permitted to continue its rise relative to both the price of oil and other prices in general.

In terms of the interpretation offered above of reserves as business inventories, one would expect that the downward revision in the expected future price of natural gas would have induced an accelerated

---

[18] This is because of the long lead time between exploration and production. See Paul W. MacAvoy and Robert S. Pindyck, *Price Controls and the Natural Gas Shortage* (Washington, D.C.: American Enterprise Institute, 1975), pp. 16-19.

[19] Ibid., p. 12.

[20] The area-wide rate making procedure, based on an adaptation of the public utility rate-making approach, tended to impart a downward bias to the regulated wellhead price. The FPC attempted to arrive at an area-wide composite average cost estimate based on a survey of cost data. Confronted with the logically impossible problem of joint cost allocation between oil and gas, the FPC systematically chose the figures at the lower end of the choice set. The Supreme Court once again ruled, in 1968, that it was within the discretion of the FPC to adopt the area-wide rate-making procedure, however arbitrary the rate may be. Permian Area Rate Cases, 390 U.S. 747 (1968).

Chart I
The Relative Wellhead Prices of Crude Oil and Natural Gas*

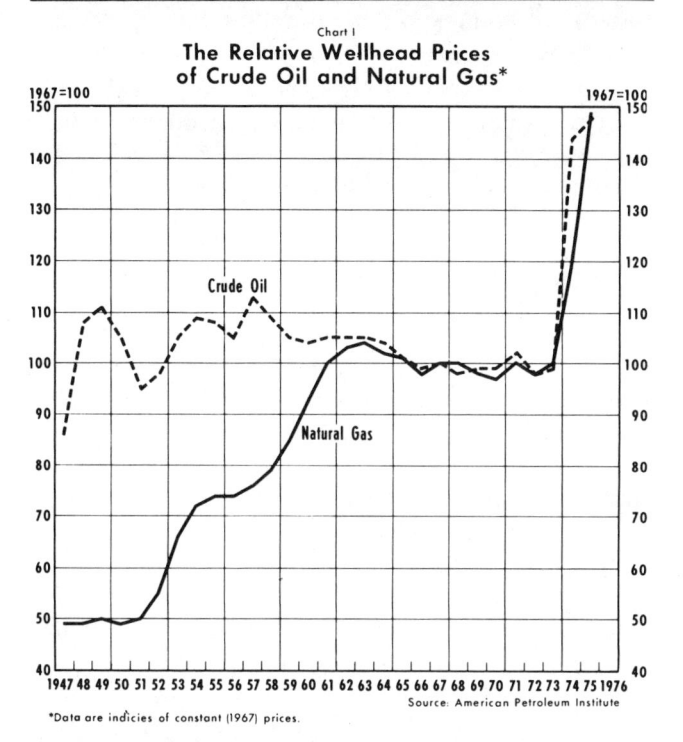

*Data are indicies of constant (1967) prices.
Source: American Petroleum Institute

Chart II
Ratio of Natural Gas Reserves to Production [1]

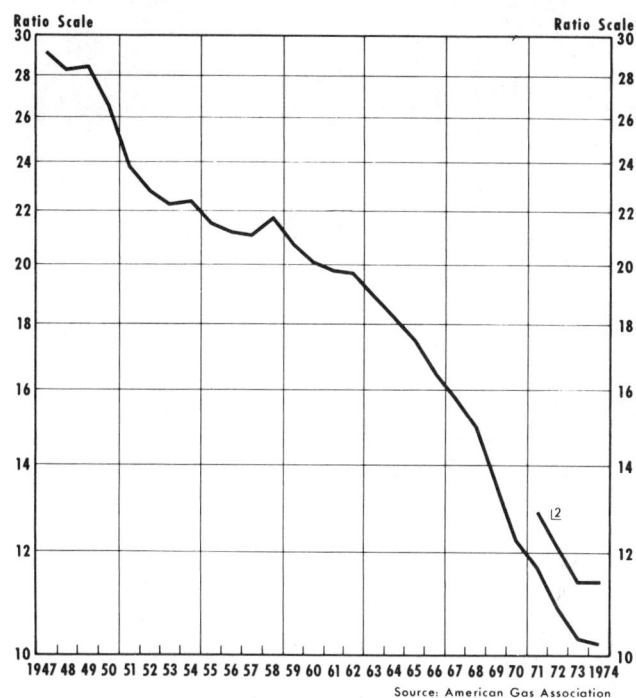

Source: American Gas Association
[1] Measured as the ratio of: the beginning and end of year figures for proven reserves of natural gas to the production of natural gas during that year.
[2] Includes 26 trillion cubic feet at 14.72 psia and 60°F in Prudhoe Bay, Alaska.

downward revision in the desired reserve-to-production ratios. Such an expectation is borne out by the behavior of the reserve-to-production ratios shown in Chart II. The chart shows that the reserve-to-production ratio was falling even before the Permian Basin proceedings in the early 1960s, indicating that the actual ratio was above the desired ratio. However, the downward adjustment proceeded at a slower rate of 1.8 percent per year after the Phillips case of 1954 but prior to the Permian proceedings in 1961, compared to the 3.7 percent per year rate in the earlier 1947-54 period. Such behavior is consistent with the earlier finding that regulation permitted a relative increase in the price of natural gas prior to the early 1960s.

The decline in the reserve-to-production ratio accelerated after the Permian proceedings began early in the 1960s. The ratio fell at the rate of 6 percent per year from 1963 to 1970. Such an acceleration in the decline of the ratio reflects the downward adjustment in the desired reserve-to-production ratio induced by the adoption of the Permian methodology.

Chart III indicates that the accelerated downward adjustment in the reserve-to-production ratio in the 1960s took the form, first, of decelerating growth of reserves, and then of outright reduction in reserves since 1968. Chart IV indicates that this slowing in reserve accumulation and the eventual reduction in reserves, can be attributed squarely to the slowing in the search for reserves as a direct consequence of policy-induced souring in the prospective returns on exploration and development activities. The Chart shows that there has been a secular improvement in the success ratios in exploratory and development efforts, possibly due to technological progress.[21] Therefore, the marked reduction in the number of successful gas well drillings since 1962, as shown in Chart IV, is primarily due to the reduction in the search activities. Production of natural gas, however, did not start decreasing absolutely until 1973.

The drawing down of reserves (inventories) by producers reconciles the apparent puzzle of an "artificially" low, controlled price and the observed increases in the quantity supplied. It is ironic that the peculiarities of the market for natural gas masked the policy-induced disequilibrium in the market, so that many new industrial and electric utility users switched over to natural gas from coal. They were attracted to natural gas because of its apparent "bargain" price

---
[21] The conclusion regarding the success ratios also holds individually for new-field wildcats, total exploratory wells and development wells.

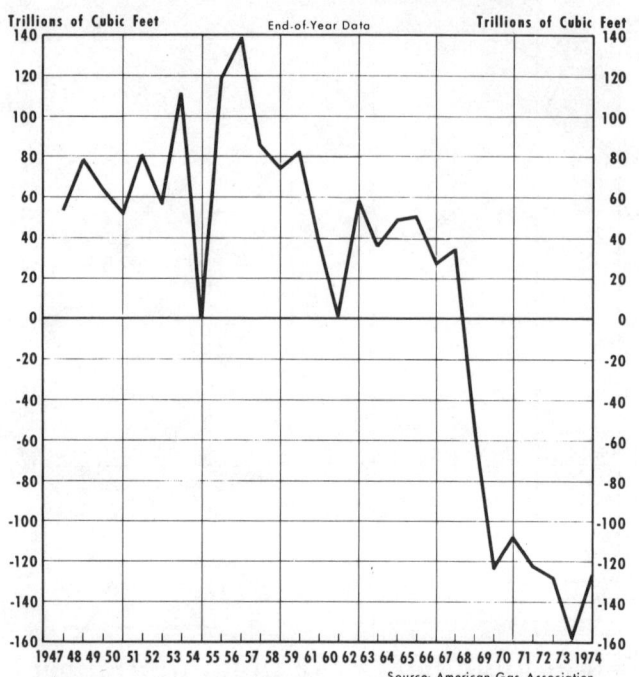

**Chart III
Changes in Natural Gas Reserves***

*This series is generated by subtracting estimated production of natural gas during the year from the reserve revisions, extentions, and discoveries during the same year.
Source: American Gas Association

and the higher cost of using coal occasioned by the passage of various environmental legislations.

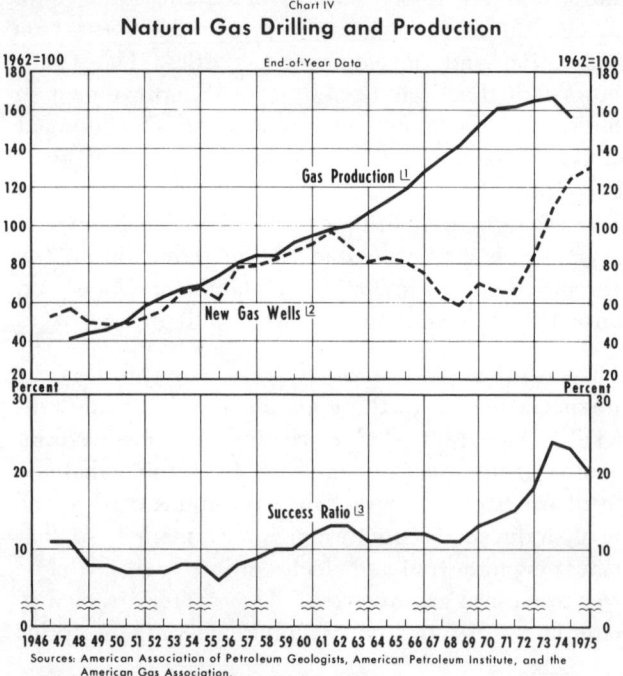

**Chart IV
Natural Gas Drilling and Production**

Sources: American Association of Petroleum Geologists, American Petroleum Institute, and the American Gas Association.
[1] Based on 13.638 quadrillion cubic feet of gas produced in 1962.
[2] Based on 5,848 new gas wells in 1962. This figure includes exploratory and development wells.
[3] Measured as the ratio of new gas wells to total wells drilled.

In view of the eventual emergence *at the controlled price* of a shortage in the market for natural gas, which led to supply curtailments, the decisions of new users to convert to natural gas must be judged with hindsight to have been ill-advised. It is doubly ironic that these victims of the unintended side-effects of public policy could now become targets of elaborate tax and administrative measures.

The Oil Market

The preceding analysis of the nature and origins of the natural gas crisis is applicable to the market for oil, the other endangered specie of energy. The adjustment capacity of the market for oil also has been attenuated as a consequence of past public policy. In contrast to the unintended shortage policy followed in the market for natural gas, a deliberate surplus policy was followed in the market for oil. As noted earlier, various state regulatory agencies followed a demand pro-rationing policy to cope with the common pool problem in the industry, which arose from the rule of capture doctrine in existence. This, in turn, arose from incompletely defined property rights over oil in the ground.[22]

In the absence of a demand pro-rationing system and of consolidation of an oil field under one or joint control, violent fluctuations arose in the price of crude oil that producers received as developed fields were intensively mined and new discoveries made.[23] The demand pro-rationing system evolved to protect the joint interests of the producers.[24] Under the demand pro-rationing system the state regulatory agencies, such as the Texas Railroad Commission, sought to alleviate this condition by setting total production targets for the particular state, and by distributing the production quotas according to a formula which favored small and usually higher-cost producers. The ever-present stripper wells — producing less than 20 barrels per day — were usually exempted from quota regulation altogether. The economic consequence of this form of allocation was higher than necessary

---

[22] Since oil is mobile in underground reservoirs, it is difficult to define and enforce property rights when the field is owned jointly.

[23] Morris A. Adelman, "Efficiency of Resource Use in Crude Petroleum," *Southern Economic Journal* 31 (October 1964), pp. 101-22.

[24] This system is a classic case of "acquired regulation." In such a situation, regulation is supplied by the state in response to the demand by the incumbents (mainly to restrain entry). For the original statement of the hypothesis of acquired regulation, see George Stigler, "The Theory of Economic Regulation," *The Bell Journal of Economics and Management Science* (Spring 1971), pp. 3-21.

resource costs of domestic oil, as higher-cost producers were rewarded.

Prior to 1948, the U.S. was a net exporter of oil, holding 31 percent of the then proven world reserves. Thus, the U.S. occupied a position of dominance, even greater than the position of Saudi Arabia today. But an accelerated pace of discovery and development by the major international oil companies of low-cost reserves in the Persian Gulf states began to make inroads into the U.S. position. Threatened by the competition from low-cost foreign oil imported mainly by the U.S. based major integrated international oil companies, other domestic oil producers and refiners, who had not developed foreign sources of oil, succeeded in persuading the government to institute a voluntary oil import program in 1957.[25]

The voluntary program failed, mostly due to the attempts of non-major U.S. producers to import from their recently developed wells in the Persian Gulf area. Unlike the international majors, which had already developed extensive networks of markets outside the U.S., these late-comers from the U.S. seized the opening under the voluntary import program to increase their market share at home. As a consequence, total imports as a percent of domestic production jumped from 19.7 percent in 1957 to 22.4 percent by 1959. Yielding to the intense pressure by a coalition of domestic producers and refiners, who demanded protection from cheap foreign oil on "security of supply" and other grounds, the voluntary import program became a mandatory import quota system in 1959.[26] As a result, a segment of the domestic oil industry was insulated from the rigors of competition in the market place. The mandatory program was to last until April 1973.

Under the Mandatory Oil Import Program, the overall import quota was set so as to freeze the share of imports at the level achieved in 1959. The distribution of import licenses among refiners was skewed in favor of smaller refiners. Such refiners received a disproportionately larger share of import licenses (in effect, subsidies), which had a market value per barrel equal to the difference between the higher-priced, regulated domestic oil and the cheaper, market-priced foreign oil.

The conventional method of arriving at the cost of the mandatory quota system is to add the estimated additional consumer costs of oil products to the cost of domestic resources unnecessarily used up to produce oil that could have been imported more cheaply. The real cost of the Program, however, would far exceed the conventionally estimated sum. The Program had sown the seed of the current energy crisis by sharply reducing the capacity of the oil market to respond to external shocks such as the effective cartelization of the Organization of Petroleum Exporting Countries (OPEC), and the Oil Embargo of 1973.

The Program set in motion a chain of events that culminated in the birth of OPEC in September 1960. The imposition of the U.S. import quota, based on a fixed share of the U.S. oil market, meant that imports could grow only at the rate of growth of U.S. production. This meant that the increased production that was just coming on stream from foreign wells developed by non-major U.S. producers had to be diverted away from the U.S. market. Precipitous price declines ensued in the world oil market and price competition forced the major international oil companies (majors hereafter) to match the decline.

It so happened, however, that the profit-sharing arrangement which the majors had with the oil producing countries was on the basis of the *posted price* rather than on the *market price*.[27] Therefore, in order to lighten the squeeze on their profits, the majors unilaterally cut posted prices in 1959 and once again in August 1960, despite strenuous protests and explicit warnings from the exporting countries.[28] The quota-induced cut in posted prices by the majors provided the spark for the exporting countries to form an organization to safeguard their common interest.

It is a moot point whether such an organization would have formed in the absence of the Mandatory Oil Import Quota Program. The point is that the quota system adopted in 1959 had a direct causal effect on the formation of OPEC, and such an untoward effect should be considered as a significant component of the cost of import programs.

The surplus policy on domestic oil, pursued by both state and Federal authorities at the instigation of some segments of the industry, reduced the incentives of the oil industry to improve efficiency and to add to

---

[25] See Dam, *Implementation*, pp. 5-8. Also see Morris A. Adelman, *The World Petroleum Market* (Resources for the Future, Inc.; Baltimore: The Johns Hopkins University Press, 1972), pp. 150-55.

[26] Dam, *Implementation*, pp. 9-14 and pp. 58-60.

[27] Yoon S. Park, *Oil Money and the World Economy* (Boulder: Westview Press, 1976), pp. 27-35.

[28] Bohi, Russel, and Snyder, *Economics of Energy*, p. 47, (p. 57 of the *Compilation*).

its stock of oil reserves. Public policy then delivered another blow to the oil market in the form of a series of price freeze and control programs instituted in 1971 to fight inflation. The domestic oil price control program had the unintended effect of killing off the mandatory import quota system. While the domestic price was being held down, the foreign price of oil increased and surpassed the U.S. level, thus wiping out the value of import licenses.

The familiar scenario of one control begetting another, in order to deal with the unintended distortions produced by the previous control, was repeated many times.[29] For example, under Phase IV of the price control program, the Cost of Living Council (CLC) adopted the technique of "vintaging" to the pricing of crude oil. A two-tier price system, with a ceiling price on "old" crude and a market-determined price on "new" and "released" domestic crude oil, was designed to encourage new exploration and production.[30] The program, while encouraging domestic exploration and development, created predictable problems of its own, due to the fact that not every refiner had equal access to *old* and *new* domestic crude oil, nor to domestic and imported crude oil.

Complaints of discrimination and charges of evading the two-tier pricing system through tie-in-sales, were often raised.[31] As a consequence of the two-tier pricing, substantial price differentials appeared in refined products reflecting different access to lower and higher-priced crude oil. The crude oil program was instrumental in creating artificial, policy-induced competitive advantages and disadvantages where none existed. A coalition of refiners, who had not developed their own domestic sources of old crude oil, lobbied actively for a crude oil allocation program under which they would receive their "equitable share" of lower-priced old crude oil.[32]

When the OAPEC (Organization of Arab Petroleum Exporting Countries)[33] embargo unexpectedly hit the U.S. in October 1973, the energy markets, particularly those of oil and natural gas, were tied up in knots due to the effects of the past policies, such as demand pro-rationing, the mandatory import quotas, and price controls on oil and natural gas. The U.S. dependence on foreign oil was to become larger than that which would have resulted in a world of open markets for natural gas and oil.[34]

The public policy response to the embargo exacerbated the adjustment problem. The Federal Energy Office — instead of focusing on the level of stocks of crude oil and refined products (which was the technique used to allocate production quotas by the Texas Railroad Commission) — focused on an anticipated reduction in U.S. oil imports, which was repeatedly overestimated. The amount of oil allocated for consumption consistently fell below the sum of domestic production and imports. As a consequence, the U.S. ended the embargo period with a higher stock of petroleum products than it started.[35]

In the wake of the embargo and the quadrupling of the crude oil price, a coalition of refiners without access to cheaper domestic old oil finally succeeded in having the newly organized Federal Energy Administration adopt the crude oil cost equalization program in December 1974.[36] The program was designed to allocate lower-priced domestic crude oil subject to price controls proportionately among refiners, and was adopted in response to the pressures to allow *all* refiners to have the equal access to cheaper domestic oil.

The principal part of the program was designed to distribute low-cost "old" domestic crude oil proportionately to *all* U.S. refiners through the issuance of tickets or entitlements. The entitlements represented rights to purchase lower-priced "old" domestic crude just as the import licenses during the mandatory oil import quota period represented rights to purchase the then cheaper foreign oil. Although the situation is reversed, the principle of resorting to political com-

---

[29] For an authoritative and revealing account of the utter frustration experienced by a former Federal Energy Office (FEO) administrator, see William A. Johnson, "The Impact of Energy Controls on the Oil Industry: How to Worsen an Energy Crisis," in *Energy: The Policy Issues*, edited by Gary D. Eppen (Chicago: University of Chicago Press, 1975), pp. 99-121.

[30] Ibid., pp. 109-110.

[31] Ibid., pp. 110-111.

[32] U.S. Congress, House of Representatives and Senate Subcommittee on Consumer Economics of the Joint Economic Committee, *The F.E.A. and Competition in the Oil Industry*, 93rd Congress, 2nd. Session, 1974, p. 17 and pp. 52-53.

[33] OAPEC was founded in 1967 by the Arab members of the OPEC.

[34] The price control on natural gas was having a delayed impact on the quantities supplied relative to the quantities demanded by then. Hence, the excess demand for natural gas spilled over into the market for oil. Bohi, Russel, and Snyder, *Economics of Energy*, pp. 81-7.

[35] Richard B. Mancke, *Performance of the Federal Energy Office* (Washington, D.C.: American Enterprise Institute, 1975), pp. 4-7.

[36] See "Allocations: F.E.A. Adopts Regulations Designed to Equalize Crude, Fuel Oil Costs," *Energy Users Report* no. 69 (Washington, D.C.: The Bureau of National Affairs, Inc., 5 December 1974), p. A-7. Hereinafter, *Energy Users Report*.

petition to alter economic outcomes remained invariant. Once again, as in the import licensing and the demand pro-rationing systems, smaller refiners (with less than a 175,000 barrel per day capacity) were to receive proportionately more entitlements than larger refiners.[37]

The system of entitlements, in conjunction with the multi-tier pricing of crude oil that was introduced earlier, had the unintended effect of increasing U.S. dependency on foreign oil.[38] The increase in foreign dependency was due to the joint effects of the "uncontrolled" price of "new" domestic oil being set below the world (the OPEC cartel) price, and the entitlement program. The former reduced the domestic production below the level that would otherwise have been attained under free (open) market pricing, while the entitlement program had the perverse effect of encouraging imports by, in effect, taxing domestic production and subsidizing imports.[39]

Figure I illustrates how a public policy, designed to deal with one set of problems through intervention in the market place, created another problem. The rise in the world (cartel) price of oil and the domestic price control on crude oil led to a demand by some refiners for crude oil allocation and cost equalization programs. Such a demand was eventually answered by the Emergency Petroleum Allocation Act of 1973 and Crude Oil Equalization Program of 1974. In Figure I, one can contrast the amount of imports that would have prevailed under free market pricing and the entitlement programs as evolved. Pw denotes the "world" price set by OPEC.[40] OPEC is assumed ready to supply all the "residual" oil demanded by the U.S. at Pw. In the absence of any domestic price control, the domestic production would be OB and the imports BC. However, under the price controls on both the "old" and the "new" domestic oil at P1 and P2 respectively, the U.S. producers would supply OE of "old" oil and EA of "new" oil. The total domestic production would now be OA and the amount of

[37] *Energy Users Report*, p. A-8.

[38] See Hans H. Helbling and James E. Turley, "Oil Price Controls," this *Review* (November 1975); Also Robert E. Hall & Robert S. Pindyck, "The Conflicting Goals of National Energy Policy," *The Public Interest* no. 47 (Spring 1977), p. 3.

[39] See Milton Friedman, "Subsidizing OPEC Oil," *Newsweek* June 23, 1975, p. 75, and Hall and Pindyck, "The Conflicting Goals," p. 3 and p. 5.

[40] The analysis abstracts from the question of how the Pw has been chosen. Presumably, if the objective is to maximize the joint profits (or wealth) of the OPEC members, a dominant-firm price leadership model would be relevant.

Figure I
The Effects of Price Controls and Entitlements

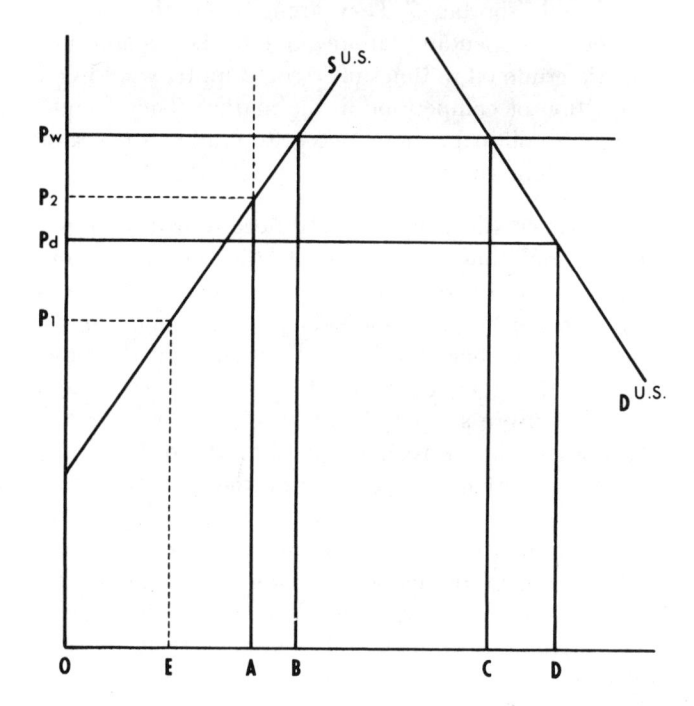

P_w: World Price (set by OPEC)
P_1: U.S. "Old" Oil Prices
P_2: U.S. "New" Oil Price
P_d: Weighted Average of Domestic and Foreign Oil *
*Assume Controls on End-Product Prices Using Pass-Through Provisions

imports would be AC, which are purchased at price Pw. The dependence on foreign oil increases by AB.

The introduction of the entitlement system worsens the situation further, especially when one assumes the existence of controls on end-product prices through pass-through provisions, for example, on utility rates. If we assume that the pricing of oil products is based on the weighted average price, denoted by Pd, of domestic and foreign oil, imported oil now increases to AD whereas the domestic production is still at OA. In view of the avowed objective at that time to achieve energy self-sufficiency by 1985 (Project Independence), it is indeed ironic that the policies chosen militated against the professed goal.

Aside from the adverse effect on foreign dependency, the crude oil cost equalization program raises a fundamental question regarding the role of public policy in the market place. Those who first asked for allocation and, then, for cost equalization of crude oil were those refiners who had not integrated backward to production of crude oil.[41] Their argument was that it was unfair for them to be deprived of the supply of crude oil by the integrated producers in times of crude oil "shortage." They argued that the price to society of impending failures, due to their inability to secure crude oil in times of "tight" supply, would be a reduction of competition in the market. They sought, through political actions, access to crude on the same terms as the integrated producers.

However, the reasoning advanced above for political intercessions runs counter to the concept of competition in the market place. The cardinal rule of competition is that individual participants in the market place bear the full consequences of their own market decisions, inclusive of those decisions regarding the future supply of raw materials. One possible strategy for an oil refiner, regarding the future source of raw materials, is to depend on the spot market for a supply of crude oil. This tends to be a higher risk strategy than the alternative one of integrating backward to the production of crude oil. A higher risk strategy is associated in the long run with a higher expected return than the alternative lower risk strategy.

In terms of this "new view" of industrial organization, then, the demands of some refiners for equal access on competitive ground is difficult to defend.[42] Furthermore, expected accommodations of their pleas tend to have effects beyond the mere redistribution of wealth from the integrated companies to those who were not integrated. It would tend to reduce the integrated oil companies' incentives to explore and develop new reserves of crude oil.

---

[41] See Eppen, *Energy*, pp. 106-107.

[42] For a systematic statement of the "new view" of industrial organization, see Oliver E. Williamson, *Markets and Hierarchies* (New York: The Free Press, 1975). For an application of the new view to the U.S. oil industry, see David J. Teece, "Vertical Integration in the U.S. Oil Industry," in *Vertical Integration in the Oil Industry*, edited by Edward J. Mitchell (Washington, D.C.: American Enterprise Institute, 1976).

An exploration into the history of two major energy markets in the U.S. reveals that the overriding uncertainty regarding the thrust and direction of public policy on energy has shrouded the energy markets. Under these circumstances, decision-makers in the energy industry were distracted from the business of securing, processing and marketing energy products in response to the perceived "energy consumption policies" of individual consumers and "energy supply policies" of fellow competitors. Instead, they have had to play the socially unproductive game of trying to anticipate and influence shifts in public policy.

CONCLUSIONS

The growing concern about an energy crisis has resulted in a repeated call for a national energy policy. Unfortunately, there are widespread misconceptions about the nature and origins of the U.S. energy problem. Past attempts by various segments of the energy industry to avoid the rigors of competition have resulted in public policies which have emasculated the energy market's ability to adjust to man-made and nature-induced shocks. It is ironic that those who now call for deregulation of the energy market are the ones that had successfully sought most of the existing regulations.

We are now faced with a "crisis," which calls for policy-mandated conservation measures that may be costly in terms of economic utilization of existing capital resources. And we seem to forget that an unfettered energy market could, and still can, bring forth ever expanding supplies of energy from higher-cost conventional sources and more exotic, alternate sources. Also, an unencumbered energy market could, and still can, induce effective conservation on the part of consumers, through the working of the first and second laws of demand. The question that remains, however, is whether the various elements of the energy industry will accept competitive market outcomes in totality or demand protection from the rigors of competition when the sledding gets tough.

45
Looking Anew at the Nuclear Future

In cooling down the failed reactor at Three Mile Island, experts from the Nuclear Regulatory Commission (NRC) had to assess somberly the risks of every feasible step, weigh them against the dangers of waiting too long, and act only after satisfying themselves that they had a reasonably clear idea of what to do. The same spirit ought to govern the public and its leaders in the intense debate about the future of nuclear power that is now beginning. As at Harrisburg, hasty judgments, formed in response either to panic or to glib reassurances that nothing much was amiss, could lock the nation into a misguided energy policy damaging to the health, welfare and productive strength of the U.S.

In the early stages of the debate, some tough questions have to be answered with an honest "nobody knows." But even before the final explanations are in on just what went wrong at Three Mile Island, it is possible to state two principles to guide future energy policy:

1) The U.S. needs nuclear power.
2) Nonetheless, the nation should reconsider just how much is required and how to get it with maximum safety.

The nature of the need should be clarified first. Fissioning atoms cannot drive cars or heat homes or melt steel, though that may become possible in some distant future. Nuclear power today can be used only to generate electricity. Last year, nuclear plants produced 12.5% of the nation's electricity, or something less than 4% of its total energy. Utilities have cut back sharply on their once ambitious plans for nuclear expansion because of rocketing costs of plant construction, regulatory and legal delays, and uncertainty about how rapidly demand for electricity will grow. President Nixon's energy planners foresaw atomic plants supplying 40% of all U.S. electricity by the year 2000. Jimmy Carter's strategists can see no more than 25% (or less than 8% of total energy consumption), and there is much doubt that even that goal can be met. Thus the fastest increase in nuclear power that realistically can be expected would come nowhere near freeing the U.S. of its dangerous reliance on foreign oil.

But nuclear power's role cannot be eliminated without dire consequences. In some areas—New England, around Chicago, parts of the Southeast—atomic plants supply about half of all electricity. Shutting them would lead to blackouts and brownouts that would gravely threaten public health and safety. Electricity bills would soar, cruelly pinching low-income homeowners, as utilities were compelled to turn to higher-cost sources of energy. Some power companies would be forced to buy still more foreign oil at prices of up to $20 a barrel, fanning inflation, weakening the dollar and tying the U.S. energy future yet more tightly to the explosive politics of the Middle East. M.I.T. Physicist Henry Kendall, a leader of the antinuclear Union of Concerned Scientists, readily concedes: "If we throw the switch and shut down all the nuclear plants next Thursday, that would represent a traumatic situation that could not be dealt with by the country."

A national moratorium on new "nukes," similar to those already in effect in several states, could lead to slower growth of electric supply, less industrial production, fewer jobs, lower standards of living. Oil cannot take over the role of nuclear power in generating electricity, even if the nation were foolish or desperate enough to speed up the already frightening increase of oil imports. Petroleum is too expensive and too much in demand for transportation, home heating, chemical output.

Of the fuels now available, only coal is abundant and cheap enough to substitute for nuclear power. But it is dangerous to mine and dirty to burn. One study sponsored by the Ford Foundation estimates that a new coal-fired plant meeting current environmental standards produces two to 25 fatalities a year. In addition, there is the threat of the "greenhouse effect," the possibility that all-out burning of coal would pour so much carbon dioxide into the air as to keep heat from escaping out of the atmosphere into space. Theoretical consequences that some scientists like to cite: warming of the earth, melting of the polar ice caps, flooding of the world's seacoast cities. In fact, there is no known way of producing energy without some environmental danger.

But even though there is no escape from keeping nuclear plants in operation and building new ones, the nation cannot let the debate end there. Three Mile Island vividly illustrated the dangers of reliance on nuclear power. Disaster was avoided, but probably not by much. Experts who never considered the possibility that a hydrogen bubble would hinder attempts to shut down a balking reactor can no longer contend that the chances of serious accident are so tiny as to be totally discounted. The radiation released was well below the Government's standards for safety, but cancer rates among people exposed to fallout from the atomic-bomb tests of the 1950s and shipyard workers who repair atom-powered vessels raise troubling questions about the long-run effects of supposedly "safe" radiation.

Still unsettled—and unsettling—is the question of how the U.S. can safely dispose of garbage from nuclear operations. Spent fuel and other wastes remain radioactive for thousands of years. At present a lot of such waste is stored under water in "swimming pools" at plant sites, but nuclear plants are running out of pool space. Some may have to shut down as early as 1983 unless a more permanent method of disposal is found. Nuclear plants are built to operate for about 35 years. By the year 2000 some worn-out ones will either have to be torn down or sealed up so that no radiation escapes. No one yet knows how to safely dismantle or seal off a reactor, though Three Mile Island may provide some insights about that.

Prudence dictates that the U.S. build nuclear plants only when practical, economical and safer alternatives are not available. There is still time to search for alternatives, while also working to tighten the safety of nuclear plants themselves. Electric generating capacity nationwide exceeds expected peak demand by 33%. That figure is not quite so reassuring as it sounds; utility-company officials contend that at least 18% "excess" capacity is required to meet unexpected surges in demand, guard against breakdowns and allow for mainte-

Reprinted by permission from TIME, The Weekly Newsmagazine; Copyright Time Inc. 1979.

nance. Still, the nation has some breathing space to figure out how many new nuclear plants are required, and how soon.

A study by the Harvard Business School indicates that the U.S. can indeed reduce dependence on nuclear power while avoiding holding itself up to ransom by foreign oil producers. It is summarized by Professors Robert Stobaugh and Daniel Yergin in the current issue of *Foreign Affairs*. The key findings:

Under present policies, nuclear power, which now provides the equivalent of the energy in 1 million bbl. of oil per day, would supply the equivalent of 3 million bbl. per day by the late 1980s. Even so, imports would rise from the present 9 million bbl. per day to 14 million. However, policies can be envisioned under which nuclear output would be only doubled, not tripled, and oil imports still held to their present level. The nation would have to adopt a rigorous conservation program (for example, better insulating of present buildings and requiring that new ones be held to tight standards). As President Carter noted in his energy speech last week, "Conservation is our cheapest and cleanest energy source."

In addition, the U.S. would have to make a heavy push on solar energy, which the authors calculate by the late 1980s could produce four times as much energy as it would under current strategies. To achieve so large an increase in solar power so quickly, say the professors, the Government would have to pay out generous tax credits and subsidies, redirect research away from huge solar satellites and "power towers" toward smaller panels fitted to individual buildings, and encourage utilities to finance and install solar gear for their customers. "Solar" in this case means not only energy from the sun itself but also from so-called biomass: burning garbage and agricultural waste.

Like all figures in the energy debate, these will be vehemently disputed, but the point remains that there *are* alternatives to both nuclear power and foreign oil worthy of consideration. One is "co-generation" of power; that is, using waste heat from factories and apartment houses to generate electricity at power plants built on site. Co-generation provides about a third of West Germany's electricity. The Army Corps of Engineers believes that electricity supplies could be increased significantly by expanding and improving existing hydroelectric power stations. Other alternatives will require technological breakthroughs. The fluidized-bed method of burning coal—essentially, burning a mixture of crushed coal and sand suspended on a column of air inside a superhot container—promises ultimately to make combustion more efficient while cutting down on pollutants. It is now in the experimental stage, but has yet to be made applicable to large-scale commercial operations. Unlocking oil from the vast deposits of shale rock in the West at present is uneconomical, produces gigantic piles of ash, and uses too much valuable water. But tests indicate that oil may be burned out of the shale underground without adding much to pollution.

These are only examples of possibilities. All may succeed; all may fail. There is no one "solution" to the energy problem. Zealots of every stripe have done the nation a disservice by touting their pet ideas (conservation, nuclear power, solar power, co-generation or whatever) as *the* solution and denigrating every other idea. Their competing overenthusiasms have confused an already difficult debate. The task is to devise a truly comprehensive energy program, investigating every feasible idea and pouring time and money into those that seem most promising.

In the most comprehensive imaginable energy program, however, nuclear power still would play a role. So the question remains: How can reactors be made safer right now? There are several approaches:

REGULATION. Experts from the NRC should be on duty in the control room of every reactor round the clock, armed with full authority to take over at the first sign of trouble, order a shut-down if that seems necessary, direct all emergency procedures for closing the plant—and damn what it may cost. At present, this responsibility is borne largely by utility-company employees, who, with the best will in the world, cannot avoid thinking about the costs to the company. In addition, computers at all U.S. nuclear plants should be wired in to a central NRC monitoring station, so that the first blip registering potential trouble would ring an alarm at headquarters.

NRC inspectors can and should keep a much closer eye on construction of nuclear plants and the quality of equipment. They are supposed to do so now, but far too much of their time is taken up poring over reports submitted by contractors. That paper work could be turned over to clerks, giving the NRC inspectors more time to go out to sites and look around. When they do so, disinterested observers agree, they do a good job. An analogy can be drawn with the space program. In its early days it was plagued by sloppy work and accidents, but now the National Aeronautics and Space Administration enforces tight safety controls on contractors. If the Nuclear Regulatory Commission had been equally tough with the utility industry, some veteran observers of the space program believe, the Three Mile Island accident would not have happened.

Power utility managers might well be pleased to turn over to the Government the burden of responsibility for monitoring and safety. Shepard Bartnoff, head of the Jersey Central Power and Light Co., one of the owners of the Three Mile Island plants, said at hearings in Washington last week that he wished an NRC inspector had been in the control room to coordinate emergency operations when the trouble started.

SITING. A Ford Foundation–sponsored study indicates that a nuclear accident at a poorly chosen site—one close to a heavily populated area or at a location where winds would carry radioactive particles toward big cities—would cause 1,000 times more damage to life and property than a mishap at a more remote spot.

Alvin Weinberg, director of Tennessee's Institute for Energy Analysis, and a physicist considered by some anti-nukes to be about the most thoughtful proponent of nuclear power, calls for severely limiting new sites for nuclear power plants. He would permit expansion only on 90 of the 100 sites where reactors are now operating or planned. Among the ten sites where he would allow no new construction: Indian Point, N.Y., near New York City; Zion, Ill., close to Chicago—and Three Mile Island. Concentrating construction at the other 90 sites, he believes, would result in the building of huge atomic complexes, staffed by groups of experts like those at the sprawling Government atomic works in Oak Ridge, Tenn.

LEGISLATION. President Carter is again expected to submit a bill to Congress to speed up licensing procedures for nuclear plants. No action was taken on a similar bill last year. Congressmen understandably are wary about putting new nuclear plants into operation more quickly. But the bill calls for standardizing reactor designs, with appropriate safeguards, and for building up a bank of preselected sites on which reactor construction would be permitted. Those provisions would enhance safety.

The nuclear issues are fiendishly complicated and the stakes the highest imaginable. The outcome will test the ability of a democratic society to solve the most involved technical questions, ones on which experts offer diametrically opposed opinions. Caution, sobriety, careful weighing of risks, which cannot be escaped, ought to be the watchwords. Slogan shouting—"Hell, no, we won't glow," vs. "Let the bastards freeze in the dark" —merely impedes progress toward America's energy future. Simply put, the nation needs to move forward to improve the safety, reliability and efficiency of all forms of energy—including nuclear, and the many alternatives. — *George J. Church*

Illustrations for TIME by Sandy Huffaker

46

The Role of Productivity Gains in Solving National Economic Problems

Remarks by

G. William Miller, Chairman
Board of Governors of the Federal Reserve System
Washington, D.C.

before the

American Productivity Center
Productivity Conference
New York, New York

October 3, 1978

Inflation is a clear and present danger which affects all our lives and all our opportunities. As far as monetary policy is concerned, the emergence early this year of inflation as a more virulent threat to our system has placed enormous responsibilities on the Federal Reserve. Monetary policy must and will be used to restrain inflation, but it needs support from other economic policies in order to avoid undesirable side effects. The task the central bank has set out for itself is to use prudent monetary policy to restrain the forces of inflation, by bringing down the rate of growth of the money supply, but to do so without triggering a recession that would work against the overall objective. It is reassuring to note that earlier this year, when it became apparent that the effort would not be left to monetary policy alone, positive initiatives were taken by the Administration and by the Congress. There have been substantial changes toward a more restrictive fiscal policy to help bring down the rate of inflation.

With this as background, I am particularly pleased to be here to participate in this conference on productivity. An initiative to achieve productivity gains is one that we can all endorse and aggressively support. A successful effort to improve economic efficiency will directly offset the upward cost pressures on prices. It will tend to make our output more competitive in international markets, and thus improve our balance of trade and help stem the deterioration of the dollar in the currency exchange markets. It will contribute to long-range increases in our economic capacity and in our standard of living. Unless the economy's productivity expands at a faster rate, we will be unable to reduce unemployment without igniting inflation. Increased productivity is the best prospect for breaking the vicious cycle of wages chasing prices and prices chasing wages.

Because it is imperative that we act now to achieve such benefits as we can from increased productivity, it is well worth our time today to look at some of the historical trends and to discuss some of the public policies that could accelerate such gains.

History shows that productivity gains have been a key factor in our economic growth and in our rising standard of living. Output per work hour

Reprinted from Federal Reserve Bank of Dallas *Voice*, December, 1978.

CHART 1

Output Per Hour, Private Business Sector

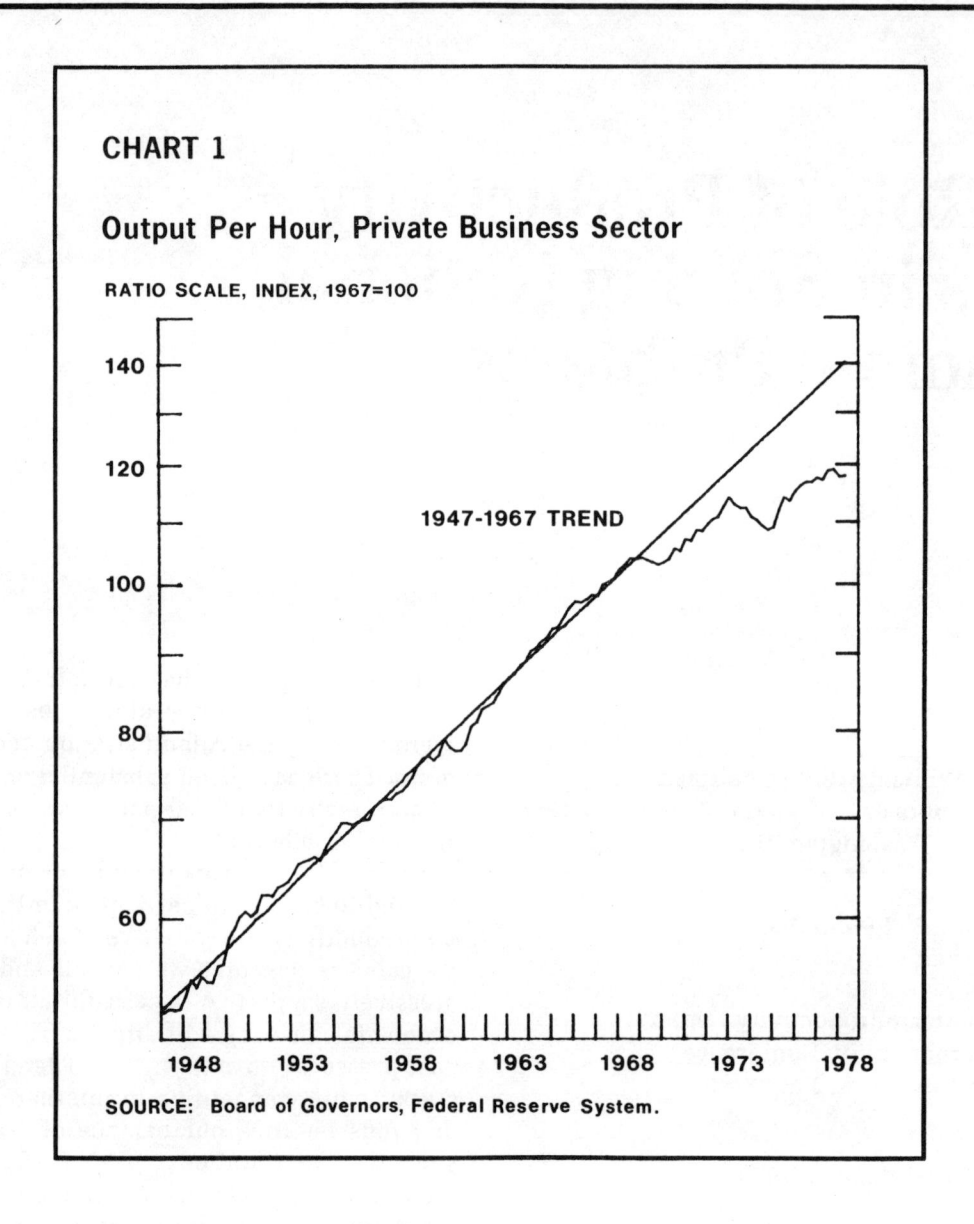

RATIO SCALE, INDEX, 1967=100

SOURCE: Board of Governors, Federal Reserve System.

in the private sector rose more than 125 percent over the past 30 years. The bulk of the improvement, however, occurred between 1947 and 1967. During that period, output per hour doubled. Since 1967, output per hour has risen less than one-fifth, only about half the average pace prior to 1967.

Chart 1 shows that output per hour is now well below its postwar trend. Even before the oil embargo and the recession of 1974-75, the rate of productivity growth had slowed down. Prior to 1967 the annual rate of growth was about 3$\frac{1}{3}$ percent; in the years 1967-72, it was only about 2 percent. Other things being equal, this added more than a full percentage point to the rise in unit labor costs. Such increases in costs are eventually reflected in final prices, and that was certainly the experience in the 1967-72 period. While we thought in those years that 2 percent was a weak performance, in the following five years things have gotten much worse. Coincident with the quintupling of oil prices and the deep recession of 1974-75, productivity fell into an unusually long and deep decline.

Chart 2 shows how output per hour has lagged during this recovery cycle. Its eventual upturn was so belated and so mild that by 1977, output per hour was up only 6$\frac{1}{2}$ percent from the 1972 level. That amounts to an average annual gain of only 1$\frac{1}{3}$ percent. Think about that for a moment: an average efficiency gain of only 1$\frac{1}{3}$ percent a year, little more than one-third the pace in the two decades ending in 1967. Even if wages and salaries had remained stable—and, of course, they did not—the productivity slowdown would have added 2 percentage points to the rise of unit labor costs. The result is a commensurate impetus to inflation.

During the years of strong productivity gains, workers and their families became accustomed to generous increases in their real incomes. America's standard of living rose dramatically; average work schedules were shortened; leisure time was increased. Over time, we came to expect an annual improvement in our real incomes. In fact, an allowance of 3 percent or more in productivity gains was included in the wage-price guidelines set in the Kennedy Administration in the early 1960's. These expectations of regular and sizable increases in the average standard of living were subsequently frustrated.

As productivity growth slowed, real income gains began to fall below individual and collective expectations. This had serious consequences for inflationary pressures. In an effort to sustain past patterns of real income growth, wages were pushed up, setting in motion a cycle of intense upward pressure on costs and prices. This occurred despite high levels of unemployment and excess industrial capacity. Thus the slowing of productivity growth helped trigger a spiral of inflationary wage-price adjustments throughout the economy.

The lower rate of productivity growth and the higher rates of inflation at home have contributed to the imbalance of our trade with other nations. Growth of productivity in the United States has been slower than that of most of our major international trading partners, making us less competitive in the international arena. Slow growth of our exports has contributed to the decline in the exchange value of the dollar, which in turn has fueled domestic inflation both directly and indirectly. Higher dollar prices for imports raise consumer prices directly, while domestic producers of competitive goods can raise their prices with less fear of losing market shares. The resulting inflation further saps confidence in the dollar. It also contributes to a lower value of the dollar in a self-reinforcing phenomenon. It is critical that we break this spiral.

Perhaps it would be worthwhile to review the trends that sustained the productivity gains in the private sector from 1947 to 1967 and to compare them with the developments of the last decade.

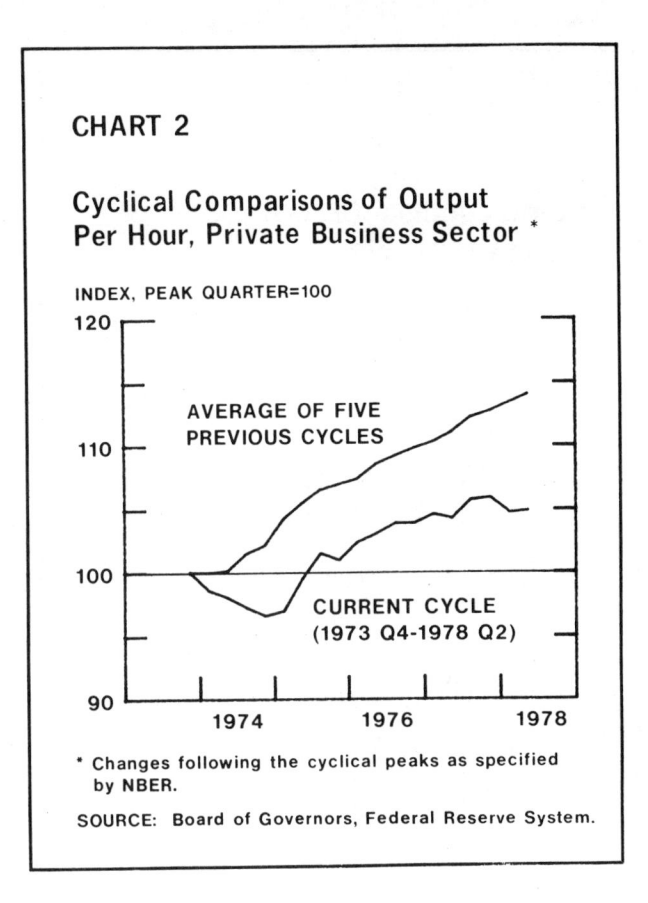

CHART 2

Cyclical Comparisons of Output Per Hour, Private Business Sector *

INDEX, PEAK QUARTER=100

AVERAGE OF FIVE PREVIOUS CYCLES

CURRENT CYCLE (1973 Q4-1978 Q2)

* Changes following the cyclical peaks as specified by NBER.

SOURCE: Board of Governors, Federal Reserve System.

The first two decades of the postwar era were marked by significant development and expansion of new technology and improved methods of operation accompanied by high rates of capital formation. Significant advances in the quality of the work force also occurred. There was a shift of resources from low- to higher-productivity sectors. Underlying some of these factors were substantial investments in research and development and in workers' educations. After 1967, however, the economic and demographic trends that supported substantial efficiency gains became much less favorable, and new trends emerged that tended to retard the growth of productivity.

A crucial factor in the slow rate of efficiency improvement has been a slackening in the introduction of new technology or, to put it more broadly, in the application of new ideas and improved ways of doing things. The effect of technology on productivity is usually associated with equipment and materials, such as an electronic device that vastly expands data processing capabilities or a new chemical that can help multiply crop harvests.

CHART 3

Average Annual Growth of the Capital Stock *

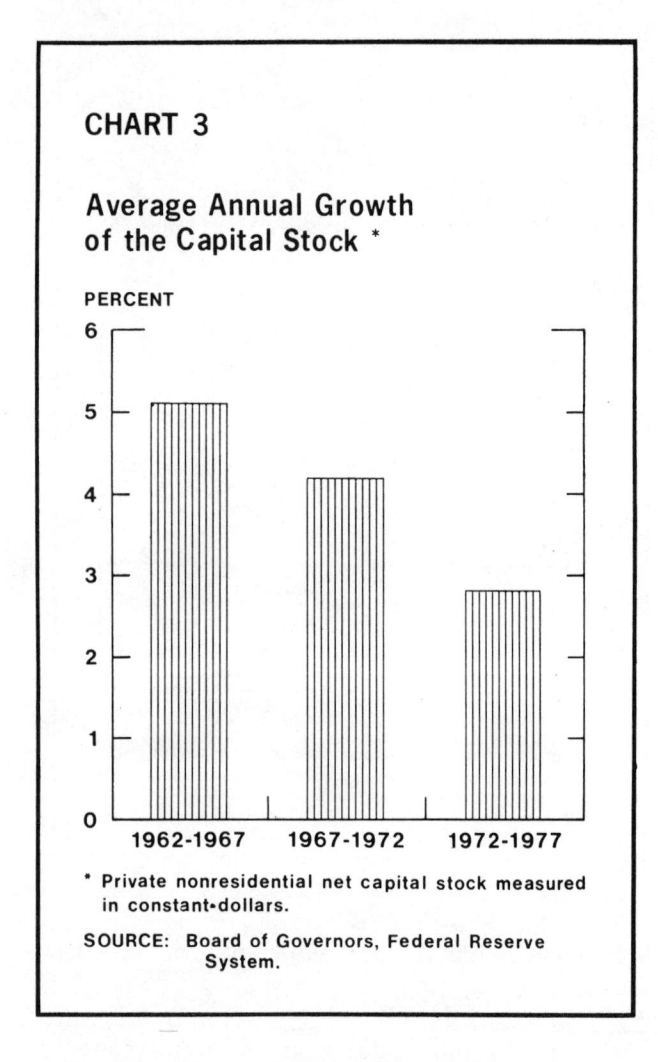

[Bar chart showing percent:
1962-1967: ~5.1%
1967-1972: ~4.2%
1972-1977: ~2.8%]

* Private nonresidential net capital stock measured in constant-dollars.

SOURCE: Board of Governors, Federal Reserve System.

But just as important are new management techniques that greatly improve the application and organization of resources, whether of labor, physical capital, or financial resources. But no matter what the form of advance in human knowledge, it frequently requires significant investment in new plant and equipment in order to exploit fully the opportunities presented.

Yet we have failed to maintain an adequate rate of capital accumulation and investment. Indeed the nation's stock of capital expanded at an annual rate of only 2.8 percent over the past five years, barely half the rate over the preceding decade. Chart 3 shows this progressive and disturbing decline.

Capital accumulation per member of the labor force has slowed even more dramatically. Compared to 1974-75, the amount of capital per person in the labor force has actually declined. This can be seen in Chart 4. At the same time, the share of capital investment devoted to environmental compliance has increased, and the imposition of environmental standards may have caused practical obsolescence of some existing plant and equipment.

In a similar vein, the massive increase in the price of energy clearly has shortened the economic life of some of our capital stock. So, in many ways, the data on the accompanying charts understate the problem that we face.

Another reason for the slower pace of productivity growth was the huge flood of inexperienced workers into the labor force. The figures are staggering. Nearly 15 million more young people and women were in the labor force in 1977 than in 1967. They accounted for nearly four-fifths—almost 80 percent—of the overall expansion of the work force over the decade. Even though these new workers enjoyed the best health, the highest educational attainment, and the best working conditions in our history, they still had to learn skills and accumulate experience before they could achieve the same productivity as employees with long tenure in a particular trade.

Improving the efficiency of the economy under these circumstances demands a comprehensive, forward-looking program—a program that will restore a climate favorable to productivity growth. Its principal elements must include, first, a commitment to conquer inflation so that investment plans can be made in an environment of more certainty and, second, greater economic incentives for private investment.

The nation's tax policies have not offered adequate incentives for new capital investment. In particular, depreciation allowances are not adequate to provide cash flows sufficient to encourage increased fixed investments in today's conditions, nor to offset the substantial risk of obsolescence. Higher inflation has made it extremely difficult for firms to predict forward costs and prices and thus has shaken confidence in business forecasts of financial conditions and general economic activity. Facing a less reliable calculation of the real cost of capital and of expected revenues, prudent businessmen set high requirements for prospective returns on investment. Capital spending inevitably is retarded.

Because we have been neglecting capital accumulation, a larger share of GNP must now be devoted to capital investments. Raising the amount of capital per worker will have a favorable impact on productivity in its own right. Also, since new

CHART 4

Ratio of Capital Stock to Labor Force

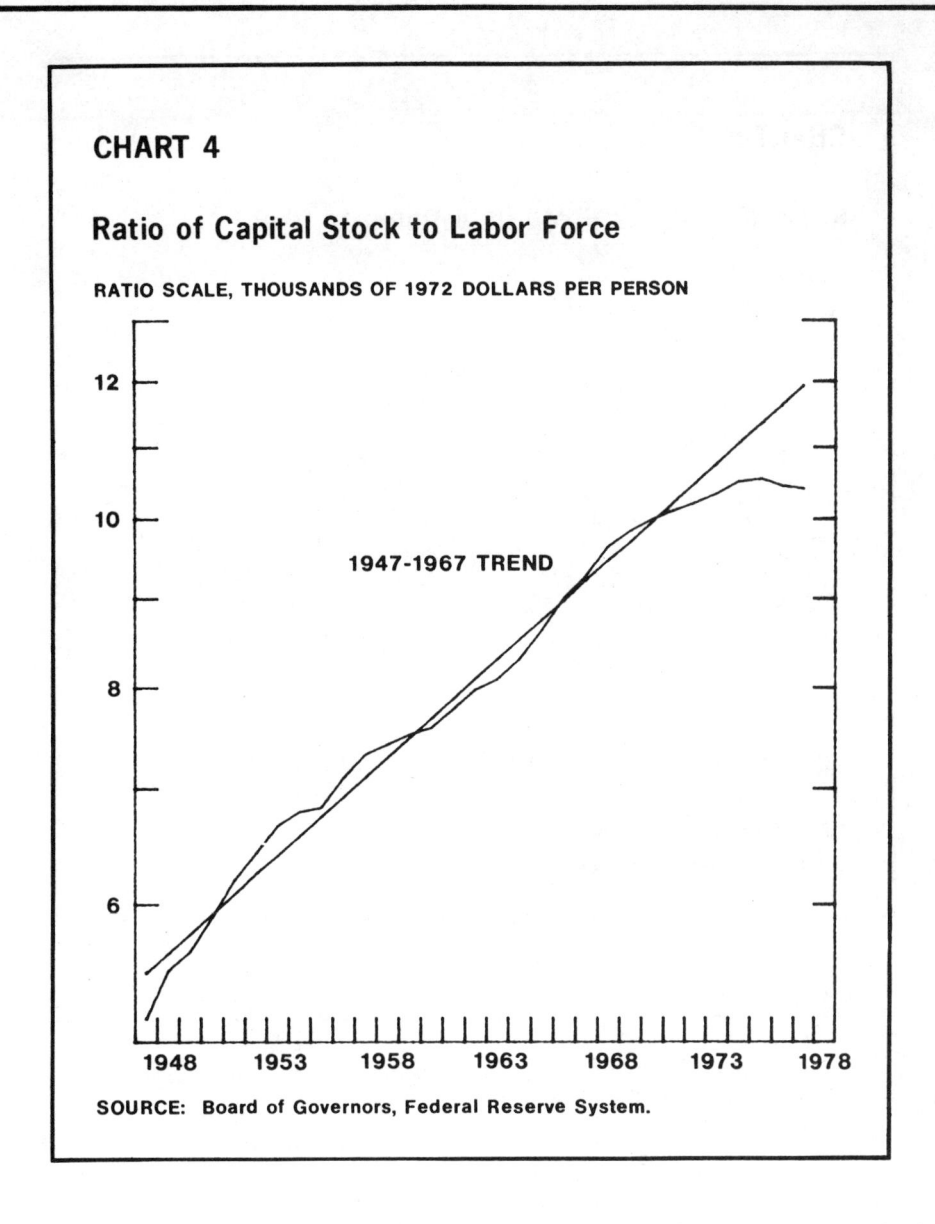

RATIO SCALE, THOUSANDS OF 1972 DOLLARS PER PERSON

1947–1967 TREND

SOURCE: Board of Governors, Federal Reserve System.

capital also generally embodies new technologies, there should be an extra increment to efficiency gains. Newer equipment and structures utilize energy more efficiently, and the resulting conservation and cost savings will contribute to achieving our overall goals.

However, it is not enough simply to reach the past peak levels of 10½ or 11 percent of GNP, reflected in Chart 5. The nation should set an ambitious objective for capital investment of, say, 12 percent of GNP for an extended period of time in order to enable us to make up for past deficiencies and to narrow the gap between our performance and that of our strong industrial competitors. The Japanese economy spends over 20 percent of GNP on capital investment; West Germany 15 percent. It certainly would be appropriate for us to seek a 12-percent level.

Another element in a long-term strategy aimed at a high-growth, low-inflation economy is extensive reform of Federal regulatory activities. We need to take a critical look at price-regulating Government programs. Price regulation in the marketplace tends to discourage or prevent full competition, which is, after all, a powerful incentive for the development and adoption of the most efficient techniques. In recent years there has been a major increase in well-intentioned laws and regulations aimed at protecting the environment and promoting health and safety. These regula-

CHART 5

Ratio of Business Fixed Investment to GNP *

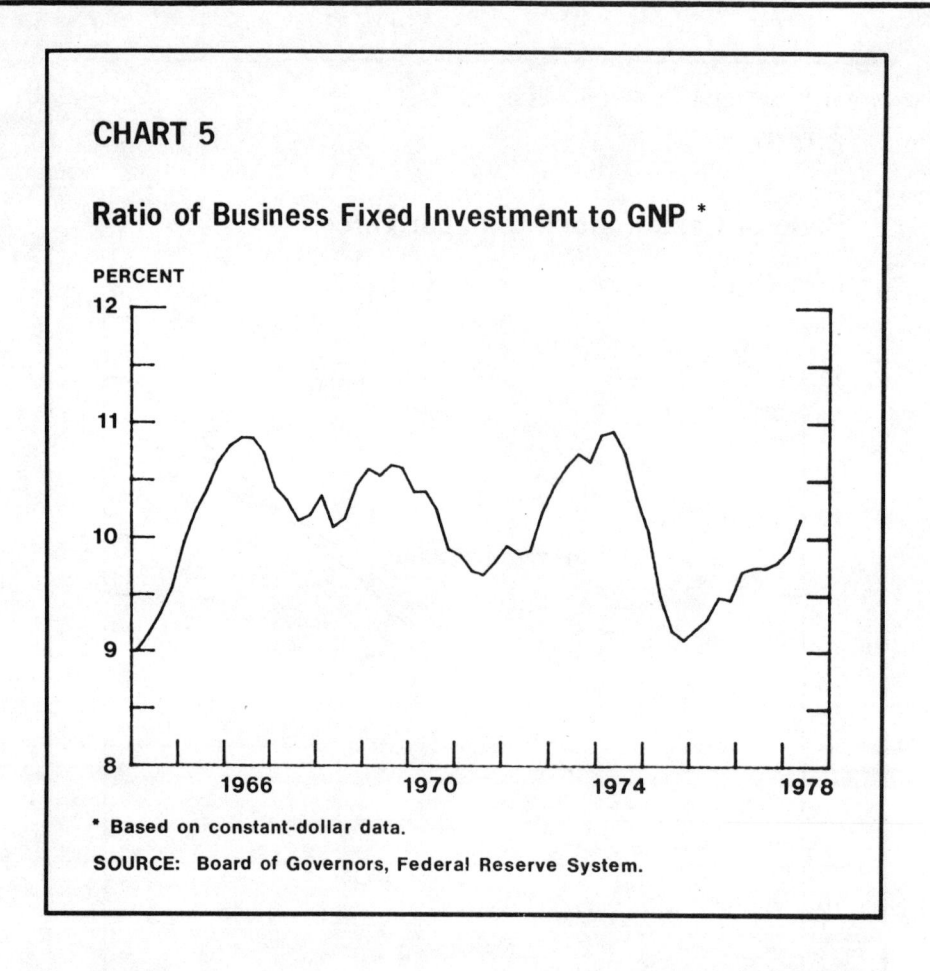

* Based on constant-dollar data.
SOURCE: Board of Governors, Federal Reserve System.

tions greatly influence when and where new productive capacity may be built and how firms may operate. Just hiring the personnel necessary to keep track of the rules, prepare the reports, and attend the hearings has swollen overall costs without any compensating increase in measured output.

In addition to requiring major expenditures, these regulations create uncertainties about the appropriate scale, location, and acceptability of major new additions to or modernization of our productive capacity. Protection of the environment and of public health and safety must be a major social goal. But the actual benefits of new forms of protection must be carefully weighed against the cost to our economy of achieving them.

Another aspect of a forward-looking growth policy is to assure that our work force continues to be ready to meet the challenge of developing new ideas and implementing new technologies. Government employment and training programs should be redesigned to provide effective skill training and work experience to disadvantaged workers. The emphasis on these programs should be on training individuals for careers in the private sector. Younger people are affected more severely than most other groups by high unemployment since early employment is essential for that on-the-job training which lays the foundation for a successful life career. With today's very high levels of unemployment among younger workers, it is possible that unless we act vigorously, a larger part of that generation will be denied the opportunities to develop the skills, attitudes, and motivation they need to become productive participants in the adult work force and to experience the self-satisfaction of personal accomplishment.

In addition to investing in human capital in the forms of direct skill upgrading, we should improve the links between the classroom and the world of work and expand apprenticeships and similar opportunities to assure that younger workers are prepared to meet the needs of their private-sector employers. Methods of raising workers' incentives to become more productive should also get more attention. Stockownership incentives, profit sharing, labor-management productivity councils are possibilities that certainly warrant closer examination and further experimentation.

We need all these government actions and incentives. But even more we need a change in attitude among managers and workers; among all citizens. America has always been a "can do" nation characterized by an innovative and competitive spirit. I am convinced that a substantial cooperative effort in the private sector, coupled with a reorientation in tax and regulatory policy, will stimulate productivity growth and will help ease inflationary pressures without curtailing growth. Such trends would be self-reinforcing, for reduced inflationary expectations would enhance confidence in our economic future. All this in turn would lessen the burden on monetary policy in the fight against inflation and improve the prospects for lower interest rates.

In the past few months we have learned a great deal about the limits of government, the importance of coordinating government economic policies, and the importance of a stronger partnership between government and the private sector. Much has been accomplished. Our fiscal program has been changed so that the prospective deficit for the year that began this week has been reduced by over $22 billion, a significant contribution to the fight against inflation. There has been cooperation with President Carter's deceleration program, although much more needs to be done and the President intends to announce other anti-inflation actions. Progress has been made in establishing elements of a national energy policy that will reduce our dependence on imported energy. We have taken steps, both through short-term bridging actions and in addressing the longer-term fundamentals, to assure a sound and stable dollar, which is essential to our economic well-being.

But much more needs to be done. In the fight against inflation, and in the campaign to raise productivity gains once again to the level that will assure increases in real incomes and increases in our standard of living, we need to have the purpose, the determination, the constancy to implement effective long-range programs. We will need to maintain our efforts for five to seven years in order to achieve the economic goals of full employment, price stability, and a sound dollar. The reward will be enhanced prospects for peace and prosperity in the world.

Black economic progress since 1964

RICHARD FREEMAN

It has become increasingly clear that black Americans have made substantial advances in the job market since 1964. Numerous recent studies, based on diverse data sets and analytic procedures, have reported sizeable declines in the differences between blacks and whites in earnings, education, and occupational position.[1] After decades of little or no improvement in the relative economic position of blacks, the advances of the 1960's and 1970's represent a major social achievement and suggest that national anti-discriminatory policies have successfully altered the job market for black workers. At the same time, however, economic parity between most groups of blacks and whites has not been achieved, nor has the high incidence of poverty, unemployment, and social ills in the black community been eliminated.

How sizeable has the decline in discrimination been since 1964? Which groups of black Americans have benefited most? Which continue to suffer serious socioeconomic ills? In what ways have blacks responded to the reduction in economic discrimination? To what extent have anti-discriminatory policies contributed to the changes? What are the lessons for policy? Because socioeconomic change is a complex phenomenon, these questions are not easy to answer. They have already generated considerable scholarly work and controversy, and will continue to do so in the future. Although the "final returns" are not yet in, it is important to assess as best we can the economic developments that have in many ways changed the life of the nation.

Measuring black gains

The amount of black economic gains since 1964 depends, at least in part, on the statistical measures used to evaluate the relative position of blacks in the market.[2] Statistical measures of relative positions serve two separate, though related, purposes. The first is to estimate the extent of marketplace discrimination, defined as differences among similarly qualified workers in wages, employment, and occupational position that can be traced to the bias of employ-

---

[1] See the bibliographical note

[2] In this paper I use the term "black" in referring to data that relate to non-whites, 90 percent of whom are black, as well as to data that relate specifically to blacks. Similarly, in several instances I use the term "white" to refer to the rest of the population, 90 percent of whom are white, as well as to whites only.

ers, employees, unions, or consumers. The ideal experiment would be to change the race (or religion, sex, etc.) of an individual and then observe what happens to his economic position. A possible practical experiment would be to present employers with job applications from workers who differ solely in race, and find out who is hired and at what pay. In the absence of such experiments or more direct measures of productivity (e.g., a batting average in baseball), observed differences in economic position must be adjusted for differences in individual abilities or other characteristics (schooling, family background, training, etc.) that can be expected to influence earnings or productivity.

Measures of relative economic position are also used to evaluate the overall economic well-being of a group, particularly to determine whether it has a higher incidence of poverty than another group. Market discrimination and economic well-being, though related, are distinct phenomena requiring separate statistical measures. Labor-market discrimination in the United States, for example, has been most severe against highly qualified blacks, although the incidence of poverty is higher among less well educated and skilled blacks. On the other hand, a group might face discrimination but have high incomes (as do overseas Chinese in some Asian countries). For historical reasons, including past discrimination, a group can come to the job market seriously disadvantaged and thus be in a relatively poor position even in the absence of current discrimination. Changes in economic discrimination and economic well-being are likely to coincide, although they need not. For example, a decline in market discrimination, which raises the relative position of black workers, may have little or no effect on certain indicators of economic well-being, such as family income, which can change along with market opportunities, but also varies according to independent characteristics, such as the number of earners in a household.

Some of the confusion and controversy over the changing economic position of black Americans results from erroneously using family-income figures to measure market discrimination or, conversely, using the labor-market status of individuals to measure overall economic well-being. For example, little can be learned about the job market from comparing the income of middle-class black families, which often have two full-time workers, with that of white families, which do not, or from comparing the income of all black families, of which a large and growing number are female-headed, with that of predominately male-headed white families. On the other hand, comparing the economic status of individual black workers with that of otherwise comparable white workers reveals little about the relative economic position of black families. So it is necessary to make a sharp differentiation between the individual and the family, and between the measures appropriate to each.

A new job market   Aggregate statistical measures of individual income or occupational position reveal sizeable gains for blacks relative to whites after 1964. Computerized cross-sectional and longitudinal data on thousands of individuals corroborate the aggregate picture. In contrast to earlier findings, evidence covering the late 1960's shows a marked convergence between the return on the educational investment of black males (especially the young) and that of white males. The impact of race on earnings fell sharply between the 1960 and 1970 Censuses. Detailed investigation of the National Longitudinal Survey shows that the occupational position of young black men entering the market after 1964 is essentially the same as that of young whites with similar backgrounds. The 1973 Occupational Change in a Generation (OCG) survey reveals marked advances in the relative position of blacks, particularly those aged 25 to 34, compared to the 1962 OCG survey. Several studies dealing with other labor-market problems have found that the traditional large negative impact of race on economic status is now much smaller than in the past.

Some of the statistical evidence that a "new market" developed for black Americans is summarized in Table I, which records the changes in several measures of the relative economic position of

TABLE I. *Comparison of Black and White Economic Positions and Average Annual Changes in Ratios*[1]

	Ratio of Black (Nonwhite) to White Position		Annual Change in Ratio	
	1950	1975	1950-1964	1964-1975
Male				
Median wage and salary	.50[2]	.73	0.6[4]	1.2
Median wage and salary, year-round full-time workers only	.64[3]	.77	0.1[5]	1.0
Median "usual weekly earnings"	—	.78	—	1.0[6]
Index of occupational position	.76	.88	0.3[4]	0.7
Relative penetration Professional, technical, and kindred	.39	.65	0.4[4]	1.8
Management	.22	.41	0.0	1.7
Crafts	.41	.71	1.2	1.2
Female				
Median wage and salary	.40[2]	.97	1.8[4]	3.5
Median wage and salary, year-round, full-time workers only	.57[3]	.99	1.3[5]	2.3
Median "usual weekly earnings"	—	.94	—	2.0[6]
Index of occupational position	.49	.87	1.4	1.6
Relative penetration Professional, technical, and kindred	.47	.83	0.9	2.1
Clerical	.15	.69	1.3	3.3

[1] Source: Calculated from Bureau of Census, *Current Population Survey*, and *Consumer Income Reports*, and from Department of Labor, *Handbook of Labor Statistics* and *Employment and Earnings*.
[2] Refers to the year 1949.
[3] Refers to the year 1955.
[4] Refers to the period 1949-1964.
[5] Refers to the period 1955-1964.
[6] Refers to the period 1967-1975.

black (nonwhite) workers. Because of the likely impact of Title VII of the Civil Rights Act of 1964 and Executive Order 11246, and the intensification of anti-discriminatory activity in their wake (including court rulings, private actions, and those of the Equal Employment Opportunity Commission, state fair-employment-practices commissions, and the Office of Contract Compliance), the table differentiates between changes in relative position before 1964 and changes from 1964 to 1975. And since market discrimination reflects the demand for labor, which depends on relative productivity and wages rather than absolute differences, all of the measures are expressed as ratios of the position of blacks to that of whites.

Three related income measures are used in both sections (male and female) of the table: annual wage-and-salary earnings, which depend on both rates of pay and time worked, and reflect changes in unemployment over the business cycle, since most of the unemployed work sometime during a year; the annual wage and salary earnings of "year-round, full-time" workers, which is obtained by eliminating the unemployed and short-time workers over the year, yielding a better measure of wage rates; and "usual weekly earnings" for all workers, including the unemployed—possibly the best available measure of rates of pay.

The fourth and fifth lines of both sections of the table turn from income to occupational statistics, which deserve particular attention since occupation is a relatively permanent phenomenon, involving long-term rather than transitory income. Unlike the income comparisons, which can be misleading if earners forego their current income in order to invest in opportunities that have the potential for higher future earnings, the occupation figures can be expected to reflect enduring economic advances. In the fourth line of both sections of the table, I estimate the economic value of a given job, calculate the proportion of black and white workers in that occupation, and then divide the black by the white measure to obtain an index of relative standing. (The incomes of all male and female workers are used to measure the economic value of a given occupation for men and women respectively.) When the distribution of blacks, relative to that of whites, shifts toward higher-income jobs, the index will rise; it will fall when the black job structure deteriorates. The fifth line of both sections measures the "relative penetration" of blacks into selected "good jobs"—the professions, management, and crafts for men, and the professions, management, and clerical jobs for women—by comparing the fraction of all black workers in those categories to the fraction of all white workers. When the value is one, blacks and whites are proportionately represented in an occupation; when it is below one, blacks are less than proportionately represented; when it is above one, they are more than proportionately represented.

Since the data in the table relate to large groups of workers and are not "corrected" for education, family background, region of employment, and the like, the comparisons are likely to overstate differences between blacks and whites that result from discrimination and to provide only rough measures of changes over time that result from changes in the job market. (More detailed analyses, based on multiple regressions, that tell much the same story as Table I, are found in the various papers cited in the bibliographical note.)

There are three basic findings in Table I. First and most important is the overall picture of relative black economic advance, especially after 1964. All of the indices show that black workers are markedly better off in 1975 than in the early postwar years. All but one of the measures (the relative penetration of black men into craft jobs) show much greater increases after 1964 than before, despite the smaller economic gap between blacks and whites before 1964 and the serious recession of the 1970's. Among men, there are at best modest increases in most of the measures before 1964, followed by sizeable changes thereafter. The income ratios rise by 0.6 and 0.1 points per annum before 1964 and by 1.3 and 0.8 points per annum thereafter. The overall index of occupational standing and the relative penetration of black males into professional, technical, and kindred jobs and managerial slots accelerated greatly after 1964. Among women, economic differences between blacks and whites declined rapidly before 1964 (in large part because of their movement out of household services into other jobs), but the table also shows a marked acceleration after 1964 in their relative median wage-and-salary income, which is roughly double the figure from the pre-1964 period, even with the rapid advances made earlier. The acceleration in the rate of relative black economic progress after 1964 is a necessary "first fact" in determining the impact on the job market of the diverse anti-bias activities that intensified in the mid-1960's.

Second, the changes indicate that the gains made by blacks after 1964 (attributed by some to the economic boom of the late 1960's rather than to more fundamental shifts in market discrimination) did not erode in ensuing years. In fact, despite the largest labor-market downturn since the Depression, the relative income and occupational position of black workers continued to rise in the 1970's. In 1969, at the peak of the Vietnam war boom, the ratio of the median wage-and-salaries income of blacks to that of whites was .67 (for men), the ratio of year-round, full-time wages and salaries was .69, while the ratio of "usual weekly earnings" was .71—all figures much below those for 1975. The rate of advance by black males in the occupational structure also continued unabated in the recession, as did the income and occupational progress of black women. The fears that the changes first reported in my 1973 Brookings paper were purely cyclical has thus been completely disproven by later developments.

Finally, Table I reveals marked differences in the relative economic position of black men and women. Because of the more rapid gains achieved by black women in the postwar period, both before and after 1964, their income and occupational attainment are closer to those of white women than the economic position of black men is to that of white men. Within more narrowly defined groups of women, in fact, the statistics show that black women do almost as well as white women. For instance, among year-round, full-time workers, black women who are college graduates earned $10,104 in 1975, compared to $11,096 for their white counterparts; black females who are high-school graduates earned $7,230, compared to

$7,400 for their white counterparts. In 1975, the principal obstacle facing black women in the job market was sex rather than race. Among men, by contrast, *overall* differences, though diminished from past levels, remain sizeable. Although the differences reflect too many factors to be attributed solely or even primarily to *current* market discrimination, the fact remains that overall economic parity between black and white men is far from established.

Winners and losers

Who has gained from the new labor market? Who remains seriously disadvantaged? Two groups of black men appear to have made the most substantial economic gains since 1964: the better educated and more skilled, especially the increasing number of highly qualified young black men who have entered colleges and universities; and those from more advantaged family backgrounds.

Consider first the economic position of black men with different levels of schooling. Prior to the late 1960's and early 1970's, the ratio of black income to white income *fell* as educational attainment rose. The rewards of going to college for black men were much below the rewards for otherwise comparable white men (perhaps accounting for some of the differences in enrollment rates). In the 1970's, the situation is quite different. At the top of the educational hierarchy, black Ph.D.'s appear to earn about as much as white Ph.D.'s ($21,200 versus $21,000 in 1973, according to National Science Foundation data). The median "usual weekly earnings" of black men with five or more years of college averages 94 percent of those of comparable white men; black graduates beginning in engineering and business fields earn about the national average; and incomes tabulated from the March 1975 *Current Population Survey* show black college men aged 25 to 29 earning 93 percent as much as their white peers, compared to sizeable disadvantages for high-school or grade-school graduates. Estimates of the rate of return on investments in college education suggest higher returns for blacks than for whites (largely because of the poorer opportunities facing young black high-school graduates). Not surprisingly, although the proportion of 18- to 19-year-old white males going to college has dropped in the 1970's, the proportion of 18- to 19-year-old black males has risen. Overall, better-educated young black males fared better after 1964 than less-educated older black males.

Occupational figures provide further support for this generalization. The relative income of black male professionals and managers increased more rapidly than that of less skilled workers. The proportion of black college men obtaining managerial jobs—historically small, relative to whites—rose sharply: In 1964, a black graduate was 41 percent as likely as a white to obtain a managerial job; by 1975, the likelihood had risen to 67 percent. Indicative of the changing opportunities for highly qualified young black men is the marked shift in their career preferences and educational choices. In the early 1960's, black college men were over-represented in education. In the 1970's, they were over-represented as business and accounting majors with intentions to work in industry.

The economic advances of the period also apparently favored young blacks from better family backgrounds. Prior to the anti-discriminatory activity of the 1960's, sociological studies of the relation between background and economic position showed that parents played only a minor role in black economic achievement. Otis Dudley Duncan's analysis of the 1962 OCG survey showed that "the Negro family [was] less able than the white to pass on to the next generation its socioeconomic status." If you were black, it did not matter much what the socioeconomic status of your parents was; discrimination dominated your position in the labor market.

Studies of the period after 1964 show a very different pattern of "status transmission." A replication of Duncan's analysis by R. M. Hauser and D. L. Featherman, using the 1973 OCG survey, reveals marked increases in the effect of background on achievement among blacks. In 1973, the impact of parental socioeconomic status on the education and labor-market standing of blacks was similar to that of whites. My analysis of older and younger men in the National Longitudinal Survey yields comparable results: Family background has only slight effects on the labor-market achievement of older black men but a sizeable impact on the position of young black men. A 10-percent increase in the index of the occupational position of one's father in 1969 would have the following effects on the hourly pay and occupational status of older and younger black and white men:

TABLE II. *Estimated Effect of a 10-percent Increase in the Index of Parental Occupational Position**

	HOURLY EARNINGS	OCCUPATIONAL STATUS
Older Men (aged 48 to 62)		
Black	0.2%	0.3%
White	2.2	2.4
Younger Men (aged 17 to 22)		
Black	1.7	2.0
White	1.6	2.3

* Source: National Longitudinal Survey.

The differential gains made by various groups of black workers can be attributed in part to the nature of the job market. Advances are concentrated among young workers because they constitute the effective "margin of adjustment" in employment. The young are not significantly hampered in the job market by past discriminatory practices and human-capital-investment decisions, which "lock" older workers into career paths and seniority ladders from which change is difficult. Improved opportunities for crafts apprenticeships or a college education will aid the 18- to 24-year-old black male but not the 45-year-old laborer. The sharp advances made recently by the highly educated and skilled also reflect the previous existence of discriminatory barriers that were most severe for the most highly qualified blacks, and the likelihood that they share the work attitudes of comparable whites. Blacks from more advantaged homes are also likely to have benefited more than poorer blacks from family investments in skills that make them more adept at responding to new opportunities. Black women have experienced a rapid improvement in economic position in large measure because experience, for whatever reason, has a lower impact on the earnings of women than men, so that improvements in starting jobs translate more rapidly into improvements in the relative incomes of women than of men.

Background disadvantages

The decline in market discrimination against young blacks and the increased role of family background in their achievement raises the possibility that differences between the backgrounds of blacks and whites—the lower income and educational attainment of black parents, the greater incidence of fatherless homes among blacks, and the social ills associated with inner-city life—have become a much more important element in economic inequality than in the past. As long as background differences between blacks and whites have not diminished greatly, the drop in job-market discrimination implies that a larger proportion of economic differences between the two groups are attributable to the "burden of background." This is a major change in the nature of racial economic inequality, which suggests the need for different social policies to deal with it.

Estimates of the importance of family background for the educational and labor-market position of young blacks versus that of whites, based on data from the National Longitudinal Survey, are given in Table III. In the calculations for education, background is measured by parental years of education, median income in the occupation of the parent, presence of a male head of household, and three indicators of "home educational resources" (presence in the home of magazines, of newspapers, and of a library card). In the calculations for labor-market position, background is measured by the median income in the occupation of the parent, since the other factors operate largely through education. By all of these measures, young blacks suffer a substantial disadvantage: The parents of the young black men in the sample average 7.9 years of schooling, versus 10.5 years for whites; 40 percent of the blacks are from "broken homes," compared to 12 percent of the whites; the index of parental occupational attainment reveals an 80-percent black disadvantage; and 45 percent of black homes have magazines, 69 percent newspapers, and 47 percent library cards, compared to 80 percent, 92 percent and 74 percent of white homes, respectively.

The impact on the educational and labor-market attainment of young men in 1969 was calculated by multiplying each background difference by regression estimates of the effect of each factor. The first line of Table III gives a measure of the initial difference between young blacks and whites in 1969. The second line shows the percentage of the disadvantage attributable to specific background resources. The next-to-last line gives the total contribution of background factors, while the last line shows the "residual" difference—usually termed discrimination.

While the table is too dependent on the specific models, measures of background, and samples used to present anything more than a rough estimate, it does tell a striking story. *All* of the differences in educational attainment appear to result from the poorer family background of blacks. Most, though not all, of the differences in occupational attainment, hourly earnings, and yearly earnings are attrib-

TABLE III. *Estimated Effect of Background Factors on the Educational and Economic Attainment of Young Black Men (1969)*[1]

	YEARS OF SCHOOLING	INDEX OF OCCUPATIONAL ATTAINMENT	HOURLY EARNINGS[2]	YEARLY EARNINGS[2]
Measure of difference between black and white attainment	1.6	.20	.33	.44
Percentage Contribution of Background				
Parental occupation[3]	31%	25%	28%	7%
Parental education	25	—	—	—
Broken home	6	—	—	—
Home educational resources	44	—	—	—
Years of schooling		40	36	34
Region and place of residence	−6	15	24	11
Total contributions of factors	100%	80%	88%	72%
"Residual" differences	0.0	.02	.03	.12

[1] Source: Based on calculations from the National Longitudinal Survey.
[2] Adjusted for years of work experience lost because of the lower age of blacks in the survey and some patterns of intermittent work experience.
[3] Because black workers have traditionally been paid less than whites in the same occupation, which is likely to affect the impact of the family on achievement, *the occupational status of black parents is measured by nonwhite median incomes, while that of white parents is measured by total median incomes.*

utable to differences in parental background, years of schooling, and region and place of residence. The effects of "residual differences" on occupational attainment and hourly earnings are relatively moderate, but high on yearly earnings. The markedly greater difference between blacks and whites in yearly compared to hourly earnings reflects the high incidence of unemployment among young blacks. For those with full-time jobs, "residual discrimination" is modest, and could be readily attributed to any of several factors not examined in the analysis. So the big problem in the labor market is not wage or occupational discrimination within businesses but lack of employment altogether. For those "in the system," particularly those with more education and better backgrounds, the improvement in the job market after 1964 has greatly reduced economic differences between blacks and whites. For those who have not entered the mainstream of the labor market, for whatever reasons, sizeable problems remain.

As evident from Table IV, the decline in job-market discrimination after 1964 has erased only part of the enormous background disadvantage of young blacks. While there has been improvement in the relative economic position of the black family, the change has been slower than for individual earners and has essentially ceased with the recession of the 1970's (see the first line of the table). In 1969, the ratio of black median family income to white stood at .61, 7 points higher than the pre-Civil-Rights-Act level of .54; between 1969 and 1975, the ratio remained roughly stable at .62. Why did family incomes rise differently than individual incomes? The major factor has been the increased proportion of black families headed by women. Between 1964 and 1969, the proportion of black homes with female heads rose from 25 percent to 28 percent; between 1969 and 1976, the proportion increased further to 36 percent. Throughout the period of decline in job-market discrimination and improved income ratios, the "deterioration" of the black family structure, which Daniel P. Moynihan first stressed in 1965, continued at a rapid pace, with an adverse impact on the rate of change of median family

TABLE IV. *Differences Between Blacks and Whites in Family Background**

	1964	1969	1975
Ratio of black median family income to white			
All homes	.54	.61	.62
Male-headed homes	.57	.71	.75
Female-headed homes	—	.61	.64
Percentage of black families with female heads	23%	28%	36%

* Source: Bureau of the Census, *Current Population Reports*, Consumer Income, Series P-60, and Special Studies, Series P-23.

incomes. As the table shows, the ratio of black incomes to white among families with fixed demographic characteristics actually rose in the 1970's.

For the young person, what matters is the position of his family. With the problems of crime, quality of education, and life in the inner cities, the differences in family income and structure create a barrier to the socioeconomic progress of young blacks. Discrimination aside, disadvantages of these magnitudes can be expected to produce sizeable labor-market differences between blacks and whites, ranging from 10 percent to 20 percent, which by their nature cannot be eliminated by anti-bias policies in the labor market and which promise continued economic inequalities into the foreseeable future.

The employment problem

Lack of jobs for less qualified and disadvantaged black workers, including teen-agers, is a large problem that has been exacerbated by the recession of the 1970's. While there is some evidence that the recession has reduced black employment opportunities somewhat less than previous recessions, the fact is that blacks suffer excessively in economic declines, and the recession of the 1970's has been particularly severe. Table V examines the employment problem in terms of the nonwhite share of various groups of men aged 16 and over and 25 to 34. While the nonwhite share of the population groups has risen, the nonwhite share of the labor force and of employed workers has remained roughly constant (or increased only slightly) from 1964 through 1976. As a consequence, the proportion of nonwhites employed has fallen relative to the proportion of whites employed. In 1964, 73 percent of nonwhite men aged 16 and over were employed; in 1969, 73 percent; and in 1976, 62 percent. By contrast, the proportions of whites employed in those three years were 78 percent, 78 percent, and 73 percent. As can be seen in the fourth and fifth lines, the drop in the total of employed workers has taken the form *not* of an increase in the black share of the unemployed (which has fallen in the recession) but of an increase in the black share of those out of the labor force entirely.

These facts highlight the sharp divergence between black Americans whose qualifications and background have won them a place in the economy since 1964 and those left out of the mainstream—such as black teen-agers, whose lack of jobs is even more severe and exacerbated by the recession. In 1964, the unemployment rate for

TABLE V. *Nonwhite Proportion of Population and Labor-Force Groups, 1964-1976**

	\multicolumn{3}{c	}{MALES AGED 16 AND ABOVE}	\multicolumn{3}{c	}{MALES AGED 25-34}
	1964	1969	1976	1964	1969	1976
Population	10.1%	10.4%	11.0%	11.1%	11.0%	11.5%
Labor Force	10.0	10.0	10.0	10.9	10.7	10.9
Total Employed	9.6	9.8	9.8	10.4	10.5	10.4
Total Unemployed	19.3	18.9	18.1	24.0	19.1	19.3
Non-Labor-Force Participants	10.7	11.9	14.8	17.0	18.7	22.9

* Source: Department of Labor, *Employment and Training Report of the President, 1977.*

18- to 19-year-old blacks was 23.1 percent, compared to 13.4 percent for 18- to 19-year-old whites. In 1969, the rates were 19.0 percent (black) and 12.5 percent (white); in 1976, 34.0 percent (black) and 15.5 percent (white). In the high-school graduating class of 1976, the unemployment rate for blacks was 46.2 percent as of October 1976, but 15.1 percent for their white classmates. Even if teen-age unemployment has no long-term consequences for the career prospects of young persons, the immediate impact is still severe. If, as is more likely, those who have an adverse labor-market experience as teen-agers suffer for much of their working life, the problem is even more critical.

Finally, it is important to remember that large groups of experienced black workers, as well as less qualified young persons, have benefited only modestly from the decline in job-market discrimination. Because male occupations require considerable investment in skills and experience and often have lengthy, formal seniority systems, experienced black workers face the problem not simply of gaining equal opportunities today but of making up past deficiencies in education and work skills. The ratio of black income and occupational standing to white among older workers increased only moderately since 1964. With some exceptions, black men aged 35 or more continued to earn much less than their white counterparts.

More striking, the labor-force-participation rate of experienced black men has declined sharply. In 1948, 95.6 percent of black men aged 45 to 54 were in the labor force; in 1964, 91.6 percent; in 1969, 89.5 percent; and in 1976, 83.4 percent. This decline may reflect the impact of the growth in female-headed families among blacks, which could be expected to reduce the incentive for men to work, or it could result from the uneven impact on male and female earnings of the lessening of discrimination, with the increased ratio of female income to male weakening the family system. The decline may also reflect the response of older black men to the recession of the 1970's. For some blacks, it may also be the result of increased Social Security Disability Insurance funds for disabled workers (disproportionately black) who leave the work force. In any case, the job-market position of many black men has been only modestly improved by reducing market discrimination. Even if economic parity were to be established among the young, differences among older workers guarantee persistent differences between black and white workers in the foreseeable future.

The lessons for policy

The magnitude and incidence of black economic gains after 1964, which have persisted in the 1970's despite the recession, and the relative increase in the number of black workers have several implications for current and future national policy toward those suffering discrimination or disadvantages. The changed job market after 1964 and the changes in corporate personnel policy and recruitment practices suggest that the national anti-bias effort, which became intense in the mid-1960's, has significantly altered the economic opportunities for black workers. Although it is hard to determine which policy instruments account for the new situation—equal-employment-opportunity laws, affirmative action, court rulings, renewed activity by state fair-employment-practices commissions—it is difficult to know what alternative explanation would be plausible. A cyclical explanation is ruled out by the continued relative progress of blacks in the 1970's. An explanation based on changes in supply is ruled out by the relative *increase* in the number of black workers. And discussions with corporate decision makers make it clear that the change in job opportunities would not have occurred in the absence of the national anti-bias effort. Of course, this is not to say that current levels of spending or activity are satisfactory or, in the long run, socially desirable. Problems of Federal reorganization, administrative change, "reverse discrimination," and the like make it clear that there is nothing "optimal" about current policies. But past efforts appear to have been effective in producing change.

Moreover, simply ending job-market discrimination and guaranteeing equal employment opportunity will not achieve parity between blacks and whites in the foreseeable future. Anti-bias policies along the lines of the 1964 Civil Rights Act and the 1972 amendments cannot alter the family structure, compensate for low social origins, or remove the burden of past discrimination. The advances of the 1960's and 1970's still leave sizeable black/white economic differences among all men (but not women) and among families.

The greater gains of blacks from more advantaged homes and the heightened impact of family background on black achievement suggest that the "burden of background" will remain a major deterrent to socioeconomic equality. What responsibility should the society take for helping blacks to overcome long-run disadvantages? To what extent should it also help whites with disadvantaged backgrounds? Since part of the background disadvantage of blacks results from past discrimination, should they merit special compensatory or redistributive programs? Or should all disadvantaged persons be aided in the same manner?

The related problems of family compensation and income differences raise more complex and controversial issues. Subsidies to female-headed homes (for instance, Aid to Families with Dependent Children) create an incentive for family disruption, which of course should be minimized. Other income guarantees to families also create incentive problems. Society need not be concerned with differences in family income resulting from differences in the number of adult earners, but it must consider the effects on the children of low-income families. Perhaps the most reasonable policy, one used in many countries, would be to provide child allowances to bring about some equalization among the young. It is difficult to see how other, less purely redistributive policies can alleviate the effect of family-income differences on the young.

As for unemployment, although it will decrease among blacks along with economic recovery, rates of black unemployment are unlikely to fall to acceptable levels. New methods of stabilizing employment in a recession may have to be found. New policies toward youth unemployment are needed to help disadvantaged inner-city blacks find meaningful first jobs and appropriate schooling and training.

Finally, the apparent reduction of job-market discrimination must not be taken to mean that the equal-employment effort should be weakened. If discrimination is a recurrent "disease," continual inoculations and monitoring are needed. On the other hand, the fact that past efforts have been reasonably successful does not imply that future efforts should be intensified or indicate which aspects of present policy should be stressed in the future. More detailed evaluations of the effects of public expenditures are required to make such judgments. Continued success in reducing market discrimination along the lines described is, in any case, unlikely to eliminate economic differences between blacks and whites in the foreseeable future. For those who remain seriously disadvantaged, anti-bias activity is not enough.

BIBLIOGRAPHICAL NOTE

Among the studies are:

1. R. Farley and A. Hermailin, "The 1960's: A Decade of Progress for Blacks?" *Demography*, No. 3 (1972), pp. 353-370.

2. R. Freeman, "The Changing Labor Market for Black Americans," *Brookings Papers on Economic Activity* (1973); "Labor Market Discrimination: Analysis, Findings and Problems," in M. Intriligator and D. Kendrick, eds., *Frontiers of Quantitative Economics* (Amsterdam: North-Holland Publishing Company, 1974); "The Changing Labor Market for Minorities," in M. Gordon, ed., *Higher Education and the Labor Market* (New York: McGraw-Hill, 1974); *Black Elite: The New Market for Highly Qualified Black Americans* (New York: McGraw Hill, 1977); and "A Premium for Black Academicians?" *Industrial Labor Relations Review* (January, 1977).

3. N. Glazer, *Affirmative Discrimination* (New York: Basic Books, 1977).

4. R. M. Hauser and D. L. Featherman, "Equality of Access to Schooling: Trends and Prospects," Center for Demography and Ecology, Working Paper No. 75-17 (Madison, Wisconsin: University of Wisconsin, 1975); and "Racial Inequalities and Socioeconomic Achievement in the U.S., 1962-1973," Institute for Research on Poverty, Discussion Paper No. 275-75 (Madison, Wisconsin: University of Wisconsin, 1975).

5. R. Hall and R. Kasten, "The Relative Occupational Success of Blacks and Whites," *Brookings Papers on Economic Activity* (1973), pp. 781-798.

6. W. Vroman, "Changes in Black Workers' Relative Earnings: Evidence for the 1960's," in G. Von Furstenberg, ed., *Patterns of Racial Discrimination*, Vol. 11 (Lexington, Massachusetts: Heath-Lexington, 1974).

7. L. Weiss and J. Williamson, "Black Education, Earnings, and Interregional Migration: Some New Evidence," *American Economic Review* (June 1972), pp. 372-383.

8. F. Welch, "Black-White Returns to Schooling," *American Economic Review* (March 1973), pp. 893-907.

9. F. Welch and J. Smith, "Black/White Male Earnings and Employment: 1960-1970" (U.S. Department of Labor, R-1666-DOL, June 1975).

48

The new face of poverty

It is younger, darker, more female— and it is increasingly without hope

Elliott Currie

In the early 1960s, Michael Harrington shocked the nation with his vivid portrayal of "the other America." Today, after a decade and a half of antipoverty efforts, that "nation within a nation" of the poor is growing, and the signs are that the condition of the poor will continue to deteriorate.

While much of the poverty of the 1960s remains, that of the 1970s is strikingly different: Today's poor are more often young, non-white, female, urban, and Northern than those whom the New Frontier and Great Society sought to help. The difference between these two populations of the poor shows how the successes achieved by the War on Poverty affected only certain groups, certain regions, and a very particular period of time.

Three forces were largely responsible for reducing poverty in the 1960s:

First was the economic expansion of that decade. Virtually all reductions in poverty — as measured by the Federal Government's official poverty definition — came before 1969. There were about thirty-nine million poor in 1959, and thirty-six million in 1964; by 1969, economic growth and tight labor markets had worked to bring the official poverty count down to twenty-four million. Since then, despite the expansion of income-support and job-creation programs, the "second nation" has grown. There were close to twenty-six million poor in the recession year of 1975; the "recovery" of 1976 brought down the count, but not below 1969 figures. The poverty *rate* — the poor proportion of the total population — has remained static since the end of the era of expansion: It was 12.1 per cent in 1969, 12.3 per cent in 1975, and 11.8 per cent in the much celebrated 1976 recovery.

The partial transformation of the South from semi-feudal stagnation was the second great factor in reducing poverty over the past fifteen years. It involved the stirrings of "Sunbelt" economic development, the work of the civil rights movement in opening access to jobs and services for Southern blacks, and — not least — the South's large-scale export of many of its poor to the North and West.

Between 1959 and 1975, the official poverty count in the United States dropped by just over thirteen million, of which the South accounted for about eleven million. In the North, the number of poor was actually higher in 1975 than in 1967. Even at the peak of the War on Poverty, the victories in the North and West were much less substantial than in the South. North Carolina's poverty population was cut in half between 1959 and 1969, but New York's dropped by only 15 per cent. California, with a poverty population of well over two million in 1959, had lost only 46,000 poor by 1969, despite antipoverty programs and growth.

The North-South divergence has been especially important for the black poor. There are more poor blacks in the North and West today than there were in 1959 — a reflection of black migration from the South, but also of the greater resistance of black poverty in the North to the conventional antipoverty strategies. The poverty rate for Southern blacks fell dramatically — by 42 per cent from 1969 to 1975 — but much more slowly — by 26 per cent — in the North.

The shift in poverty from South to North is tied to the decline in rural as opposed to urban poverty — a shift that occurred mainly through the transformations of the rural South. At the end of the 1950s, well over half of the nation's poor lived in non-metropolitan areas; in 1975, about two-fifths did. Of the thirteen million dropped from the poverty rolls since 1959, fewer than two million were urban. The poverty rate in America's central cities dropped by only 17 per cent throughout the 1960s and early 1970s, and it was fractionally higher in 1976 than in 1967.

To the extent that the antipoverty strategies of the 1960s worked, therefore, they worked best for the rural — especially the southern — poor. They barely dented the poverty of the inner cities of the North and West. Only part of the difference was due to the movement of poor Southerners North and poor farmers to the city: Another factor was the stubborn persistence of the more "modern" poverty of the urban North. In the recovery of 1976, central city poverty actually increased, while it dropped outside the cities; the number of inner-city poor was higher by more than a million in 1976 than it was in 1974.

The expansion of the welfare state

Elliott Currie has taught sociology and criminology at Yale and the University of California, Berkeley; he monitors criminal justice for Pacific News Service.

Reprinted by permission from The Progressive, 408 West Gorham Street, Madison, Wisconsin 53703. Copyright © 1978, The Progressive, Inc.

has been the third great force against poverty since the mid-1960s. But if the welfare state helped reduce poverty, it also highlighted how serious the poverty was — as evident in the technical distinction that is now drawn between pre-transfer and post-transfer poor.

Pre-transfer poverty is a measure of the number of poor before income transfers from the Government — public assistance, Social Security, unemployment compensation, food stamps, and other benefits — are included. It serves as a measure of how the American economy has failed to reduce poverty. About 17.6 million American households were poor before Government transfers in 1972 — two million more than in 1965. Those households included almost forty million Americans — almost a fifth of the population — either living in or precariously near poverty through dependence on public aid. The number has definitely gone up since 1972. Between 1968 and 1972, official — post-transfer — poverty was reduced by almost a million people; at the same time, more than 3.5 million lost their livelihoods and became dependent on the welfare state: The rate of pretransfer poverty increased by more than 5 per cent.

So the despised practice of "throwing money at problems" has been the only thing that has kept poverty in America from becoming much worse over the last ten years — the only buffer against an economy that, left to itself, actually increases rather than decreases the population of poor. But the data also show that the welfare state has worked better for some people than others — better for the old than for the young, better for men than for women, better for whites than for blacks.

Social Security has been the most significant antipoverty measure over the past fifteen years, and the only measure that has kept the poverty count from rising much faster since the end of the 1960s. The poverty rate among the elderly dropped 41 per cent between 1969 and 1976, while the rate for related children under age eighteen *rose* by 14 per cent. Of the families raised above the poverty line by cash transfers from the welfare state in 1972, two-thirds were made non-poor by Social Security payments, only 5.5 per cent by public assistance. Just over half of the people who escaped from poverty since 1966 have been over age sixty-five. This does not mean that the elderly live well; rather, it shows more than anything else how poverty in the 1970s is less and less poverty of the old and more and more poverty of the young.

And not just young, but female. Aside from the sharp drop in Southern poverty, the most striking change in the second nation since the 1960s has been the sharp rise in the number of poor who are single women or living in female-headed households.

In absolute terms, there are more poor women today than there were in 1959. Poverty among single women (unrelated individuals, in Census jargon) and among people in families headed by a woman increased from ten million to 12.5 million from 1959 to 1976, while among single men and people in male-headed families it dropped from about twenty-nine million to less than 13.5 million. Women have always been poorer than men — in 1959, the female poverty rate was two-and-a-half times the rate for males — but today they are much more so; women's poverty rate by 1975 had jumped to four-and-a-half times the rate for men.

And the second nation is darker than it was in the early 1960s, despite the impact of civil rights legislation and affirmative action. The number of black poor increased by 10 per cent between 1969 and 1976; the recovery in the latter year saw white poverty decline by almost one million, while nonwhite poverty rose by some 50,000 people. In 1959, the rate of poverty among blacks across the country was just over three times the rate for whites; by 1976, it was closer to three-and-a-half times the white rate.

These are the poor who are beyond the capacity of the welfare state to reach. A new strain of poverty has arisen in the 1970s, highly immune to the remedies of the past decade. Today's poor will not be affected by economic growth, civil rights and Southern development, and the rise of welfare benefits. These traditional strategies have sputtered out in the "age of scarcity" of the 1970s. The era of easy expansion is over, and the emphasis in Washington is on belt-tightening.

The nostrums being peddled by the Carter Administration offer little hope for the new poor. If any antipoverty strategy can be found in the vague proclamations periodically emanating from Carter's Washington, it is the shopworn idea of putting the poor to work — most evident in Carter's welfare reform plan.

But the problem is not that the poor won't work — most of those who can work do — but that the work they have is neither stable enough nor rewarding enough to raise them from poverty. Just under half of the heads of poor families worked during 1976; a fifth worked year-round. There are well over one million American families with two or more earners who stayed poor in 1976, including close to 300,000 with three or more workers. Contrary to the popular image of the poor as lazy consumers of Government largesse, the poor are as likely to work for their entire income as anyone else.

More than 1.2 million poor families obtained all their income from earnings in 1976 — and, among whites, the poor were slightly more likely to get their entire livelihood from work alone than the rest of the population.

Moreover, as MIT economist Bennett Harrison has shown, over a period of several years the vast majority of welfare recipients mix public assistance with work at some point. Without upgrading the jobs available to the poor, simply devising rules that force them into the labor market cannot make a difference in their standard of living.

Most of the non-working poor, on the other hand, are those who have been effectively excluded from the labor market — through disability, discrimination, or lack of supportive arrangements for child care or other services. Efforts to force these people to work have necessarily foundered in the past, and will fare no better in the future.

Ultimately, there are only three ways to eliminate poverty in America, other than by manipulating the statistics and causing the poor to disappear through numerical sleight of hand. We can upgrade the jobs the working poor now hold; we can create more and better-paying public jobs for the rest of the employable poor; and we can substantially raise benefit levels for those who can't work even when a decent job is assured.

Why haven't we done these things?

'In the "age of scarcity"... the War on Poverty threatens to become a War on the Poor....'

The answer illustrates another difference between the poverty of the 1960s and that of the 1970s — a difference in the way we think about poverty and its remedies. In the 1960s most antipoverty warriors believed — or at least publicly stated — that it was in everyone's best interest to abolish poverty in the United States. Making the two nations into one would bring benefits to the entire society. It followed that once the plight of the poor was made visible, the necessary steps would be taken to reduce it.

Today, we can no longer hold that rosy view. It is increasingly clear that American society is divided into those who are hurt by poverty and those who benefit from it.

The latter category is powerful and effective; it includes employers whose profits depend on keeping wages below poverty levels and affluent taxpayers whose accustomed standard of living depends on keeping the cost of social services down. All of the measures that would be effective against the urban poverty of the 1970s would require a major redistribution of income from those groups to the poor; that is why the measures have not been taken, and why the battle against poverty now requires a political struggle on a level the antipoverty warriors did not conceive.

For still another difference between the poverty of this decade and the last is that in the 1960s we managed to raise the standard of living of millions of poor people without changing the overall distribution of income and resources. It is highly unlikely that we can do that again. A number of studies have shown that though poverty measured in absolute terms decreased in the 1960s, when measured in relative terms — the poor defined as all those with an income below a certain proportion of the median — there was virtually no change.

Control over resources abroad gave us an expanding economic pie at home, which enabled us to reduce poverty without altering the distribution of income between rich and poor. In the "age of scarcity," the War on Poverty threatens to become a War on the Poor — an escalating confrontation over dwindling resources which the rich, so far, show every sign of winning.

49

America's War on Poverty— Is It a No-Win Struggle?

All the government programs tried and all the billions of taxpayer dollars spent have failed to reduce the number of poor. Now there's growing doubt among voters and officials that there is any answer to the problem.

Some 15 years after being officially declared, America's war on poverty is still bogged down in the trenches, little closer to victory than when it began.

Government authorities and ordinary taxpayers alike are growing discouraged by this blunt fact: Despite all the innovative programs and the hundreds of billions of dollars spent, the number of people classed as poor remains essentially unchanged from what it was a decade ago. In fact, experts today cannot even agree on what poverty is, let alone how to eliminate it.

Now the Carter administration's drive to cut inflation by holding down federal spending makes it unlikely that any major new attempts to aid the poor will be launched soon.

Some authorities argue that the government's own statistics prove that poverty programs have been an unmitigated failure and should be scrapped. Others contend that their studies show the exact opposite—that, for all practical purposes, real deprivation no longer exists in this country and victory over poverty should be declared.

What most people see is a confusing hodgepodge of complex programs, riddled with fraud and waste, which have shot up in cost by nearly 300 percent in the past decade while leaving the poverty rolls virtually unaffected.

One out of 5. This magazine's Economic Unit estimates that in 1977 some 160 billion dollars in social-welfare spending went to the 1 American in 5 whose income from nongovernment sources placed that person below the poverty level. The figure encompasses cash payments such as Social Security as well as other forms of government benefits—from medical care to public education. In 1968, that type of spending totaled 43.7 billion.

In 1968, 25.4 million people were living in poverty after receiving all their cash-income benefits from the government. Today, even in a growing economy and an expanding job market, the number of Americans listed as poor remains at a seemingly impenetrable 24.7 million.

While the proportion of poor people is declining slowly as total population increases, experts believe that a general perception of inadequate progress against poverty is a major cause of mounting public dissatisfaction. Economist Robert Plotnick of Dartmouth College observes: "Disenchantment with parts of the Great Society, perhaps ill-founded but certainly a political reality, has fostered disinterest in new approaches to social ills, not a willingness to continue experimenting."

Public apathy was apparent last year when President Carter's sweeping proposal to reform the welfare system failed to get off the ground in Congress. Calling for a kind of guaranteed income for people unable to work and government-created jobs for those who could work, the plan

Reprinted from "U.S. News & World Report."

$160 Billion to Ease Poverty's Pinch

Benefits paid by federal, state and local governments to persons below the official poverty line before receiving aid—

- 1965: $30.9 bil.
- 1968: $43.7 bil.
- 1972: $78.5 bil.
- 1974: $101.9 bil.
- 1976: $142.8 bil.
- 1977 (est.): $160.0 bil.

Note: years ended June 30, except for 1977 when year ended September 30.

Thus, government assistance of all kinds has soared to **five times** what it was in 1965. On top of this are the billions in private charity that Americans give each year.

Source: Robert Plotnick, Department of Economics, Dartmouth College; 1977 estimate by USN&WR Economic Unit.

carried a price tag as much as 20 billion dollars higher than the current system. Opponents said the approach was too costly and complicated. Any White House plans for reforms in 1979 are sure to be sharply limited.

Congress appeared to signal a further shift away from the concerns of the poor with the passage last year of a 21.4-billion-dollar tax-reduction measure that reversed past practice by giving more relief to middle and upper-income people than to the least affluent.

Tax-limitation measures voted in California last June and similar steps taken by other states in the November 7 general election, plus the election of many fiscally conservative candidates, added more thrust to the trend.

Poverty: Confusion Over Figures

Helping to fuel a growing sense of frustration over programs for the poor are the government's own statistics, which many authorities insist paint a much darker picture of intractable poverty than actually exists.

Most growth in antipoverty spending in the past decade has been through "in-kind benefits" such as food stamps, medicaid, medicare and social services. The Census Bureau ignores these benefits in its poverty estimates. Anyone whose annual cash income falls below a certain level, $6,191 for a nonfarm family of four, is deemed automatically by the government to be poor.

The Rand Corporation, a private research-and-analysis organization, found in a 1974 study that—in addition to cash payments—the average New York City welfare recipient got the equivalent of $500 in food stamps, $1,600 in health care and $128 in social services. In today's dollars, the amounts would be higher. In addition, many benefited from rent-subsidy, nutrition, education and other programs, none of it counted as income by public officials. The Connecticut Public Expenditure Council, a citizens' group, reported last July that welfare benefits in several states now exceed incomes of families at the poverty threshold.

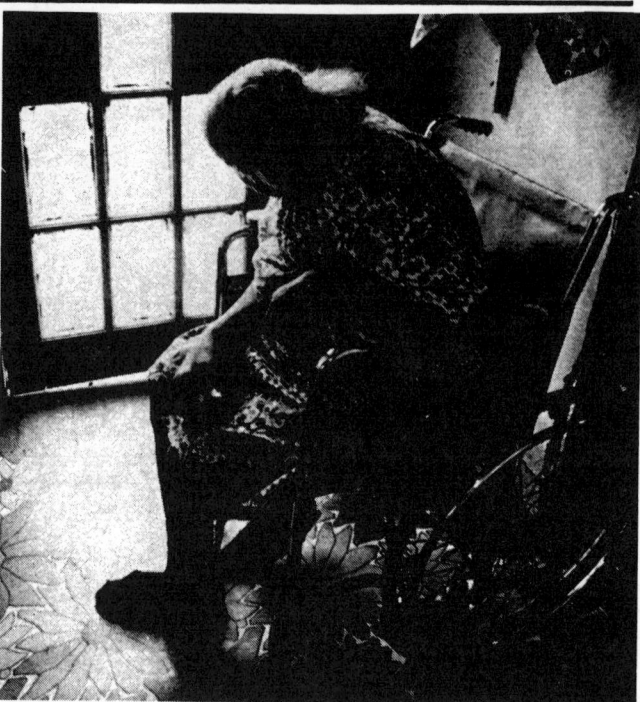

The growth of noncash benefits has led many private authorities to urge that the government's whole concept of measuring poverty, including its method of determining the official poverty level, be re-examined.

A judgment call. Alice Rivlin, director of the Congressional Budget Office, declares: "You can argue whether the line for determining poverty ought to be higher or lower. That's a judgment that society must make from time to time. But you can't argue that because benefits don't come in the form of cash, they're not benefits."

When the CBO compiled its own poverty estimates, taking into account the value of major noncash benefits received by individuals, a more promising picture emerges: Instead of 10.7 million families and unrelated individuals living in poverty in 1976, the total was estimated at 6.6 million—still high for an affluent nation but down by half from the level of a decade earlier.

Some private economists carry this approach another step to include unreported income and assets. Government studies show that public-aid recipients frequently fail to disclose such information, which might reduce benefits. When all such income sources are counted, actual poverty shrinks still more—to an estimated 3 percent of the population instead of the official 11.6 percent.

This theory of uncounted benefits and income leads Prof. Martin Anderson of Stanford University to assert that, in terms of abolishing real poverty, government programs have been "a smashing, total success."

But Dartmouth's Plotnick argues that "the need for income assistance remains as high today as it was in 1965, or higher," adding: "A major goal of the Great Society and the war on poverty was to markedly decrease the number of persons who were unable to earn themselves and their dependents out of absolute poverty. Manifestly, this has not occurred in the past 15 years.... The number of absolute pretransfer poor persons has actually risen by 4 million."

While not denying that countless individuals have been helped, critics question effectiveness of all the education, motivation, job-training and similar programs designed to

Most long-term welfare recipients are the old, children and the sick. Others draw public aid only for brief periods.

And Where The Money Goes

Benefits received by the poor in 1976—

Major Programs	Amount Paid
Social Security, railroad retirement paid to those below the poverty line	$ 44.8 bil.
Education	$ 18.3 bil.
Public assistance, Supplemental Security Income	$ 14.9 bil.
Medicaid	$ 11.2 bil.
Medicare	$ 10.5 bil.
Public-employe pensions	$ 9.9 bil.
Food stamps	$ 4.7 bil.
Unemployment insurance	$ 4.4 bil.
Veterans' programs	$ 4.1 bil.
Workers' compensation, temporary-disability insurance	$ 3.3 bil.
Public housing	$ 1.1 bil.
Other medical programs	$ 6.9 bil.
Other housing, social services	$ 8.7 bil.
Total	**$142.8 bil.**

Source: Robert Plotnick, Department of Economics, Dartmouth College.

Profile Of Today's Poor

Out of 24.7 million Americans with incomes below the federal poverty level—

Race: White 66.4%, Black 31.3%, Other 2.3%

Age: 18-64 45.8%, Under 18 41.4%, 65 and over 12.8%

Region: Northeast 20.0%, North Central 22.6%, South 41.5%, West 15.9%

Source: U.S. Dept. of Commerce

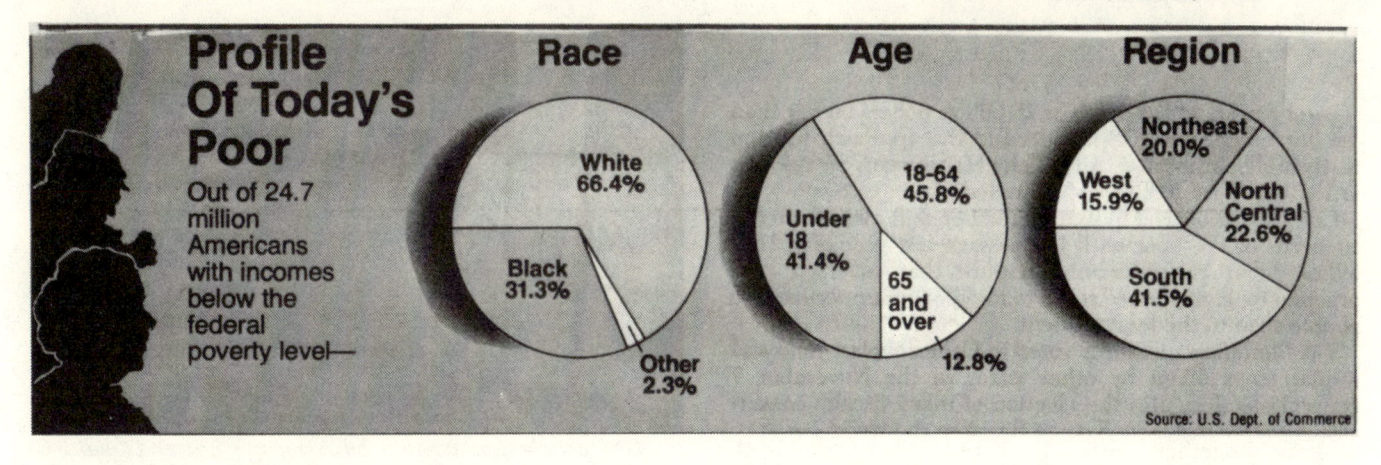

open new vistas for the disadvantaged. "We are keeping people from starving," comments Martin Abramowitz of the Massachusetts Public Welfare Department, "but we are not very good at dealing with the effects of poverty."

Welfare: Part of the Problem?

Without government help, some 43 million Americans—20 percent of the population—would be classified as poor. Why this figure has remained stagnant for the past dozen years, despite the addition of millions of new jobs and rising wages in a growing economy, puzzles many experts.

Helping to explain the paradox is the fact that more people are reaching old age than ever before. Many were lured into early retirement by rising Social Security and private-pension benefits. Once out of the job market, they found their incomes slipping below the poverty line.

Also contributing: a rapid decline of jobs on farms and in decaying urban areas, particularly in the Northeast. Inflation also has driven people into poverty as prices climbed faster than income.

Compounding the poverty problem is the welfare system itself, which some studies indicate has given marginally employed people an attractive alternative to work.

What has happened, explains Sar Levitan, director of the Center for Social Policy Studies at George Washington University, is that people earning around the minimum wage—now $2.90 an hour—see their jobs "as no better than welfare." For such people, "continuing on welfare is a very reasonable substitution for working, and that is a very real problem," Levitan told a House subcommittee.

Experts also are troubled by the results of recent experiments in Seattle and Denver indicating that when cash-income subsidies are given to low-income people, they work less and have more frequent family breakups.

A major development of recent years has been a sharp rise in female-headed households, a third of which have incomes below the poverty line. In other cases, fathers desert their families, or at least move out of the house, in order to qualify wives and children for aid.

Weak points in welfare programs are quickly spotted and just as quickly exploited. After benefits were expanded and eligibility requirements relaxed in Aid to Families with Dependent Children, participation tripled. More recently, lower eligibility standards have contributed to a rash of claims under the Supplemental Security Income program for the aged, blind and disabled.

The Poverty Population: Ever Changing

While the poverty rolls are proving frustratingly hard to reduce, they are constantly changing. Although a hard core stays on public aid for years, millions more work their way into self-sufficiency, only to be replaced by newcomers leaving the job market for one reason or another.

Research has shown that the "welfare class," those depending on public aid for most of their income most of the time, is much smaller than previously supposed. Martin Rein and Lee Rainwater of the Massachusetts Institute of Technology–Harvard University Joint Center for Urban Studies report that the welfare class represents only about one fifth of the current welfare population. Other recipients, they add, "are typically people who use welfare only during periods of crisis—marginal, unstable employment and family disruptions are the common problems."

Fewer than half of those whose incomes dip below the poverty line receive public aid, and for those who do, welfare is typically not a lifetime sentence. A majority of recipients stay on the rolls less than three years.

Most people drawing welfare are too old, too young or too unhealthy to work. Of those able to hold jobs, only a small percentage are willfully unemployed, officials report.

Still, the public conviction persists that far too many welfare recipients are shiftless malingerers taking unfair advantage of a loosely run system. Secretary of Health, Education and Welfare Joseph A. Califano, Jr., calls this "the welfare myth." One sociologist's conclusion: Many Americans find that denigrating the poor is "psychologically necessary" in order to feel better about themselves.

Can Poverty's Cycle Be Broken?

Surprisingly, despite years of research, wide disagreement still prevails among specialists over the causes and nature of poverty. At opposite poles are the sociologists, who see poverty primarily as a "situational" problem characterized by misfortune, and the anthropologists, who believe a large segment of the poor is caught in a self-perpetuating "culture of poverty."

Whatever put them there, millions of people find themselves trapped in a cycle that apparently has no beginning and no end: Insufficient income breeds poverty, which produces cultural and environmental obstacles to motivation, which result in poor health and inadequate education, which lead back to low income. Thus, a legacy of poverty passes from one generation to the next.

A recent study in Los Angeles County found that 37,000 of 176,000 female-headed families receiving welfare were second-generation recipients. According to Keith Comrie, director of the county's Department of Public Social Services, many are young mothers under age 17 who had never seen their own mothers or fathers work. Some come from neighborhoods where half the families are on welfare.

Contributing to an apparent hardening of American attitudes toward the poor, some authorities believe, are the changing demographics of the poverty population.

Not only is it older, with more female-headed households; it also is becoming increasingly black and Hispanic. In 1960, poverty claimed 17.8 percent of the white and 55.9 percent of the nonwhite population. By 1977, only 8.9 percent of all whites but 29 percent of nonwhites remained below the poverty level. Today, about a third of the poor in this overwhelmingly white nation are black or Hispanic.

In Prospect: a Permanent Underclass

Experts say that unquestionably the growing "blackness" of the poverty population adds a new dimension to the problem: racial discrimination. The University of Michigan reports that more than three fourths of the Americans who remain poor year after year are black.

Investigators say that while other racial and ethnic groups have climbed the income ladder, the black poor feel an economic and social isolation previously unknown in this country. "Negroes are the first group in American history whose only hope of getting off the bottom is not by standing on someone else's shoulders but by eliminating the bottom altogether," concludes Stephan Thernstrom in the classic study *On Understanding Poverty*.

Concern that America is creating a permanent underclass comes not only from the white majority but from successful blacks. Last summer, *Atlanta Journal* reporter Chet Fuller traveled the South, posing as an unemployed black looking for work. Among his greatest surprises was the attitude of poor blacks he met along the way. "They are beginning to hate" middle-class blacks, Fuller wrote. "We have let them down as much as the white man. The gulf that separates us from them grows steadily. Soon it will be too broad to close. Already they have stopped looking to us for help."

New Approaches for the Hard-Core Poor

While the dream of eliminating poverty in America is by no means dead, confidence in solutions of the past is fading.

One program that officials say looks promising is the Community Services Administration's effort to help establish labor-intensive business enterprises in poor areas. Aided by public and private capital, dozens of these community-development councils have been formed, some with notable success. In Harlem, residents own and operate a multimillion-dollar business in real estate, home improvement and auto-parts manufacturing. In Mississippi, a similar company makes blue jeans for a major retail chain.

But many liberals insist that for the bulk of the employable poor, the best answer lies in broader enforcement of affirmative-action programs that open up more well-paying jobs. Also essential are better educational opportunities, contends George Washington University's Levitan, who notes, "The sheepskin is still the best guarantee for exit from poverty."

For the hard-core unemployed, "sheltered jobs" and more intense job training coupled with strong work incentives are being advocated. Congress has funded 660,000 public-service jobs for 1979, many but not all of which are targeted for the unemployed poor. President Carter's original welfare-reform plan called for the creation of 1.1 million such jobs that the able-bodied poor would have been required to accept or face a reduction of benefits. The revised version, now being hammered out by the White House, is expected to include far fewer jobs for the poor.

Experts warn that any major effort to get at the root causes of poverty will be expensive for taxpayers. But with both President and voters in an antispending mood, observers doubt that Congress will approve any sweeping changes that will greatly increase social-welfare costs.

Some authorities note that the cost of all cash and other benefits to the poor soon will exceed by several billion dollars the amount of income needed to bring everybody at least to the poverty level. They advocate replacing the present welter of aid programs with a single cash payment to the poor. Economist Milton Friedman has suggested that this be accomplished through a negative income tax in which the government would "pay" those with insufficient incomes.

For many Americans, reared in a society that values self-reliance and hard work, such proposals are condemned as an acceptance of failure. Instead, at least 20 states have adopted programs requiring the able-bodied poor to work for their benefits, either in public or private jobs.

And so the search goes on for new ways to help those who are being left behind economically. More and more people, however, are beginning to agree with the dour assertions of specialists in poverty legislation such as Representative L. H. Fountain (D-N.C.), who told a House subcommittee: "There may be no really good or final answers." □

This article was written by Associate Editor Donald C. Bacon with the aid of the magazine's bureaus.

Cheats—Profiteering In the War on Poverty

It may be argued whether the war on poverty has helped America's poor, but everyone agrees that some not-so-poor people have cheated taxpayers out of millions of dollars.

In one state after another, swindlers and opportunists—"poverty pimps," New York's Mayor Edward Koch calls them—have bored into programs for the disadvantaged.

"To be blunt," writes black economist Thomas Sowell, "the poor are a gold mine."

Bolstering that assertion are reports such as these—

- The Community Services Administration awarded 1.5 million dollars to develop an industry to create jobs in Crystal City, Tex. After two years, no business was started, but $500,000 had been spent for administration. The CSA suspended funding.

- A former head of a New Jersey antipoverty agency has been convicted of conspiring to receive thousands of dollars in kickbacks from consultants. She allegedly used some of the cash to buy a luxury car.

- Amid reports of improper spending, fraud and other abuses, authorities in Los Angeles have called for a grand-jury investigation of a local poverty group known as GLACAA.

- An audit of most of New York City's 367 antipoverty agencies found mismanagement and possible corruption in 34.

Legacy of the '60s. Leaders of local groups often are chosen by the poverty community itself, a legacy of the 1960s when militants demanded more representation for poor people. In many cases, they discovered that they could spend money for almost anything without a complaint from Washington.

Gilbert Archuletta, legislative analyst for Los Angeles, observes: "People expected those who had little administrative ability to handle multimillion-dollar programs."

The House Manpower and Housing Subcommittee criticized the federal Community Services Administration for failure "to demand or enforce sufficient financial or programmatic discipline on its grantees."

The CSA now is demanding stricter accounting and is withholding funds from several mismanaged organizations. Travel has been curtailed. At least a dozen officials have been indicted or convicted for fraud.

50

Cheer number two for meddlesome bureaucrats.

Feeding the Hungry

by Nick Kotz

"Wherever we went and wherever we looked," the doctors retorted, "we saw children in significant numbers who were hungry and sick, children for whom hunger is a daily fact of life, and sickness in many forms an inevitability. The children we saw were more than just malnourished. They were hungry, weak, apathetic. Their lives are being shortened. They are visibly and predictably losing their health, their energy, their spirits. They are suffering from hunger and disease, and directly or indirectly, they are dying from them—which is exactly what 'starvation' means."

The physicians were describing conditions not in Biafra or the Sahel, but right here in America in 1967. This bleak medical report by doctors sent around the nation by the Field Foundation and other investigations, concluding that 10 to 15 million Americans suffered from hunger or malnutrition, stimulated some of the largest social welfare programs of the Great Society. Until hunger developed into a political issue in the late 1960s, the federal government's food aid programs were modest and intended principally to help farmers get rid of excess food supplies without depressing prices. But since 1967, Congress has enacted more than a dozen food aid laws and now appropriates more than nine billion dollars annually to feed the poor.

In the conservative political climate of the late 1970s, however, the food programs, like many other Great Society initiatives, have come under attack as wasteful,

Nick Kotz is the Pulitzer Prize winning author of Let Them Eat Promises: the Politics of Hunger in America *(Doubleday Anchor Books, 1971). His research for this article was supported by a grant from the Field Foundation.*

corrupt and ineffective. Clichés abound about "Welfare Mary" who signed up under a dozen different names for food stamps, or about well-dressed shoppers using food stamps for sirloin steak. But an evaluation of these programs shows that government efforts to feed the poor are working effectively and with relative efficiency. There is far less raw hunger in the United States than there was 10 years ago, and there has been progress in meeting the problems of malnutrition.

Last year the Field Foundation again dispatched doctors into the country's worst pockets of poverty. The Field medical team concluded:

> ... there are far fewer grossly malnourished people in this country today than there were ten years ago. Malnutrition has become a subtler problem. In the Mississippi Delta, in the coal fields of Appalachia and in coastal South Carolina—where visitors ten years ago could quickly see large numbers of stunted, apathetic children with swollen stomachs and the dull eyes and poorly healing wounds characteristic of malnutrition—such children are not to be seen in such numbers. ... This change does not appear to be due to an overall improvement in living standards or to a decrease in joblessness in those areas. In fact, the facts of life for Americans living in poverty remain as dark or darker than they were ten years ago. But in the area of food there is a difference. The food stamp program, the nutritional component of Head Start, school lunch and breakfast programs, and to a lesser extent the women-infant-children (WIC) feeding programs have made the difference.

The largest federal initiative has been the food stamp program. It has grown from a $288 million budget serving 2.8 million people in 1968 to a five billion-dollar budget serving 15 million people today. Recent studies reveal that practically all food stamps go to people who need them the most. The Congressional Budget Office concluded that 87 percent of food stamp benefits go to families living below the poverty line, including several million people living on incomes less than what is needed to buy a decent amount of food alone. The CBO study also showed that food stamp benefits have lifted four million people above the poverty line, including several million working poor. In fact, food stamps are virtually the only government aid offered to the working poor.

Middle-class citizens also have benefited. When the unemployment rate rose above nine percent in 1974-75, participation in the food stamp program rose from 14 million to 19 million participants. In fact, food stamps today help more Americans than any other social program except social security.

A good sign that food stamps are going where they are most needed is the program's impact in the nation's worst pockets of poverty. In 1968, the Citizen's Board of Inquiry on Hunger and Malnutrition identified 256 "hunger counties" with high percentages of poor people, high infant mortality rates and weak or nonexistent food aid programs. A recent Agriculture Department study revealed that annual food aid expenditures per person in those "hunger counties" has increased over $100 per person, from $26 per person in 1969 to $127 per person today, while the national average increase is only $44. Retail food sales in those counties have been raised substantially by food stamp buying power.

In a miserable shack in the Mississippi Delta, for example, the Field doctors visited a very poor black family of four adults and a half-dozen young children. There was no plumbing or drinking water in the house. Heat was provided by unsafe open fires. The children were not receiving needed educational or health services. But in the midst of all this, in the one working refrigerator, there was fresh milk and meat. "This food, purchased with food stamps, was the one difference from the situation ten years ago," the doctors reported, "and the children's health and liveliness reflected this [difference]."

Researchers have had trouble determining the exact amount of food stamp aid that is translated into increased food purchases, and the precise effect of that aid on nutritional well-being. The congressional Budget Office has estimated that 57 percent of the food stamp dollar goes to added purchases of food while 43 percent simply frees money for meeting other needs. In effect, hard-pressed poor people who lack money for housing, health care and other necessities as well as food, are juggling their meager resources to meet their most pressing needs. Recent research provides a strong antidote to the classic "food stamp sirloin" myth. Donald A. West, an agriculture economist at Washington State University, compared the food spending practices of middle-class food buyers with those of poor people who used food stamps and poor people who didn't. All three categories of people allocate their food dollars quite similarly among the various food groups. For instance, all spend about 36 percent for meat, poultry and fish, and 13 percent for milk products. But the more affluent buyer spends his meat dollars on more beef and veal while the food stamp buyer spends more on pork and poultry. The middle-class buyer spends more on finished bakery goods while the food stamp buyer spends more on flour. The middle-class buyer spends more on ice cream and yogurt while the food stamp buyers spend more on milk and eggs. The poor family that is eligible for food stamps but not participating in the program allocates its money much as does the food stamp family. But out of necessity, it simply spends less on food.

The effect of food stamps on nutrition is less clear. The two most quoted studies indicate that food stamp participants have slightly better diets than eligible nonparticipants or participants in the old surplus commodity distribution program. The poor need nutritional guidance. (But, other studies show, so does everyone else.)

The food stamp program has some problems. The program now reaches only about one-half of those eligible for it. Participation is even lower in many rural areas. Many eligible people remain ignorant about benefits. Others are put off by hostile attitudes of program administrators, or have trouble getting to food stamp issuance offices, or wish to avoid the stigma associated with participating in a welfare program.

Even after getting an application, applicants often are subjected to endless trips to the food stamp office to bring in further documents verifying their rent, income, etc. In their zeal to prevent fraud and to protect their own records, issuance officers force applicants to make their way through a frustrating bureaucratic maze. Food stamp offices in rural areas often are remote from people's homes and only open for limited hours. Old people have special problems participating in the food stamp program, although 2.3 million elderly benefit from a fast-growing special program for senior citizens.

Until now, many people have stayed out of the program because of the high cost of food stamps. A family of four, for example, with $300 monthly income must pay $83 to get $182 worth of stamps. The 1977 food stamp revisions, which finally will go into effect early in 1979, should solve this problem. The purchase requirement has been eliminated, so the family with $300 income will simply receive its $99 in bonus stamps. In theory at least, the new law also greatly simplifies the application procedures, and ends the need for various verification documents. The true test, however, will be how state and local welfare agencies decide to implement the new law.

The National School Lunch program began after

World War II primarily to help farmers get rid of surplus commodities. In 1968, three million poor children received free lunches and 300,000 got breakfasts. Today, 10.6 million school children receive free lunches, 1.3 million have their lunches subsidized, and 2.6 million receive free breakfasts. One million preschool children get free breakfasts and lunch in Head Start and other child care centers.

Recent research indicates that the school breakfast and child care programs are nutritionally valuable. The Congressional Budget Office reports that more than a third of America's children get off to school in the morning with less than two-thirds of the needed calories, iron, and vitamins A and C, and many have nothing at all for breakfast. Children with inadequate breakfasts are known to function less well at school both emotionally and in cognitive learning abilities. It is heartening, therefore, that the CBO study reports a marked improvement in the nutrition of poor children who attend the school breakfast program. Beyond any question, poor children would benefit by substantial expansion of the school breakfast program. But such expansion is vigorously opposed both on philosophical grounds that providing breakfast is a parental responsibility and because of the reluctance of school administrators to take on another responsibility. As for the pre-school feeding program, a doctor in the Field team reported, "There was a sharp contrast between the bright-eyed, happy and alert little ones we saw in Head Start centers and the dull listless infants and children we saw who did not participate."

One of the most dramatic success stories in food aid is the Supplementary Feeding Program for Women, Infants and Children (WIC), which has grown from a $14 million experiment in 1974 to a $270 million effort serving 1.3 million people today. In the WIC program, pregnant women, their infants and young children who are at nutritional risk are provided health examinations, nutrition education and supplementary nutritional food packets. There is an established connection between a mother's diet and the low birth weight of infants, and a link between low birth weight, infant mortality, birth defects and mental retardation.

WIC has been studied in detail by the Center for Disease Control of the US Public Health Service. CDC reported: "Children entering the WIC program have a high prevalence of anemia, presumably caused by iron deficiency, a high prevalence of linear growth retardation, a high prevalence of overweight. Children in the program for one year experience considerable improvement in hemoglobin and hematocrit values (by which anemia is measured), and a slight improvement in linear growth. The proportion of low birth-weight babies born to WIC mothers is the same as the general population which probably represents a considerable improvement over what might have been without WIC." A Yale Medical School study of WIC participants in Danbury, Connecticut showed a growing impact over several years in reducing the fetal death rate. An infant growth study showed that WIC participants caught up with the general population in all parameters of health. The infant death rate on seven Montana Indian reservations dropped from 31.5 per thousand in 1972 to 16.6 in 1975 after introduction of WIC.

Right now the WIC program reaches only 1.3 million of the eight million people who are eligible for it. It isn't available in areas without a government health clinic to administer it, and there are administrative problems, such as office opening hours, similar to those of the food stamp program. An odd and unnecessary requirement is that poor women and infants have a proven nutrition deficiency *before* they are admitted to the program.

The United States still lacks an adequate system for monitoring the nutritional health of its citizens, especially the poor. The best information today comes from the Center for Disease Control and from the Health and Nutrition Examination Survey conducted by the National Center for Health Statistics. CDC and HANES surveys indicate some improvement in nutrition among the poor since 1968. But malnutrition still persists, causing under-average growth, obesity, anemia and dental caries.

A new complaint from government efficiency experts as well as economic conservatives is that the poor are now getting multiple benefits from a variety of food aid programs. But even with all these programs the poor are hardly being nutritionally over-indulged. The food stamp program is based on a so-called "thrifty food plan," a diet on which a highly skilled homemaker supposedly can sustain her family for brief periods of time. Even taking advantage of all the food programs, a family cannot bring itself up to the level of the Agriculture Department's "low cost food plan," which is considered sufficient to meet long-run nutritional needs.

The major change needed in government food programs is an effort to reach the millions of eligible Americans who, for a variety of reasons, are not participating. State and local governments should be compelled to follow the laws about outreach programs for the elderly, children, minority groups and the working poor.

The food programs are relatively popular with the public and enjoy unique bipartisan support in Congress at a time of political conservatism when it is unlikely that Congress will provide major initiatives for jobs, housing, welfare reform or health care. (They also get strong support from the food industry.) No legislation is needed. There is an unusual opportunity to take programs of the 1960s which actually produced results and to build on that success. Those who worry about more federal food aid encouraging a "dole mentality" should be reassured that a hungry child cannot learn and an ill-fed adult cannot compete for or hold a job.

51

Young Blacks Out of Work: Time Bomb For U.S.

Angry at society, poorly educated and lacking job skills, their numbers are reaching explosive proportions. Massive public and private efforts have failed so far to solve one of the nation's most perplexing problems.

Drifting further and further out of the American mainstream is a growing army of the unemployed whose intractable joblessness baffles the experts.

A minority within a minority, these are black youths and adults being left behind not only by the white majority but by an expanding black middle class.

Poorly educated, untrained for available jobs, often unmotivated to seek any type of gainful work, they cluster in big-city slums to form a subculture that leans heavily on welfare, crime, drugs and alcohol.

Some had jobs but lost them in the recent recession or when urban employers started moving out to the suburbs. Others, however, are well into their 20s and 30s without ever having held a job successfully.

Authorities have tried many ways of solving the problem. But antidiscrimination laws, taxpayer-financed education and job-training programs have failed to reach what has turned into a seemingly impenetrable core of the unemployed and unemployable.

Result: Reaching and helping this alienated segment of society has become a pressing domestic problem, a source of explosive friction between the races and a major challenge to local leaders, Congress and the White House.

Although many individual blacks have made enormous strides, the civil-rights era has proved something less than an economic boon for blacks as a whole. The wide disparity between the median incomes of black and white families has narrowed only slightly since the 1950s.

Unemployment among blacks has consistently held at about double the rate for whites, until this year when the gap began to widen even more. In October, 15 per cent of the black labor force was jobless, compared with 6.1 per cent of the white. For black teen-agers, the rate was a towering 40 per cent, against 14.8 per cent for white teen-agers.

It is this chronically high rate of joblessness among black youth, who should be benefiting most from a rainbow of new opportunities opening up in recent years, that is most discouraging to black leaders, economists and government officials. The proportion of young blacks working or looking for work has been dropping steadily through periods of prosperity as well as recession.

Accounting for only one tenth of the black labor force, but one quarter of the unemployed, the black population from ages 16 to 20 is "the most serious part of the over-all problem of black unemployment," says Bernard E. Anderson, associate professor of industry at the University of Pennsylvania's Wharton School of Finance.

Soaring expectations that marked the black-rights movement of the 1950s and 1960s have given way in many areas to intense frustration and anger. Unable for whatever reason to earn a living, many fall into a lifetime routine of handouts and public charity. Others strike out at society in general through such activities as robbing, prostitution, looting and random arson. A significant portion withdraw to their own shadow world of drugs and liquor. Comments a State employment counselor in Atlanta, whose clientele is about 90 per cent blacks: "The people who come through here have a hopeless 'what's the use' attitude. It's usually their last resort."

YOUNG BLACKS ARE DROPPING OUT

Young black men and women—born since the Supreme Court struck down racial segregation in 1954, afforded better educational opportunities than previous generations, the focus of special aid for a decade—would seem to hold the best hope of breaking the race's cycle of poverty.

But instead of expanding, the job market for young blacks appears to be contracting. The official unemployment rate for black teen-agers climbed from 35.4 per cent in 1972 to 39.3 per cent in 1976. Monthly rates this year have ranged as high as 45.4 per cent.

Official statistics take into account only those actively seeking work. They do not include "discouraged" people who say they want to work but are not looking for a job. Counting these potential workers, the National Urban League estimates that black teen-age unemployment has soared well above 50 per cent. In a few areas, such as Oakland, Calif., authorities say it is as high as 70 per cent.

WHO ARE THE UNEMPLOYED?

Out of total unemployment of	6,221,000
Whites	4,774,000
Blacks	1,348,000
Other races	99,000

AMONG YOUTH—

White teen-agers	1,131,000
Black teen-agers	328,000

UNEMPLOYMENT RATE

All Americans	7%
All whites	6.1%
All blacks	15%
White teen-agers	14.8%
Black teen-agers	40%
White-collar workers	4.1%
Blue-collar workers	8.3%
Service workers	8.3%
Farm workers	4.3%

Note: Figures for October, 1977; unemployment rates seasonally adjusted.

Source: U.S. Dept. of Labor

Latest figures show that only about a quarter of the nation's black teen-agers have jobs, down from 38 per cent two decades ago. "There is nothing now on the horizon to change these trends," warns a study for the Joint Economic Committee of Congress.

Much of the black unemployment problem is concentrated in the central cities—areas where business is often in decline and job opportunities are dwindling.

The discouraging pattern is repeated in city after city: Blacks moved in from the rural South and other regions after World War II. Whites and middle-class blacks fled to the suburbs. Plants, factories and shops soon followed, causing a loss of jobs and tax revenue. Local services including public education began to slip, prompting more businesses and affluent residents to pull up stakes. It is a cycle of deterioration that continues today in many American cities.

Stranded in urban slums have been those least able to cope with a demanding and competitive society—the young, the old and the disabled. For them, broken families, poverty, isolation and despair have become the norm.

Adding to the problem: While white birth rates have declined sharply in recent years, the rate among low-income blacks has remained high. Black children born in record numbers in the 1950s and 1960s are now reaching maturity, making job prospects for this age group bleaker than ever. The young black population will continue to expand at least into the mid-1980s, according to official projections.

Meanwhile, blacks are being squeezed by a changing job market that increasingly puts a high premium on good education, motivation, skill and experience.

Although the educational gap between blacks and whites measured by years of schooling has narrowed substantially, the difference in the quality of their education has not.

Black leaders frequently blame the urban public schools for turning out graduates who are ill prepared for work. "The young people can't fill out a work application because they can't read," complains a National Urban League official in Los Angeles. Some trace the present difficulty to the late 1960s when educational standards were lowered in many urban black communities to meet militant demands for courses stressing racial pride.

Now there is a shift back to fundamentals. But it comes too late for many thousands of youngsters who have emerged from school as functional illiterates.

Even those graduating from high school with job skills may find that they have been trained in a field that is already vastly overcrowded or one that is becoming obsolete. In Brooklyn, youngsters at one vocational center are learning to operate printing presses of a type that haven't seen commercial use in decades. In Dade County, Fla., schools are training cash-register operators despite a surplus of these workers in the area.

Employers say many young black job seekers not only are unskilled but frequently show little understanding of what work is all about. Many have never been taught the importance of getting to work on time, taking orders from a superior, grooming themselves or getting along with others.

"When you've grown up in a family with no father present, an unemployed mother, and maybe a brother who's in jail, the world of work is something you naturally don't know much about," says a black leader in Philadelphia.

IN THE GHETTO: DWINDLING HOPES

For a closer look at the problem, visit a typical slum neighborhood in New York City's South Bronx.

Here are areas of extreme poverty, long since deserted by those on their way up the economic ladder and now ruled by street-wise hoodlums and hostile youth gangs. Many of the streets are barren of commercial activity, pocked with fire-

U.S. NEWS & WORLD REPORT, Dec. 5, 1977

YOUNG BLACKS OUT OF WORK
[continued from preceding page]

gutted buildings and heavy with a feeling of hopelessness. Loitering teen-agers and young adults eye passers-by suspiciously. Out of school, nothing to do, resentment building, they simply wait for something to happen.

Youngsters in areas such as the South Bronx often wind up in trouble with the law, which gives them a police record that makes them that much less employable. Drug addiction takes a heavy toll. Teen-age pregnancy is common.

Many turn to an array of social-welfare programs—from disability benefits to Aid to Families With Dependent Children—that can be more lucrative than a low-paying job.

A Labor Department official explains: "More people are seeking alternatives to work." In the 1960s, welfare claims by mothers with children grew rapidly. "Now," he says, "we have a 'disability explosion' among males, particularly nonwhites, that has gone almost totally unnoticed."

Previously, many aimless youngsters were drafted into the armed forces, where some learned skills and discipline. Now most ghetto youths shun voluntary enlistment. Says Andrew Young, U.S. Ambassador to the United Nations: "When we did away with the draft, we closed the door of opportunity, in a sense, to a large segment of our society."

Complicating the problem for blacks is the fact that they are running into increasing job competition from white women, who are joining the labor force in large numbers, and illegal immigrants, who are often preferred by employers because they "work hard and scared."

Industries that formerly hired masses of low-skilled people have automated or relocated abroad where labor is cheaper. Even the small shops and "mom and pop" stores that once provided early work experience for young people have all but disappeared from the hostile inner-city environment.

Other potential employers generally are uninterested in hiring and training young people. Many have minimum-age requirements that exclude persons below age 22 or so.

Last year, 1,500 employers in New York City were asked to join in a subsidized on-the-job training program. "We got absolutely no positive response," notes a city official.

Some businessmen say they would be willing to hire young applicants and train them, but not at the required minimum wage. Whether the wage floor, soon to rise to $2.65 an hour, inhibits employment is hotly debated by economists. After examining the issue, the Joint Economic Committee concludes: "The weight of academic research is that unemployment for some population groups is directly related" to the statutory minimum wage. Still, Congress defeated a recent effort to enact a lower minimum wage for youth, although it cut some of the red tape for small businesses that want to hire a few students at reduced wages. Among those opposing a youth wage differential was organized labor, which fears it would mean fewer jobs for adults.

JOBS THAT GO UNWANTED

What puzzles many ordinary citizens is that even when jobs are scarce, there are sometimes few takers for menial and hard-labor positions that are available to the uneducated and unskilled.

In many urban areas, there are shortages of domestics, yard workers, janitors and kitchen helpers. But young blacks, instilled with racial pride, frequently say they want no part of what they derisively call "dead end" or "jive" jobs.

Recent stress on the importance of meaningful jobs, says black economist Walter E. Williams, of Temple University, "is unfortunate because it creates false and unrealistic labor-market expectations among our youth."

Comments the University of Pennsylvania's Professor Anderson: "The difference between many white kids and inner-city black kids is that a white kid can take a menial job knowing he'll eventually move on to something better. A black kid sees his father and his mother—all the people he knows—doing that kind of work. For him it's not just a way station; that's his destination. So why hurry to get there? That job will be around when he's 25 or 30."

Even better jobs in the suburbs often fail to attract inner-city applicants. One reason: In many localities, public transit is expensive and spasmodic beyond the city limits.

A suburban Philadelphia firm once tried to stimulate its hiring of inner-city blacks by providing free bus service to and from the plant. The experiment failed. Those who took jobs soon quit, citing the inconveniences of rising early and being confined on a bus for hours a day. "It was a new experience for them," notes Andrew Freeman, former executive director of the Philadelphia Urban League.

Why do some cling to the slums even though job opportunities and living conditions might be better elsewhere?

Representative Shirley Chisholm (Dem.), of New York, observes: "People want to live where they feel comfortable, where they know their neighbors and have a sense of identity. So it's not easy when you offer them something—maybe out West where they have all this fresh air and can get the kids out of the ghetto. They won't jump and go, even though it might be a better situation for them."

GOVERNMENT: EMPLOYER OF LAST RESORT

Indications are that the unemployed of all ages overwhelmingly want to work if given the opportunity. In Detroit, a rumor that General Motors or Chrysler is hiring will bring thousands of job seekers of both races to the plant gates. Last summer, hordes of New York youngsters, many of them black, swarmed an office that was taking applications for Government-subsidized summer jobs.

Although experts agree that ideally some way should be found for private industry to absorb more of the nation's unskilled and semiskilled millions, the Government increasingly is stepping in as the employer of last resort.

Included in the Comprehensive Employment and Training Act (CETA), which Congress expanded this year, are programs to create public-service jobs and help disadvantaged persons to compete in the job market. Funded at 12.8 billion dollars, CETA programs are expected to serve 5.6 million, including 1.8 million minority youth, by next year.

POPULAR VIEW: NO SPECIAL TREATMENT

Most Americans oppose granting preferential treatment to minorities and women in getting jobs or entering college, according to a recent Gallup Poll.

The survey found that, despite claims of past and present discrimination, 81 per cent of those questioned felt that ability as measured by test scores should be the main consideration in hiring and admitting people to schools. Only 11 per cent favored preferential treatment, and 8 per cent had no opinion.

Also enacted largely as a response to persistent joblessness among minorities was the Youth Employment and Demonstration Projects Act of 1977.

Budgeted at 1 billion dollars, this statute sets up a number of experimental and demonstration programs to train and prepare disadvantaged young people for entry into the labor force. More than half of the 443,000 initial participants are expected to be minority-race members. Authorized under the Act are a Young Adult Conservation Corps and several urban-training efforts to supplement existing CETA programs. In addition, Congress extended the Job Corps training program and a summer work-experience program for youth.

But as federal manpower programs expand, so does criticism of their long-range effectiveness.

The summer youth program, for instance, has been widely cited for waste and for failing to give participants useful work to do in return for their pay. Opponents charge that youngsters are assigned tasks without supervision and later return to the street no better off than they were before.

Backers claim that many of the summer-jobs program's early deficiencies have been overcome. Still, studies of this

Often, few takers can be found for the hard or menial jobs available in many areas despite high unemployment generally.

and other work programs have found that few participants successfully make the transition to "real jobs" in the private sector when their training or subsidized job is over.

Another problem: Evidence of substantial misuse of CETA funds has surfaced in city after city. Instead of providing jobs for the hard-core unemployed as Congress intended, some local administrators have been found to be favoring less-needy people, including relatives of officials, and using program money to help meet regular city payrolls.

In New York, for example, a study found that relatively few of the 20,000 workers hired under the newly expanded public-service-employment program had been picked from low-skilled minorities. Many were middle-level workers previously laid off by the city during its financial crisis.

As big and expensive as federal job programs have grown in recent years, they are minuscule in comparison with the problem they address. For instance, after funds to create jobs for youth were spread around the country, New York received authority to hire only 6,000 people. The city has half a million teen-agers potentially eligible.

THE SEARCH FOR BETTER SOLUTIONS

What's the answer?

Manpower experts and black leaders are divided on many of the causes as well as the solutions to black unemployment. But many agree with Professor Anderson's observation that "no amount of economic growth" is going to solve all the problems of depressed inner-city areas.

Most foresee an expanding role for the Government in creating jobs for people who cannot compete in the labor force. To be effective, they add, such programs must be better targeted to reach the truly needy. Already before Congress are several bills to aid the chronically unemployed, including President Carter's proposal to create some 1.4 million jobs for welfare recipients. At the same time, labor specialists doubt that the Government is financially able or administratively capable of providing all the jobs needed.

In addition to a robust and growing economy, any long-term solution, they say, should include these elements:

• Greater public and private effort to improve conditions in the urban communities so that business and industry will want to return. City services need to be restored, slums cleaned up, and crime and graft brought under control. Some cities may have to offer tax breaks or other incentives to lure employers back.

• Greater access to jobs in the suburbs and beyond for inner-city residents.

• More emphasis on education, career counseling and job training. Studies indicate a need for programs that allow young people to continue their education while they work, rather than having to choose between the two.

• Continued vigilance in eliminating racial discrimination as a factor in private employment.

• More stress by the black community on self-help and the rewards of the work ethic. One encouraging trend: Successful blacks are increasingly eager to work with the disadvantaged and serve as positive role models for ghetto youth.

Calvin Pressley, of the New York City Opportunities Industrialization Center, a black-run organization that prepares black youngsters for jobs in private industry, puts it like this: "The only way we're going to affect this large market of unemployed and untrained is to provide them with quality training for quality jobs. The key is opportunity. That's what most people are looking for. Very few are looking for a handout."

This article was written by Associate Editor Don Bacon, aided by the magazine's bureaus in New York, Chicago, Detroit, Atlanta, San Francisco, Los Angeles and Houston.

Copyright 1977 U.S. News & World Report, Inc.

Short and Long Run Unemployment Burdens

Martha S. Hill and Mary Corcoran
Survey Research Center
The University of Michigan

Typically unemployment is measured at a point in time, over a survey period, or during one year; and it usually affects only a small proportion of workers, though those who are unemployed may lose substantial proportions of their potential income while not working. Such short-run "snapshots" of unemployment may, however, be consistent with several long-run scenarios. Observed unemployment could result from a long-run process in which a large proportion of workers spend some time unemployed, each only losing a relatively small fraction of their potential total work time. Or it could result from a process in which the same small proportion of workers are unemployed over and over again, with their unemployment time forming a large fraction of both their short- *and* their long-run potential work time. Which of these scenarios is closest to the truth obviously affects the distribution and severity of the unemployment burden.

Evidence from a Panel Study

Using data from the Panel Study of Income Dynamics, a longitudinal study begun in 1968 of over 5000 American families, we have examined long-run unemployment experiences and compared them with short-run snapshots. We restricted our sample to men aged 35-64 in 1976 who were household heads and in the labor force every year of the ten-year period 1968-1977; this yielded a sample size of 1251 individuals. While such prime-age male workers have traditionally had lower unemployment rates than other subgroups of workers — the young and females — they constitute a large segment of the labor force and their unemployment is therefore important in the aggregate. Further, a prime-age male household head is often the primary or only earner in his family, so his unemployment is likely to have a stronger effect on family well-being than that of other household members.

About one in ten (10.3 percent) of our sample reported some unemployment in 1976, with those unemployed losing a substantial fraction (28.8 percent) of their expected work time[1] and a comparably large fraction (21.2 percent) of their expected after-tax labor income.[2] Underlying this snapshot was a long-run unemployment picture in which a much larger percentage (38.4 percent) of workers experienced some unemployment between 1967 and 1976 and in which the average costs (as a percent of expected work time or after-tax labor income) for those unemployed were much lower.[3] The 38.4 percent of our sample who were unemployed suffered average losses amounting to 5.3 percent of expected ten-year work time and 4.2 percent of expected ten-year after-tax labor income.

Relative Burdens Among Workers

These averages, however, mask an important finding. Although exposure to unemployment in the long run is quite widespread, and average long-run costs (measured as a percentage of expected work time or after-tax labor income) are low compared to short-run costs, there is a small group for whom both long- and short-run costs are large. Indeed, it appears that a small percentage of workers shoulder the bulk of the group's unemployment burden.

In investigating the distribution of the unemployment burden we concentrate on time spent unemployed, since preliminary analysis showed that length of time unemployed is the dominant component of after-tax income losses from unemployment in both the short run and the long run.[4] We investigated the long run distribution of the unemployment burden by constructing a Lorenz curve depicting the cumulative percentage of total unemployment hours for the prime-age male household heads by the cumulative percentage of the sample, both those unemployed and those not unemployed, for the years 1967-1976. This analysis indicates that five percent of the sample accounted for almost half (46.6 percent) of all the work hours lost by the entire group because of unemployment between 1967 and 1976 (see the chart). During this period, these men averaged 96 weeks, or 19.1 percent of their expected ten-year work time, unemployed. For them unemployment resulted in average losses of $19,114 in after-tax income, or 15.4 percent of their expected ten-year after-tax labor income. They also shouldered a large short-run unemployment burden. Three-quarters (77.3 percent) of this small group were unemployed in 1976, and those who were unemployed accounted for over half (56.0 percent) of the 1976 unemployment hours of prime-age male household heads. Interestingly, those bearing the bulk of the unemployment burden constituted a larger fraction of the short-run unemployed than of the long-run unemployed. The three-quarters of the group who were

---

[1] Expected work time is defined as the sum of employment plus unemployment hours for a given time period. Proportion of work time lost is the ratio of unemployment hours to expected work time.

[2] Proportion of expected income lost is the ratio of lost disposable income to expected after-tax labor income. Lost Disposable Income = [(Hourly Wage) x (Hours Unemployed) x (1-Average Tax Rate)] − Unemployment Compensation. Expected After-Tax Labor Income = [(Reported Labor Income) + ((Hourly Wage) x (Hours Unemployed))] x (1 − Average Tax Rate).

[3] Although costs as a percentage of expected work time or after-tax labor income decreased as we extended the time period from one to ten years, the reverse held for absolute costs. The average man unemployed in 1976 lost 14.8 weeks of work and $2445 in disposable income. This compares to averages of 27.3 weeks and $5113 for men who reported some unemployment between 1967 and 1976.

[4] We decomposed after-tax income losses due to unemployment into these components: unemployment time, after-tax wage, and fraction of after-tax earnings' losses recovered through unemployment compensation. In doing so, we found that both in 1976 and 1967-1976 the variance in unemployment time accounted for much more of the variance in after-tax income losses than did the variance in the other two components of these income losses.

Reprinted from ECONOMIC OUTLOOK USA, Autumn 1978, by special permission. Copyright 1978 by The University of Michigan. A more complete discussion of this topic is available from the authors at the Survey Research Center, P.O. Box 1248, Ann Arbor, MI 48106.

LORENZ CURVE* FOR 1967-1976 UNEMPLOYMENT HOURS

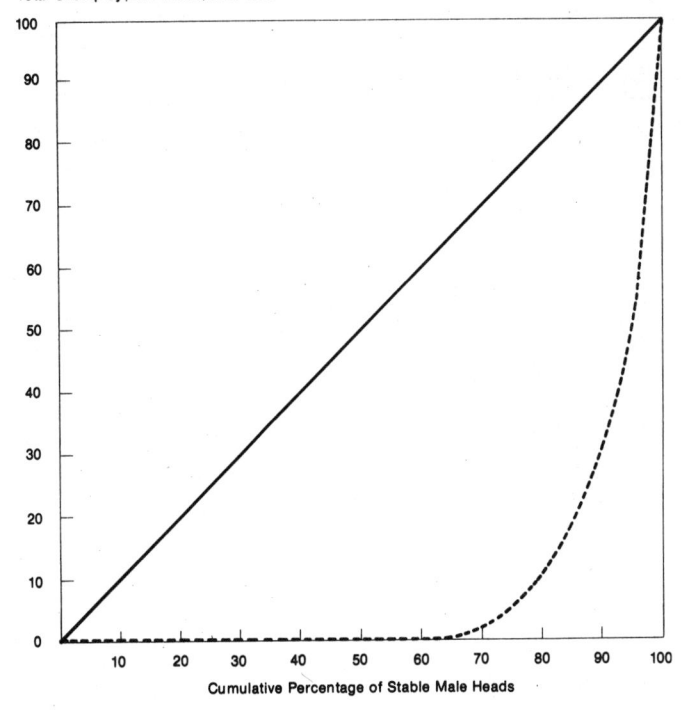

*Increasing divergence from the diagonal denotes increasing inequality in the distribution of unemployment.

Note: Plot based on men aged 35-64 in 1976 who were household heads and who reported themselves working, temporarily laid off, or looking for work 1968-77; 60% experienced no unemployment during the ten years.

Source: Panel Study of Income Dynamics, SRC.

unemployed in 1976 comprised 38.3 percent of the 1976 unemployed, whereas the entire group comprised only 13.0 percent of the 1967-1976 unemployed.

Although this analysis shows a very strong concentration of the unemployment burden among these male household heads, it may well understate the concentration at the family level. Analysis of Panel Study data for all household heads and wives as of 1975 showed evidence of extensive unemployment cumulating within families. In 1975, wives in households where the husband was unemployed for 14 or more weeks were themselves more likely to be unemployed at least 14 weeks.[5]

Race and Poverty Status Differences

Since we were particularly interested in knowing if blacks or the working poor shouldered a disproportionate share of the unemployment burden, we examined race and poverty status differences in some detail. Prime-age black male household heads were one and one-half times as likely to become unemployed during 1967-76 as well as in 1976 as were prime-age white men who headed households. More than half (53.6 percent) of the blacks were unemployed some time during 1967-1976 as compared to about one-third (37.2 percent) of the whites. However, blacks and whites unemployed during this period averaged about the same number of weeks unemployed (28.9 and 27.2 weeks, respectively), and blacks were not significantly more likely than whites to experience chronic (at least five weeks in each of three or more years) or substantial (50 or more weeks total) unemployment over the ten year period.

Poor male household heads were also disproportionately subject to unemployment. About two-thirds (68.2 percent) of the poor household heads in our sample reported some unemployment between 1967 and 1976, as compared to about one-third (37.5 percent) of the non-poor.[6] And, unlike race differences, poverty status differences in average weeks of unemployment and incidence of chronic or substantial unemployment were quite sizable. During 1967-76, those poor household heads who were unemployed averaged 45.6 weeks of unemployment, compared to 26.3 weeks for unemployed non-poor heads. And the poor were four to five times as likely as the non-poor to experience repeated or lage amounts of unemployment over the ten-year period.[7]

Factors Associated with Unemployment Experience

We performed a number of multivariate analyses with several demographic and job characteristics as predictors of unemployment.[8] These analyses showed that workers with less than eight years of schooling, in blue-collar jobs, and in the construction industry were more likely to experience some unemployment in 1976, and in the de-

---

[5] In 1975, 2.6 percent of all households contained a wife with 14 or more weeks of unemployment, and 6.3 percent contained a head with 14 or more weeks of unemployment. If the head's and wife's likelihood of exposure to extensive unemployment were statistically independent, we would expect to find 0.164 percent [(.026) x (.063) = .00164] of all households with both the head and wife unemployed at least 14 weeks. However, the actual figure was 0.4 percent, a value which was statistically different from 0.164 at the 99 percent confidence level. This cumulative unemployment may, of course, result from the wife entering the labor force as a result of her husband's being unemployed for a protracted period.

[6] We define poor by computing the ratio of ten-year family income to ten-year needs. Family needs are calculated using the Orshansky index. Whenever the income-to-needs ratio was less than 1.25, we defined a family as "poor." One might argue that our analysis is circular since unemployment might push families into poverty. However, of the 110 poor in our sample, only three would have attained ten-year family income/needs ratios of 1.25 or greater if they had received their usual earnings when unemployed.

[7] About six percent of the non-poor segment reported 50 or more weeks of unemployment, compared to 23 percent of the poor segment. About six percent of the non-poor also reported that they were unemployed at least five weeks at least three of the years 1967-1976 compared to 33.2 percent of the poor.

[8] Each analysis had a different dependent variable but the same set of independent variables. The dependent variables were:
  If Unemployed Sometime During 1976,
  If Unemployed Sometime During 1967-1976,
  If Unemployed at Least Five Weeks in 1976,
  If Unemployed at Least Five Weeks in 1976 and in Two Other Years 1967-76,
  If Unemployed at Least 50 Weeks During 1967-1976, and
  If Unemployed at Least Five Weeks in Three Years 1967-1976.
The independent variables included:
  Race,
  Age in 1976,
  Education in 1976,
  County Unemployment Rate in 1976,
  Region in 1976,
  Industry in 1976,
  Occupation in 1976, and
  If Belonged to a Union in 1976.

cade 1967-1976, to be unemployed at least five weeks in 1976, to be repeatedly unemployed over the ten-year period, and to be unemployed a total of at least 50 weeks over the ten-year period. Race differences in unemployment became insignificant when other demographic and job characteristics were controlled. Whites with comparable levels of education and in similar occupations in similar industries were just as likely as blacks to be unemployed either in 1976 or 1967-1976, suggesting that job sorting (that is, the mechanism by which blacks and whites end up in different kinds of jobs) may be the key to race differences in unemployment incidence. Controls for demographic and job characteristics did not eliminate poverty status differences in unemployment, however. Even with the controls, the poor remained more likely to experience several years of substantial unemployment. But perhaps our most disappointing finding was that all our demographic and job characteristics accounted for only ten percent of the variance in our chronic unemployment measures. We are still far from adequately identifying those workers who experience substantial and repeated unemployment.

These results, in many respects, raise more questions than they answer. Over the long-run we found two distinct groups of unemployed male household heads. The first includes most of those unemployed. For these workers unemployment is an infrequent occurrence with low relative costs of time and money over the long run. The other group is small, experiences extensive and chronic unemployment, and suffers severe losses of time and money, whether measured in the short run or the long run. This second group is obviously very important; it is a group which is not being integrated into stable employment with present policies even though each of its members has at least a ten-year history of labor force participation. But we do not know very much about who makes up this group and why they accumulate so much unemployment, questions of obvious concern to policymakers. All we know is that schooling and occupation make some, though not much, difference. But whether work attitudes matter, whether early experience produces cumulative impacts for particular types of workers but not others, etc. are questions that we cannot answer at present.

Federal Reserve and Treasury Support the Dollar

On November 1 the Federal Reserve and the Treasury announced measures to strengthen the dollar in foreign exchange markets. In a joint statement, the Secretary of the Treasury and the Federal Reserve Board Chairman declared: "Recent movement in the dollar exchange rate has exceeded any decline related to fundamental factors, is hampering progress toward price stability, and is damaging the climate for investment and growth. The time has come to call a halt to this development."

The Federal Reserve Board announced the following specific measures:

- Approval of a 1-percentage-point increase in the discount rate at Federal Reserve banks from $8^1/_2$ to $9^1/_2$ percent. The discount rate is the rate charged member banks when they borrow from their district Federal Reserve Bank.
- Establishment of a supplementary reserve requirement, in addition to existing reserve requirements, equal to 2 percent of time deposits in denominations of $100,000 or more.
- Increases in the Federal Reserve's reciprocal currency (swap) arrangements with the central banks of Germany, Japan, and Switzerland by $7.6 billion to $15.0 billion.

The prearranged credit lines with the three countries are part of a network of reciprocal short-term credit arrangements with 14 central banks and the Bank for International Settlements, commonly referred to as the swap network. The foreign currencies made available through the expanded short-term credit arrangements with the foreign central banks can be used by the Federal Reserve to buy dollars in exchange market support operations.[1]

The reserve requirement action, which increased required reserves by about $3 billion, should help moderate the recent rapid expansion in bank credit. Together with the increase in the discount rate, the higher reserve requirements should increase the incentive for member banks to borrow funds from abroad, thereby strengthening the dollar in foreign markets.

---

1. One noteworthy aspect of the swap increase is that Japan is included, with an increase from $2 billion to $5 billion. The United States has not used this swap line in the past, and the increase could augur intervention in the yen as well as the German deutsche mark and the Swiss franc.

Reprinted from Federal Reserve Bank of Dallas *Voice*, November, 1978.

Dollar's value has progressively weakened over past year

EXCHANGE RATE INDEXES (MARCH 1973=100)

- SWISS FRANC
- GERMAN MARK
- JAPANESE YEN
- TRADE-WEIGHTED DOLLAR

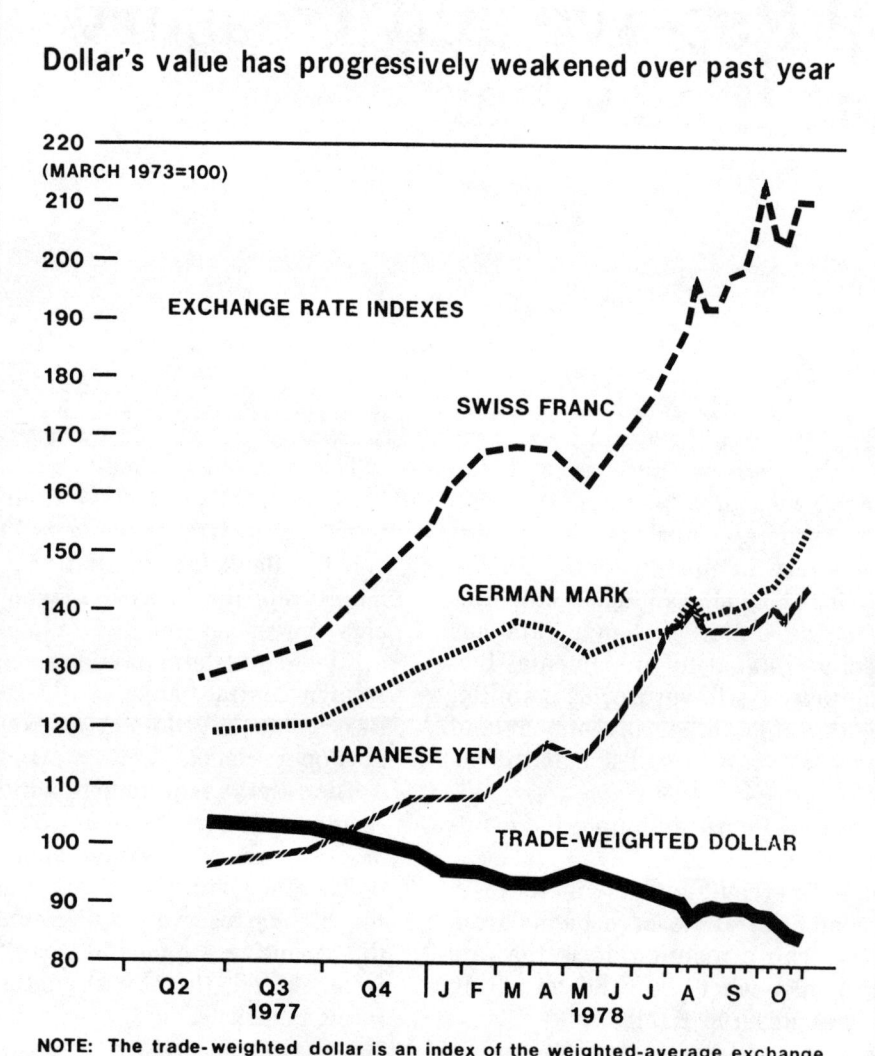

NOTE: The trade-weighted dollar is an index of the weighted-average exchange value of the U.S. dollar against currencies of ten other countries. Weights are the 1972-76 global trade of each of the ten countries.

SOURCE: Board of Governors, Federal Reserve System.

Foreign countries have achieved much sharper reductions in their inflation rates

TABLE 1. Changes in Consumer Price Indexes of Seven Major Countries

(Percentage changes at annual rates)

Country	Three years ended 1977-Q2	1977-Q2 to 1978-Q2	Change	Forecast, 1978-Q2 to 1979-Q2
Germany	5.0	2.6	−2.4	3.3
Japan	10.5	3.7	−6.8	5.4
France	10.5	9.0	−1.5	11.0
United Kingdom	19.1	7.6	−11.5	8.8
Canada	8.9	8.9	.0	6.9
Italy	17.7	12.1	−5.6	13.5
Trade-weighted average of six countries[1]	9.8	5.5	−4.3	6.6
United States	7.5	7.0	−.5	7.7

1. Weights are the 1972-76 global trade of each of the six countries.
SOURCES: Federal Reserve Bank of St. Louis.
Organisation for Economic Co-operation and Development.
Federal Reserve Bank of Dallas.

To augment the measures taken by the Federal Reserve, the Treasury announced the following measures:
- Issuing up to $10 billion of Treasury securities denominated in foreign currencies, intended primarily for sale to private foreigners.
- Drawing $3 billion in foreign currencies from its reserves at the International Monetary Fund and selling $2 billion of its IMF Special Drawing Rights (SDR's) for foreign currencies.
- Increasing its gold sales to at least 1,500,000 ounces monthly beginning in December, up from 300,000 ounces currently and about double the previously announced level of 750,000 ounces that was to have begun in November.

To the extent that the gold is sold to foreign residents, increased gold sales will help reduce the U.S. trade deficit and absorb excess foreign-held dollars. The currencies acquired from the IMF, the sale of SDR's, and the issuance of foreign-currency-denominated Treasury securities—together with the amounts available through the Federal Reserve swap lines—provide up to $30 billion in foreign currencies for support operations in exchange markets.

The goal of these measures is to reverse the decline in the dollar's value abroad. By showing an intention to support the dollar, the Treasury and the Federal Reserve hope to stem unwarranted diversification out of dollars by private and official foreigners. In the long run, the recovery of the dollar will depend on actions by the Government to change underlying inflationary expectations.

The value of the dollar in foreign exchange markets has progressively weakened for over a year. Since September last year, it has fallen against virtually all major currencies except the Canadian dollar. During that period, it has declined 28 percent against the German mark, nearly 47 percent against the Japanese yen, and over 55 percent against the Swiss franc. The trade-weighted average value of the dollar, a broader measure of its value, has declined about 20 percent in the past year.[2] In the period from the end of August to the end of October, the dollar declined 7.6 percent on a trade-weighted basis, reaching a new low and precipitating the actions of the Federal Reserve and the Treasury.

2. This measure of the dollar's value takes into account the amount of foreign trade with different countries. The greater a country's exports and imports, the more that country's currency exchange rate affects the trade-weighted average value of the dollar. Thus, the index is a better measure of the dollar's value in international markets than is any single-country exchange rate.

Increased competitiveness and relatively slower growth expected to reduce deficit in U.S. current account

TABLE 2. Current Balances of Major Countries
(Billions of dollars)

Area	1974	1975	1976	1977	Forecast 1978	Forecast First half, 1979
United States	−2.3	11.6	−1.4	−20.2	−25.0	−18.0
Japan	−4.7	−.7	3.7	11.0	17.5	13.0
Germany	9.8	4.0	3.8	3.8	5.0	3.0
Other major European countries	−22.4	−4.5	−10.4	−.6	4.0	5.5

NOTE: The current balance is the sum of the merchandise trade balance, net services, and private and official transfers.
SOURCE: Organisation for Economic Co-operation and Development.

A major reason for the recent bearish sentiment against the dollar has been a reversal in relative rates of inflation in the United States and other countries in the past year. Until recently, the United States had a lower rate of inflation than did its major trading partners. As shown in Table 1, the rate of inflation in the United States, as measured by consumer prices, was 2.3 percentage points less than the average inflation rates in major trading countries in the three years ended in the second quarter of 1977. Although the United States reduced its rate of inflation during the next year, anti-inflation policies in other countries were more successful so that, on average, their inflation rates fell more than 4 percentage points. Consequently, during the past year the inflation rate has been higher in the United States than abroad. Moreover, by estimates of the Organisation for Economic Co-operation and Development (OECD), the rate of inflation in the United States is likely to remain somewhat higher through 1979.

Another reason for the dollar's decline has been a persistent U.S. current account deficit since early 1976 (Table 2). This deficit in the balance of international payments tended to increase net foreign claims on U.S. assets (and decrease U.S. claims on foreign assets). Thus, the net stock of dollar assets in the hands of foreigners has been increasing during a period when domestic inflation was making the dollar a less attractive asset to hold.

Paradoxically, much of the deficit in the balance of payments has been a result of the relative strength of the U.S. economy. As shown in Table 3, real GNP has been growing more rapidly in the United States than for foreign economies since 1975 (the last year the U.S. balance of trade was in surplus). The more rapid rate of growth of the domestic economy tended to increase the demand for foreign goods, pushing up total U.S. imports. By contrast, the relatively slow growth of the foreign economies caused them to demand fewer exports from the United States. We have posted larger and larger trade deficits, while our trading partners have been posting large surpluses. But this difference in growth rates has already begun to be reversed, and the OECD projects a faster growth rate abroad than in the United States for the first half of next year.

The more rapid rate of inflation in the United States since the beginning of 1977 is partly responsible for the trade deficit. Taken by itself, the higher inflation rate makes U.S. goods less competitive in foreign markets. However, in a system of floating exchange rates, as has existed since 1973, the exchange rate of a currency will tend to decline in order to offset domestic inflation and maintain international competitiveness. In fact, the value of the dollar in foreign exchange markets has recently fallen by more than enough to compensate for the higher U.S. inflation rate; from early 1977 to mid-1978, the cost of U.S. goods relative to the cost of foreign goods, adjusted for changes in exchange rates, fell about 6 percent. It is expected that the increased competitiveness of U.S. goods will help strengthen the U.S. current account balance by next year.

The actions announced by the Federal Reserve and the Treasury serve as bridging measures to support the dollar until more fundamental forces

Growth strong in United States in past but slowing relative to growth abroad

TABLE 3. Changes in Real Gross National Product of Seven Major Countries

(Percentage changes at annual rates)

Country	1975	1976	1977	Forecast 1978	Forecast First half, 1979
Germany	−2.5	5.7	2.4	2.5	2.8
Japan	2.5	6.0	5.1	5.5	4.5
France	.1	4.6	3.0	3.8	3.8
United Kingdom	−2.1	2.3	.7	2.8	1.8
Canada	1.1	4.9	2.6	4.0	4.0
Italy	−3.5	5.7	1.7	2.0	3.0
Trade-weighted average of six countries[1]	−.8	4.9	2.7	3.4	3.3
United States	−1.3	6.0	4.9	3.8	3.0

1. Weights are the 1972-76 global trade of each of the six countries.
SOURCES: Federal Reserve Bank of St. Louis.
Organisation for Economic Co-operation and Development.
Federal Reserve Bank of Dallas.

have time to take hold, assuming further progress in slowing domestic inflation. Exchange market intervention by the Federal Reserve and foreign central banks provides direct support for the dollar. The increase in the Federal Reserve discount rate and the supplementary reserve requirement on large time deposits put immediate upward pressure on short-term interest rates in the United States. Higher yields on dollar-denominated securities make them more attractive to investors, both domestic and foreign, and thereby increase the demand for dollars.[3]

Whether the measures announced by the Federal Reserve and the Treasury mark a permanent turnaround for the dollar will depend on whether the factors that caused the dollar's decline are moderated or reversed. If inflationary expectations are reversed, and if current forecasts of lower U.S. growth than that abroad do materialize, we may not need to utilize the entire support package.

3. Investors also take into account differences in rates of inflation in different countries when comparing rates of return on financial assets. Although nominal interest rates have generally been higher in the United States during the period of the dollar's recent fall, the higher inflation here has made real interest rates much lower.

54
Our Sick Dollar Starts To Regain Its Health

Is the turnaround going to last? What does it promise for Americans? For a look at how experts here and abroad size up the U.S. currency—

The dollar has risen from its sickbed and, suddenly, is back in fashion on the world's financial markets.

Since last fall, U.S. money has recovered about 40 percent of the value it lost against major foreign currencies in a long slide that began nearly three years ago.

Today, investors, speculators and corporate money managers abroad are rushing to buy dollars in exchange for holdings of Japanese yen, West German marks and Swiss francs—the currencies that had been giving the dollar the most trouble. Only six months ago the rush was in the opposite direction.

Foreign confidence in American greenbacks had plunged to its lowest point since World War II. A global flight from the dollar was in high gear. The dollar's price in most major foreign currencies was plummeting.

What has happened since then to reverse the tide? Is the dollar now on the way to full recovery? If it is, what does that mean to individuals and businesses? Here are answers to these and other questions as supplied by experts in New York, Geneva, Washington and other world centers:

Just how much has the dollar recovered?

Its value is up 8.9 percent since last October 30, as measured against 10 major currencies weighted according to how much heft the issuing country carries in world trade. That is when the dollar hit a postwar low. At that point, it had fallen 23.3 percent from its postrecession peak in June, 1976.

Despite some daily ups and downs, the greenback has recovered about 40 percent of the ground it lost. One dollar now buys about 22 percent more Japanese yen than it did last fall, about 16 percent more Swiss francs and 10 percent more West German marks.

The dollar has lost ground against Canada's dollar this year. But among major countries, Canada alone had seen its currency do worse than the greenback during the long slide.

Does this mean that the dollar's troubles are over?

Not if the U.S. doesn't show progress soon in licking inflation, if it isn't able to reduce its dependence on foreign oil and if the trade deficit is not reduced significantly.

These were the problems that led to the dollar's decline in the first place.

Europeans doubt that President Carter can slow the wage-price spiral quickly enough. If U.S. inflation continues to race ahead at twice Germany's rate and three times that of Switzerland's, foreign confidence in the dollar sooner or later will weaken again, predicts Fritz Leutwiler, president of Switzerland's National Bank.

How long will the recovery last?

Most experts believe that optimism about the dollar will prevail for the next few months, at least. But they are skeptical about the long run.

There are signs that the herd instinct, which helped bring the dollar low by causing hordes of speculators to unload their dollar holdings, now has reversed and is helping the rise. That means the recovery may be fragile. A run of bad news could quickly produce a renewed battering of the dollar.

For one, Otmar Emminger, president of the Bundesbank, West Germany's central bank, doubts that the dollar's comeback will last. Many European bankers think a new setback could come before year's end.

The governments of Europe and Japan are anxious to keep the dollar from rising too much because that would push up the costs of imports from the U.S. as well as Mideast oil prices, which are denominated in dollars. That would add to already rising inflation rates in those countries.

The Bank of Japan, that nation's central bank, has just raised its official discount rate for the first time in more than five years in an attempt to dampen the inflationary surge there. For Ja-

Bounding Back...

What U.S. dollar buys in foreign currencies—

		Change From Oct. 30, 1978
215.200	Japanese yen	UP 21.5%
21.110	Israeli pounds	UP 20.4%
23.990	Brazilian cruzeiros	UP 17.7%
1.708	Swiss francs	UP 16.1%
30.050	Belgian francs	UP 10.8%
2.057	Netherlands guilders	UP 10.2%
1.893	German marks	UP 9.9%
4.357	French francs	UP 9.0%
4.384	Swedish kronor	UP 7.3%
.903	Australian dollars	UP 7.2%
843.200	Italian lire	UP 7.0%
36.700	Greek drachmas	UP 5.7%
68.350	Spanish pesetas	UP 2.0%
.483	British pounds	UP 1.3%
22.790	Mexican pesos	No change
1.141	Canadian dollars	DOWN 2.6%

SINCE STRIKING an all-time low last October 30 in comparison with 10 leading foreign currencies, the value of the dollar has gone up 8.9 percent.

Note: Figures as of April 18. Source: Federal Reserve Board

Reprinted from "U.S. News & World Report."

pan, there is another problem, too. Depreciation of the yen as the dollar rises would make Japanese goods cheaper in the U.S. That would add to Tokyo's difficulty in paring its 12-billion-dollar-a-year trade surplus with the United States. Failure to trim the surplus could increase already strong protectionist pressures in Congress and lead to limits on Japanese imports.

Will the dollar's comeback help American consumers?

Yes. Americans going abroad already are able to get more foreign currency for their dollars, as the table on page 35 points up.

On prices here at home, short-term ups and downs won't have much effect. But just as devaluation of the dollar boosts consumer prices, so an increase in the dollar's value—if it sticks—will eventually reduce inflationary pressures by enabling each unit of currency to buy more goods.

How large the impact will be is a matter of debate among economists. Prices usually come down more slowly than they go up.

One rough estimate, from Allen Sinai, monetary economist at Data Resources, Inc.: For every 10 percent the dollar climbs, consumer prices will be half a percent lower than they otherwise would have been at the end of a year.

What's behind the dollar's buoyancy?

There is no single cause. Monetary experts cite a long list of factors. Chief among them is the series of sweeping actions jointly ordered last November 1 by President Carter and the Federal Reserve Board, which is responsible for monetary policy.

Among the steps: A sharp increase in U.S. interest rates, aimed at attracting foreign-held dollars back to this country.

Another key move was a pledge to buy as many dollars from foreign holders as necessary to keep the value from sliding any further.

Other actions: A quadrupling of gold sales to sop up dollars, and sale for the first time by the government of foreign-denominated securities in a bid to lure foreign investors into lending the U.S. their currencies so they could be used to buy still more dollars.

Since the November actions, there has been a sharp reversal in currency flows. Central banks in Europe and Japan have been forced to sell millions of dollars in the markets to protect their currencies against massive devaluations.

As a result of the dollar's new strength, the Treasury Department announced plans on April 18 to cut in half the amount of gold on sale at its monthly auctions starting in May.

Last fall, dollars changed hands like hot potatoes. Potential buyers waited for the greenback to fall even further, while exporters earning dollars were getting rid of them as quickly as possible. Now, those who have dollars are hanging on tight; those who want them are scrambling. Foreign investors have been switching from hard currencies with low interest rates to higher-yielding dollar investments. Mideast oil money has been flowing into dollars.

Still other money has been coming back to the U.S. from foreigners who have been buying U.S. stocks and others who have been purchasing land and businesses here at prices that have seemed to be bargains because of the dollar's skid.

At the same time, American multinational corporations have been bringing home the earnings of foreign subsidiaries rather than holding the money abroad where its value could erode. When the dollar was falling, they left the money in overseas currencies.

How did Carter's rescue program help?

It erased an impression abroad that the administration was not only following a policy of "benign neglect" toward the dollar, but even favored a cheap dollar to help American industry sell more goods abroad. This view of U.S. aims dated back to Washington's devaluation of the dollar in 1971 and helped to erode confidence in the dollar, Europeans say.

With his rescue package, Carter created "a new basis of confidence," says West Germany's Emminger.

The measures were a signal of a fundamental change in attitude, notes Princeton University economist Peter B. Kenen. And they were read that way abroad. Zurich bankers saw the actions as an indication that Washington had changed its basic "currency philosophy." The message: The U.S. government now recognizes that the value of the dollar cannot be left entirely to chance and to the whims of speculators.

Why wasn't something done sooner?

Monetary authorities in both the U.S. and abroad did not want to interfere with the new system of floating exchange rates, which was intended to allow currencies to be valued by free-market forces.

But a "bandwagon effect" caused massive selling of the dollar by speculators, forcing its value far below what most monetary experts felt was justified by hard economic facts.

Why is foreign confidence in the dollar rising today when the U.S. economy is still in such a disarray from inflation and other problems?

It comes down to a question of whose long-term prospects look best.

The new round of oil-price increases was bad news for the U.S. but even worse news for the oil-poor Europeans and Japanese.

Foreign observers believe that the cost of adjusting to the latest oil shock will be lower in the U.S. than overseas. Carter's deregulation of domestic-oil prices is seen as a major plus, an indication this country is finally addressing its oil-import problem seriously. The result: A boost for the dollar.

Recent monthly figures that indicate the U.S. is making progress in reducing the trade deficit have been encouraging to foreigners. So has a run of other statistics showing a small decline in the U.S. money supply for the past six months and scattered indications that the economy's growth is easing. With those things happening, they reason, a downturn in inflation cannot be far off.

Over all, what is the long-term outlook?

In the end, the dollar's fate hinges on stopping the price spiral, agree experts in the U.S. and abroad. Concludes a Zurich banker: "The dollar could stage a lasting comeback as the world's strongest and safest currency in the '80s, but only if the Americans win their inflation battle—and that remains to be seen." □

Copyright 1979 U.S. News & World Report, Inc.

OPEC's Billions

Bruce K. MacLaury

THE WORLD IS STILL RECOVERING from the shock of radically higher energy prices triggered by the October 1973 war in the Middle East. In the months following the oil embargo and the quadrupling of oil prices, it seemed possible that the strains imposed on world markets and financial institutions, and indeed on national economies, would cause a fracture in one or another part of the complex linkages that make up the world economic system.

The increase from about $40 billion to $120 billion in the export earnings of the world's oil exporters between 1973 and 1974 was probably the largest bonanza in world history, exceeding even the inflow of gold and silver into Spain in the sixteenth and seventeenth centuries. The strain of this massive redistribution of world income compounded existing economic difficulties on every front.

Among industrialized countries, the unanticipated jump in the prices of petroleum and its products added substantially to inflationary pressures that were already a major source of concern. At the same time, the transfer of purchasing power from oil importing to oil exporting nations had the same depressing effect on demand in the oil importing countries as would a tax, the receipts from which were hoarded rather than spent.

The need to use a greater portion of existing income on higher-priced petroleum left less for other purchases. The result was the recession of 1975, the deepest since the 1930s. Although rates of inflation came down during the recession, they remained unacceptably high in most industrial countries as wages and prices continued chasing each other.

Bruce K. MacLaury is president of the Brookings Institution. This article is based on his remarks before the Western Finance Association in Honolulu.

Recovery from the 1975 recession has been slow—even halting—in many industrial countries and investment outlays have lagged. Whether these countries have entered a period of slower growth in the long run is an unanswered question.

Linked to the difficult domestic adjustments required by the oil shock were equally difficult balance of payments problems. Exploding OPEC surpluses inevitably implied equally large payments deficits for the rest of the world. While conceptually the surpluses and deficits must offset each other in the aggregate, there was no reason to think that they would do so on a country-by-country basis. On the contrary, there was every reason to expect that the surplus countries would direct their rising financial assets to a small number of financial centers, leaving to institutions in those centers the task of redistributing these claims on an international basis. Indeed, this was at the heart of the much-discussed recycling problem—the tensions and financial risks that were created by the mismatch of claims and liabilities on

Photographed from *Brookings Bulletin*, Fall, 1978. Reprinted by permission of the *Journal of Financial and Quantitative Analysis*, November 1978, University of Washington.

financial institutions in the private sector, and on the major international banks in particular.

Many observers, myself included, seriously questioned whether financial markets and institutions could cope with the unprecedentedly large financial transfers that the oil price increase set in motion. As it turned out, the recycling problem has been accommodated with less disruption than seemed likely at the time. More generally, the resilience of world economic relationships has proved greater in the face of the oil shock than we had any right to expect.

It seems worthwhile to review key aspects of the adaptation process of the past few years in order to determine what risks still lie ahead as a result of continuing OPEC surpluses. Let me anticipate my conclusion by saying that in my judgment, there is substantially less danger to financial stability from OPEC surpluses—past, present, and future—than seemed likely only a short time ago.

OPEC Surpluses Are Dwindling

The first evidence to support this conclusion is the diminished size of OPEC surpluses themselves. The massive jump in the current account surpluses of OPEC countries, from $6 billion to $67 billion between 1973 and 1974, looked like the beginning of a sequence of large surpluses with no end in sight. Before long, however, it became clear that early projections of massive reserve accumulations were exaggerated.

The major misperception was the speed with which OPEC imports would expand to absorb the enlarged export receipts. For the OPEC countries as a whole, imports increased by roughly two-thirds in both 1974 and 1975. While the pace of increase has slowed in the last couple of years, the only countries in continuing substantial surplus are Saudi Arabia, Kuwait, and a few other oil producers along the Persian Gulf.

The presumption had been that even the more populous oil exporting nations would have required more time to expand their imports. In practice, even the sparsely populated exporting countries—Saudi Arabia in particular—have managed to develop plans, begin massive projects, and commit funds for imports at a rate that could hardly have been foreseen.

A second factor that has contributed to narrowing OPEC surpluses has been the lower than expected demand for their oil exports. The slackness in world demand is the result of several forces. One, of course, is that Europe and Japan have not fully recovered from the recession. Unemployment in Europe remains as high or higher than it was at the bottom of the recession, and industrial production is only now regaining 1974 levels.

At the same time, new petroleum production in countries outside the OPEC group has added to world supplies and reduced demand for OPEC oil. The Alaskan pipeline is now bringing oil from the North Slope, and production is increasing from the North Sea. While these sources are not expected to provide long-term expansion possibilities to meet growing world demand, they have contributed to a softening in world petroleum markets for the time being.

Another development that has turned out more favorably than had been expected is the apparent response to higher petroleum prices in the United States and in the industrial world generally. In the United States, for example, energy use in the period 1965-73 grew faster than real gross national product—4.3 percent as against 3.7 percent a year. Since 1973 energy consumption per unit of real GNP seems to have declined. On the assumption that U.S. oil prices will move gradually toward world levels, one of the major oil companies is now making projections for the 1980s on the assumption that energy use will increase at only two-thirds of the projected growth rate of real GNP—2.3 percent as against 3.4 percent a year during 1980-90.

For these reasons, among others, the world price of oil seems likely to remain roughly stable in real terms at least through the early 1980s, barring major political or economic disturbances.

The combined effect of rapidly rising OPEC imports and slowing demand for OPEC oil exports has been a substantial drop in the current account surplus of oil exporting countries. After hovering in the range of $35–$40 billion from 1975 to 1977, the surplus is expected to decline to $20 billion or less in 1978, and to narrow further through 1980.

If these projections turn out to be approximately correct, then it is hard to see how diminishing OPEC surpluses in an expanding world economy could be a major cause of financial instability over the next few years.

OPEC Reserves

Stability in world financial markets is not assured simply by the absence of large OPEC surpluses, though that certainly helps. Previous surpluses have resulted in large accumulations of reserves in a small number of countries. The shifting of those reserves from one form of asset to another could have disturbing consequences for financial institutions, domestic financial markets, exchange rates, and rates of money creation.

The magnitude of OPEC reserves is very large in both relative and absolute terms. OPEC's net external assets at the end of 1977 were $155 billion. Given projections of continuing though diminishing surpluses over the next few years, those assets could well reach $200 billion by 1980.

Whenever financial assets of this size are concentrated in a few hands, one must acknowledge the possibility of disruptive shifts motivated by either financial or political considerations. Ironically, the early concern was not that aggressive reserve manipulation constituted a threat, but rather that the conservative reserve management policies of countries like Saudi Arabia might expose U.S. and other financial institutions to substantial risks. The preference of these reserve managers for short-term deposits at major banks, for example, tested the ability of those banks to cope with unprecedented inflows.

In 1974 nearly two-thirds of the exceptionally large OPEC surplus was invested in short-term instruments, mainly foreign currency deposits. In the three subsequent years, however, only about one-third of the smaller surpluses went into short-term deposits, with two-thirds going into a variety of longer-term investments. Thus, insofar as extended maturities constitute more stable reserve holdings, there has been a noticeable change toward greater stability following the first turbulent year of OPEC surpluses.

On the other hand, shifts in the currency composition of OPEC reserves during the past year may have contributed to exchange rate fluctuations and to the weakness of the dollar. According to the latest annual report of the Bank for International Settlements, direct flows of OPEC funds into the United States fell by a quarter from 1976 to 1977, including a slowdown between the first and second halves of last year when the dollar, for a variety of reasons, began to weaken. Specifically, in the first half of 1977, when new OPEC deposits in reporting banks grew by $8.5 billion, 90 percent of those deposits were denominated in dollars. In the second half of the year, nearly all of the $5 billion increase in deposits was denominated in currencies other than the dollar.

There is no reason to suppose that these marked changes in the currency composition of OPEC reserves were occasioned by anything other than financial considerations. Nor are there grounds for saying that these particular shifts "caused" the decline of the dollar, any more than did similarly motivated shifts by other participants in the market. Nevertheless, the evidence that OPEC reserve holders are at times willing to shift out of dollars, even though this lowers the relative value of their remaining dollar assets, makes it imprudent to ignore the potential impact on exchange rates and financial stability that their large reserve holdings can have.

Growing Debt of Less Developed Countries

A third problem that was thought to threaten the stability of world financial institutions was the sharply rising debt of the less developed countries. Indeed, the oil importing LDCs did encounter severe balance of payments problems in the first two years following the oil price increase. As a group, their current account deficits ballooned from $11 billion in 1973 to nearly $40 billion in 1975, then fell back to about $25 billion in 1976. During that three-year period (1973–76), the external debt of these countries jumped from $80 billion to $140 billion. Nevertheless, there is less concern today that defaults by developing countries will snowball into a major threat to world financial stability.

This changed perception reflects several factors. In the first place, these countries have experienced a sharp reduction in their current account deficits in recent years —a much faster response to domestic restraint than had seemed likely. For example, the current account positions of Argentina, Brazil, Mexico, South Korea, and Taiwan improved as a group by some $5 billion last year. This improvement, plus even sharper improvement in 1976, means that the current deficits of oil importing LDCs are no larger today, allowing for the expanded value of trade, than they were before the oil price increase.

It is significant that the payments position improved in those very countries—Brazil and Mexico in particular—that have the largest debts outstanding to private foreign banks. Although defaults on debts to foreign governments or international lending institutions would be serious matters, they would be unlikely to have the same adverse repercussions on financial markets as would defaults on debts to private lenders. In this sense, the improvements occurred where they were most needed.

But the current account improvements, important as they are, don't tell the whole story. Capital inflows into the oil importing LDCs last year were larger than required to finance their collective deficits, with the result that their reserves rose by roughly $10 billion for the second straight year. With this increase, LDC reserves were nearly as large in relation to imports as they had been before the oil price increase. Even more surprising, the non-oil developing countries, which had borrowed nearly $30 billion from banks in the three years 1974–76, actually became net lenders to banks last year.

Adjusting development plans to bring about these improvements has undoubtedly been difficult and in some cases painful, in terms of slowed growth. Yet, on balance, the relatively advanced developing countries have maintained their momentum, in both exports and domestic expansion, better than most of the industrialized countries in the aftermath of the oil shock. Since the notion of "debt burden" has meaning only in relation to some measure of ability to pay—GNP or exports, for example—sustaining growth is of critical importance, quite apart from its implications for improving living standards around the world.

So the initially rapid rise in LDC debts associated with the sharp rise in oil prices seems to have been brought under control. This doesn't mean that some countries won't have difficulty in meeting repayment schedules. Nor does it mean that the poorer LDCs don't need additional concessional assistance in financing energy imports. But it does mean that LDC debt as such is less threatening to international financial stability than it seemed only a few years ago.

Bank Exposure on Foreign Loans

The fourth and final concern arising from OPEC surpluses and their effects on international financial stability is in some ways the obverse of the LDC debt issue: the risks for banks, and for U.S. banks in particular, inherent in their increased exposure on international loans. But while LDC debts and foreign bank loans are obviously related issues, they are by no means identical.

For one thing, developing countries were not the only ones whose payments positions were made more precarious by the oil price increase. A number of industrial countries encountered similar problems and became higher risks for bank lending. In addition, loan losses are only one kind of exposure banks encounter in their international operations. As is evident from the collapse of the Franklin National Bank, foreign currency losses can be equally troublesome.

Finally, most LDC debt does not in fact represent exposure for *private* banking institutions. Of the $140 billion of external LDC debt outstanding at the end of 1976, only half was owed to private creditors (as distinguished from governments), and only a third of that, or $24 billion, was without a guarantee from governments or other public entities.

Substantial losses on even a part of the $24 billion in nonguaranteed bank debt could pose serious problems for the world banking system and for confidence in general. But in assessing this risk, one should recall that only ten advanced developing countries were responsible for nearly three-quarters of the non-oil LDC bank debt outstanding at the end of 1976, and that Brazil and Mexico alone represented half the total. Thus, one's concern about bank exposure on LDC loans turns heavily on an assessment of the risks in a relatively small number of countries, which for the most part have made substantial progress in reducing their external deficits.

If the risk on bank loans to LDCs depends heavily on the distribution of those loans among particular countries (and indeed among particular borrowers within those countries), it is also true that the risk to world financial stability from possible defaults depends on the ability of particular banks to absorb such losses, and hence on the distribution of LDC loans among lending institutions.

Bank regulators in a number of industrial countries have taken steps to increase their ability to monitor the exposure of their banks on foreign credits, including improved supervisory procedures and means of evaluating foreign loans. Such measures are no guarantee against problem loans or possible losses, nor are they a substitute for good credit analysis by the lending institutions themselves. Nevertheless, they are evidence that the special risks associated with foreign lending, particularly during a period of rapidly changing economic and financial circumstances around the world, are receiving systematic attention.

It is also significant that U.S. banks, which had played a leading role in extending credits to non-oil developing countries in the early aftermath of the oil price increase, were less actively involved last year. For a variety of reasons, including relatively more attractive lending opportunities at home as well as concern about the size of existing foreign credits, the growth in U.S. banks' foreign assets slowed from nearly $12 billion in the first nine months of 1976 to less than $3 billion in the comparable period last year.

Summing Up

As I indicated at the outset, OPEC surpluses now represent a smaller threat to world financial stability than they seemed to only a short time ago. This judgment is based on several related but separate observations.

First and most obvious is the substantial decline in OPEC surpluses themselves, and the prospect of further reductions in the years ahead.

Second, while one cannot rule out politically motivated shifts of existing and future OPEC reserves any more than one can rule out another oil embargo, the increasing interdependence of oil exporting and industrialized countries makes such actions more costly and less likely.

Third, shifts of OPEC reserves from one currency to another based on financial considerations are clearly possible, and in fact occurred last year. But such shifts are by their nature self-limiting, and OPEC reserves, despite their size and concentration, are only one factor among many operating in exchange markets at any given time.

Fourth, the specter of developing countries going bankrupt as they pile up debts to sustain pre-1973 levels of energy imports has diminished greatly, if not disappeared.

Fifth, international banks and the regulatory authorities seem better equipped to monitor and limit the various risks associated with massive international capital flows, even as the size of those flows—at least as related to OPEC surpluses—has diminished.

It is important to understand what these observations do *not* mean. Specifically, they do not mean:

That the world, having absorbed the 1973 oil price increase, could swallow another major hike without disruption as great or greater than before.

That all developing countries have adjusted to the new levels of energy prices.

That declining OPEC surpluses have diminished the urgency of reducing U.S. petroleum imports.

That there should be any less concern about the stability of the international financial system simply because it has survived the shocks of massive OPEC surpluses.

The last point needs emphasis. If the threat to world financial stability from OPEC surpluses and their related distortions has diminished, as I believe it has, that threat has been replaced by the potentially disruptive effects of intractable payments imbalances among the major industrial countries themselves. This year, for example, the combined current account surplus of Japan, Germany, and Switzerland is likely to be as large as OPEC's. And there seems little likelihood that the record U.S. deficit will decline much this year.

So long as payments imbalances of these magnitudes persist, we must expect continued instability in exchange rates and in financial markets generally.

56
Trade Wars 3: The Politics of Oil

The Embargo—And Its Friends

When the prices of gasoline and other petroleum products exploded in 1973 and 1974, the increases were widely blamed on the oil embargo which Arab countries slapped on the West in the aftermath of the October 1973 Mideast war. However, the embargo did not actually cause a shortage of oil. Nor did it end the major companies' profitable reign over much of the world's oil trade. Rather, it led the majors to work in partnership with OPEC — at the expense of consumers around the world.

When the embargo was declared in late 1973, official expressions of shock and surprise in the developed countries were less than candid: there had been embargoes in the 1956 and 1967 Middle East wars; radical Arab forces had already been calling for the use of the "oil weapon" against Israel and the U.S.; and in May 1973 the Saudi government warned U.S. oil companies that another war was on the way.

The Arab embargoes during the two earlier wars had had little effect, since U.S. oil production, combined with oil the major companies produced in non-Arab countries, had been sufficient to fill the gap. But by 1973 Arab oil had become more important to the industrial capitalist countries. This time a prolonged, complete cutoff *would have* had a serious impact.

The Shortage That Wasn't

In fact, the 1973-74 embargo had no measurable effect on total oil output. In 1973, production by the eleven leading members of OPEC increased at exactly its average growth rate for the preceding twenty years. Throughout 1973 and 1974, the output of the five top *Middle East* producers was at or above the level it would have reached by maintaining its traditional growth rate.

There are three reasons why the embargo was ineffective. First, some oil continued to "leak" out of the Arab countries. Second, Iran, a non-Arab country with ties to Israel as well as the U.S., sharply increased production. Third, knowing that war was coming, Saudi Arabia produced a lot of extra oil beforehand; from January 1973 until the war broke out in October, Saudi output was 36% higher than in the same period of 1972.

The shortages of gasoline that did occur in the U.S., then, were not caused by the embargo, but by the extremely "cautious" rate at which the companies rationed their more than ample stocks of oil. In March 1974, after winning staggering price increases in the midst of the gasoline panic, the companies decided that such "caution" was no longer necessary, and gasoline suddenly flowed freely in the U.S. once again.

More important than the embargo's effect on oil supplies was the accompanying price increase declared by OPEC. Within a few months the price of OPEC oil nearly quadrupled; Saudi crude went from $3.01 to $11.65 a barrel. The companies, while publicly bemoaning the OPEC increase, were able to more than make up for it by raising the prices they charged their customers.

For instance, from 1972 to December 1974, the average price of crude oil in the U.S. went up 96%, while the price of gasoline increased 95%, home heating oil jumped 142%, and oil bought by electric utilities leaped 224%. Profits rose even on gasoline sales: its costs include not only the price of crude oil, but also the operating costs of refineries, tank trucks, gas stations, etc. — which rose much less than 95%.

As a result, oil company profit

Excerpted from *Dollars & Sense* magazine, 38 Union Sq., Room 14, Somerville, MA 02143 (monthly, $7.50/year).

rates shot up. Back in the 1950's and 1960's, Exxon's average profit rate of 12.6% (as a percentage of net worth) was the best in the industry. In 1974, all the majors' profit rates exceeded 20%.

Why Not Sooner?

If the oil companies could get away with such tremendous price and profit hikes in 1974, why didn't they do it earlier? The obstacles to price increases were primarily not economic (since people have little choice about continuing to drive their cars and heat their homes, whatever the price), but rather political (too great an increase might lead to popular pressure for serious government regulations and restrictions on the companies). OPEC's actions provided a political opportunity to raise prices and profits, by focusing much of the public hostility on "greedy Arabs" rather than on greedy Anglo-Saxon executives.

The oil crisis illustrates the contradictory relationship of the major companies to OPEC. On the one hand, the companies undoubtedly preferred the old days, when the U.S. could simply overthrow troublesome governments like Mossadegh's in Iran (see page 12), or use its domestic oil production to wash away an Arab embargo.

On the other hand, those days were clearly over. Libya's unilateral price hikes and the awakening of OPEC militance occurred in the early 1970's, at a time of declining U.S. power. Opposition to the war in Vietnam had made additional U.S. foreign interventions impossible, and falling U.S. oil production had made OPEC more indispensable to the industrial countries.

So, by the time of the embargo, the companies had decided, "if you can't beat 'em, join 'em." Beneath a veneer of rhetorical antagonism, the companies and OPEC together could control the worldwide sale of oil, at the high post-embargo prices.

> **Back in the 1950's and 1960's, EXXON's average profit rate of 12.6% (as a percentage of net worth) was the best in the industry. In 1974, all the majors' profit rates exceeded 20%.**

Of Price Hikes, Petrodollars & Power

OPEC is a convenient scapegoat, easy to blame for the decline of U.S. economic strength around the world. But the events of the last five years don't point to OPEC as the cause of U.S. problems. In fact, there is a lengthy list of dire predictions about OPEC that haven't come to pass:

OPEC has not continued to make drastic price hikes. From early 1974 through the scheduled 1979 increases, the price of OPEC oil will have risen only 25%, while U.S. consumer prices will have climbed roughly 50%. Credit for this moderation belongs to Saudi Arabia, the OPEC country with the closest ties to the U.S. government. Saudi Arabia has actually argued for slower price increases than the rest of OPEC before, during and after the 1973-74 embargo.

OPEC has not used its oil earnings ("petrodollars") to upset the world monetary system or the economies of the developed countries. A surprisingly large, and steadily growing, fraction of OPEC's income has been spent on imports, for crash industrialization programs and in many cases for military build-ups. Saudi Arabia, by far the richest OPEC nation, has also given out extensive foreign aid, largely replacing U.S. aid in the Middle East and northern Africa. So the surplus left over for investment in the developed countries, while large (OPEC's foreign investments totalled $155 billion at the end of 1977), is no longer growing rapidly.

The financial position of OPEC countries varies widely. Despite import booms, Libya, Saudi Arabia, Kuwait and the smaller Arabian states continue to receive far more income than they can spend. It is these few nations that own the bulk of the "petrodollars" invested abroad. All other OPEC nations, by sometime in 1977 or 1978, were spending more on imports of goods and services than they received for their oil.

So the widespread worry about

how OPEC will use its surplus boils down to the question of how a few countries, chief among them Saudi Arabia, will choose their investments. The general pro-U.S. orientation of the Saudi regime makes it unlikely that they will withdraw their investments as a weapon of Middle East politics. And on a strictly financial basis, the large size of Saudi investments in the U.S. may now give them a significant stake in the value of the dollar.

OPEC has not thrown out the oil companies. As a result of negotiations begun in the early 1970's, there has been a gradual increase in the share of oil production owned by the OPEC governments. However, the takeover has been far from complete, and in many cases the companies have lucrative contracts to operate the oil fields they once owned.

The increased government ownership has led to a slow rise in oil sales outside the control of the major companies, particularly to the national oil companies of some Third World countries, and to Japanese, French and other "independent" companies. However, the bulk of OPEC oil, including much of the government-owned oil, still moves, profitably, through the hands of the major companies.

OPEC has not weakened the U.S. relative to other developed countries. High oil prices have clearly been a blow to consumers — far more severely, it should be noted, in the Third World than in the industrialized countries. As the only industrial country with large domestic oil supplies in the mid-1970's, the U.S. may well have been the least seriously hurt of the consuming nations. While U.S. industry suffered from the initial blow of higher prices in 1974-75, it actually gained some relative advantage over its harder-hit counterparts in Europe and Japan.

More recently, however, OPEC's ties to the U.S. and the dollar have provided an advantage to Europe and Japan. OPEC's oil prices are set in dollars, so as the dollar has declined in value relative to the mark, the yen and other currencies, oil has become cheaper in strong-currency countries.

In effect, OPEC's income is fixed in dollars; as the dollar declines, so does OPEC's purchasing power in Europe and Japan. This wouldn't matter if all of OPEC's imports came from the U.S.; but in 1977-78, only 22% of OPEC's imports of manufactured goods were from the U.S., while 35% came from Germany and Japan, the leading strong-currency countries.

Protests about this, and threats from some OPEC members to go off the dollar standard, have been vetoed by Saudi Arabia. It is the only country with a real veto, since it always can, and frequently does, threaten to defy OPEC by selling its vast oil production to the U.S. at a lower price if it is outvoted.

OPEC has not caused the decline of the dollar. If trade and investment are considered together, more money enters the U.S. than leaves due to OPEC. From 1974 to 1977, the U.S. spent $106 billion on imports from OPEC (95% on oil), and took in $70 billion from exports to them, for a $36 billion trade deficit. However, at least $38 billion of OPEC investments, possibly much more, entered the U.S. in the same period. Moreover, profits made by U.S. corporations in OPEC countries and returned to the U.S. (almost all oil profits) run around $3 billion a year. If anything, trade and investment with OPEC have strengthened the dollar over the last five years.

The cause of the dollar's weakness, therefore, must be found in U.S. relations with other countries, particularly in the loss of relative advantages over the other developed countries. In the inter-capitalist struggles of the 1970's, Saudi Arabia in particular and OPEC in general have, appearances to the contrary, remained some of the staunchest allies of the U.S. While some of the power over world oil must now be shared with the sheiks of the dunes and palaces of Arabia, much of it still resides with the grandsons of the robber barons, in the upper floors of American skyscrapers. ■

Sources: Blair, *The Control of Oil*; Stork, *Middle East Oil and the Energy Crisis*; *Petroleum Economist* 7/78, 8/78; *Petroleum Intelligence Weekly* 1/1/79; *Brookings Bulletin* Fall 78.

WHO HOLDS OPEC PRICES UP?

In the past, cartels such as OPEC have often fallen apart when the sales of their product drop, since producers begin cutting prices to win customers away from each other. This failed to happen in the 1975 recession, when world oil use dropped sharply, because the major oil companies carefully planned cutbacks in OPEC production to match the decline in consumption.

Most observers believed that OPEC was not sufficiently unified to enforce such cutbacks on its members. In public statements after the fact, both the Saudi oil minister, Sheik Yamani, and Exxon's chairman of the board, Clifton Garvin, agreed that the initiative and planning for the 1975 cutbacks came from the companies.

57

HENRY C. WALLICH

Evolution of the International Monetary System

Our current "dissynchronized" world business cycle, with national growth rates that don't match, has helped prolong the present expansion, but at the same time has aggravated international monetary instability.

The world business cycle is passing through a phase of great significance for the world economy and the functioning of the international monetary system. The growth rates of the U.S. economy on one side and most industrial countries on the other have been converging. Until early 1978, the United States was expanding at a rate above its long-run potential, while most other countries were expanding well below their potential. According to many projections, we are entering a phase in which the rate of growth of other industrial countries will, on average, exceed that of the United States.

What we are witnessing is a dissynchronized world business cycle, a condition, in other words, where national cycles are out of phase with each other.

Much of the turmoil that we are observing in the world today can be traced to this dissynchronization.

Before examining what a dissynchronized business cycle has done to the world, however, we should remember the experience we had with the previous cycle, culminating in 1973-74, which was almost perfectly synchronized. All major countries, at that time, were moving in step and were then operating at peak capacity. Widespread shortages prevailed. There was no way in which excess demand in one economy could be compensated for by excess supplies in another. Consequently, competing buyers drove up prices mercilessly all over the world. When the bubble burst, inventories

HENRY C. WALLICH is a Member of the Board of Governors of the Federal Reserve System. This article is based on a paper he delivered at the Conference of the "Zeitschrift für das Gesamte Kreditwesen," Frankfurt, Germany, November 10, 1978.

Reprinted from *Challenge:* The Magazine of Economic Affairs by permission of M. E. Sharpe, Inc., White Plains, New York.

were excessive, orders vanished, and, with the additional burden of a quadrupled price of oil, a severe recession became inevitable. It was then that the thought took hold that if the world economy were to continue to be cyclical, as it has been for 150 years or more, somewhat less synchronization would be helpful. Peaks and valleys would be smoothed out, shortages in one country could be overcome by excess supplies elsewhere, the danger of a severe recession greatly reduced.

Effects of dissynchronization

That wish has been granted. Five years later, we find ourselves in a dissynchronized expansion. Are the results what we expected them to be? Let me begin with the good features, which do not seem to have attracted a great deal of attention. The United States, and most other industrial countries, are now almost four years beyond the trough of the recession as it was recorded in the United States in early 1975. Continued expansion is expected in the United States at about its long-run potential rate of roughly 3 percent. Other economies, after some slow starts and a few relapses, are now growing at somewhat faster rates. Since the length of cyclical expansion, at least in the United States, has historically been from two to three years, the longevity of the present expansion is a distinct achievement, probably attributable in no small measure to the dissynchronized pattern of the present cycle.

The dissynchronized pattern, however, has not been particularly favorable to the functioning of the international monetary system. The reason is that dissynchronized behavior produced imbalances of trade which affected exchange rates. These, in turn, affected rates of inflation which reacted back on exchange rates. Moreover, as the cycle advanced, the approach to full employment generated inflationary pressures in some countries, while excess capacity still was pushing down inflation elsewhere.

During the present cycle, it was the United States that was leading in cyclical phase. The United States, therefore, found its imports rising rapidly, while its exports were lagging and a large current account deficit developed. Japan and Germany, expanding slowly, had the opposite experience. Some countries fell in between.

The ensuing divergent pattern of deficits and surpluses set in motion exchange rate movements which in turn began to influence price developments. The declining exchange rate contributed to inflation in the United States. Rising exchange rates in Germany, Japan, and Switzerland helped to reduce inflation there. The inflation differential further weakened the dollar while the currencies of countries in strong surplus strengthened.

Meanwhile, as the United States economy began to approach the full-employment zone, renewed price pressures began to make themselves felt. Previously, the United States had succeeded in bringing inflation down from a peak of around 12 percent in 1974 to the 5 percent zone shortly following the 1974-75 recession. More rapid expansion, however, and policies supporting this expansion, as well as the institutional peculiarities of U.S. collective bargaining, kept the rate of inflation from falling further. A declining dollar and mounting economic activity caused the U.S. inflation rate to reaccelerate from the 5 to 6 percent range after a period of perhaps two years during which it had remained relatively constant.

In the countries whose economies were lagging, an opposite pattern occurred. Maintenance of substantial slack helped to bring down inflation. Policies designed to accomplish this objective were supported, in the case of Germany, Japan, and Switzerland, by a rise in exchange rates. The latter, in turn, responded both to a movement toward current account surplus and to diminishing inflation. In this way, the leading industrial countries developed sharply contrasting patterns. Some countries, including the United Kingdom and Italy, fell in between, suffering both high inflation and slow growth. These eventually found themselves compelled to restrain their economies in order to remove current account deficits which threatened further exchange rate depreciation and inflation.

Rates of inflation, interest, and exchange

It is noteworthy that during this period of contrasting movements, some features of the separate economies involved came into good alignment, while others did not. In the major countries, interest rates came roughly into alignment with rates of inflation. Low-inflation countries had low interest rates, countries with higher inflation had higher rates. Particularly in the United States, Germany, Switzerland, and to some extent Japan, differences among rates of inflation were roughly equal to differences among interest rates. Real interest rates, that is, nominal interest rates adjusted for current inflation rates, were not very different among these countries. Where nominal interest rates were high, they nevertheless were, if not negative, at most barely positive in real terms.

Exchange rates, on the other hand, behaved very differently. For the most part, their movement failed to reflect nominal interest rate differentials, frequently exceeding these differentials very substantially. Likewise, exchange rate changes were greater than needed to reflect the change in purchasing power. Over prolonged periods, exchange rates, especially for the dollar, the yen, and the Swiss franc, but only to a lesser degree for the DMark, considerably under- and over-shot exchange relations based on relative price movements.

For the behavior of exchange rates, and the associated behavior of current account deficits and surpluses, a variety of factors may be held responsible. One of them is the well-known J-curve phenomenon. An exchange rate movement that, over two or three years, may be expected to bring about greater balance in the current account, may in the short run produce the opposite effect, or perhaps a delayed effect. The volume of exports and imports does not respond instantaneously to changing prices and/or exchange rates. It takes some time before the more favorable exchange rate—for the depreciating country—and the less favorable rate—for the appreciating country—can have their full effect.

A similar J-curve phenomenon may occur in capital markets, although it has been less clearly demonstrated in that context. A rise in interest rates may be expected to attract capital to the country where it occurs. A rise in interest rates, or the expectation thereof, has an adverse effect upon longterm financial and real assets. Bonds, the stock market, and perhaps other assets tend to decline as interest rates rise. The capital losses that investors could sustain from such moves can far exceed any gains that would accrue to others from investing at the new rates. While asset markets seek to establish a new base, therefore, the effect of rising interest rates is not necessarily to attract capital to the countries where the rise occurs. If investors move abroad during this period, the exchange rate may suffer. Once an adjustment has taken place, of course, the widened interest differential may well produce a much enlarged inflow of capital with attendant consequences for the exchange rate.

Pressures on the international monetary system

All this demonstrates that in a dissynchronized expansion, considerable pressures are likely to converge upon the international monetary system. Exchange rates may undergo movements that do not necessarily correspond to their values in any long-run equilibrium. For that reason, it is perhaps not exclusively of historical interest to inquire how a dissynchronized business cycle would have fitted into the precepts of the old Bretton Woods system. That system was exposed to dissynchronized cycles only rarely and in moderate degree, such as in 1958-59 and the latter half of the 1960s. The prevailing view in those days was that "when the United States catches cold, the rest of the world catches pneumonia." This implied a cycle led by, and synchronized with, the United States cycle. Nevertheless, the Bretton Woods system had one clear standard that could have been applied to a dissynchronized cycle: under the Bretton Woods code, only fundamental disequilibrium could justify and require an alteration in exchange rates. A cyclical disequilibrium, with other sources of imbalance absent, was to be ridden out. The ensuing current account deficit was to be financed and dealt with by other adjustment measures, but not by exchange rate depreciation.

In recent years, market forces have told us that the Bretton Woods prescription would probably not have been adhered to had it still been in effect today. They have told us this by moving exchange rates around rather sharply. The world has fared better under floating rates because in all probability it has been spared a series of exchange rate crises that could have provoked counterproductive controls on capital movements. But the Bretton Woods precepts are not without their lesson. They remind us that there is a difference between a cyclical and a fundamental disequilibrium. That difference, of course, was never clearcut. No one would argue that the disequilibrium experienced by the world today is purely cyclical. For the United States, it is overlaid by the problem of oil imports. For Germany and Japan, it is overlaid by a variety of structural changes, including a slowing of long-term growth and reorientation toward lesser dependence on exports. Something similar could be said for numerous other countries.

But the cyclical component is important, and the Bretton Woods precept that cyclical movements should not give rise to permanent exchange rate changes ought not to be altogether forgotten. Nor does today's floating rate system, to which there appears to be no practical alternative, relieve us of the need to take adjustment action. "Adjustment" was one of the key words of the Bretton Woods system. Its successful implementation frequently eluded us, and the Bretton Woods system came to an end. But the need for adjustment has remained under the system of floating exchange rates.

Contrary to the views frequently expressed before floating began, floating exchange rates do not allow a country to adopt any kinds of domestic policies it chooses. A country that were to ignore the effect of its policies upon inflation and upon its exchange rate would quickly discover, from the behavior of both, the limits of its freedom of action.

Value of the dollar

The United States has been very conscious that the value of the dollar depends on its domestic policies, and that the value of the dollar is enormously important both for its domestic well-being and for its international economic and political relations. A number of actions attest to this.

First, the United States has brought its cyclical expansion to a soft landing at a rate of growth consistent with its long-term growth potential. This was accomplished by a reduction in the budget deficit which in 1976 stood at $66 billion. Early in 1978, the budget deficit for fiscal year 1979, which began October 1, 1978, was still projected at $60 billion. Now the deficit for fiscal year 1979 is expected to be less than $40 billion. It is recognized that such a deficit is still too large for a fully employed economy, and a reduction to $30 billion is expected for 1980.

Second, the Federal Reserve has tightened monetary policy, by seeking to limit the growth of the monetary aggregates. While the target for M_1 (currency and demand deposits) of 4 to 6.5 percent has been overshot by approximately 1.5 percentage points, it should be recognized that the M_1 target was extremely modest, considering that nominal GNP was expected to rise at a rate of 11 percent. The Federal Reserve is aware of the need for adequate monetary restraint. Recent increases in the discount rate, the latest by a full percentage point to an unprecedented level of 9.5 percent, as well as in the federal funds rate, which is the principal focus of impact of Federal Reserve policy, attest to this. So does the increase in reserve requirements on large time deposits by almost $3 billion; the successful achievement of our targets for M_2 (M_1 plus bank time and savings deposits other than large negotiable certificates of deposit) and M_3 (M_2 plus deposits in thrift institutions) also is evidence of a policy of restraint.

Third, the United States has instituted a program of wage and price restraint. While the program is voluntary, it does not lack means of enforcement, through the procurement mechanism and through the action of regulatory agencies that set prices for certain regulated industries. The use of the tax system to encourage wage restraint, through a real wage insurance, is also being proposed by President Carter.

Fourth, the United States has finally enacted energy legislation. A great effort to intensify conservation of energy and develop substitute sources for oil and gas is still ahead of us. Nevertheless, it should be noted that increases in the price of energy have been proportionately no smaller than in most other industrial countries. They have gone less far only because they started from a generally much lower level. The response of U.S. consumers and particularly of U.S. industry to higher energy costs has been about the same as abroad.

Fifth, the United States has also instituted an export promotion program. The United States is a relative latecomer to this practice, which has been followed far more energetically for a long time by a number of its competitor countries, including Japan, Germany, France and the United Kingdom. Some of these countries today are concerned about their own large surpluses and about the U.S. deficit. These concerns could be eased if more effective agreements could be arrived at to restrain competition in export promotion. The United States has been trying to facilitate such agreements.

Finally, to support its policies, especially the President's wage and price program, the United States also has strengthened its capacity for intervention in the exchange markets by putting in place a package of $30 billion of foreign exchange resources, including sale of Special Drawing Rights (SDRs), drawings on the International Monetary Fund, sale of foreign currency obligations by the Treasury, and enlargement of swap facilities on the part of the Federal Reserve. An increase in gold sales beginning in December 1978 was also announced. The United States expressed its determination to intervene, in cooperation with the governments and central banks of Germany and Japan and the Swiss National Bank, in a forceful and coordinated manner in the amounts required to correct the situation in the exchange markets.

Under the impact of these policies and developments, the U.S. current account deficit today gives promise of substantial reduction over time. Econometricians have estimated that the full effect of the cyclical gap between the United States and the rest of the world accounts for something like $10 to $20 billion. That is to say, if the entire world were to move to full employment, the U.S. current account, which amounted to about $20 billion over the last 12 months, would be reduced by that order of magnitude. It has also been estimated that every percentage point of depreciation of the dollar, after adjustment for inflation, that is, in real terms, should reduce the deficit by $750 million to $1 billion over a period of two years. The dollar has depreciated, in real terms, about 12 to 15 percent over the last 18 months which again would imply a substantial reduction in the deficit. An improvement of 30 to 40 percent is a reasonable expectation.

Moves toward stability

These developments should help the international monetary system regain a much greater measure of stability than it has recently shown. It is universally recognized that the stability of the system can only be attained by greater domestic price stability resting on appropriate fiscal and monetary policies. Actions in that direction are now under way in all countries.

In addition, evolution is progressing along two lines. Within Europe, action is afoot to create an area of monetary stability among countries willing to achieve a sufficient convergence of their policies to be able to sustain among themselves a system of fixed though adjustable exchange rates. Within the membership of the International Monetary Fund, arrangements have been put in place for surveillance of members' policies with respect to exchange rates and with respect to domestic policies affecting the exchange rate system. The European effort, if designed properly, can make an important contribution not only toward stability among the countries concerned, but also toward the strengthening and stability of the international monetary system and to the central role of the IMF within that system.

These developments characterize the present state of evolution of the international monetary system. The system cannot be static, and gradual change must be expected. The system must be capable of dealing with both synchronized and dissynchronized cyclical developments. It will best be able to accomplish this task, the advantages and difficulties of which I have tried to set forth here, if evolution proceeds in an environment of international cooperation and freedom of movement for goods and capital.